# CHIEF SEATTLE

## AND THE TOWN THAT TOOK HIS NAME

# CHIEF SEATTLE

## AND THE TOWN THAT
## TOOK HIS NAME

---

### THE CHANGE OF WORLDS
### FOR THE NATIVE PEOPLE AND
### SETTLERS ON PUGET SOUND

---

## DAVID M. BUERGE

SASQUATCH BOOKS
SEATTLE

This work is dedicated to Cecile Hansen, chairwoman of the Duwamish Tribe, who has devoted her life in the effort to gain federal recognition for her people, the first signatories of the Treaty of Point Elliott.

> *Holy Seattle, thrice born and*
> *Always among your people;*
> *Visit these words well meant,*
> *And greet us again, birds*
> *Homing under the eaves*
> *In the house of your name.*

---

Printed in the United States of America
Published by Sasquatch Books

21 20 19 18 17      9 8 7 6 5 4 3 2 1

Editor: Gary Luke
Production editor: Em Gale
Design: Tony Ong
Maps: David M. Buerge
Copyeditor: Elizabeth Johnson

Cover image of Chief Seattle: Courtesy of the Burke Museum of Natural History and Culture, catalog number 1994-1/5.
Cover image of Seattle: Courtesy of the Library of Congress, 75696660

Library of Congress Cataloging-in-Publication Data
Buerge, David M., author.
  Chief Seattle and the town that took his name : the change of worlds for the native
    people and settlers on Puget Sound / David M. Buerge.
  Seattle, WA : Sasquatch Books, 2017.
  Includes bibliographical references and index.
  LCCN 2017004912 | ISBN 9781632171351 (alk. paper)
LCSH: Seattle, Chief, 1790-1866. | Suquamish Indians—Biography. | Seattle Region (Wash.)—
Biography. | Puget Sound Region (Wash.)—Biography.
LCC E99.S85 B84 2017 | DDC 979.7004/97940092 [B] —dc23
LC record available at https://lccn.loc.gov/2017004912

ISBN: 978-1-63217-135-1

Sasquatch Books
1904 Third Avenue, Suite 710
Seattle, WA 98101
(206) 467-4300
www.sasquatchbooks.com
custserv@sasquatchbooks.com

SUSTAINABLE FORESTRY INITIATIVE

Certified Chain of Custody
Promoting Sustainable Forestry
www.sfiprogram.org
SFI-01268

SFI label applies to the text stock

*(Photo facing title page) E. L. Sammis photograph of Seattle, chief of the Duwamish and Suquamish people, cofounder of the city of Seattle, taken in 1864.*

# CONTENTS

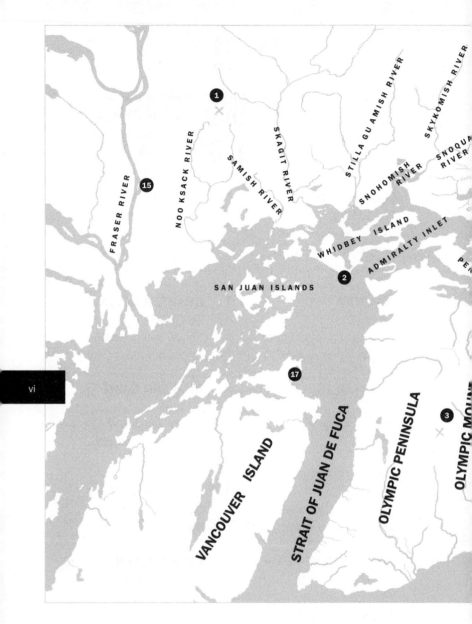

1. Mount Baker
2. Point Partridge
3. Mount Olympus
4. Snoqualmie Falls
5. Snoqualmie Pass
6. Yakima Pass
7. Nachess Pass
8. Təko′bad/Mount Rainier

9. Mount Saint Helens
10. Mount Adams
11. Basha′l, Leschi's birth village on Maschal River, near Eatonville, WA
12. Fort Clatsop, Lewis and Clark, 1805–06, near Astoria, OR

13. Fort Astoria (Pacific Fur Company), 1811–13, at Astoria, OR; Fort George (North West Company), 1812–21; Hudson's Bay Comany, 1821–48; Clatsop Methodist Episcopal Mission, 1841–44, on Clatsop Plains

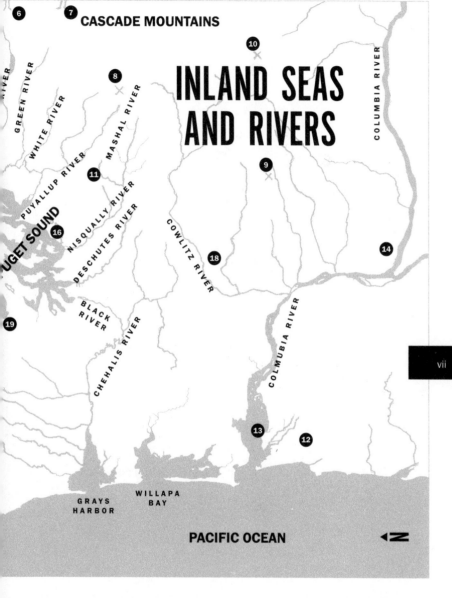

CASCADE MOUNTAINS

# INLAND SEAS AND RIVERS

PUGET SOUND

COLUMBIA RIVER

COLMUBIA RIVER

COWLITZ RIVER

NISQUALLY RIVER

DESCHUTES RIVER

PUYALLUP RIVER

WHITE RIVER

GREEN RIVER

MASHAL RIVER

BLACK RIVER

CHEHALIS RIVER

GRAYS HARBOR

WILLAPA BAY

PACIFIC OCEAN

N

**14.** Fort Vancouver, HBC, 1825–60, at Vancouver, WA; Fort Vancouver Anglican Chaplaincy, 1836–38; Methodist Episcopal Oregon Mission School, 1835–44; Fort Vancouver Roman Catholic mission/St. James mission, 1838–46; Vancouver Barracks, US Army, 1849

**15.** Fort Langley, HBC, 1827–60, at Fort Langley, British Columbia, Canada

**16.** Fort Nisqually, HBC, 1833–40; Puget Sound Agricultural Company, 1840–69, at Dupont, WA

**17.** Fort Victoria, HBC, 1841–64, at Victoria, British Columbia, Canada

**18.** Cowlitz Farm, Puget Sound Agricultural Company, 1839–69, near Toledo, WA; St. Francis Xavier Roman Catholic Mission, 1839–74

**19.** Skokomish Congregationalist mission, 1874–1907, at Skokomish Indian Reservation

STRAIT OF GEOR[GIA]

VANCOUVER ISLAND

COWICHAN RIVER

**1**

COWICHAN LAKE

# STRAITS

SOOKE HARBOUR

PORT SAN JUAN

CAPE FLATTERY

STRAIT OF JUAN DE FUCA

**4**

CLALLAM BAY

FAL[SE] DUNGE[NESS]

N

1. Maple Bay
2. Fort Victoria, Hudson's Bay Company trading post, 1843–64, at Victoria, British Columbia, Canada
3. Fraser River
4. Nunez Gaona, 1792, at Neah Bay, WA
5. Yənus, at Port Angeles, WA

6. Point Partridge
7. Gooseberry Point
8. Whatcom, American settlement, 1858–1903, at Bellingham, WA, 1903–present
9. Sehome, American settlement, 1854–1903, at Bellingham, WA
10. San Juan Island; American Camp, 1857; English Camp, 1857

11. Port Discovery/Discovery [Bay]
12. Port Townsend, WA, American settlement, 1851–present
13. Fidalgo Island
14. Indian Island
15. Marrowstone Island
16. Hadlock Portage
17. Tsit'tsibus, Irondale, WA

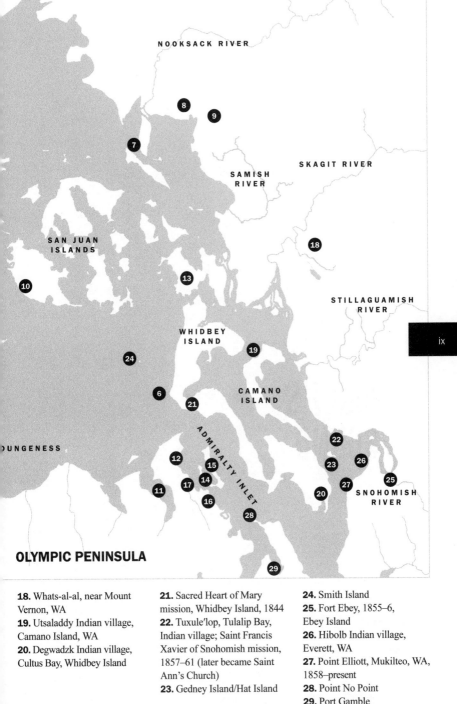

**OLYMPIC PENINSULA**

18. Whats-al-al, near Mount Vernon, WA
19. Utsaladdy Indian village, Camano Island, WA
20. Degwadzk Indian village, Cultus Bay, Whidbey Island
21. Sacred Heart of Mary mission, Whidbey Island, 1844
22. Tuxule'lop, Tulalip Bay, Indian village; Saint Francis Xavier of Snohomish mission, 1857–61 (later became Saint Ann's Church)
23. Gedney Island/Hat Island
24. Smith Island
25. Fort Ebey, 1855–6, Ebey Island
26. Hibolb Indian village, Everett, WA
27. Point Elliott, Mukilteo, WA, 1858–present
28. Point No Point
29. Port Gamble

GOLDSBOROUGH CREEK

OAKLAND BAY

HAMMERSLEY INLET

HARST[...]
ISLAN[...]

LITTLE SKOOKUM INLET

TOTTEN INLET

ELD INLET

DANA PASSAG[E]

BUDD INLET

HENDERSON

PUGET'S SOUND

X

BLACK LAKE

BLACK RIVER

DESCHUTES RIVER

1. Squaxin Island
2. Black River Portage
3. Tumwater Falls
4. Medicine (Sxuda'dap) Creek
5. Sequalitchew Creek

6. Point Defiance
7. St!sch!a's, Indian village at Tumwater, WA; New Market, American settlement, 1845–63

8. Smithfield, settlement at Olympia, WA, 1846–present; Chinook Street, 1849–55

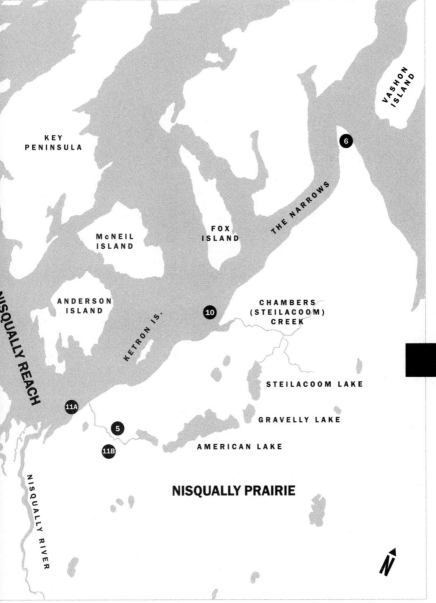

**9.** Saint Joseph of Newmarket Roman Catholic Mission, 1848–60, near Olympia, WA

**10.** Ch!tikwəb, Indian village at Steilacoom, WA, 1850–present; Steilacoom Barracks/Fort Steilacoom, 1849–68

**11A.** Fort Nisqually, Hudson's Bay Company trading post, 1833 location **B.** HBC trading post, 1843 location; Nisqually Roman Catholic Mission, 1839; Fort Nisqually Methodist Episcopal Mission, 1840–42

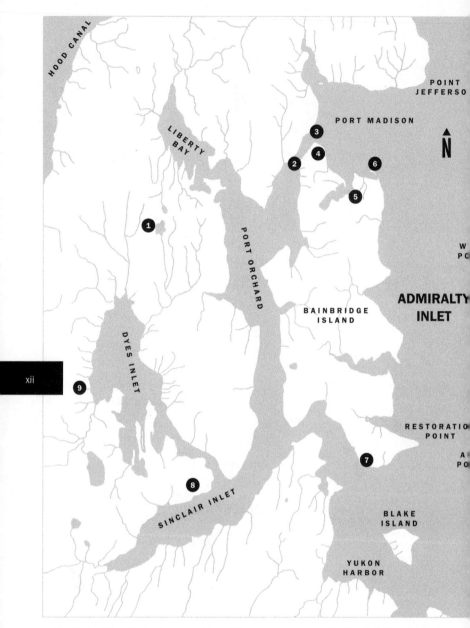

1. Island Lake, Kitsap Peninsula
2. Agate Passage
3. Txwchə′kup Indian village/
Lu′luƛ! A′lal /Old Man House, at
Suquamish; Saint Peter Roman
Catholic Mission, Suquamish,
1861–present
4. Agate Point, Bainbridge Island

5. Meigs's Mill
6. Point Monroe,
Bainbridge Island
7. Beans Point,
Bainbridge Island
8. Bremerton, WA, 1901–present
9. Chico, settlement, 1889

10. Shə′lshol village, Ballard,
Seattle, WA
11. Baba′kwəb, "Meadows,"
village
12. Dzidzəla′ləch, "Little
Crossing Place," village

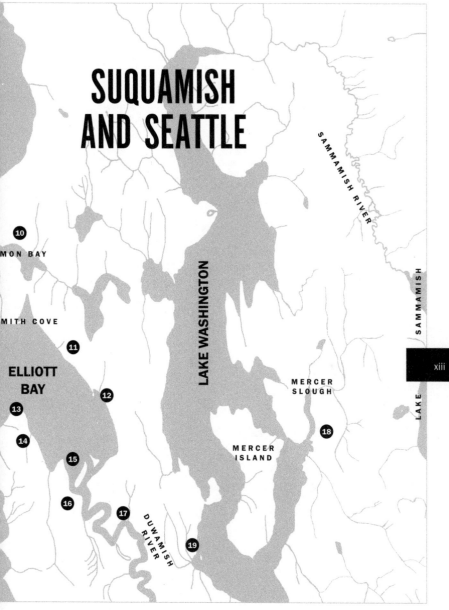

# SUQUAMISH AND SEATTLE

SAMMAMISH RIVER

LAKE WASHINGTON

SAMMAMISH

LAKE SAMMAMISH

MON BAY

MITH COVE

ELLIOTT BAY

MERCER SLOUGH

MERCER ISLAND

DUWAMISH RIVER

**10**

**11**

**12**

**13**

**14**

**15**

**16**

**17**

**18**

**19**

**13.** Duwamish Head/Holderness Point; New York Alki, American settlement, 1851–1902
**14.** Skwǝdks, Indian fishing camp, West Seattle, WA
**15.** T!ula′ltu, "Herring House," village

**16.** 45KI23 archaeological site, Seattle, WA
**17.** Txwkwiltǝd, "Fishing Spear," village, Seattle, WA
**18.** Sa′tsakał Indian village at Factoria, Bellevue, WA

**19.** λ!i′tchus, "Island," village, Pritichards Island/Atlantic City Beach Park, Seattle, WA

# DUWAMISH AND SEATTLE

Gray rectangles on the map identify longhouses, the number per site derived from Claimants' Exhibits W-2 and Y-2, in the Court of Claims of the United States, the Duwamish, et. al, Tribes of Indians versus the United States of America, No. F 375, File October 3, 1927.

LAKE SAMMAMISH

MERCER SLOUGH

MERCER ISLAND

LAKE WASHINGTON

UNION BAY

HORSE TR

LAKE UNION

SALMON BAY

SMITH COVE

ELLIOTT BAY

1. West Point
2. Smith Cove–Salmon Bay portage
3. Shə′lshol, "Threading a Bead," village
4. Baba′kwəb, "Meadows," village
5. Elliott Bay–Lake Union portage

6. Lake Union–Union Bay portage
7. Dzidzəla′ləch, "Little Crossing Place," village; Fort Decatur
8. The Nose/the Point
9. Elliott Bay–Lake Washington portage
10. Ba′kwəb, "Prairie Point"/ Alki Point

11. ƛ!iłchus village, Pritchard Island/Atlantic City Park, Seattle, WA
12. Sa′tsakał village, Factoria, Bellevue, WA
13. Lake Washington–Lake Sammamish portage
14. Skaita′w, village of Skaitilbabsh, Renton, WA

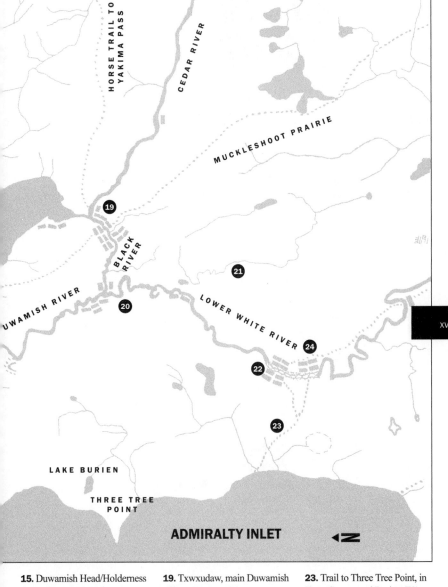

HORSE TRAIL TO YAKIMA PASS

CEDAR RIVER

MUCKLESHOOT PRAIRIE

**19**

BLACK RIVER

UWAMISH RIVER

**20**

**21**

LOWER WHITE RIVER

**24**

**22**

**23**

LAKE BURIEN

THREE TREE POINT

ADMIRALTY INLET

**15.** Duwamish Head/Holderness Point, Duwamish Indian Subagency, 1856–61

**16.** T!ula′ltu, "Herring House," village

**17.** 45KI23 archaeological site

**18.** Txwkwi′təd, "Fishing Spear," village, Seattle, WA

**19.** Txwxudaw, main Duwamish village, Renton, WA

**20.** Seattle's ambush site, Tukwila, WA

**21.** Tskwa′litsh, Upriver Portion, Kent, WA

**22.** Stək!, "Logjam," village, Kent, WA

**23.** Trail to Three Tree Point, in Kent, Seatac, and Burien, WA

**24.** Ch!ut!əp!altxw, "Flea's House," village, Kent, WA

# DUWAMISH WATERSHED,

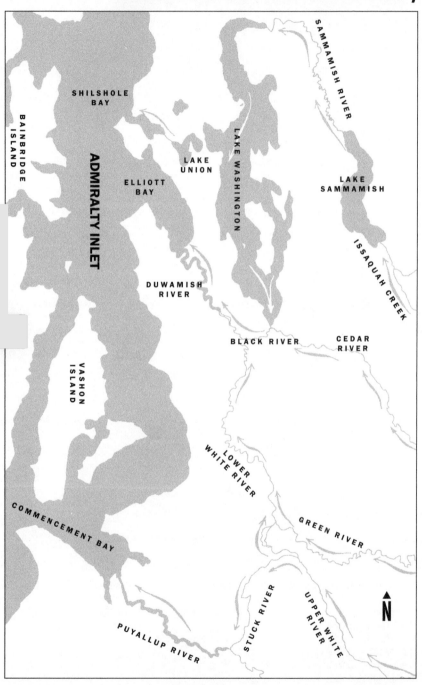

**1800s**

# ANCIENT AND MODERN

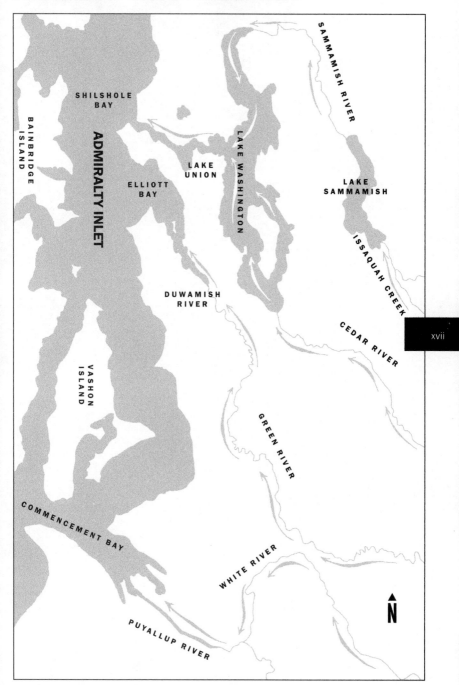

**Present day**

Seattle's burial site at Suquamish. The story poles carved by Squaxon tribal artist Andrea Wilbur-Sigo replaced a framework holding aloft carved canoes erected during the 1976 national bicentennial.

# INTRODUCTION

January days dawn typically cold and gray on Seattle's rain-slick streets. Near Pioneer Square, the historical heart of the city, where potholed asphalt slopes down to Elliott Bay, the bluffs of a small island once gave way to a gravelly beach. The island, its bluffs, and the beach have been buried for over a century beneath urban fill, but the slope still mirrors that of the old landscape. In a place where written history does not go deep, the power and dynamism of the modern city is a thin blanket resting on the lineaments of an older and largely forgotten world.

Out on the bay container ships lit up like billboards ride at anchor waiting to deliver cargoes from Asia, and ferries cross steely waters, looking like so many illuminated palaces. Around me, streetlights still shine, but the city already thrums with the low rumble of traffic and construction. Workers in yellow rain gear and residents holding their coats close hurry, heads down, through drizzle to work, but I sit in my car on my own errand. Today is January 12. On that day in 1854, in colder, clearer weather, over one thousand native people disembarked from scores of canoes hauled up on the beach and gathered around driftwood fires. Joining them were about one hundred American settlers, new neighbors only recently arrived.

If I could take you back to this same spot that January day, we would find ourselves, absent the fill, balancing unsteadily atop the bark-shingled roof of the Seattle Exchange, a log cabin store built with native help for David Swinson Maynard, a Vermont doctor with a medical degree from Middlebury College, who had arrived when the place was an Indian village. Everyone had assembled to hear Isaac Ingalls Stevens, the first governor of Washington Territory, announce plans for upcoming treaties with the Indians.

After Stevens made a brief speech, a large old Indian with a powerful voice stepped forward. In the west, a pale moon hung openmouthed in the sky over the Olympic Mountains. In the hybrid settlement bearing his name, Chief Seattle spoke compellingly about change and continuity, love and loss, justice, kindness, and the power of the dead.

Another pioneer doctor, Henry Allen Smith from Ohio, penciled snatches of what he heard in his diary. Edited and published thirty-three years later, what Smith wrote is considered to be one of the greatest orations ever delivered by a Native American. But the anniversary of that speech, which I mark this morning, passes without notice. Indeed, none of its anniversaries have ever been noted. How is this possible?

In the Pacific Northwest, written history begins late in the eighteenth century, when European and American explorers took possession of the last great temperate swath of North America. Following them, traders, missionaries, settlers, government officials, and naturalists left impressions of the land and its inhabitants that historians interpreted and organized into a record of life in this far corner of the world. In these accounts, native people in their tens of thousands were generally treated as features of the landscape—resources that study and exploitation might render useful. Such utilitarian motives rarely lent themselves to reflections on the deeper themes Chief Seattle addressed on that January day.

In the twenty-first century, we wrestle with the contradictions of that history. We have learned that the dominance many of us assumed as a birthright leaves us vulnerable to unexpected shocks. The power and influence our ancestors acquired make us soft targets even as the pursuit of wealth breeds poverty. Uneasily, many search for meaning in the words passed down to us from a man we hardly know.

It is no small thing to be the largest city in the world named after a Native American. Although Seattle was a person of considerable stature in his day, very little is actually known about him. His preliterate people do not show up in the historic record until the 1790s, and their genealogical memory did not extend many generations beyond. The earliest references to him and his people come from the logs, journals, reports, letters, and accounts written by those who arrived to claim and exploit the land. Missionaries who played a crucial role in this conquest described their native charges from a somewhat different perspective, recording their languages and myths to more effectively convert them. The emphasis in all these writings was on utility. It was only when ethnographers, anthropologists, and linguists interested in native cultures and societies for their own sake made records of what native peoples actually thought and said in their own languages that we began to realize how unique their world was. But by then, it had been largely swept away.

The first historical reference to Seattle appears in an 1833 journal entry made by William Fraser Tolmie, a young Scottish doctor hired by the Hudson's Bay Company to tend to its local employees. Tolmie described Seattle, then in middle age, as "a brawny Soquamish with a roman countenance & black curley hair, the handsomest Indian I have seen." Nearly two decades later, a government official, Indian agent Edmund A. Starling, mentioned a significant detail about Seattle in a report to Governor Stevens. Describing native traditions of leadership, he wrote:

> Sometimes a free male or chief will take a slave, and raise her to the condition of one of his wives. The condition of their issue I could never entirely comprehend. Seattle, one of the most sensible and influential chiefs on the Sound, was born of parents of this condition. His father was a chief or Tyee and his mother being a slave. He is chief at present of the Sowquamish Tribe. 'Tis a stigma, however, upon him, which were it not for his known good sense, would take much influence from him that he otherwise would have.[1]

A handsome nobleman or the son of a slave? In the *Journal of Occurrences at Nisqually House*, the daily log kept by chief traders at the Hudson's Bay Company post near the head of Puget Sound, few native leaders have as many negative epithets associated with their names as Seattle. He was described as violent and troublesome, "a blackguard," "a villain," and "a scamp," and one distressed writer recorded his wish that Seattle's own people would murder him. He has since been described as a friend to the whites, their enemy or their stooge, a counselor to his people, and a traitor to his race. Ambiguity is his hallmark.

Even though Seattle was in his sixties when Americans gained power on the Sound, they wrote most of what little is recorded about him and had the most dealings with him. It may surprise many that long before he died, he was quoted in the *New York Herald*'s morning edition. Even so, what was written about him is often superficial and contradictory. Indeed, the paucity and ambiguous nature of what we know about Seattle has allowed him to be refigured to suit a variety of purposes. He has been described as a war leader, a peacemaker, a gifted orator, a savage who communicated only in signs and grunts, a friend, a traitor, a drunk, a supporter of temperance, a religious leader, a philosopher, and an environmental saint.

Like Jesus and King Arthur, other iconic figures about whom little is known for sure, he has become a malleable symbol. Aside from his oft-repeated name, the only literal mark he left in history was a short line marked across another, an *X* made beside the English version of his name on the Treaty of Point Elliott. Signed in January 1855, this fateful document that ceded native lands to the federal government identified Seattle as "Chief of the Dwamish and Suquamish tribes." He died in 1866, but his passing made no news. The records of the few utterances attributed to him have been refracted through diverse cultural mediums and show evidence, as does Smith's version of Seattle's speech, of having been reworked to support each writer's particular agenda.

Some will question whether there is enough historical fabric to piece together a decent garment for a man who died unnoted more than a century and a half ago. Recently, when historian, writer, and regional gadfly Knute Berger wanted to learn more about Chief Seattle and asked for a biography of him at the Seattle Public Library, he was directed to one published for a juvenile audience in 1943. There was little else.

For much of my life, I never gave Seattle the man much thought. For me, growing up in rural Snohomish County and visiting Seattle only rarely, the city with its fascinating waterfront redolent of the sea always beckoned as a place of wonders. Then in 1973, while teaching on Vashon Island, I met Marshall Sohl, a tall, bearded, and utterly charming man, the peripatetic historian of the island, who handed me a roll of microfilm with the words "I think you will find this interesting." It contained anthropologist Thomas Talbot Waterman's *Puget Sound Geography*, a list of hundreds of native place names, villages, and mythic sites that he recorded while interviewing native informants in the early decades of the twentieth century.

A place I thought familiar assumed an entirely new guise—new to me, anyway—with a supernatural dimension I could only compare to the mythic landscape of the classical world. It was utterly fascinating, and it inspired a decades-long search for more understanding. Involvement in an archaeological field school near the mouth of the Duwamish River in

1980 led to my astonished discovery that a Duwamish Tribe still existed and had a tribal office in Burien, a suburb of Seattle. Ancient history suddenly became modern. I became a student of the Duwamish Tribe, and their friendship gave me confidence to carry on the work.

It was while I was standing in one of the test pits at the archaeological site that I met David Brewster, then publisher of *Seattle Weekly*, who gave me the opportunity to explore cultural and historical themes, drawn from my studies, in the columns of his newsmagazine, which helped hone what writing skills I have.

When it was first suggested that I should write a biography of Seattle, I refused, saying it would be virtually impossible, given the lack of primary sources. That was twenty years ago. For a variety of reasons, and curious to see if it actually could be done, I began researching the man and writing a manuscript. In the intervening years, I came to understand why no one else had undertaken this quest, but by then I was too deep into the project to quit, and the work never failed to fascinate me and those with whom I shared it. "When's that book coming out?" they would ask.

Native Americans, who vastly outnumbered white settlers in 1854, today represent less than 2 percent of Washington State's population. Their precipitous decline began nearly a century before American industrial society overwhelmed, deracinated, and compressed them into the mold that a dynamic modern superpower demanded. But they survived, and what they remembered and gave scholars like Waterman provided glimpses of Seattle's ancient world. Still, the fragmentary nature of their knowledge and the loss of native languages by the forced assimilation of native children in schools means that much of what we know comes from personal recollection and isolated accounts. Only by examining these and how they fit together can one begin to understand the outline of a complex society and a culture of great antiquity. But gaining a glimpse of an ancient world is not the same thing as trying to follow the life of an individual from it. Little is known about Seattle's early life, and the actions of his later years can be seen only through cultural lenses clouded and askew. There is, for example, the simple problem about how to pronounce his name. Given the difficulty English speakers have reproducing the sounds in native languages, my choice to use the form taken by the city is not entirely arbitrary.

The modern Suquamish and Duwamish regard Seattle as one of many leaders who led them, defended them, and held Americans to the promises made to them in treaties. In the small community that took his name and grew to become a thriving city, the roles he played at its founding have been overshadowed by subsequent events or edited by historians. A romantic bronze statue of him standing life-size at a busy intersection, clad in a Hudson's Bay Company blanket, raises its right arm in dramatic greeting. A few bronze busts scattered around town preserve what was imagined to have been his stolid countenance, and a bland profile is the image used in the city's logo. Only one photo of him is known to exist.

Some maintained that Seattle gained fame from the city named after him rather than for any particular accomplishment on his part. In a city constantly trying to define itself and anxious to be considered world-class, the ignorance surrounding him has made him an icon of convenience. Seattle is the most isolated city of its size in the continental United States, eight hundred miles north of San Francisco and twelve hundred miles west of Minneapolis–Saint Paul. Until quite recently, it was regarded as a distant outlier, mostly irrelevant to the larger national narrative. As a result, its residents cherish the icons they have. Several years ago, when an ice-cream company erected a billboard showing the bronze statue of Seattle holding one of its parti-color cones in its upraised hand, the resulting storm of public outrage forced the company to quickly remove the offending image and apologize.

Clearly, the man occupies a unique place in the hearts and minds of locals and, increasingly, in many around the world. Smith's version of Seattle's speech has had a lot to do with that. Shortly after Smith had it printed in 1887, which in this book comes at the end of Chapter Nine, others began questioning whether Seattle had actually said what Smith wrote, a debate that continues today. Its grip on the popular imagination is immense, so much so that several spurious and apocryphal utterances attributed to Seattle have been penned by writers eager to present him in roles that would have astonished him. Books, movies, plays, and choral and orchestral works have been crafted to present his purported messages. Paradoxically, this intense focus has kept scholars from exploring Seattle's life, keeping him hidden in plain sight.

This book is about Chief Seattle and his relationships with the invading peoples who entered and seized his peoples' land. By weaving together threads from surviving accounts, spun from often disparate sources, the weft of Seattle's actions drawn through the warp of his character helps reveal the patterns of his life. Exploring how the famous speech came to be and how it was received and altered may tell us more about ourselves than him, but doing so brings to light unfinished business requiring our attention—a wrong done long ago, long ignored, and needing to be made right. This, too, can help us understand why Seattle looms as controversially in our world as he did in his own.

A Native American writer would doubtless produce a biography different from mine. So why do I, yet another white man, think myself qualified to write this? I was challenged to, and the challenge has been worth the effort. In the 150 years since Seattle's death, with the exception of the biography written for a young audience, no one, native or nonnative, has done so. It is long past due. This book is not intended as casual reading for a blithe audience, but as a gad to provoke reconsideration of an important and poorly understood figure.

We begin with questions. Who was Seattle? Into what kind of world was he born? What did he do? What sort of person was he? Why did settlers name the town after him? Is he a worthy eponym? Is the city bearing his name worthy of it? Do the life he lived, how he thought, and what he hoped and worked for still have meaning today? I hope to answer these questions in the following pages. The thrum of the modern city will serve as a proper chorus for the recitation of his deeds.

# CHAPTER ONE

*"There was a time when our people
covered the whole land."*

The Suquamish Cemetery, located near the Port Madison Indian Reservation across Puget Sound from the city of Seattle, holds the grave of Chief Seattle. A modern memorial there, dedicated in 2011, features two twelve-foot cedar uprights, carved by Squaxin artist Andrea Wilbur-Sigo of the Squaxon Island Tribe, depicting episodes from Seattle's life: as a child at the arrival of the Vancouver expedition in 1792, as a warrior, and as an orator. A marble cross, dedicated atop the grave mound in 1890, estimated his age when he died on June 7, 1866, at eighty years, putting his birth around 1786.

By that year, the United States, independent little more than a decade, reached to the Mississippi River. Its three million people were spreading into the trans-Appalachian West, bringing revolution with them and driving native people from their ancient homelands. Long distance isolated the new nation from what would be called the Pacific Northwest, but in that decade American sailors visited its outer coast in ships prophetically named *Lady Washington* and *Columbia Rediviva*.

Despite the region's isolation, the awful heralds of Euro-American contact—disease and violence—had preceded them, ravaging native people and altering their societies. Seattle was born during this tumultuous period, and to understand who he was we need to understand what we can of his world.

The Pacific Ocean penetrates the region via the Strait of Georgia and the Strait of Juan de Fuca. Hood Canal, Admiralty Inlet, and Puget Sound reach over a hundred miles into the region's lowland. Collectively, these bodies of water were called Xwa'ltsh or *e whulj*, "salt water" in Xwəlju'tsid, the modern name for the native language spoken on the Sound, which means, literally, "saltwater language." Prevailing westerlies ensure a maritime climate and produce a small rain shadow east

1

of the Olympic Mountains and a larger one from the Cascades onto the Columbia Plateau. As a result, only the Skokomish River, flowing from the eastern Olympics, is as large as those rivers flowing westward from the Cascades: the Nooksack, Samish, Skagit, Stillaguamish, Skykomish, Snoqualmie, Snohomish, Duwamish, Puyallup, Nisqually, and Cowlitz. All of the river names identify the peoples that lived beside them.

Great western red cedar trees enabled the peoples of the Sound to become builders and artisans in wood, and the water yielded a rich, sustainable life thanks to sophisticated fishing methods. This rich environment bore the imprint of an ancient habitation, and a long human presence gave rise to cultural and linguistic differences.

Prior to the twentieth century, the Duwamish River had the most complex watershed in Western Washington. It entered Elliott Bay amid a clutch of delta islands, and upstream it received waters from many tributaries. The Americans named its lower course the Duwamish, a stream entering ten miles up they named Black River, and another heading into the Cascades became Cedar River, but to the Duwamish people all three made up the single Txwxudaw. The whispered prefix, *Txw*, "place," was followed by the root noun *daw*, "inside." The addition of a suffix, *ahbsh*, "people," described villagers living inside, identified as the Duwa'bsh, the modern day Duwamish.[1]

Groups closely related to the Duwamish lived on lakes and rivers connected with the main stream, and on Elliott Bay, Salmon Bay, Lake Union, Lake Washington, the Sammamish River, and Lake Sammamish. Others lived on a tributary, the White River, which received the waters from the Green River. At that confluence, the upper White River split into two distributaries: one going north as the White River, and another going south, the Stuck River, that flowed into the Puyallup River and Commencement Bay. Today, owing to changes made in the last century, the Cedar River flows into Lake Washington, the Black River has disappeared, and the White River has been diverted wholly into the Puyallup River. To add to the confusion, the Green River now flows through the old White River channel into a much reduced Duwamish River, which runs through dredged and straightened waterways past artificial islands into Elliott Bay, hemmed in by modern cargo cranes, busy wharves, and the towering cityscape of downtown Seattle.

Directly across the Sound, the Suquamish lived on the Kitsap Peninsula and Bainbridge Island. Their name derives from the native name for Agate Passage, Txwchə′kop, that describes the narrow waterway separating the peninsula from the Island. Here the Dxwsəq!wəbsh, the Suquamish, had an important and ancient village. The modern tribe translates their village placename, Dxwsəq!wəb, as "Place of Clear Salt Water." Near the beginning of the twentieth century, anthropologist Thomas Talbott Waterman suggested that the name referred to the actions of powerful currents in Agate Passage that kept its water clear in contrast to weaker currents in nearby Liberty Bay that allowed the build-up of debris and marine growth. Alternatively, modern anthropologist Dr. Nile Tompson theorizes that the root of the name, *wuqw*, meaning "drift," referred to a great flood when lines connecting ancient canoes to a mountain top parted and the ancestors of modern groups drifted to their traditional locations. If debate about ancient place names complicates understanding, we must accept that the effort to create a cogent narrative of events is dependent on weighing varied and sometimes conflicting interpretations.[2]

The Suquamish dominated the northern Kitsap Peninsula. Farther south and on Hood Canal, a deep fjord separating the Olympic and Kitsap Peninsula, lived the Twana people. The S'Klallam people lived along the Strait of Juan de Fuca. The non-Salish-speaking Chemakum lived at the northern entrance of Hood Canal and Port Townsend Bay, and farther south, the Sxomamish, or "Swiftwater People," lived on Vashon Island. On the east side of Puget Sound, the Skagit and the Snohomish lived north on Whidbey and Camano Islands and the mainland rivers, and the Skykomish and the Snoqualmie lived along their named tributaries.

At one time, several thousand people lived in Suquamish and Duwamish winter villages in longhouses that commonly sheltered several related families. Village location often conferred strategic advantage. For example, the main Duwamish village, Txwxudaw, at the confluence of Lake Washington's outlet and the Cedar River, at the present city of Renton, gave its families access to river, aquatic, and land resources that made them wealthy and significant. Likewise, the Suquamish on Agate Passage had a reputation for wide and influential connections.[3]

Villages generally included one or more shed-roofed or gabled longhouses, each measuring about thirty by sixty feet, sheathed with hand-hewn vertical wall planks, the style favored by the Duwamish and their neighbors, affixed to a robust wooden frame. Abutting the inside walls, a wide bench built some three feet above the earthen floor provided space for sleeping and sitting. Each family had its own hearth near the center of the house, and looms, storage boxes, baskets, tools, nets, floats, clothing, and blankets filled the airy interior. Rarely holding more than thirty individuals, house groups, a northwestern iteration of the ancient hunter-gatherer band, were often headed by siblings united by blood ties and marriage. This extended family shared food and organized itself into a self-sufficient cooperative strengthened further by intermarriage with other villages that broadened a house group's economic base.

This was especially important for the Suquamish, who lived in the Olympic rain shadow and had no large rivers in their homeland. They hunted on their peninsula and fished its creeks, but because salmon runs on rivers were huge, it was essential for them to marry into groups that operated large river fisheries, such as the Duwamish. Seattle's Suquamish father, Shxwiyehəb, married Sxila'ts!a, a Duwamish woman from the village of Stək!, meaning "Logjam," on the lower White River. The Suquamish also intermarried with the Twana of Hood Canal, the S'Klallam, and others like the Snohomish. Likewise, the Duwamish inter-married with neighboring groups and with families east of the Cascades.

People like Seattle, with parents and other relatives from several groups, moved freely between them, taking advantage of their villages' resources. Native marriages were ratified and maintained by exchanges of goods between the groom's and the bride's families. Just as the fin-gering inlets of the Sound and its entrant rivers gave the people a geo-graphic identity, a ramified kinship system bound them together socially and economically. Men brought woodworking, hunting, fishing, and leadership skills to the house group, and women, their abilities as weav-ers, basket makers, wives, mothers, and grandmothers. Women knew where and when shellfish were best collected, which plants were used for medicine, how to cultivate root crops in their gardens, and where to pick berries in burned-over areas. In villages seeking to keep their sons close, marriage was patrilocal: the bride went to live with her husband's family. But matrilocality, where the groom lived with the bride's family, was not uncommon.

If a husband died, the marital alliance connecting his birth family to his wife's was maintained by her marrying her husband's brother or another male relative. Such a marriage was called *sba'lusəd*. Conversely, if a husband's wife died, her family was expected to supply him with another. Genealogical memories of Seattle's halfsiblings indicate that Shxwiyehəb had at least one other wife than Sxila'ts!a, although her name is unknown. [4]

Some householders practiced polygyny, the custom of having many wives. However, because a man had to be wealthy to support his wives comfortably and bring gifts to his in-laws, he rarely had more than two or three. Stories of men boasting more underscored the generality of smaller families.

Multiple wives were often sisters who got along well, but families or kin who could not afford a dowry sometime sought connection with a wealthy man by offering him their daughters as concubines, and the man might accept them to advertise his wealth and enrich his household with their industry. If he accepted, they became legitimate, albeit socially inferior, wives, and their children could share in the family inheritance, which included, presumably, its names.

Family members visited often, and Seattle's earliest memories would have been of visiting kin as his family pursued its annual round of activity. Since he did not receive an adult name until he was an adolescent, and we do not know his childhood nickname, in what follows we shall refer to him as the Child or the Boy.

---

For native people, the year began in March, when the voices of frogs signaled winter's end. To celebrate renewal, people sang songs and painted themselves with vermilion, the color of life. "The frogs have begun to sing in the marsh, and the Indians in their camps," wrote pioneer Caroline Leighton. "How well their voices chime together!" The Child would have heard the tale of Mink, a lascivious bumbler who killed his nephew Land Otter while seeking supernatural power. Fearing angry relatives, he hid with his frog sisters in a swamp, where they keened over his troubles. Smearing his body with pitch, he crept into Land Otter's house, but passing too near the hearth, he burst into flames, frightening the relatives, who fled outdoors and changed into birds.[5]

Like Land Otter's relatives, the Child's family left the longhouse to gather food as the world warmed. His father and uncles taught him how to hide in blinds with a bow and arrow, and wait for hungry elk to come crashing through swamps in search of brilliant yellow skunk cabbage. Tipping their arrows with wooden plugs, hunters knocked songbirds out of trees and plucked, dried, and cut their downy skins into spirals, which, wrapped around yarn, were woven into extraordinary feather blankets.

By April, groves of alders red with swelling buds, beautiful under a pale-blue sky, signaled the pregnant time, "plant life in bud and sprout," recalling the *gwal*, "the capsizing of the world," which ended the mythic age and ushered in the human era. As a Child, he would have learned that one of the first plants to bloom, the twinflower (*Linnaea borealis*), was named "Eyes of Du'kwibał," meaning "Eyes of the Changer," after the great culture hero who changed the titans of mythic times—the Elip Tillicum, or "First People"—into a host of supernatural powers. They helped the Earth bring forth her myriad children: fern fiddleheads, horsetail roots, and tender salmonberry shoots, which provided welcome greens to a diet of dried fish. In villages along the Duwamish River, people in tune with its flow might feel its supernatural nudge and sing the smelt upstream to spawn. The run was famously large, and at night the Duwamish and their kin trooped to its banks with dip nets to scoop them up under the flare of pitch-wood torches.

As days lengthened, a family might join two canoes together with house planks to haul bulky gear and sheltering mats to temporary campsites. Far inland, people plucked knots of wool from trees, where shedding mountain goats had rubbed against rough bark, but when the blooming western dogwood signaled that butter clams were ripe, it was time for families to head to the beaches. With ironwood digging sticks, women collected the fat mollusks or, on lakes, worked the water-chestnut-like wapato bulbs from the shallows with their toes. Beating lake water with branches, they drove schools of peamouth and chub into basket weirs placed on entrant streams.

The Child's mother and aunts carried him and his cousins to lowland gardens, where women practiced what is called "dibble agriculture." Pressing with their chests against perforated elk-horn handles fitted crosswise at the end of digging sticks, they dug up camas bulbs and other root crops. So closely were these handles identified with their owners that women were often buried with them. The bulbs and roots steamed or dried in stone ovens were often ground into flour to make a dark flatbread.[6]

In late spring, willows issued their heavy fragrance. "This is the time when the ducks go north," said elders. "Everything becomes good, peaceful. Out in the bay, upon beds of kelp, porpoise gives birth to her young." It was time to collect cedar and spruce roots and the inner bark of the cedar: raw material for a long list of items, from baskets and baby diapers to sanitary pads. The Child watched women weave large, beautiful baskets patterned with colored and textured fibers. Some were fine enough to be watertight and used to brew soups and teas heated with hot rocks.

By May, the last families left the longhouses. Late in his life, Seattle told Catherine Maynard, David Maynard's wife, that he was born on Blake Island, noted for its clam beds and for sculpins that were speared in shallow water, in a house built by his father. People generally lived in temporary camps on the island, and it is possible that Seattle's birth there came as an early surprise to his mother.[7]

If a bumblebee hovered near a woman upriver, folks said he was telling her to make baskets quickly, because the berries were about to ripen. Inland calendars followed the moon, and the lunation during which salmonberries ripened, happening about the time the first migrating salmon appeared, was called "Moon of Yellow Salmonberries." Among saltwater villagers who knew that the moon governed tides, a suffix added to the name changed its meaning to "Tide of the Yellow Salmonberries."[8]

Beginning in late June, a succession of salmonberries, elderberries, blackberries, and salal berries attracted gangs of women and children to clearings, where they gathered and pulped the berries into loaves and dried them for storage in baskets lined with maple leaves. Berry picking required dexterity and discipline, and when girls experienced their first menstruation, a thin stick placed between their teeth was inspected periodically to see if it had more than one set of toothmarks, which would indicate that they had talked or eaten berries while picking, both taboo.[9]

The summertime reappearance of anadromous salmon, acclimating themselves in river estuaries, called for celebration. Salmon were regarded as an immortal race living in longhouses under the sea. The mythical Salmon Sisters were said to have kidnapped Star Child, a hero born of heaven and earth who lived with them and married Chum Salmon Woman, sealing an alliance between his human kin and the Salmon People, who agreed to travel upstream every year and sacrifice their robes of flesh. The Child, and later the Boy, absorbed the land's storied magnificence, but also the spirited conversations among gathered kin in their richly allusive language, especially the women, whose humor, joy, anger, and pathos spun a skein of stories around the people and their rigorous lives.[10]

The Duwamish who lived on rivers had a more elaborate first salmon ceremony than the Suquamish, who trolled the Sound throughout the year, but both greeted the first fish of the season with reverence, cooking it in special ways and making sure everyone in the community ate a piece during a sacramental meal before ritually disposing of its bones. With his male relatives, the Boy learned to spear the big chinook and coho salmon lurking at the surface and to troll for black cod near promontories. At night, he speared flounder and sole in shallow lagoons by torchlight.

Groups typically followed regular itineraries, returning periodically to villages to store the food they had gathered, and it was said that if one knew the family, one knew where they were at any given time. In fields as large as one thousand acres on Whidbey Island, bracken fern roots, an important source of carbohydrates, wild onions, and carrots were cultivated, along with stinging nettles, whose tough, thin fibers were woven into durable nets.[11]

Fields were burned periodically to keep out unwanted plants, and the flames were often directed to surrounding tracts of timber. Early pioneers recalled August days when smoke so clouded the air that they needed a compass to navigate the Sound, but these seemingly wasteful fires helped maintain a mosaic of old and newer growth, prevented more disastrous fires, and kept trees spaced so that light could support undergrowth for browsers such as deer and elk.[12]

As pickers gathered the last berries in mountain meadows and hunters stalked mountain goats among the peaks, ice crystals in the upper atmosphere gave the sky a harder brilliance, and evening frosts signaled summer's end. But in the lowlands, the greatest food-gathering activity of the year was just beginning. Honoring their ancient covenant with · Star Child, the Salmon People ascended rivers in miraculous numbers. Fence weirs built across river channels were supported by heavy log tripod platforms, where men with dip nets scooped up salmon milling before weir screens. Tossed into canoes, the fish were brought ashore, where women gutted them and hung them over smoky fires.

One observer noted that weirs were built where the views of forests and mountains were the most beautiful, but most fishing was done at night, under the blaze of torches, making the weir sites shimmering spectacles, ravishing to a child's mind. With their technology, the people could have captured every fish, but that would have made no sense. River groups agreed to remove screens periodically to allow enough fish upstream to spawn and keep the run healthy. Spaces between weir stakes were also calibrated to allow smaller fish to ascend unimpeded. The fishery was so well managed that when the settlers arrived, it is estimated that returning salmon numbered in the millions.[13]

Large migrations of ducks and geese also arrived in the fall. Hunters paddled silently along marsh edges, with fires flickering on earth bedded in their canoes, to lure curious birds out to the light, where they were snagged by an underhand toss of a multipronged spear. The vision of these drifting evening fires had to have been magical, but even more remarkable were the great nets hoisted into the air to snare birds in flight.

These were no ordinary nets. One belonging to the Boy's uncle, Lə'k!lax, was housed in a great roller. It was attached to a rope unreeled across Agate Passage, a distance of more than seven hundred feet. The margins of these nets were woven from willow and nettle twine, but the inner parts, which absorbed the powerful collisions, were woven from Indian hemp (*Apocynum cannabinum*), imported from east of the Cascades. Its fibers are so strong that a single strand pulled will often cut the holder's hands before breaking. In fog or at night, the nets were hoisted between tall poles across habitual flyways. On a signal, the birds were "started up" and flew the normal escape path now blocked by the net, which was dropped immediately for hunters to dispatch its struggling catch.[14]

These food-gathering strategies were not done so much to ensure an adequate food supply, rarely a problem in so bounteous a region, but to obtain the surpluses necessary to support the time-honored customs of feasting and gift giving. And the individuals whose breeding, wealth, and strategic marriages ensured that these customs were done properly were by definition noble. In Xwəljutsid, these nobles were called *sia'b*. In the Chinook Jargon of the nineteenth century, a trade patois made up of a few hundred native, French, and English words, they were called *tyees*.[15]

In early historic times, the majority of people on Puget Sound lived in a familial society of free individuals ordered by the rules and etiquette of kinship, with a small substratum of slaves. But lineage, ability, and fate worked to divide free individuals into two broad groups: *sia'b* and commoners. *Sia'b* came from wealthy lineages with honored names and powerful connections with the spirit world. They married wives outside the village group and built houses at in-laws' villages for their visits. *Sia'b* directed communal food-gathering activities; they were the ones who hosted feasts celebrating important social events and marital alliances, and it was their daughters who were sought-after in marriage. *Sia'b* organized ceremonial activities and were memorialized at death with lavish canoe burials, sometimes featuring the ritual killing of slaves. The broad kin networks they established produced an extensive cousinage. Ethnographer Thomas Talbot Waterman estimated that in historic times the term *sia' b* applied to about one-third of men and women. Since wealth largely determined rank, its acquisition and the rules governing its manipulation mattered a great deal.[16]

Commoners, like commoners everywhere, did most of the work. Skill in hunting, fishing, gathering, woodworking, weaving, and basketmaking distinguished men and women, as did one's ability as a warrior, a shaman, an herbalist, or a healer. Individual skills could gain a person renown and wealth, and with intelligence, good character, and good marriages, he or she might be counted among the *sia'b*. But such social mobility was virtually nonexistent for slaves.

Slaves, particularly young women and children captured during raids, were widely traded. Unions between the enslaved and the free were taboo, and resulting children were considered debased, although in troubled times, initiative and skill might overcome their perceived debility. Even if those enslaved by raiding groups were reclaimed by their own people, the taint of enslavement often stayed with them, as was the case with one of Seattle's grandmothers. Suquamish elder John Adams said that the grandmother of Ts!agwəɫ, one of the Boy's younger siblings, had been captured by northern raiders and made a slave.

Settlers who struggled to pronounce native names often conjured an English equivalent. On their tongues, Ts!agwəɫ became Suquardl or, more commonly, Curley. Native people who found Western *r*'s challenging sometimes pronounced it "Kelly," but for our purposes, Curley he will remain. The kidnapping of his grandmother was said to have happened "way back," probably in the mid-1700s, and even though she was later recovered, the taint of slavery passed to her descendants. "Yet Curley became a great man," Adams said. "A speaker anyway."[17]

Because the Boy and Curley were siblings, the taint affected both. Curley was born around 1810, a generation after the Boy, which suggests that he was born from one of Shxwiye'hub's younger wives, making him the Boy's half brother. That Seattle was similarly tainted suggests that the kidnapped grandmother was paternal. Because he and Curley were living in turbulent times, their abilities outweighed the stigma of their ancestry, but as we shall see, jealous memory could still thumb the balance.

The abundance of late summer and fall made it the season to hold celebrations. A gambling match might last several days and include feasts and athletic contests, such as shinny, a ferocious version of field hockey; wrestling; or jumping contests. But grandest of all

Ts!agwəɫ, Seattle's half-brother Curley, from a damaged sketch made by surgeon John Y. Taylor from the USS *Decatur*, 1855–6. With Seattle, he welcomed Americans to Elliott Bay.

were potlatches. The word "potlatch" comes from Vancouver Island and means "to make a ceremonial gift," but this give-away feast so beloved of anthropologists had different names among groups from Alaska to Oregon. In Xwəljutsid, it was called a *sgwi'gwi*, meaning "come, come"— which identified a gathering that required an invitation. Because Seattle hosted many *sgwi'gwis*, they deserve examination.[18]

A *sia' b* hosting a *sgwi'gwi* might spend years amassing property that would be distributed to invited guests. The order in which this was done and the value of each gift defined the giver's social relationship with each recipient. *Sgwi'gwi* were hosted in large houses built to celebrate the birth of a child, a daughter's coming-of-age, a marriage, or the assumption of an ancestral name, but their primary purpose was to demonstrate a host's relationship with a powerful wealth-gathering spirit and so affirm rank within the community. Not surprisingly, the potential for slighted feelings and discord during the distribution of gifts was great, but a successful *sgwi'gwi* kept these in check. Outside of war, the *sgwi'gwi* was the principal means by which the game of power on the Sound was played.[19]

A *sgwi'gwi* that might last several weeks typically began when parties of guests sprinkled with eagle down arrived in big canoes and advanced in a singing line toward shore. Visitors sometimes satisfied their sense of honor in a shoving match orchestrated during the landing, when the host's people briefly barred their advance. When hosts and guests finally sat down to feast and servers distributed the courses, speakers voiced welcomes, gave thanks, recalled the illustrious lineages of those assembled, and announced the purposes and intentions of the host. Interspersed with feasting were entertainments, games, and initiations into secret societies.

Like the *sgwi'gwi*, secret societies were institutions of the nobility. Individuals sponsored by secret-society members were carried off to a hidden place and put under the spell of the society's tutelary power. Made savage by supernatural possession, they were presented to the membership, accompanied by attendants restraining them with short leashes so they would not bite onlookers. These initiates made wild were ceremonially reintegrated into civilized society, emerging from their ordeal with enhanced social standing. Suquamish initiations were often held deep in the forest near Island Lake, north of Dyes Inlet on the Kitsap Peninsula, and Seattle appears to have hosted one on Elliott Bay in 1850.[20]

The distribution of gifts in a *sgwi'gwi* took place at its end, when good feelings prevailed. In a dramatic conclusion, the host sang the song of his wealth-giving power, and a master of ceremonies—the speaker—called guests forward to receive their gifts. Afterward, the recipients loaded up their canoes and headed home. In their general contempt for native culture, later Western observers anglicized the Jargon term for the potlatch host, *hyas muckamuck*, "[one who provides] plenty of food," into a term of mock importance, "high mucky-muck." It remained for the disciples of the great anthropologist Franz Boas, years later, to understand that such dramatic reaffirmations of kinship and association, where individuals could demonstrate their wealth, generosity, and success, enabled native societies to maintain their form and vitality even as they endured wrenching change.

As autumn declined to winter, dead salmon lay heaped on upstream gravel bars, where bears, raccoons, and even ducks fed on the rotting flesh, making their own distasteful. It was the time of "leaves fluttering down," a time to "put your paddles away," when families returned to longhouses, where preserved food filled boxes and baskets or hung from ceiling racks. In the effort to reestablish old household rhythms or establish new ones, the people were aided by the return of their guardians, the *skala'lətut*, a word related to dreaming, which described a race of supernaturals who, like their human counterparts, had completed a circuit around the world and returned home.[21]

Because of religious persecution, modern Native Americans are often guarded when speaking about familial religious beliefs and practices. My description is based on what native informants told anthropologists early in the last century, knowledge crucial to an understanding of Seattle and his world. Projecting human understanding and action onto the animating forces of nature gives rise to a conception of them having supernatural dimension and will. In nature myths, natural forces and phenomena are described as manifestations of the Elip Tillicum, the First People, comparable to the Greek titans. Other supernatural beings, among them the *skala'lətut*, were believed to empower human capacities.

It was believed that these beings were encountered during quests begun at puberty, when adolescents kept vigil in isolated places and fasted in hopes of entering into a relationship with a guardian power. This guardian power came to a person in a vision and, if disposed, taught the supplicant its song and gave them a skill. They could be identified with living or nonliving things, or forces that revealed themselves in human traits, like brashness (Blue Jay), handsomeness (Skate), hunting skill (Wolf and Cougar), carpentry (Beaver), and basketry (Crow). Hazelnut got individuals out of tight situations, just as hazelnuts often shot away when struck. Thunder made one a powerful speaker.

Residing in deep water, the most valuable powers provided wealth and influence, and as a youth, Seattle dove for one of these. Such belief explained the multifaceted human psyche, visions, and dreams, and the complexities of social relations, and connected the human, natural, and supernatural worlds in a meaningful cosmos. In our own time, we still speak of skills as "gifts," and many identify angels as guardians. Guardian powers normally spent the year traveling around the world as the people did, and just as people returned to their winter villages, the powers also returned with them, revealing themselves during a ceremonial season called *spegpugud*, "the time of the winter dances."[22]

The return of one's power was believed to induce illness or lassitude. To cure this spiritual malaise, to "feed the power," a host invited witnesses to the house, sang the spirit's song, and demonstrated its gift. This might be the ability to handle fire without injury, to miraculously heal self-inflicted wounds, or to animate material objects. Others helped find lost objects or inspired the gift of prophecy. Guests often joined by singing and dancing their own songs, which added to an intense religious atmosphere.

A remarkable ceremonial demonstration of power held during the winter solstice was called the "Spirit Canoe." The full moon rising on a frigid world was *xa'xa*, the "holy" or "dangerous" moon, when infants, the sick, and the aged often died, a time of awe when ghosts hungry for human company traveled from the Land of the Dead to seek and kidnap souls in the living world. If a shamanic diagnosis of symptoms—particularly loss of property—indicated soul theft, a crew of ceremonialists was hired to travel the dark road, find the abducted soul, and return it to its owner.[23]

The Duwamish were famous for their spectacular Spirit Canoe ceremonies, which took as many as seven consecutive nights to enact, and the few surviving ritual objects they created for them represent examples of a remarkable Puget Sound Salish art form. The way to the land of the dead was well known but difficult, largely because things there were opposite those in the living world: skeletons walked backward; canoes and bowls had holes in them; and day there was night here, so that those making the journey did so on winter evenings, when they could surveil ghost country in spectral daylight.

Spirit Canoe audiences paid rapt attention, since what the crew encountered could affect the coming year. For example, success collecting berries flitting about a spectral meadow could improve the coming harvest. The people joined in the crew's singing and struck roof planks with poles to provide a powerful, rhythmic accompaniment. Once the kidnapped soul was recaptured, the crew fled the angry ghosts, mimed by village boys armed with bows, who sent blazing splints ricocheting off roof planks onto the dance floor. The ceremony reached its dramatic crescendo when the crew returned and its leader presented the soul to its owner amid a scene of terrible excitement. One who witnessed this as a small child recalled decades later that he had been "frightened out of his wits."

Ghosts figure mightily in the speech Seattle delivered in January 1854, when his people believed they were about, and its elegiac tone accurately reflected the season's mood of awe. Winter was also when elders recited creation myths, describing successive worlds populated by races that rose and fell in great cycles of time, giving rise to the fundamental rhythms of existence. Myths told how Muskrat and Beaver created the world with mud brought from the bottom of the primal sea and how the Four Winds fought over the land. Legends further recalled changes to the land; when the great mountain they called Təko'bad, which we call Rainier, moved into place, it had its head torn off in a fight and grew to new height.[24]

In one cycle, Southwind married Northwind's daughter, who bore him a son, but Northwind's people killed Southwind and his relatives, except for his mother, who hid on a rocky hill. Northwind built an icy weir across the Duwamish, to block salmon, and sent Raven to foul the grandmother's face. Southwind's son grew up in Northwind's village but eventually discovered his grandmother, who told him his true origin and his name, Stormwind. As the old woman wove baskets, the two plotted revenge. Stormwind washed her face, making it possible for her to shake out the rain from her baskets. The flood this raised destroyed Northwind's ice weir, and Stormwind drove him out, but, because he was kin, he was allowed to return for annual visits, bringing winter with him.

Along the White River, the full moon following solstice was called "Stuck Fast," after ducks that awoke to find their feet frozen in lake ice, making them easy prey for hunters. On the Sound, vast schools of herring made the water hiss like a rain squall as they spawned in eelgrass beds. At the village of T!ula'ltu, "Herring House," on the west bank of the Duwamish River estuary adjacent to Elliott Bay, men, in the bows of canoes paddled by their wives, swept oar-like rakes through the mass, impaling fish on sharp hardwood pegs. People ashore scooped them up with dip nets or laid fir boughs in the water for the fish to plaster with eggs. On Dyes Inlet, herring were caught in tidal catchments made of beach stones. Fresh herring eggs were considered a treat, especially when they popped deliciously between the back teeth, and they were also stuffed into salmon skins or deer intestines and cured like sausage.

To hurry river floods that signaled the salmon to return, the Boy would have joined male friends swinging bull-roarers, whose sound mimicked the voice of Stormwind. At the base of the Grandmother's Hill, women washed the mineral-streaked stone to cleanse the old woman's face so she could again shake rain from her baskets.

In myth, at the end of the mythic age, Du'kwibał, the Changer, traveled up-country, transforming the world—creating humans from wood, fire, or balls of mud. All were weak and vulnerable, so he taught them how to flourish, and then everything changed. During a great flood, the ancestors tied their canoes to the mountaintops, but the mountains collapsed, the ropes parted, and the people drifted to their respective homelands. It was a cosmic catastrophe, a literal turning-over as the mythic world capsized and another took its place. As islands and mountains ceased their wanderings and took root, human society took form.[25]

These accounts were recited by weeping elders and heard in awe, for the people believed that the spoken word could bring about the very changes it described. Reciting the deeds of Stormwind helped drive out winter's cold, just as the tales of Star Child reminded the Salmon People of their ancient promise. The stories of Du'kwibał reminded listeners that the world could change. And should these changes build like a wave and threaten once again, some said that Du'kwibał or one like him would return to help his people.

Prophecies warned that this world would end as surely as earlier ones had. People said to have died and visited the land of the dead came back with stories about the end times, and in the years preceding Seattle's birth, epiphanies coming out of the sunrise suggested apocalypse was at hand.

---

One day, interior people rode out of the Cascades on elk-size creatures with large antlerless heads. These first horses were used by the native groups who lived beside grassy fields, much more so than those who lived downstream cared to, gliding along waterways in their lissome canoes. By the early 1800s, horses were still a curiosity among river and saltwater groups, and the Whidbey Island Skagits told a story about Sneetlum, a wealthy headman living on Penn Cove, who brought a horse into his house and kept it there until it died because no one knew what to feed it. Horses made it easier for those living on the eastern slope of the mountains to bring trade goods over the passes and to winter in the more temperate western valleys, where their owners married into western nobility. However, the word Tu'bshədəd, identifying these traders, also meant "warrior," underscoring the fact that not all the visits were peaceful.[26]

As they bartered dogbane fiber and dried biscuit-root, the traders reported the approach of a very different people, speaking new languages and preaching a new religion. From the ocean coast came reports of strange vessels carrying beings skilled in metalwork. All along Puget Sound, people struggled to make sense of this. An echo of their wonderment may survive in a legend describing a flood that turned the White River valley into a lake and divided the river, sending a southern distributary pouring into Commencement Bay through a new channel named Stəx, "pushed through," the modern Stuck River. It was said that whales thrashing in the lake plowed the new channel to the Sound, and that one whale, with a spruce tree growing from its head, traveled north to British Columbia, where it was killed by people who grew rich selling its blubber. This strange tale may recall the appearance of tall-masted trading ships on the Strait of Juan de Fuca around the time of the flood.[27]

Then terrible sickness swept the population, killing thousands. During winter dances, it was common for individuals to manifest symptoms of illness to mark the arrival of their supernatural guardians, but now entire communities writhed in the grip of something horribly new. This was smallpox. Anthropologist Robert Boyd, whose *The Coming of the Spirit of Pestilence* is the definitive work on the cataclysmic impact of diseases introduced on the Northwest Coast, times the initial appearance at around 1775, when Westerners appeared off the coast and the disease spread inland, erasing as much as a third of the population.[28]

The hand of death drew forth a religious response. A group on the Skagit River attributed its salvation to a dance introduced by a prophet, La-hail-by, who learned it in a dream and taught it to his family. As death stalked the village, his family members stayed in their longhouse and danced in rows facing south, stopping only to sleep and eat. Over days, the east ends of the rows moved slowly forward, the west ends back, until all faced west. At this, La-hail-by told them to stop. The sickness had passed.[29]

To them, magical protection could at least explain why some survived. Restorative powers were also attributed to the use of the sweat lodge and a tea made from stinging nettles, but Boyd noted that sweating in steam followed by an icy plunge would likely have increased mortality. Nevertheless, the community reassembled itself, not as families returning in the fall laden with foods, but as survivors seeking familiar forms amid cataclysm or weaving new ones from grief and resolution. As old leaders died, a new generation confronted a radically different situation. The Spirit Canoe may have become more elaborate as the ranks of the dead grew and people sought to combat mobs of lonely ghosts. Amid the tumult, reports of new beings promising salvation and the resurrection of the dead gained a rapt hearing.

The flood carving out the Stuck River channel left a mile-long *stək!*, "logjam," blocking travel on the lower White River. Short-term logjams

The site of Flea's House, the White River–Duwamish settlement where Seattle was raised as a boy, located on the bank of the White River (now the Green River), in what is now the city of Kent, WA. Flea's House was a community of mythological significance.

appeared frequently, but this one remained long enough for bushes and trees to grow where silt collected on its surface. It marked the division of the downstream floodplain, known as the Tskwa'litsh, a brushy tangle of swamp and forest, from its more densely wooded upper half. Shortly after the jam appeared, five noble families from the Black River pulled up their house posts and rebuilt longhouses at the jam's strategic downstream end. They became known as the Stək!a'bsh, "the Logjam People," and in short order, they became notorious for arrogance and for their abuse of those living a mile upriver in a village called Ch!ut!əp Altxw "Flea's House."[30]

A myth about Elk Woman said that when she married Flea and moved to his village, his gigantic kin tried to asphyxiate her by burning fresh bones in their fires. She clubbed them and tore them apart with her teeth, leaving the house spattered with blood. The drops returned to life as tiny fleas, a plague upon humanity but no worse, thanks to Elk Woman.[31]

The myth became an allegory. Flea's House had been an important village with noble families living in large houses in an area rich in resources. Its members were said to be endogamous, choosing marriage partners from their own number. This was not uncommon among larger villages, where members of a long-standing house group might marry those from another, but along the White River, or at least among the Stǝk!a′bsh, the residents of Flea's House came to be regarded as low.

The Black River families' move to the logjam was a provocative act, difficult to imagine happening unless conditions made it possible. The decimation of the local population by disease could explain it. Less able to resist the inroads of a stronger group, a smaller population would also be less able to procure surpluses required for feasting and ceremony, rendering them low in the estimation of their affluent neighbors. Lethal epidemics like smallpox, which scarred and often blinded survivors, would have made orphans from Flea's House poor marriage choices. Until archaeological work is carried out, we can only speculate if Flea's House devolved in this way—abused, informants said, as "a people like slaves to Stakabsh [Stǝk!a′bsh]."[32]

The antipathy between Stuq` and Flea's House worsened when the Stǝk!a′bsh planned a trail from their new village to the clamming beach at Three Tree Point and asked the Flea's House people for help. They refused, but when the Stǝk!a′bsh finished their trail, the Flea's House people cut a path to intersect it. The Stǝk!a′bsh tried to block the spur by felling trees across it, and when this didn't work, they captured the Flea's House headman and lynched him with a noose woven from hazel withes. Thereafter, the Stǝk!a′bsh missed no opportunity to humiliate the people of Flea's House. When they sent out formal invitations for a *sgwi′gwi*, they called the Flea's House people by tipping over a canoe and pounding on it. The Stǝk!a′bsh traveled between the two villages on a dry road along the levee, but those from Flea's House had to use a muddy path and wash away their footprints. It was not just Flea's House that suffered the Stǝk!a′bsh's arrogance. Oral histories describe them at odds with Vashon Islanders, the S'Klallam, and the Snoqualmie. Raids turned the river into a bloody highway for most of a century.

Differing accounts of Seattle's ancestry are rooted in this conflict. Native informants told Waterman that he was the child of Shxwiye′hǝb, a Suquamish man, and Sxila′ts!a, a woman from Stǝk!. A colleague of Waterman's, anthropologist John Peabody Harrington, heard that the Boy grew up at Stǝk!. But one of anthropologist Arthur Ballard's

White River informants, Charles Satiacum, said that the Boy and his father and grandfather were from Flea's House. A Harrington informant, Jim Bass, claimed that the Boy's mother was from Flea's House, and that his father was not a chief, that in fact his father and mother were *alsh*, "cousins" or "age-mate friends." This suggests theirs was an endogamous marriage, and writing half a century before Waterman and Harrington, Indian agent Edmund Starling reported hearing that Seattle's mother was a slave.[33]

We know that in the later 1850s, enmity developed between Seattle and groups from the southern tributaries of the Duwamish River, which participated in the Yakima War. Is it possible that allegations of Seattle's connection to Flea's House reflected this enmity? But Starling heard about Seattle's slave ancestry prior to the Yakima War, and the specificity of the claims underscores the genuine tumult roiling the Boy's world at the time of his birth. If some of his paternal ancestors did come from Flea's House, then they may have lived there when it was an important village, enjoying marital links with Duwamish and Suquamish nobility. Native informants remembered Shxwiye'həb being constantly at war with the Twana on Hood Canal and with the Chemakum living at its mouth, and coveting the land of the Duwamish, all of which strongly suggests that he was a war leader. His attacks on the Chemakum and the Duwamish were said to have greatly reduced their numbers. These stories may telescope memories of kinship links binding the upriver Duwamish, specifically those at Flea's House, to the Suquamish, seeking access to the river fishery, with the depopulation caused by epidemics. Shxwiyehəb's truculence mirrors that of the Stək!a'bsh and prefigures the irascibility of his son.

Sxilats!a was the daughter of a White River woman and a Duwamish man from a Black River family. If the White River woman hailed from Flea's House, she probably gave birth to Sxilats!a among her people, as was customary. Besides Seattle, Sxilats!a had other children, whose names have come down to us in one form or another: Xtsha'tshidax, baptized David, and another baptized John. She also had two daughters, one the settlers called Nancy, and her sister, Ann. This Ann, or Anne, may have been the woman named Quitsdeetsa who we know later married the settler Abner Tuttle.[34]

Shxwiye′həb may have had another unnamed wife from White River, possibly a *sba′losed* marriage, who birthed the Boy's half brothers: Curley; K!ubaii, also written as Guba′i'i, and Xoxwa′tkəb, both said to have been from White River; plus a fourth son, known as Dodo or Labs; and a daughter, the Boy's half sister, whom settlers called Sally. She married the headman of Herring's House and became a Methodist. Another of Curley's sisters was Kickumulow, mother of the man settlers called Yarkekeeman, Indian Jim, or Denny Jim.[35]

Shxwiye′həb was a noble name from a lineage with links to Hood Canal. By marriage, he was Seattle's link to the Suquamish, to their great warrior, K!itä′p—Kitsap, after whom the peninsula is named, to the Twana and possibly the Skagit. Sxilats!a was the Boy's link to the Duwamish and the chief Kwia′xtəd. The name Seattle, now the most famous of all Puget Salish names, was said to have been inherited from her people, although by Harrington's time, informants said no one knew about any earlier Duwamish Seattles.[36]

From all of this data, we may reconstruct a plausible scenario of events surrounding Seattle's birth. In the late 1700s, disease swept the Duwamish River valley, reducing the population and decimating Flea's House. Accompanying this catastrophe, winter storms blocked travel on the lower White River with a logjam. As groups struggled to recover, noble Black River families erected longhouses at the logjam, usurping the traditional rights of their devastated neighbors upstream. The Duwamish lands Shxwiye′həb coveted may have once been his own.

Although the Boy was said to be from the noble village of Stək!, it was also said that he grew up "a mile above their village," at Flea's House, and that "he was not really a noble." The putative slave ancestry on his father's side, combined with the taint of endogamy and the humiliation of Flea's House remained with him all his life, reaching Edmund Starling's ears in the 1850s in believable form. As recently as the 1950s, George Adams, a Washington state legislator and member of the Skokomish tribe, derided Seattle as "an ex-slave who lived at Fleaburg."[37]

Around the time of the Boy's birth, strange beings in tall ships showed up near the northern entrance of Puget Sound, where a Skagit story recalls a first encounter: The people thought the Changer had returned in a great canoe. But when his crew gave them a liquid to drink, it confused them and inspired one to sing his guardian spirit's song out of season. The Skagits could not imagine the Changer allowing such an embarrassing faux pas, but if the strange beings were not his emissaries, who could they be?[38]

Then Schwiyehəb's kinsman Kitsap made a prophecy. Holding a trade bead in his fingers, possibly during a winter dance, he told listeners that the strange beings who brought beads like this would soon visit them. Within the year, on a spring afternoon, a group camping on a windy point near Kitsap's house observed a white birdlike thing approaching from the north. As it approached and increased in size, some fled, fearing that Gedney Island, near the mouth of the Snohomish, had broken the ropes holding it in place and gone adrift, a sign that the world was literally coming apart. Others stood transfixed as the terrific shape passed majestically before them. Later that evening, it returned nearer the point, folded its wings, and became a whale with trees growing from its back. In the branches clambered beings white as ghosts.[39]

Brave souls paddled out for a closer look. They were hailed in a strange nasal language and beckoned with trinkets. After accepting some, they hurried back. It was as Kitsap foretold: strange beings had come to trade. Before dark, a small boat lowered from the craft traveled west and then looped back, propelled eerily by beings facing backward, like ghosts would in the land of the dead, pulling on what looked like herring rakes. Some in brilliant colors and shining metal got out and walked around like resplendent birds before returning to their craft. One was George Vancouver, the thirty-four-year-old captain of HMS *Discovery*, out of Falmouth, England, on a voyage of exploration and diplomacy. The next day, May 20, 1792, he brought his ship nearer the encampment at the western edge of a lush meadow. His descriptions of "huts . . . poor and miserable . . . constructed something after the fashion of a soldier's tent" are the first Western description of native life on Puget Sound.[40]

Men, women, and children were drying fish and shellfish over fires while others were "busily engaged like swine, rooting up this beautiful meadow in quest of a species of wild onion and two other roots," Vancouver wrote. He wove this comment into his narrative along with notes kept by the ship's doctor and naturalist, Archibald Menzies, a graduate of the University of Edinburgh, who had visited the Northwest

Coast once before the 1780s. Menzies discovered a new plant in the meadow, but neither he nor Vancouver were much impressed by the people who looked like those they had seen along the Strait of Juan de Fuca, described as "equally ill made, and as much besmeared with oil and different colored paints, particularly with red ochre and a sort of shining chaffy mica."

Native memories of the encounter with *Discovery* preserve a sense of wonder very different in tone. While many at the point fled to the woods, others followed the strange vessel's progress, exclaiming "ƏchidaaÍ ƏchidaaÍ" ("Wonderful! Wonderful!") over and over again. The oil and paint they wore were the accoutrement of formal greeting, and throughout the time the British remained, the native people maintained a scrupulous etiquette toward their sensational guests.[41]

Three hundred years before, a similar scenario occurred when people on the island of Guanahani in the eastern Lucayas (Bahamas) swam to Christopher Columbus's flagship, *Santa Maria*, and called out, "Come see the men who came from the heavens! Bring them something to eat and drink!" This was the transcendent moment of discovery, when an old world met the new. With a terrible prescience, Columbus observed that the "Indios" would be "good and intelligent servants," assuring his king that "with 50 men all of them could be held in subjection and can be made to do whatever one might wish."[42]

Contact overwhelmed Guanahani, whose inhabitants vanished in fifty years. Its wave swept through the Caribbean into Mexico, Central America, South America, the Gulf and Atlantic Coasts, the Mississippi watershed, the boreal forest, the Southwest, the Great Basin, and California, reaching Puget Sound in 1792, where the old hubris still echoed in the British imagination. The discovery of charred skeletons at what was probably a burned-over cemetery near Port Townsend led Menzies to fancy it the site of a barbarous immolation, "for," he wrote, "it is the known practice of the American tribes on the opposite coast to burn their victims." For the discoverers, the new land had vast potential, but its "savage" inhabitants did not.[43]

Shortly after *Discovery* moved nearer to shore, someone in a canoe tossed an animal skin on board, as payment for the gifts given the previous day. When Vancouver and his officers visited the encampment around noon, two men welcomed them with a meal of boiled roots and clams. Later, the two men led the intoning of a traditional Suquamish greeting from canoes. It was, Vancouver wrote, "principally sung by one man, who at stated times was joined in chorus by several others, whilst some in each canoe kept time with the handles of their paddles, by striking them against the gunwhale or side of the canoe, forming a sort of accompaniment . . . by no means destitute of an agreeable effect."[44]

After some coaxing, the two men clambered on board, under the ship's towering masts and its web of rigging, to the crew's curious stares. Vancouver invited both into the stern cabin, where he presented each a garment of blue cloth, pieces of copper and iron, and other trinkets. Back on deck, he watched them trade everything except the copper for the shiny buttons and buckles of the crew's dress.

The Indians were mystified when crewmen directed them to dip pieces of hardtack into a container of what looked like pitch, but after watching the British consume it with exaggerated relish, they did likewise, discovering the sweetness of molasses. Still convinced it was a type of pitch, Kitsap, probably one of the two, later used some to plug cracks in his canoe and was shocked to discover that it dissolved in water.

On May 22, Vancouver noted that canoes that had passed from the village point to the eastern shore the previous day had returned with nearly eighty people paddling dugouts shaped differently than the high-prowed canoes that had circled *Discovery*. These were river canoes, riding lower in the water and squared at each end, carrying river people, the Duwamish, who Vancouver thought resembled the Suquamish except that "they were infinitely more cleanly." On May 24, the native visitors stashed mats, gear, food, and barking dogs picturesquely in their craft and paddled off. The next day, several returned with the gift of a whole deer captured after a hunt on Blake Island. In return, Vancouver delighted them with the gift of a sheet of copper.

On May 26, *Discovery*'s tender, the brig *Chatham*, dropped anchor off the village point, and ship's clerk Edward Bell observed that while the native people's readiness to exchange goods for copper indicated they were aware of the maritime trade farther north, the great amount of goods they exchanged for it suggested they had never dealt directly with Westerners. In return for foodstuffs, arrows, horn bracelets, and other manufactures, they received cloth, brass buttons, buckles, hawk's bells, iron implements, glass beads, and sheet copper. We can only imagine what they thought when Vancouver's crew assembled to watch sailors have their wrists tied to *Discovery*'s shrouds and their backs bloodied by lashes from the cat-o'-nine-tails, or the absolutely thunderous salute fired by *Discovery*'s cannon on May 29 to celebrate the anniversary of King Charles II's restoration to the English throne. And then the magical ships disappeared. *Chatham* left first, and on the morning of May 30, *Discovery* slipped around the low headland christened Restoration Point and headed north.[45]

Thirty-two years passed before Euro-Americans left record of another encounter with native people on this part of Puget Sound. Vancouver's description of the region encouraged its eventual colonization and settlement, but his visit had a profound and lasting impact on the Suquamish and Duwamish who, in a matter of days, had become the richest people on the Sound. If the British were not supernatural beings, they certainly enjoyed relations with extraordinary supernatural powers. How did they come by these? Even as a youngster among the throng, the impressions of those stirring days remained with the Boy, and years later he would tell incoming Americans that he remembered the great Vancouver.

# CHAPTER TWO

*"Why should I murmur at the fate of my people?"*

The kind of trade initiated by Captain George Vancouver on Puget Sound had been going on farther north for a generation. In 1774, the Spanish sent Captain Juan José Pérez Hernández north on the frigate *Santiago* to determine if Russian landings in Alaska threatened Spain's sway in the Pacific. By August, Hernández was trading at Nootka Sound on the west coast of what is now Vancouver Island. The Spanish response prodded the British to send Captain James Cook to the Northwest Coast two years later in search of the fabled Northwest Passage. Instead, his men discovered that the lustrous sea otter pelts native groups traded for baubles brought a fortune in China. So began the maritime fur trade, when scores of ships from many nations headed to the Northwest Coast.

Vancouver had been a young lieutenant on Cook's voyage, and his 1792 visit came as the result of the so-called "Nootka Incident" in 1789, when Spanish authorities seized several British trading vessels after their crews built a post on Nootka Sound without permission. The resulting diplomatic row threatened war between the two powers, and Vancouver was instructed to strengthen Great Britain's claims to the region and reach an amicable agreement with Spanish officials. Ultimately, Spain allowed the British and others to trade on the coast north of the 42nd parallel.

The resolution of the crisis opened the Northwest Coast to British and American colonization, and the effect of Western contact on the native peoples transformed their societies. For the survivors of populations decimated by smallpox, the infusion of trade goods and firearms brought about wrenching change. Distribution of the new goods during potlatches enhanced the status of noble hosts but also sharpened rivalries, as groups sought access to the burgeoning trade or went on slave raids to rebuild their populations. And if sheet copper, mirrors, and glass beads failed to sufficiently awe rivals, muskets, powder, and shot would make a deeper impression.

The violent fallout showed up in the logs of the Spanish explorers who were sent north to strengthen their government's claims prior to negotiations with Vancouver. Coming out from Dungeness Bay on the Olympic Peninsula to trade with members of Manuel Quimper's expedition in 1790, the S'Klallam told the Spaniards that they were under attack from marauding groups coming from Vancouver Island. During the exploration of Puerto de la Bodega y Quadra (Discovery Bay), on the peninsula's north shore, Quimper's pilot, Juan Pantoja, found "canoes closed with boards and capes, very well tied, which had inside some human skeletons." Other scattered remains cast gloom over the lovely inlet, and departing, Pantoja expressed relief at "getting out of this slaughter house of human beings." He did not speculate about the cause of death, but a grimmer spectacle farther west suggested warfare. "From the Puerto de Quimper [Dungeness Bay] to the Ensenada de Rojas [Clallam Bay], some 18 leagues," he wrote, "we saw on all the beaches a number of skeletons fastened to poles on the shores," a S'Klallam warning to foes across the strait.[1]

Vancouver also observed the skeletons at Discovery Bay, as well as human heads impaled on tall poles at the entrance to Admiralty Inlet, which appeared to support Archibald Menzies's view that they were the result of barbaric warfare. Whatever the cause, Vancouver rightly concluded that the country had suffered a great and recent depopulation. That this was accompanied by conflict was borne out by the native people's desire to obtain weapons. The S'Klallam sought muskets and swords from Vancouver's men, and on the island named after him, *Discovery*'s Master, Joseph Whidbey, observed a village headman wearing English and Spanish short swords.[2]

This instability produced shifts in population. Lummi legends tell of their move from the San Juan Islands to the resource-rich mouth of the Nooksack River after overcoming devastated groups or marrying into them. The latter outcome presented a familiar pattern, where feuds among neighboring groups or even the attacks of invaders could be resolved by sexual politics. Native people believed strong powers made strong people, and what better way to share power but through intermarriage, so that the children of such unions could access their families' supernatural ties? Conflict surely antedated Euro-American contact, but depopulation, burgeoning trade, and the introduction of firearms harrowed traditional societies and heightened the need for peacemaking.[3]

Like disease, conflict spread from points of contact with Western traders. Fighting followed the Samish, linguistically akin to the Lummi, south and east from their home islands to the fishery at the mouth of the Samish River. Legends of the neighboring Nu-wha-ah recount raids on groups from Vancouver Island to the Puyallup River, led by a famous war leader, Chadas-kadim, and his son.[4]

A Lower Skagit legend describes a massacre of residents farther south, at the mainland village of Whats-al-ul, near the modern town of Mount Vernon, carried out by raiders from the village of Utsaladdy on Camano Island. A later attack by survivors forced the Skagit to move from Camano to Whidbey Island. The Skä'häkachet, a group on Whidbey said to have no warriors, were absorbed by the Snohomish, who moved from their river to southern Whidbey. The Snohomish, in turn, fought with the Chemakum, on the northeast corner of the Olympic Peninsula, who ultimately found themselves at war with all their neighbors. They were probably the ones who impaled the heads on the stakes that Vancouver saw, to warn away their foes.[5]

Like falling dominoes, the conflict spread into central and southern Puget Sound. The Boy's father, Shxwiye'həb, fought frequently with the Chemakum, whom the Suquamish accused of encroaching upon their territory. It is significant that Shxwiye'həb's ability to drive an arrow through the side of a canoe was one of the few memories of him. He led raids against the Twana on Hood Canal and against the Duwamish, and it was during this tumultuous period that the Boy grew up.[6]

There are few specifics of Seattle's early life, save a photograph of him in later life that may show a slightly flattened head. Pioneer Arthur Denny recalled that Seattle's head "was not flattened by far as much as the ordinary Indian," and Lieutenant Thomas Phelps, an officer on the sloop of war *Decatur*, which defended the town in 1856, described him as an "intelligent Flathead Indian," which, in the confusing parlance of the time, meant one whose head had not been flattened. The *sia'b* customarily tied a slat to a baby's head, so that as the skull developed, it expanded in back rather than in front, making the forehead follow the line of the nose. A sketch of Curley shows his head to have been flattened. Seattle's flattening was apparently not as pronounced, but this did not preclude his becoming a chief. The naturalist George Gibbs, who knew Seattle and wrote the first detailed ethnography of Washington

Territory's Indians, wrote that Seattle was chief of his mother's tribe, the Duwamish. Because his father was Suquamish, the Boy often visited the people at Agate Passage, where he gained a reputation for sensibility that set him apart from the arrogant Stǝk!a'bsh.[7]

On the White River, the Boy's people taught him how to make himself agreeable to the powers that would make him a man of worth. But prophecies of apocalypse, unsettling rumors, devastating epidemics, and the appearance of strange beings unsettled native society. And shortly after Vancouver departed, another episode in the fearful sequence struck people on Puget Sound like a thunderclap.

Groups on the outer Northwest Coast were the first to suffer epidemics. If a group's population declined and it could not produce the surpluses needed to maintain its previous stature, it became poorer in the eyes of its neighbors. To bring back enough young women and children to rebuild their population and kill enough men to stymie revenge attacks, afflicted groups began raiding. The appearance of raiders in their great canoes on Puget Sound became more frequent. Seattle's daughter Angeline recalled that when her father was still a child, northern raiders carried out an attack on Salmon Bay, a deep inlet immediately north of Elliott Bay. At night, warriors in long black canoes stealthily threaded their way through the bay's narrow entrance—called the Shǝ'lshol, which means "Threading a Bead," and attacked the Shǝlshola'bsh village, killing and capturing many.[8]

In the years following, the Boy sought a guardian power. These were generally described as guardian spirits, the *skala'litǝt* or the more dangerous *xuda'b*; the latter identified with shamans, or those encountered in a secret society, the Sxǝdxǝdǝb, whose gifts initiates sought in dramatic rites. Adolescents were taught by family trainers to identify the proper spirit powers and then sent to isolated haunts to carry out a quest. While there, in a dream vision, the power received the supplicant, taught its song, and gave a special power that could be called up when the song was sung. The supplicant might also be given a special name, as Jacob, in the Old Testament, received the name Israel from the supernatural being he wrestled with at the Jabbok River Ford.

According to a Suquamish informant, Amelia Snaetlum, Seattle had Thunderbird power. In the lists of supernatural spirits, this power,

Xwi'kwadi, is prominent. "It meant wealth and it healed wounds, so that the person who had it was very brave." It was not the great Thunderbird of legend, however, but a creature the size of a seagull, or, in Seattle's case, a duck. Its power was awakened by singing its song and shaking small wooden duck-shaped rattles with pebbles inside.[9]

It is possible that Seattle found his power in Lake Burien, today a pond in a suburb south of Seattle. The lake's location near Stuq' and Flea's House and its native name, Xwi'yəkw, "Thunder," suggest to me that this is the place where the Boy went on his quest—spending days alone, fasting and rubbing himself with rotting fir bark to cleanse himself before diving with a heavy stone that took him down to the power's house. Seattle's people believed he could call thunder from the skies, and they said that when he was angry, his voice thundered. In a neat turn of phrase, Snaetlum said that when Seattle was angry and shouted, "The one he was angry at would shake. It was a big power, that power of Seattle."[10]

When a well-born boy outgrew his nickname, he received an ancestral name, announced by a relative during a ceremony hosted by his family. It was at such an event that the Boy received the name of a maternal ancestor. What comes down to us as "Seattle" or "Sealth" or, more accurately, "Siʔaʔɬ," has been variously translated as "Honorable One" and "Good Blood Child," but Nile Thompson suggests "Siʔaʔɬ" may have been a shortened version of an ancestral name or even an adult nickname. During his lifetime white listeners heard three syllables with the emphasis on the middle one. Because I think the way we pronounce the city's name more closely approximates the contemporaneous pronunciation, I write his name as "Seattle."[11]

Later events indicate that he was also initiated into the Secret Society. I interpret Angeline's claim that he inherited the chiefship when he was a boy as the social recognition that came with his reception of a powerful guardian spirit, an ancestral name, and his induction into the Secret Society, making him an acceptable choice as a leader. Among adults, Seattle learned to cherish the ability to capture attention with language, to turn a phrase and to wield words like the speaker who silenced a carping critic by asking, "Are you running a race with me?"[12]

Seattle was an ambitious young man, and he soon gained a reputation for bravery and martial skill, which was described in an account of his early years written by Samuel F. Coombs, a pioneer merchant, Wells Fargo agent, and student of native culture. Shortly after arriving in the Puget Sound region as a young man from Maine in 1859, Coombs observed the aged Seattle presiding at a very large gathering of native people. Impressed by his demeanor and authority, he hired a translator to ask how Seattle came to be a leading figure. The elders traced his rise back to an event that occurred when he was only twenty years old—around 1806 if his estimated birth date is correct.[13]

In Coombs's account, downstream villagers learned of an imminent attack by upper Green and White River raiders, who had earlier enslaved some of their kinfolk. These raiders were related to the Tu'bshədəd, equestrian interior folk who traded in goods and slaves and had married into upriver groups. As headmen planned a defense, Seattle, whose name Coombs writes as Sealth (easier to pronounce than the Xwəljutsid form, which ends with a voiceless lateral alveolar fricative), solicited support for an attack.

Suspecting that the raiders would come downriver at night, Seattle and others felled a tree across a sharp bend, positioned so that it rested only inches above the water. In the dark, the raiders did not see the obstruction until they collided with it, and in the confusion, Seattle and his fighters ambushed them with arrows and spears. Of the raiders' five canoes, three capsized, and the cries of their comrades drove the crews of the last two ashore, where they beat a hasty retreat.

The weapons used, as described by Coombs, were bows and arrows, tomahawks, and knives. A concentration of projectile points discovered in Green River, where the ambush is said to have happened, may actually come from this encounter. Coombs's account does not describe Seattle cutting off the heads of his foes, a fairly common practice of Puget Sound warriors, who collected trophy heads. In this, it seems he followed the example of Kitsap, a war leader who disliked the practice, opining that hanging heads in front of the village was "showing off."[14]

Seattle's victory continued the seesaw of violence along the lower White River. The aggressive response by tidewater and downriver groups—the Duwamish, whom Gibbs generalized as Seattle's mother's people—against upriver and inland groups calls to mind the conflict between the Stək!a'bsh and the inhabitants of Flea's House. The significance of Seattle's first success as a war leader, following in his father's

CHIEF SEATTLE'S GREAT VICTORY ON WHITE RIVER

An engraving depicting Seattle's successful ambush of upper-river raiders that accompanied an account of the chief's life that appeared in the *Seattle Telegraph* newspaper. The writer, Samuel Coombs, interviewed native elders for the story.

footsteps, is underscored by the fact that Coombs's informants remembered it half a century later.

Other parts of the story are problematic. Coombs wrote that after the victory, at a grand council of six tribes—the "Ole Man House [Suquamish], Moxliepush [lower White River], Duwamish, Black River, Shilshole and Lake tribes"—Seattle was elected head chief, and leaders of the six tribes became his subchiefs. Coombs said that Curley was named subchief of the Duwamish from the bay to the confluence of the Black and White Rivers, but this would have been unlikely since he would have been only four or five years old at the time. According to Coombs, when the lower White River, Black River, and Lake people objected, Seattle organized another expedition on the rivers and lakes, during which he threatened war and took hostages to ensure their loyalty. From what we know about how head chiefs were selected, it seems unlikely that so many groups would confer leadership on a twenty-year-old no matter his success. This part of the account sounds more like what happened about a decade later, when the Suquamish chief Kitsap organized a confederacy to meet a threat from the north. Coombs's references to hostages may recall diplomacy sealed through intermarriage in which Seattle played a role; indeed his own marriage may have been a result.

Over his lifetime, Seattle was known to have had four wives—two of whom appear to have been *sba'losəd* marriages—and several concubines. Having an honored name and success as a war leader, Seattle first married a Duwamish headman's daughter. Intergroup ties fostered well-connected marriages, but individual desire was not ignored, and there were courting rituals. If a boy liked a girl, he could leave the punt pole he used to propel his river canoe leaning against her family's longhouse. If she used it, it signaled her agreement to marry him. A Suquamish girl's choice could also be made public when a boy wearing a belt with cords attached whirled around in a dance. If a girl grabbed one, it showed that she fancied him, and if the families agreed to the match, a marriage went forward.[15]

What would this have been like? Ethnographer Herman Haeberlin, a student of Franz Boas in the early twentieth century, described a traditional wedding between a Suquamish bride and a Puyallup groom during which both families exchanged gifts over several months, because such celebrations "should never be hurried." At the final ceremony, the families sat across from one another, and the bride's father passed gifts to the groom's family. Then the bride, wearing many dog-wool blankets, was led to her in-laws' side along a road of woven mats. The image of the bride seated in her luxurious white cone of blankets calls to mind the great Cascadian volcanoes, which, in myth, are given a female persona. A common suffix ending women's names, *tsa*, as in Sxila′ts!a, was derived from the word for blanket and signified worth—similar to how the Latin name Antonia means "priceless" or "praiseworthy." After the groom's family presented its gifts, the couple stood up and clasped hands, and the headmen made speeches. There were athletic contests and a feast, and the day ended with gambling and singing.[16]

We do not know the name of Seattle's first wife, but she died shortly after bearing their only child, a daughter, around 1811 or 1812. The baby had a childhood nickname, Wee-wy-eke, and several adult names—Sabolits!a and one variously rendered as Kick-is-om-lo or Ka-ki-is-il-ma. Seattle pioneer Catherine Maynard thought these sounded too harsh for such an attractive woman and gave her the name by which she is better known, Angeline.[17]

Seattle park historian Don Sherwood preserved an account that said Angeline had been born near Pritchard Island, in Seattle's Rainier Beach neighborhood, on the southwest shore of Lake Washington. The island's name, X̱!i'lchus, "Little Island," identified a winter village there. Women often returned to their mothers' households to give birth, so this may have been the home of the mother of Seattle's wife. The people living there, the Skaitil'babsh, took their name from the Skaita'w, a powerful long-haired merman, a wealth-giving power who made his people prominent enough to be listed in the Point Elliott Treaty, as "the Sk-ta'hl-mish," right after the Duwamish and the Suquamish.[18]

Following his first wife's death, Seattle married a woman whose name is remembered as Owiyahl, daughter of Sakhumkun, a headman. Her later burial at Alki Point identifies Herring House as her birthplace. Whether this marriage was polygynous (made before his first wife's death) or *sba'losəd* (made after) is not known, but Seattle's tie with this important village grew stronger when its presiding headman, Tsutsa'lptid, whom settlers named Dick, married Seattle's half sister Sally.

Seattle's second wife raised Angeline and bore him three sons and many daughters. One son, Sa'kw!al, possibly the eldest, became a noted warrior. Some confusion surrounds the names of two other sons, whose baptismal names, George and James, may celebrate prominent Hudson's Bay Company officials George Simpson and James Douglas. Most sources give George's native name as See-an-ump-kun (whose name sounds similar enough to his maternal grandfather's to suggest he inherited it). But a list of Suquamish and Duwamish headmen drawn up in 1854 identifies him as Schwoo-yehm, separate from a "See-a'h-num-kan," who is also listed. The latter may be James, more commonly known as Jim, who may also appear on the Treaty of Point Elliott as Sloo-noksh-tan, signing for the Suquamish. Two daughters died young; another, possibly baptized Ann, married a headman of the Sts!apa'bsh, or Sammamish, a group living along the meandering Sammamish River.[19]

By the late eighteenth and early nineteenth century, Western influences pulsing into the Sound from the Strait of Juan de Fuca were joined by others coming from the south. In 1792, American captain Robert Gray brought his brig, *Columbia Rediviva*, around Cape Horn from Boston into the north Pacific. Crossing the perilous bar of a fabled river, he named it "Columbia's River," after his sturdy ship, giving his country its first opportunity to realize ambitions seeded during colonial days, when royal charters mapped land grants reaching from the Atlantic to the

Pacific. Great Britain and Spain quickly challenged the claim, but Lewis and Clark's 1805–06 sojourn at the river's mouth strengthened it.

Along with its strategic value, the river's rich peltries made it a prize. Chinese demand for sea otter furs sent the first wave of maritime traders to the Northwest Coast, but European and American demands for fur also inspired overland expeditions that blazed paths for future emigration. Marten and ermine, whose pelts lined the sleeves and collars of high-fashion garments, had been nearly trapped-out in Europe, and North Americans were quick to tap their abundant sources. On both sides of the Atlantic, the top hat made from felted beaver fur defined style for the rising middle class, and increasing demand for beaver pelts drove trappers farther and farther west. Captain Gray's discovery of the Columbia excited trading companies, which doubled as agents of national expansion, and in 1811 members of John Jacob Astor's Pacific Fur Company, headquartered in New York, traveled by sea and land to the mouth of the great river and built Fort Astoria, beating both Russian and British efforts.

The British seized the fort during the War of 1812 and renamed it Fort George, but a year later the fort was sold to the North West Company, a fur trading company headquartered in Montreal, and its trade produced the same effect in the south that the maritime trade had in the north. The Chinook, in whose territory the fort stood, exchanged furs, hides, and food for metalware, blankets, and beads. This and their acquisition of firearms made them powerful middlemen, distributing goods obtained from Western traders to their native neighbors from whom they collected slaves for a profitable trade.

Furs from the Puget lowland made their way to the fort, but a bloody fight in 1818 between Iroquois trappers employed by the North West Company and the Cowlitz, a group determined to control trade on that river, barred access to the most convenient portage route to Puget Sound. That same year, British and American diplomats agreed that the 49th parallel would define the boundary between their respective claims from the Great Lakes to the Continental Divide. The following year, the Adams-Onís Treaty made the 42nd parallel the boundary between Spanish and American claims from the Continental Divide to the Pacific, and the 1824 Russian-American Convention set the boundary between Russian and American claims at N 54°40', the line also agreed to in an Anglo-Russian convention defining British claims. In this way, Great Britain and the United States jointly occupied the vast region called Oregon. By this time, because of the Louisiana Purchase, the United States extended from the Atlantic to the Continental Divide, and the treaties assured its expansion to the Pacific.

Although few Europeans and fewer Americans were in Oregon at the beginning of the nineteenth century, their commercial forays had increasing impact. Trading and raiding on Puget Sound continued to provoke religious ferment as groups struggled with destabilizing change. It is in this context that we can imagine winter dances, when the powerful war leader Seattle advanced down the firelit length of a longhouse, shaking his duck-shaped rattles and singing Thunder's song in his booming voice.

Winter dances, initiations, and the *sgwi'gwi* required large houses to provide a proper setting for invited guests, and here we come to Old Man House on Agate Passage—the most remarkable structure erected on Puget Sound—built by the Suquamish with outside help. Longhouses on Puget Sound could be up to 120 feet long, and a *sgwi'gwi* house at Herring House was recalled to have measured sixty fathoms in length and ten in width (360 by 60 feet). Native buildings even larger were built with steel tools and mill-sawn lumber, but at the beginning of the nineteenth-century, woodwork was done with stone tools, and planks and beams were split and hewn by hand. Building a large house required skill and a vast expenditure of labor, and in its time, Old Man House was extraordinary.[20]

The name comes from the Jargon word *oleman*, meaning "old or worn out," literally "old man." It is the translation of the Xwəljutsid Lu'luƛ!, A'lal, which described its bleached ruin. Tsu-suc-cub, a name given to it in 1895 by *Seattle Post-Intelligencer* reporter Joseph Costello, is a version of Dxwsəq'wəb, the name for its location on Agate Passage.[21]

The first written description of it was made in 1841 by members of a United States Exploring Expedition commanded by naval lieutenant Charles Wilkes. In May of that year, a survey of the west side of the Sound carried out by Lieutenant William Maury discovered Old Man House while traveling north from Port Orchard. In his journal, passed midshipman Joseph Sanford described a structure he estimated as two hundred feet long and one hundred feet wide, whose roof was supported by twenty sets of wooden uprights supporting immense cross timbers. In his log, Wilkes gave a more precise measurement of 172 by 72 feet, but this was the remnant of a much larger building. In 1855, Major Hugh A. Goldsborough of the US Coast Survey visited the site and noted less obvious remains that outlined a single structure 520 feet long and 60 feet wide. Originally, it had thirty-seven pairs of fifteen-foot-high uprights in front and ten-foot-high in back, all fashioned from wooden slabs two to three feet wide and five to eight inches thick. When Goldsborough saw them, a few still held immense rafters fashioned from tree trunks, including one tapering from twenty-two to twelve inches in diameter. Native informants told him the building had been erected forty years before by one of Seattle's brothers, putting its construction sometime after the turn of the eighteenth century.[22]

In the early twentieth century, Suquamish informants identified the structure with Seattle's relative, the Suquamish head chief Kitsap. His father, a Green River man descended from the Yakama, east of the mountains, married into the Suquamish. Wealthy and powerful, he lived in a longhouse at the south end of Bainbridge Island, west of Restoration Point. He was said to have acted as Vancouver's guide, bringing him to the head of Puget Sound. By 1815, he was nearing middle age and was remembered as a "tall, broad and thick man, able to snap an elk's antler with his hands . . . a ruthless, domineering leader, who killed his own uncle when the latter opposed him."[23]

Sam Wilson, grandson of Seattle's last wife, told freelance writer and local historian Ernest B. Bertelson that the inspiration for Old Man House came to Kitsap in a dream about a great building where his people could greet the white men when they returned. Kitsap directed women to clear brush and logs from a cattail swamp at Agate Passage. With large clam shells and antler picks, they excavated a great rectangle, heaping basket loads of earth along the sides, while men downed huge cedars with fire and stone tools, sectioning them into rafters or splitting and shaping them into timbers and planks. The project took four years, during which Kitsap invited groups from as far south as the Cowlitz River to help raise his grand edifice, arranging competitions to hoist the immense rafters onto notched uprights.

Kitsap's apartment in Old Man House was in the center, fortified, and painted red and black, befitting a warrior. Two carved images—

one of a man with muskets and a cocked hat and another of a man wearing a top hat and a frock coat leading a child—flanked his apartment and may recall memories of Vancouver's crew. The figure of a great Thunderbird over his apartment may have represented Kitsap's guardian power, Tubcha'dad, a variant of Tu'bshədəd, described as "an eagle like a man." This may be associated with the story of the battle between an eagle and a water serpent that turned a narrow tidal channel into the broad Agate Passage, a mythic recollection of terrific seismic activity along the Seattle fault a thousand years ago.[24]

Seattle and his aged father, Shxwiye'həb, along with a man called Tsu-lu-cub and four other headmen, were also said to have occupied prominent apartments in the house, identified by uprights bearing carved images of human figures or geometric shapes painted white, black, and red. Another name associated with the site, Itakbw, refers to something gathered or jammed together in one place, perhaps like people in Old Man House. A Snohomish version of the name, Ita'kəbiwx, appearing in later written records as Etakmur, meaning "Mixed People," may refer to the connections the Suquamish enjoyed with many neighbors, but it may also have served as an insult questioning the noble ancestry of Suquamish families.[25]

Images carved on Figurehead Rock, a large beach boulder located at the tide line near Agate Point, may depict figures associated with the *sgwi'gwi* and secret-society initiations associated with Old Man House. Ethnographers propose that figures carved on boulders in the intertidal zone communicated with marine powers when submerged. The markings on Figurehead Rock inspired awe well into the early twentieth century, and a recollection that Kitsap carved one of them argues for the boulder's connection with Old Man House.[26]

Kitsap's pedigree, his apartment in Old Man House, and his house on Rich Passage marked him as a wealthy man. His ability to shoot an arrow more than two hundred feet up from a canoe into the woods at Point Defiance, near Tacoma, celebrated his strength; the arrows of his only competitor in this feat, his brother Təli'but, could not top the cliffs. But Suquamish memories of Kitsap focus less on his wealth or the strength of his arm than they do his strategic vision and leadership.[27]

The scale of Old Man House required many groups to help build it. Did Kitsap build it to hasten Vancouver's return, like members of cargo cults did in the South Pacific after World War II, building landing strips to coax the return of wartime cargoes? Our knowledge of events on Puget Sound in the decades after Vancouver is fragmentary, but it is possible to construct a narrative that can better account for its construction.

Raids like the one that devastated the Shəlshola'bsh required an organized response. The *sgwi'gwi*, secret-society initiations, and winter dances were ways traditional society generated leaders. Seattle's success blunting a raid during a chaotic time was another. Added to this, the written accounts of Euro-American traders returning to the region provide context that can help us comprehend the significance of Old Man House in the opening decades of the nineteenth century.

---

Fort George remained an outpost of the North West Company until its takeover in 1821 by the rival Hudson's Bay Company (HBC), headquartered in London. The enormous reach of trading houses, capable of fielding expeditions and supplying outposts around the globe, mirrored that of nations that required maps of entire continents to define their claims. In 1818, the United States and Great Britain agreed in the Treaty of Joint Occupation that the Oregon Country, one of the last uncolonized part of temperate North America, would remain free and open to members of both nations for a period of ten years. They agreed further that the 49th parallel, the US northern boundary to the Rocky Mountains, would provide the logical line of division for a future partition of Oregon. However, many British believed the Columbia River would serve as a better border than an imaginary line in the woods, particularly since its muscular course would keep Puget Sound within their sphere.

Bearing this in mind, in 1824, a decisive thirty-eight-year-old Scot, George Simpson, newly appointed governor of the HBC's vast Northern Department of Rupert's Land, which included the Oregon Country, traveled across the continent and down the Columbia to Fort George, determined to put the fur trade west of the Rockies on a firmer financial footing than had the Nor'Westers. A new headquarters, Fort Vancouver, would rise on the north bank in a drier, more cultivable region, away from the rainy coast and the truculent Cowlitz, who were blocking the portage to Puget Sound. By the time Simpson reached Fort George, plans for an expedition to flank the Cowlitz, locate a site for a new trading post on the lower Fraser River, and bring the Puget lowland firmly into the company's grasp had taken shape in his mind.

The expedition would be led by James McMillan, a forty-one-year-old Scot who had traded in the region since 1811. On November 18, 1824, he, three clerks, an interpreter, and thirty-six other men left Fort George in open boats, battling surf, wind, and rain through Willapa Bay and Grays Harbor and up the Chehalis River, to a portage from Black Lake, which brought them to Puget Sound on December 5. From Eld Inlet, they paddled through Dana Passage, camping at Anderson Island before picking up Snohomish interpreters at a mainland village. On December 7, they camped across from Vashon Island, and before breakfast the next morning they arrived at a Suquamish village to call on a chief known from previous encounters—unnamed in their reports, but possibly Kitsap.[28]

Journals kept by clerks John Work and Francis Annance provide our first glimpses of the Sound since 1792. They tell us that beaver had been virtually trapped-out on the Nisqually River and that men from Fort George had traveled as far north as the Skagit River, but they also reveal a region gripped by fear. With few exceptions, Vancouver's surveyors had been welcomed by friendly groups, alarmed neither by their visit nor their weapons, but by 1824 the approach of unfamiliar armed men in canoes inspired panic. "Saw some Indians, who all fled into the woods, leaving their canoes on the beach," wrote Annance as they reached the Sound. It was the same when the party reached Whidbey and Camano Islands. "Saw few lodges, the poor natives all fled to the woods . . . Every thing flees before us," he wrote. "All these tribes," wrote John Work, "appear much alarmed on our approach . . . All strangers are considered by these as parties of neighboring tribes coming on war excursions."

The most feared were the Cowichan, from the mouth of the Cowichan River on Vancouver Island, who dominated the mouth of the Fraser River, the expedition's goal. Locals described them as "a barbarous and wicked people." If the Suquamish chief McMillan sought on December 8 was Kitsap, he and most of his people had made themselves scarce when McMillan and his party arrived—gone fishing, according to the nervous few left behind. Like others, the Suquamish avoided the Cowichan by hiding in the woods.

Slave raids had led the Cowichan far from their homes in search of human merchandise, and by the early 1800s they dominated the Strait of Georgia. By spreading havoc on the Sound, they likely intended to eliminate rivals and make the HBC come to them, which is exactly what McMillan did. Once his party reached the Fraser, they were relieved to find the Cowichan more than happy to trade. After scouting a post site on the river, McMillan's men returned to Fort George via the Cowlitz River on January 30, unmolested. Having been successfully outflanked, the Cowlitz people concluded that they would be better served if their portage carried the company's trade. All of this delighted the parsimonious Simpson, who gloated that the whole enterprise had been carried out for less than ten pounds.[29]

To halt Cowichan depredations, Kitsap envisioned an alliance strong enough to attack them in their home waters. If by doing so Puget Sound were to become an attractive avenue for trade, so much the better. The confederation Kitsap engineered stretched from central Puget Sound to the Columbia River, and Old Man House was its nexus. The groups he brought together there demonstrated their commitment by adding apartments that increased its majestic scale, expressing their aspirations through architecture.

Memories of Seattle's father's encouraging production of canoes may recall his role providing river groups in the confederation more seaworthy vessels. Haeberlin's account of the Suquamish-Puyallup marriage, and even Coombs's description of Seattle's hostage-taking, may echo efforts to solidify the coalition.

One story about Seattle may reflect these efforts. It happened "when a great number of tribes were gathered together for a raid" and drawn-up canoes covered the beach. When a Snohomish man several canoes away began to taunt Seattle, he leaped up, sprinted over five Snohomish canoes, and, in an astounding show of strength, grabbed the man, hoisted him up bodily, and jumped back over each of the canoes while avoiding Snohomish warriors swinging at him with their knives. He threw the man down when he reached his own canoe, a feat akin to the descriptions of strength and daring Homer celebrated in the Iliad. By intimidation and diplomacy, the confederation took shape until Kitsap felt confident enough to mount an attack whose scale became the stuff of legend.[30]

The photoethnographer Edward Curtis wove a vivid account from several versions of Kitsap's raid provided by Puget Sound informants in the early 1900s, and details come from other sources. The attack likely took place around 1825, after the first McMillan expedition. Kitsap and other Suquamish men took the lead, joined by a contingent from Stək! and the Sammamish. There were men from the Puyallup and the Nisqually, from groups at the head of the Sound and Squaxin Island, from the upper Chehalis, and from the distant Cowlitz, under their chief, Wieno. Although not mentioned in the Curtis account, Seattle is likely to have been among the Suquamish warriors.[31]

More than two hundred canoes moved north to Whidbey Island, where they augmented supplies by pillaging Snohomish and Skagit camps before coasting along the San Juan Islands and crossing Haro Strait to Vancouver Island. Near Victoria harbor, they attacked a Sooke village, taking many prisoners. The Sooke chief told them that Cowichan and neighboring Sanetch raiders were headed for S'Klallam country across the Strait of Juan de Fuca and would arrive that very day. Knowing that if Kitsap's force was attacked by the raiders upon their return, he and the prisoners would be killed, he advised Kitsap to release them and head for home.

Ignoring his warning, the allies pillaged the Sooke village, even taking time to harvest camas in a nearby meadow. When they finally pushed off with their captives and booty, they were surprised by dark canoes rounding a point. Equally surprised, the Cowichan and Sanetch attempted to parley, but Kitsap and his warrior roused their men to battle fury, singing their warrior powers' songs and taunting their foes. Blood flowed when the allies ran spears through their prisoners in front of the northerners and threw their bodies overboard. In one Twana account, lice streamed from Kitsap's hair, the mark of Tubcha'dad, the warrior power described as an eagle like a man.[32]

Faced with such resolve, the Cowichan and Sanetch struck up their own war chants, drew their canoes together, and backed water, drawing the attackers forward. Dividing into groups, the northerners rammed their large canoes into the smaller Puget Sound craft, showered them with arrows, and stabbed crewmen struggling in the water with short spears. The allies fought desperately, but as wreckage and bodies filled the inlet, Kitsap's fleet disintegrated, and the surviving allies broke for open water. Kitsap, Təli'but, and others escaped in their canoe, with Təli'but prostrate after he had torn out an arrow that had struck him in his eye. Kitsap kept oncoming canoes at bay with his archer's skill, scooping up floating arrows as his ran out, while those shot at him passed harmlessly through his hair. By one account, only forty allied canoes returned.

Seattle's later boast of slaying a great chief may recall his role in the melee. Despite its disastrous end, the attack persuaded the Cowichan to halt raiding on the Sound, and when the eldest son of the old Suquam chief (probably Kitsap) came to trade at Fort Langley, he was given protection by the Cowichan chief Shashia. Subsequent intermarriage between Cowichan and Puget Sound groups strengthened ties; a sister of Seattle's first wife married a Cowichan, his daughter Angeline married a half-Cowichan man, and Seattle regularly traveled to the Fraser River in the fall to fish.[33]

The Suquamish and their neighbors had regained their old confidence, so that when McMillan's second expedition left Fort Vancouver in 1827 and traveled down Sound to build Fort Langley on the Fraser, the journal kept by clerk George Barneston described a much less fearful place. Once again, they visited a Suquamish village, but this time the chief was there to receive presents from the Hudson's Bay Company men.[34]

Two days later, on July 6, McMillan and his men camped at Point Jefferson, in view of Mount Baker's magnificent cone, and received a visit from "the old Suquam Chief with about 30 of his tribe," bringing venison to trade. This was likely Kitsap and his retinue eyeing the newcomers and their gear intently enough so that McMillan's men were relieved when their visitors left at day's end. This scene captures the outcome of Kitsap's vision. The alliance birthed in Old Man House had halted depredations from the north so that when Vancouver's heirs returned they were met as men rather than supernaturals. In Seattle's catalog of memories, this was never forgotten.

On July 9, near the tip of the Kitsap Peninsula, Barneston added new names to his journal as the HBC met with other Indians. One of them, Washkalagda, a Whidbey Island Snohomish headman, hailed from the wealthy village of Degwadzk on south Whidbey's Cultus Bay, a place famous for abundant crabs and sharks. The Snohomish were not about to let the Suquamish hog the trade, but both would learn that trading with the company was not the same as trading with Vancouver.

But just months after Fort Langley rose beside the Fraser, S'Klallam raiders attacked a company express, a group engaged in a swift errand that was bringing Christmas mail from Fort Vancouver to Fort Langley, killing its leader, Alexander McKenzie, who was a clerk at Fort Langley, and four other men, and carrying off one of their native wives. The S'Klallam would maintain that the killings happened over a matter of honor, but HBC chief factor John McLoughlin, the man Simpson appointed to administer all seven hundred thousand square miles of Oregon from Fort Vancouver, believed they were murdered for loot. Determined to let nothing hamper the company's movements between posts, he resolved to nip their effrontery in the bud. Simpson, who was rarely impressed by underlings, thought McLoughlin decisive and formidable, calling him "such a figure as I should not like to meet in a dark Night in one of the bye lanes in the neighborhood of London." Tall and muscular, with a snowy mane, piercing blue eyes, and a volcanic temper, he was not one to be trifled with, and the S'Klallam did not help their cause by daring him to avenge their deed.[35]

In the summer of 1828, McLoughlin sent chief trader Alexander McLeod and sixty-three heavily armed men in canoes down the Cowlitz portage and Puget Sound to rendezvous with the armed schooner *Cadboro*, sail against the S'Klallam, and, in McLeod's words, "let his guns settle the dispute." Some native groups saw opportunity. When McLoughlin announced his intention to chastise the S'Klallam, several groups on the lower Columbia offered assistance, eager to be counted as allies when the likelihood of being asked was small. On the Sound, McLeod received a more meaningful offer from the Suquamish.[36]

Clerk Francis Ermatinger, keeper of the expedition log, described their meeting with the Suquamish on June 29. One of them wore a powder horn traded by the S'Klallam, which had belonged to one of the murdered men. When this was snatched away, his companions sought to allay tensions by offering themselves as auxiliaries. Through interpreters, McLeod barked that the company fought its own battles but offered the group's spokesman a present and allowed the Suquamish to tag along.

The next morning, McLeod traded two small canoes for a larger one and then headed north, with four Suquamish canoes following. A short time later, McLeod's men spied two men in another canoe and chased them to the beach. They were also Suquamish, and their chief, whom Ermatinger described as "the old Indian," coaxed them from the woods to which they had fled and provided information about the S'Klallam.

Shortly after McLeod left Fort Vancouver, the anxious S'Klallam had sent word to McLoughlin that they wished to negotiate, but it was too late. At the Hadlock portage, near Port Townsend, McLeod's men opened fire on a waking S'Klallam village, killing eight men, women, and children. Once on board *Cadboro*, they sailed west and anchored off a large S'Klallam village at Dungeness, where the kidnapped wife was being held. McLeod ignored the efforts of the Whidbey Island Snohomish headman Washkalagda to peacefully resolve the issue and directed fire on a canoe of S'Klallam seeking to parley, killing one. Then *Cadboro* blasted the village with cannons. Twenty-seven were killed; canoes were destroyed, and the place looted. On their return, McLeod's men torched a longhouse at Port Townsend two hundred paces long. The kidnapped woman was freed, and many of McKenzie's possessions were retrieved, while not one of McLeod's men was even wounded. The S'Klallam had received a lesson in free trade, Western style. If the "old Indian" was Kitsap, this is one of our last glimpses of him. In one Suquamish account, it was said that he lusted after the daughter of one of his slaves. His wife warned him to leave her alone, and when he tried to force himself on the girl she scratched his face. Enraged, he split her skull open with a rock. The girl's mother went to the woods to cry out her grief, and when Kitsap later died, some thought she had directed killing power his way. But during his lifetime, Kitsap's dream of close relations with the strange white beings he had met years before remained intact, and the Suquamish kept to the course he charted, even allying themselves with the newcomers against a neighboring group in what would prove a fateful precedent.[37]

A year later, McLoughlin sent a party to chastise the Clatsop at the mouth of the Columbia, the western portal of trade. The HBC's wealth and armaments made it formidable, and its reputation for decisive action underscored its value as an ally. That much was obvious; a more intriguing question, however, was how company men came by their wealth and power. And how was it that these newcomers survived the waves of sickness that continued to decimate native people?

In the fall of 1830, McLoughlin wrote his London superiors from Fort Vancouver: "The Intermittent Fever (for the first time since the trade of this Department was Established) has appeared at this place and carried off three fourths of the Indian population in our vicinity." Scholarship identifies the malady as malaria, and Boyd estimates that it wiped out 88 percent of native people in the Willamette Valley and spread as far as Southern California. The Indians believed it came from an American ship, the *Owyhee*, trading on the lower Columbia, whose captain threatened to release among them a disease he said he had trapped in a bottle if they did not trade with him.[38]

Later that year, the ship visited the Strait of Juan de Fuca, where the Snohomish believed the captain loosed the malady. Skagit oral history recalls that barely two hundred out of one thousand Skagits survived. The captain, John Dominis, had likely heard how in 1811 the chief of the outnumbered traders at Fort Astoria had held a corked bottle he claimed held smallpox and threatened to release it if attacked. Dominis, it seemed, had also played the Indians for fools, but the trick would have terrible consequences.

Traditional curing practices exacerbated malaria's impact. Those stricken with it sought to assuage their chills and fevers by steaming themselves in sweat lodges and plunging into cold water. Those who did not quickly die of shock often developed fatal pneumonia, further decimating a population just beginning to rebound from its earlier devastation by smallpox. Although whites suffered the same symptoms, quinine and acquired resistance kept more of them alive.

Malaria and the wreck of company vessels had complicated the HBC's efforts to compete with Americans on the Sound, but the company expected success to come from a network of posts and stations along the coast. One, at Nisqually Prairie, where the Cowlitz portage reached the Sound, would link Forts Langley and Vancouver and fulfill Simpson's strategy of cementing ties with Russian Alaska by shipping it food raised on the extensive grasslands. In April 1832, McLoughlin sent Archibald McDonald, chief trader at Fort Langley, north from Fort Vancouver to drum up trade and scout a location for the new post. Where the prairie met the Sound near the mouth of Sequalitchew Creek, an imposing village headman named Lahalet allowed them to build a small storehouse and leave three to guard it and plant a garden. (Today the site is in the small city of DuPont, midway between Tacoma and Olympia.) In May, McDonald returned as chief trader for the new Fort Nisqually and built a dwelling house on the verge of the oak-studded prairie. The grassland was "boundless & picturesque," in the words of William Fraser Tolmie, a twenty-one-year-old medical student from Glasgow who had been hired by the company as a surgeon.[39]

Tolmie's diary and the *Journal of Occurrences at Nisqually House*, the fort's log, provide the first sustained Euro-American observations of life on Puget Sound. As he acquainted himself with locals, making creative stabs at names and affiliations, Tolmie described familiar figures like Watskalatchet—Barneston's Washkalagda—"who from dressing in European style & sporting bushy whiskers, is styled The Frenchman." He also introduced a new cast of characters, among them the aforementioned Lahalet; Chiatzazen, a shaman and ceremonialist; Babyar [the "babbler"]; and Challicum, a Suquamish "chief of some note & well disposed towards the whites."[40]

In these accounts, Challicum also appears as Challicoom, Chilialucum, Chilialiucum, Shallicum, Zallicum, and Tslalacom. He is probably the Tsu-lu-Cub mentioned living at Old Man House, and the Tsalcom mentioned by later Suquamish informants.

A tall, imposing figure, weighing over two hundred pounds, he was older than Seattle who outlived him by two decades. He was also an eloquent speaker and a crack shot. Sam Wilson, a Suquamish informant, told anthropologist Marian Wesley Smith that he had a Suquamish father and a Skagit mother, and was related to a noble Skagit family, possibly that of Sneetlum, the Whidbey Island chief. Dr. Thompson takes it further, proposing that his name, a nickname, and ancestors hailed from a village at the head of the sound named Ch!ti'lkw, itself named after the smallflower woodland-star (*Lithophragma parviflorum*), also known as the Indian pink, which was common in the area. Its people, called the Ch!tilkwəbsh, were ancestors of the modern Steilacoom Tribe, located near the present town of Steilacoom. The Suquamish write his name as Challacum, and that is the form we shall use to identify this Suquamish chief who played so significant a role in the region and was, in many ways, Seattle's foil.[41]

That neither Tolmie nor the *Journal* mentions Kitsap suggests that by then he was dead. His violent personality brought him many enemies, and a grandson, William Kitsap, recalled that he was murdered and that his body was buried in a secret location to prevent his foes from desecrating it. It was not secret enough, however, to prevent grave robbers from the Smithsonian Institution carrying off his bones in later years, but his people never forgot how he succeeded in bringing many groups together in alliance that achieved what none could have accomplished alone.[42]

A week after McDonald and Tolmie reached Nisqually Prairie, they traveled north by canoe to rendezvous with the *Vancouver*, an overdue supply schooner. Near Hood Canal, they caught up with Challacum, known to McDonald from earlier surveys, in a large canoe crewed by his extended family, with hampers full of camas bulbs and dried cockles. After a lunch of dog stew, they sighted *Vancouver* near Challacum's well-stocked summer home near the northern tip of the Kitsap Peninsula, where the tyee impressed Tolmie with his generosity, providing food without asking for payment.

Married to a Skagit noblewoman from Whidbey Island, Challacum summered on the lower Sound and wintered at Old Man House. Living near the much-abused Chemakum, he could keep his eye on the turbulent S'Klallam and direct action on Whidbey, where several groups competed to dominate that gateway to the inland sea. Tolmie noted Challacum's possession of McKenzie's double-barreled shotgun, but the fact that the company made no effort to retrieve it evidenced the good relations the tyee enjoyed with them. To supply the chief's retinue during his frequent visits to the fort, they allowed his servants to cultivate a potato garden nearby.

In early July, Tolmie traveled down Sound on another errand. McDonald's replacement as chief trader at Fort Nisqually, Francis Heron, a moody Irishman from Donegal, solitary and given to drink, was dissatisfied with the fort's location and sent Tolmie to examine a low point jutting from Puget Sound's eastern shore. Native people called it Sbə'kwabəks, "Prairie Point," from *ba'kwəb*, "prairie," and the suffix *ks*, "point." It was favored by Jean Baptiste Ouvre, a Hudson's Bay Company middleman, who traded with Indians away from the post for furs. He had explored the area (Ouvrie's River was the initial name given to the Duwamish), and

Tolmie thought it promising, noting the presence of the "Tuamish Indians, of whom we saw several parties along the coast, miserably poor and destitute of firearms." In view, west from Prairie Point, he noted, was the homeland of "the warlike Soquamish with whose chief T. Zallicum [Tyee Challacum], we are on friendly terms."[43]

Seattle's stature among the Duwamish and Prairie Point's location near to Herring House, his wife's village, suggest that Seattle played a role in this effort. Other prospective sites were on Whidbey Island (in Challacum's bailiwick) and near the mouth of the Deschutes River at present-day Olympia, where a *sia'b* named Gray Head, whom we shall meet later, resided. Heron's plan ultimately came to naught—Fort Nisqually remained where it was—but Seattle bided his time.

Tolmie, who had studied for the ministry, took an interest in the religious ferment sweeping native communities on the heels of the epidemics. Heron, also religious, harangued the people, contrasting their miserable state with a better life to come if they followed Christian teachings. Heron's catechism, his exposition of Christian doctrine, was delivered in short segments. These were translated by Heron's native wife into the language of the interior Spokane that Washkalagda, the "Frenchman," understood and translated in turn into Xwəljutsid. Despite the difficulty, the lessons were received "with breathless attention by young & old" gathered around a fire.

For an hour, the Frenchman and the shaman Chiatzazen explained the new religion in a dialog, after which "a simultaneous hum of approbation followed every pause." As Tolmie headed to bed, the Frenchman led his people in the *samanowash*, a circle dance, followed by prayers when all prostrated themselves. This is our first reading of a Chinook Jargon term, *samanowash*, a variant of Tamanowus, which meant anything religious. From the native perspective, Heron's wealthy, well-armed people obviously enjoyed good relations with powerful spirits, and the supernatural knowledge he was eager to share had to be important. Heron would have agreed, and the company was as eager to parlay its spiritual advantages as the Yankees were to boast of their power over disease.[44]

On August 3, 1832, Tolmie noted that several hundred Suquamish, Snohomish, Twana, and Puyallup had assembled on the beach, anticipating the arrival of a supply ship. "They are now haranguing each other," he wrote, "& a few are performing the Samanawosh." The next day, Heron invited the Frenchman, Challacum, Chiatzazen, Lahalet, and Babyar into the dwelling house to walk with him a little farther down the road of faith. Joining them, Tolmie said, was "Sialah . . . a brawny Soquamish with a roman countenance & black curley hair, the hand-somest Indian I have seen." This was Seattle, making his striking debut in Western history, a wealthy middle-aged war leader consequential and intimidating enough for an HBC headman to invite him into his house with other chiefs and ask them to change their way of living.[45]

Following the biblical practice of publicly admitting sins, Heron invited the headmen to confess their "evil actions beginning with the murders & next the thefts." Steilacoom admitted murdering four men, and Lahalet said he had killed the people responsible for the murder of an uncle and his uncle's slave. The Frenchman claimed that he had not killed anyone, and Babyar, "after coughing, blowing & humming fre-quently," said he hadn't either, but later he remembered killing five men, stealing their property and two slaves. Chiatzazen protested that he hadn't harmed anyone, that "he had for a long time been a physician & conductor of the religious ceremonies . . . but afterwards acknowledged himself the murderer of five, (besides those killed by his medicines)," Tolmie added parenthetically. Seattle announced that he "in his youth slew a great chief & stole a fathom of very fine payaquas [shell money] from the Klalum [S'Klallam]."

In Tolmie's account, Seattle's confession reads like a Homeric boast, but in an effort to distance them from a savage past, Heron had the headmen mark a piece of paper binding them to abjure murder and theft. The British lion that blew people away with cannon invited lambs to lie passively beside it. If Seattle and the others shared meaningful looks, they humored Heron by fingering the unfamiliar quill offered them and scratching marks next to what he assured them were their names. Afterward, Heron triumphantly announced to the people outside what their leaders had promised and asked them to solemnize the deed by performing another *samanowash*. And just as Kitsap learned that molas-ses would not patch a canoe, his followers would soon discovered that written words worked no better with promises.

# CHAPTER THREE

TO 1847

*"Your God seems to us to be partial."*

The 1830s, the age of Andrew Jackson in the United States, were marked by expanded white male suffrage, faith in manifest destiny, and a cupidity nurtured by the spoils system and laissez-faire economics. Having reached the Rocky Mountains, the nation of seventeen million looked to the Pacific, but if Jacksonian democracy celebrated the common man, it was still the white man, and the same decade saw expansion of black slavery into the old Southwest and the ethnic cleansing of tens of thousands of native people from their ancestral lands. The names of the Seminole chief Osceola, the Wampanoag sachem Metacom, the Cayuga war leader and orator Logan, and the Shawnee chief Tecumseh—all victims of earlier conflicts—weighted the folklore of white conquest. The expulsion of the Cherokee in 1833 by whites hungry for their land convinced distraught Protestant missionaries determined to save the Indians from damnation and white rapacity to convert them well in advance of the frontier.

If the Pacific Northwest had been snared in the nets of imperial ambition, native people still lived broad and autonomous lives. "Indeed," historian Gray H. Whaley writes in *Oregon and the Collapse of Illahee*, "nationality often mattered less than personal conduct in an evolving colonial world where neither the people nor the relations among them remained fixed for long." In the *Journal of Occurrences*, native groups constantly strove with one another to gain advantage and, despite disease, vigorously involved themselves in feuds sparked by insults, paranoia, and clashing interests. Amid the tumult, the Hudson's Bay Company and its native customers struggled to find common ground.[1]

Ethnographic work done in the early twentieth century highlighted the qualities that native groups looked for in a leader: a wealthy person from a leading family whose personality, life, and longevity imparted the gravitas necessary to be taken seriously. In dangerous times, Kitsap's war leadership mattered, but during the HBC's mercantile regime the peace it imposed paid better dividends than war, and Challacum amply fulfilled the requirements for a peace chief. In company records he is mentioned frequently, and in them he and Seattle emerge as very different figures.[2]

In the summer of 1833, relations between native people and the company soured when the chief trader at Fort Nisqually, Francis Heron, increased the price of a blanket from one beaver skin to two. For years, the company had charged what markets would bear: three skins for a blanket in the Rocky Mountains and two in the interior, but along the coast it dropped the price to one to drive American traders out of the Sound. That being achieved, it sought to rebalance its ledger by raising the coastal price to two. Angry groups boycotted the blanket trade, holding on to furs and loudly threatening to bring them to American ships, which they claimed were on the Sound. Heron knew differently and trusted his inventory to overcome resistance. Grudgingly, the people accepted the new price, masking their resentment over the company's tightfistedness.[3]

In September, Seattle and others were rewarded at the fort for unloading the supply schooner *Cadboro*. Each received five brass rings, a four-inch twist of tobacco, and a meal of potatoes, salted salmon, molasses, and rum. The rum was liberally "bailed out," and many got roaring drunk. Bleary camaraderie prevailed, but on the beach, fighting broke out, and Heron sent Jean Baptiste Ouvre to break it up. Still experimenting with names, Tolmie found Lahalet "in the clutches of the brawny Soquamish Siasch, & his son & receiving from them a vigorous pommelling from which he was rescued by O." Rivalry between competitive headmen was sharp, and rum didn't help, but how quickly Seattle could go from words to fisticuffs was on display.[4]

Trade continued desultorily, but when business called him away to Fort Vancouver, Heron left Tolmie in charge. Seeking the young man's measure, Challacum sent Atchilum, a Chinook who lived in a longhouse on the beach, to warn Tolmie that a party of S'Klallam, led by the son of a chief killed during Alexander McLeod's assault on his village, were preparing an attack. Atchilum added that "it would grieve him [Challacum] much, that evil should happen to us, who have always treated him kindly & that if we wish it he will remain as a protector until Mr. Heron arrives." Asking around, Tolmie concluded that Challacum's message was meant to intimidate as well as ingratiate. He had Atchilum thank Challacum, but he also pointed out that any violence would be severely avenged by the whites, who were far more powerful now than when McKenzie was murdered. If threats continued, he added, the company would pack up and leave.[5]

The next morning, Tolmie reminded the headmen of the company's largesse by providing them a breakfast of venison, molasses, and biscuits. But when some canoes came up missing, he confronted Challacum in Atchilum's longhouse and publicly accused him of stealing them. Surprised and humiliated, Challacum exploded in a finger-waving tirade, which Atchilum nervously declined to translate, claiming Challacum "spoke bad." Tolmie cut him off, repeated his threat to abandon the post, and stormed out.

As he strode back to the dwelling house, Atchilum caught up to warn how narrowly he had escaped death. Pointing a finger, he explained, signaled a dire threat among his people, and he advised Tolmie to prepare for an attack. Tolmie thought this unlikely but issued muskets and ammunition to employees anyway, with the order to keep them loaded. He also had company clerk John McKay keep the night watch with him in his room. The next morning, he sought to sooth Challacum with friendly words and gifts, but ordered his men to erect picket walls connecting the dwelling house to the storehouse.

The Indians took a dim view of this: building defensive walls in another's territory was a serious affront, and the headmen protested vehemently. When their anger appeared to cool, Tolmie good-naturedly offered Challacum his rifle in a test of marksmanship. The tyee's first bullet pierced the target's bull's-eye at sixty paces. The message was clear: the company might build a palisade, but anyone peeking over it to get off a shot had better be quick. Once again, the headmen became "ugly customers," complaining loudly as they waited to pass through the entryway one at a time to trade.

Near the end of October, the confrontation trailed off as people left to go fishing. Finally, Challacum, Seattle, and the other Suquamish left, much to the relief of Tolmie, who sought solace in the writings of Saint Paul. When Heron returned, he extended the palisade and strengthened it with two corner bastions.

Seattle's size earned him the company nickname Le Gros, "the Big One," and his daughter Angeline recalled that while his father and Curley were tall and slim, Seattle was robust. Tolmie's mention of Seattle's son at Lahalet's beating on the beach reintroduces Sa'kw!al, then in his early twenties, possessing the same menacing temperament of his father.[6]

Despite Seattle's belligerence, it was reported that he treated his slaves and concubines well. "Indeed, many of these so-called slaves," pioneer merchant Samuel Coombs wrote, "afterwards became Chief Sealth's principal lieutenants." According to Coombs, the slaves were hostages who had been taken from local groups after Seattle's success on the lower White River. However, one of his slaves, Yutestid, whom Angeline knew from her youth, was said to have been born of a Cowichan mother and a man from the head of the Sound. That Yutestid's head was flattened but he could not speak his mother's people's language point to his capture as an infant with his mother during a raid. He may have been one of the slaves Angeline recalled her father had purchased, "out of pity from another who treated them cruelly." Seattle may also have inherited slaves or received them as part of a dowry. Concubines were not slaves, and some may have taken his name as their surname. Slaves fished, hunted, and gathered for their masters, and Seattle's made him wealthy enough to host feasts and the *sgwi'gwi*.[7]

Seattle's bloody success on the White River, his role in building Kitsap's confederation, and his likely participation in the raid against the Cowichan and in the company attack on the S'Klallam marked him as a war leader. A bellicose temperament and thundering voice made him feared, and his explosions of violence that are recorded in the *Journal of Occurences* mark him as the kind of person the Company did not usually call upon for services.

It had trouble enough retaining customer loyalty. To native people, distributing goods outside one's house group was a ceremonial activity defining rank. At Fort Nisqually's counter, however, a noble could expect no more in return for a beaver skin than would a slave, and when the chief trader gave extra gifts—a twist of tobacco, a few musket balls, a capote, or a dram of rum—it was more a reward for services rendered than to honor the recipient's status. Nobles who asked for gifts were labeled "beggars," "scamps," or "rogues," and on occasion they were publicly humiliated, but because the goods and services the company provided were valued, the fort and its rude traders were grudgingly accepted.

With the passage of time, cordial relations developed between the company and those it favored. The company encouraged staff to marry native women, and many native women were eager to marry into its powerful network. Lahalet, the Frenchman, Challacum, and Sneetlum, a Whidbey Island Skagit headman, were employed as couriers by the HBC. Challacum also escorted company officers on trips and undertook sensitive missions on their behalf. He and his son received training as a trader. By trading industrially mass-produced metalwork and textiles for furs, and by introducing new crops, agricultural techniques, horticulture, and stock raising, the HBC profoundly transformed native life.

The company also provided religious instruction, although it was a latecomer in the missionary business. In the 1780s, the Spanish sent Franciscans to Fort San Miguel on Nootka, at the south coast of Vancouver Island, to tend the Spaniards' spiritual needs and preach to native people. Their dramatic masses, brilliant vestments, and gleaming sacred vessels focused on the figure of the crucified Christ, the God-man who died and went to the land of the dead but returned with a message of hope detailed in the *Doctrina Cristiana*, a catechism explaining doctrine and beliefs that the friars translated into native tongues.[8]

The Christian message also came with the coureurs de bois—a rugged band of French Canadian, Scots, Orkneymen, Métis, and Indian engagés (employees) that companies hired and sent into the woods to collect and transfer furs. To discourage settlement and maintain the Indian trade, they paid the engagés' passage home after they were discharged or retired from service, but some remained out west, where they appear in historical records as free men or free hunters. Their familiarity with Euro-American ways and French, the language of trade in the northern half of the continent, made these men invaluable marriage partners. Like the Tu'bshədəd riding over the passes into the Puget lowland, they were welcomed into the nobility, where they became important middlemen, trading in goods and expertise, as well as knowledge of the new religion.

When the HBC absorbed the North West Company in 1821, its new charter required it to foster the moral improvement and religious instruction of its engagés and native clients. Historians tend to snicker at the idea of fur traders working as missionaries, but many HBC officers took this work seriously. George Simpson began Sabbath observances at Fort George, reading out of the Anglican Book of Common Prayer to employees and visiting Indians, and he ordered the same done at other posts. John McLoughlin held Anglican services in English at Fort Vancouver and other services in French for his Catholic employees, prior to his conversion to their church. Many were sincerely religious, like Francis Heron and William Fraser Tolmie. For others, a litany of blasphemous oaths and curses voiced the sum of their Christian knowledge, but the faithful did their best to teach through word and example. In 1834, Catholics who had settled in the Willamette Valley were concerned enough about their faith to petition Bishop Joseph-Norbert Provencher at Red River, in what is now Manitoba, to send them priests.[9]

An earlier appeal had been made, in 1831, by a delegation of Nez Perce and Flathead Indians from western Montana. After traveling over one thousand miles to Saint Louis, they met William Clark, of Lewis and Clark, and asked him for help. He sent them to Catholic bishop Joseph Rosati, whose priests instructed them. Two who died, baptized Narcisse and Paul, were buried in the cathedral cemetery. Two others heading home on a Missouri River steamboat sat for portraitist George Catlin but were never heard from again. Two years later, however, a sensational account of their visit appeared in the *Christian Advocate and Journal*, a Protestant publication in New York. The Indians' plea for instruction, likened to "the Macedonian Call," in Acts 16:9 in the New Testament, gave American missionaries what they were looking for: the possibility of converting Indians well in advance of settlement. In 1834, the Missionary Society of the Methodist Episcopal Church and other groups sent missionaries to the Oregon Country, a region many Americans had come to view as theirs by right of earlier claims and the designs of Providence.[10]

Heron and Tolmie preached in the Chinook Jargon. Listeners complained that it confused them, but Heron's replacement, one-time seminarian William Kittson, about forty, an English clerk from Montreal, persevered, preaching against shaman cures. And with malaria raging on the Cowlitz River, the people were desperate for hope.

Seeing opportunity, the Suquamish chief Challacum volunteered as a catechist to translate the religious instruction he received from company officials into the language of his listeners. In 1834, he told Kittson about "the Juggler," a young man who claimed that spirit beings had presented him with a written paper and eighteen blankets during a vision. Wearing a coat covered with dollar coins, he gave the blankets away at winter dances, promising to make the distribution an annual affair. His popularity grew until it was discovered that he had acquired his wealth by robbing graves. Kittson preached against the "So-qua-mish Juggler" but agreed with Challacum's decision to banish the fraud rather than kill him, and in March 1835, Challacum informed him that the "'thief of the dead" had been banished from his lands.[11]

While Challacum joined in the company's civilizing mission, Seattle continued to menace. On September 28, 1835, the *Journal of Occurrences* reported that middleman Jean Baptiste Ouvre and Seattle had quarreled: "It is said he threatened Ouvre with his gun. This is the second time." Seattle was threatened with consequences should he do so again, the writer noted, concluding that "he is at best a scamp and like Challacum, a black heart ready to pick a quarrel."[12]

In October, the *Journal* recorded the exchange of ten beaver skins by a Skagit man nicknamed the Borgne, meaning "One-Eyed" or "louche," for Seattle's daughter. We know the Skagit by his native name, Daxwsəb, which Americans later rendered as Dokubcub, who was a man of Cowichan and Skagit parentage living on Whidbey Island. The marriage produced two daughters and a child who died in infancy. The Duwamish recall that Daxwsəb abused Angeline, but she escaped the marriage by winning a test of wills. According to one story, her habit of sleeping late so shamed her husband that he finally told her, "There is a canoe. Take it and go home to your people." After her return, Seattle very likely hosted a *sgwi'gwi* in order to remove the stigma of divorce so she could "marry honorably again," which she did.[13]

Divorce often threatened blood feud between families, and few figures in HBC accounts had as many negative epithets associated with them as Seattle, so when Daxwsəb was murdered during the winter of 1837–38, it is not hard to imagine Seattle's involvement. True or not, Seattle's penchant for violence was real, as subsequent events would demonstrate.

A resurgence of violence on the Sound began in 1835 with another outbreak of smallpox, ravaging groups from California to Alaska. In March 1836, a strep infection swept Fort Nisqually, and as deaths mounted, so did paranoia. "The process of blaming," wrote Kittson, "has commenced with a vengeance." He blamed the mortality on the people's lifestyles and shaman cures. The shamans blamed company tobacco.[14]

Among those most affected were the Snohomish, whose fierce reputation suffered as disease came amid a series of disasters. After their raiders attacked a Hood Canal village, a Skokomish man who had lost sons directed hate magic at them. In Twana oral history, its efficacy was confirmed when a steep bluff at the southern end of Camano Island collapsed, sending a great wave onto a Snohomish encampment on the west side of Gedney Island, killing many.[15]

Late in 1836, the Whidbey Island Snohomish suffered attacks by the Skykomish, who lived on that mainland river, and these became so violent that couriers from Fort Nisqually were afraid to travel to Fort Langley. A month passed before an express braved it through, and after three Snohomish headmen were killed, many sought protection at Fort Nisqually. Trade declined, and Kittson sought native help to end the cycle of revenge killings.

The Cowlitz agreed to mediate. In February 1837, a six-canoe peace mission of forty Cowlitz men and women led by Wy-he-noo (likely the Wieno of Kitsap's raid), and fifty others in canoes led by Watskaladga, the Frenchman, left Fort Nisqually for the Skykomish River. After a brief shoot-out, the aggrieved parties negotiated a peace accord, and travel on the Sound resumed, bolstering Kittson's hope that trade would return to earlier levels. But people would come to trade only when they felt safe, and at this point Kittson looked to Challacum and others to broker a general peace.[16]

One outcome of his effort was the appearance at Fort Nisqually of the Snoqualmie, who lived along a tributary of the Snohomish River. They were a numerous people whose ambitious headmen would lead them on feared plundering raids, but initially Challacum was able to use them for his own purposes. In October, he and a Skagit group arrived at the fort accompanied by several Snoqualmie, who had come to retrieve kin enslaved by a Nisqually headman. Five days later, Challacum and the Snoqualmie left with the ransomed slaves, the speed of the transaction suggesting that he had deftly used the threat posed by the Skagits and Snoqualmie to engineer the exchange. Challacum had become an indispensable man.

Challacum's preference for peace was real. Kitsap had kept a lid on violence on the Sound, but after his death, the S'Klallam ventured to carry out a raid on the Suquamish that killed several people. Angry Suquamish planned their own raid, and when Challacum asked what they intended, they said they wanted revenge, but he told them not to; he didn't want any more killing. "They obeyed the chief," recalled Suquamish informant John Adams. "He was good and didn't want trouble."[17]

But in January 1838, Challacum had to settle a dispute among his own Suquamish that threatened the general peace. With a gun from the Sahewamish, at the head of the Sound, Seattle had killed a Skykomish shaman, causing such outrage that Kittson vented in the *Journal of Occurrences*, "I wish they would determine on shooting the villain."

Shamans were sometimes murdered if they were believed to have caused a death by failing to cure or by casting a fatal spell, and we know that after Angeline married Daxwsəb in late 1835, one of their children died young. Infant mortality was always high, and smallpox added to the toll. Still, a grandfather's rage provided a plausible motive for murder.[17]

Kittson wanted Seattle dead, but blood money satisfied the aggrieved kin. Because the fatal weapon had come from the Sahewamish, they were also deemed culpable, so Challacum negotiated on their behalf. Tensions kept Seattle on his guard. In April, he and fifteen armed companions traded at the fort. After gambling the night away, they left the next morning, much to Kittson's relief.[18]

By the mid-1830s, the Pacific Northwest was entering a period of momentous historic change, marked by the arrival of more missionary groups prior to the advent of American settlement. On the eve of this transformation, we have data that gives a close-up look at the Duwamish and Suquamish. An 1838–39 HBC census of the Puget Sound region counted a total Duwamish population of 415: 111 men, 109 women, 82 boys, 50 girls, and 11 slaves. The total Suquamish population was 576: 150 men, 165 women, 110 boys, 79 girls, and 72 slaves—the most slaves of any group on the Sound, total or per capita. The Duwamish had no horses, 12 guns, and 11 canoes; the Suquamish, no horses, 21 guns, and 119 canoes—the last exceeded by nine only by the S'Klallam, who had twice the population.[19]

The Suquamish were more populous than the Duwamish, wealthier, and more consequential, and in the narratives of the time written by those who valued order and profit, Challacum, who supported Hudson's Bay Company values, received the most attention. At Seattle's age, a *sia'b* was expected to smooth relations between contending parties rather than inflame them, as he did, and as missionaries entered the region Challacum's rising star eclipsed Seattle's.

In September 1834, Methodist missionaries Jason and Daniel Lee and lay assistants, inspired by the Indians' plea at Saint Louis, had arrived in the Willamette Valley, thirty miles south of Fort Vancouver. A year later, the Presbyterian missionary families of Henry and Eliza Spaulding and Dr. Marcus and Narcissa Whitman arrived at Fort Vancouver, where they met the Anglican reverend Herbert Beaver, sent by the HBC to serve as chaplain, and his wife, Jane. The Spauldings traveled east, to the Nez Perce, and the Whitmans went to Waiilat, "Place of the Ryegrass," on the Walla Walla River, to develop a mission among the Cayuse. Nine months later, fifty-two people, including married couples and sixteen children, arrived by sea, raising the American missionary colony's numbers to seventy-five.

The Willamette Valley Catholics' 1834 petition and another sent a year later brought no priests, but in 1838 Bishop Joseph Signay of Quebec was able to send two—Francis Norbert Blanchet and Modeste Demers—with the company's annual brigade to Fort Vancouver, where they arrived on November 24. Less than two hundred engagés had been allowed to retire on farms south of the Columbia, and the number of Euro-Americans throughout Oregon did not exceed 350—less than one for every five hundred native people. But anxious to retain the allegiance of its mostly Catholic settlers, the company welcomed the priests, a fact not lost on the Americans, who were as nationalist as they were Protestant.[20]

Blanchet, appointed vicar-general (an administrator responsible to a bishop) of the Oregon mission, was forty-three, nineteen years a priest, diminutive, tough, intelligent, and steeped in the devotional faith of the Quebecois. Demers, twenty-six years old and more genial than the dour vicar, was as enduring. Both had worked with native groups: Blanchet among New Brunswick's Micmac, and Demers among the Red River Métis.

Three weeks after their arrival, Blanchet visited Cowlitz Prairie, where Quebecois Simon Plomondon and his native wife ran HBC's Cowlitz Farm, which became the nucleus of a French Canadian community. After selecting land for a mission dedicated to Saint Francis Xavier, Blanchet appointed farmer Francois Fagnant catechist to teach wives and children prayers and instruct them in religion until his return.[21]

Having mastered the Chinook Jargon, Demers translated the Sign of the Cross, the Lord's Prayer, and several hymns from the French, and early in 1839 he and Blanchet carried out a Catholic mission at Fort Vancouver, lasting nearly five months—a catechetical boot camp. In March, Blanchet returned to Cowlitz Farm, drawing large crowds of Indians interested in hearing the priests whom French Canadians regarded as spiritual guides, and on April 6, Challacum and ten Suquamish showed up, their feet bleeding from three days on a rough trail.[22]

Seeking to give this important catechist a vivid idea of Catholicism in the short time available, Blanchet came up with an absolutely brilliant idea. On a squared stick, he carved rectangles, representing centuries, and dots, representing years, fashioning a vertical time line, starting at the accepted date of Creation (c. 4000 BC) to the current date. Beside these, ascending symbols represented Creation, the Fall, the Flood, the Covenant on Mount Sinai, and other historical highlights in the Holy Land, including the birth of Jesus, his ministry, Crucifixion, and Resurrection, and the Gospels. To ensure that neophytes would not be misled by American Protestants, a line deviating to the side alluded to the errors of the Reformation. This Sahale Stick, or "Stick of Heaven," had great success as a mnemonic device, and its symbols were soon inked onto large parchment sheets, allowing for even more detail. (This type of large-scale diagram came to be known as a "Catholic Ladder.") In the eight days in April that Challacum was at Cowlitz Farm, Blanchet pounded all he could into the *sia'b*'s head.

The hundreds of Indians who gathered to attend these missions effectively sidelined the American missionaries David Leslie and William Wilson, who had been assigned to Fort Nisqually. Challacum, the Frenchman, and Sneetlum, the Whidbey Island Skagit headman, did not show up at a May mission as expected, but as Blanchet was about to leave, six Indians and Challacum's wife arrived by canoe with a request: Her husband was too sick to travel. Would Blanchet visit him and his people on Whidbey Island? Presenting the Sahale Stick carefully sheathed in sewn skin, she begged Blanchet to come and preach its message.

Regarding the invitation as heaven-sent, Blanchet hired a canoe, an Indian crew, and Ouvre as interpreter, loaded supplies, and reached Challacum's camp after a rough two-day passage. But as they approached, people raced along the shore calling out in French, "Who goes there?"[23]

He had landed in the middle of a fight. A marital dispute had escalated into conflict between the Skykomish and the S'Klallam, leaving two dead. The S'Klallam had raided Challacum's camp, but Challacum told Blanchet that the cross he wore around his neck had allowed his people to defeat the S'Klallam, "because," he said, "they did not know God, sang no canticles at all, nor made

The Catholic Ladder, a visual religious chronology of world history, from creation to the mid-nineteenth century, distributed by Catholic missionaries. The timeline starts at the bottom with horizontal bars representing centuries and dots representing years. The thirty-three dots in the middle represent Jesus's life. Each sample was inked by hand on parchment.

any sign of the cross." Besides offering eternal salvation, the Christian God could also come in handy in a fight. Challacum had used sickness as an excuse to stay on contested ground, where the priest might prove a powerful tool in his effort to master a dangerous situation.

With a parchment Catholic Ladder six feet long and fifteen inches wide rattling in a sunny breeze, Blanchet placed an altar cloth on a rough-hewn board and lifted a gilded chalice from his traveling kit before the marveling eyes of his audience. When he ignited a mixture of incense and dry grass in his censer by striking a wooden match, the people were mute with astonishment. They had never seen matches before and thought the priest must possess great power indeed to conjure flames.[24]

Then it was Blanchet's turn to be astonished. As he began making the Sign of the Cross and speaking in the Jargon, the people made the same motions and mouthed the same words. Starting a hymn, the people joined in, singing the words and melody exactly as he had taught Challacum at Cowlitz Prairie. It was the same with the Frenchman and his Snohomish, and Snaetlum and his Skagit. Blanchet wept with joy. Over several days, he feasted with the people, celebrated masses, and, in the presence of a great wooden cross that men had erected on a beach bluff, he had parents line up to have their children baptized. He directed the parents to voice for their children baptismal vows: that they believed in God, in Jesus Christ, and in the power of the seven sacraments; that there was only one road to heaven; that they would follow this road made by Jesus, taught by the priests, and not other roads "lately made by men;" that they renounced the devil; and that they would "desire to know, love and serve the great Master of all things." For four hot hours, the line inched forward on the sun-drenched prairie beside a cobalt sea. The children were tired, frightened, and crying, but Blanchet baptized all 122 of them.

On Tuesday, June 2, he baptized nearly one hundred more children, near the mouth of the Snohomish, and brokered a truce between the S'Klallam and the Skykomish, who offered two guns to satisfy the blood debt for the two S'Klallam killed.

In the summer of 1840, Blanchet sent Demers on an even more extensive mission. Challacum took him to Agate Passage, where the priest instructed the Suquamish and baptized seventeen children, celebrating Mass beneath a large wooden cross erected beside Old Man

House. Enthusiastic crowds met him at a mainland Snohomish village, at Whidbey Island, and at a Skagit fort. Then it was up to the Lummi villages and to Fort Langley on the Fraser River, where Demers preached to a crowd of three thousand, his arm aching from shaking so many hands. In a scene recalling the deeds of missionary saints, groups who had arrived armed left their weapons at his feet.

By the time Demers returned, weary and exalted, to the Cowlitz mission in September, he had baptized 765 children, and his enthusiastic report convinced Blanchet that an Indian mission on the Sound would prosper. Thanks to the efforts of Steilacoom and his brothers in faith, a peaceful native Catholic commonwealth seemed in the making. In September 1842, Blanchet sent Jean-Baptiste-Zacharie Bolduc, a young priest from Quebec, recently arrived by sea, to the Saint Francis Xavier Mission at the Cowlitz Farm to prepare for a permanent mission on Whidbey Island.[25]

Seattle appears in none of these accounts. The loss of *Journal of Occurrences* volumes covering the period from 1840 to the end of 1845 limits our understanding of events, but other sources point to his continued role as a war leader. A fanciful depiction places him on the Snoqualmie River, where, chased by enemies to the brink of Snoqualmie Falls, he leaped from a canoe to a rock at the brink, afterward named Seattle Rock, while his pursuers plunged to their deaths. The story is mute regarding his escape, but seems to preserve a memory of him raiding on the upper Snoqualmie River. We know that a Klikitat woman and her daughter Mary Sam, were captured during a raid carried out by Suquamish near the falls in the late 1830s or early '40s and taken across the Sound by Tyochbid, a Suquamish headman. And a Twana story describes a Yakama party heading down the Snoqualmie that ignored warnings and was swept over the falls. The Seattle story echoes both while emphasizing his reputation for ingenious surprise.[26]

Violence also continued to haunt the White River. The raiders Seattle had ambushed earlier were a mix of river and interior people, the latter wintering on the headwaters of westward-flowing streams. One group frequenting the western slope was an Upper Yakama band led by Owhi, a large man with a deceptively benevolent visage, and his brothers. Sometime around 1840, he was said to have murdered one of Seattle's cousins, and in revenge Seattle and Curley led an attack against Yəla′kwo, a village at the confluence of the Green and White Rivers, where Owhi presumably had kin, killing ten and enslaving many women and children.[27]

Anthropologist Marion Wesley Smith described four types of warfare waged on the Sound. The most organized were attacks like Kitsap's, carried out by a coalition of groups against an invader. Next in scale were the raids for fame, slaves, or property. Loss of life was not essential to these raids' success, or to a third type of warfare, a sham battle, during which fighting men from contending villages confronted each other and made aggressive displays while negotiations went forward amid beating drums and power-singing. The affray between the Skykomish and the Snohomish in 1837 was an example of this third type. In all cases, success was often sealed by marital alliances, establishing peaceful kin ties between foes. But destruction of life and property was the goal of the fourth type of warfare—the revenge party. Seattle's murder of a shaman is an example of this type, and given the bloody history of the White River valley, the attack on Yəla′kwo seems like another. But if the raid again blunted the threat posed by upriver people, it also added to the local legacy of bitterness generated by Seattle and his downriver kin.[28]

It was this violence, chief trader William Kittson argued, that kept outlying groups from visiting Fort Nisqually and caused the local fur trade to decline. Farming and stock raising seemed to him a better way to defray the costs of supplying posts in the region, and settlement that had been discouraged by the Hudson's Bay Company could serve British interests north of the Columbia vis-à-vis the Americans. In 1838, the HBC's governing committee, in London, organized the Puget Sound Agricultural Company (PSAC), which ultimately planted 3,000 acres in wheat on Cowlitz Prairie and devoted 167,000 acres of Nisqually Prairie to raising cattle and sheep. The profits from meat, grain, dairy products, hides, and wool, sold in Russian Alaska and Hawaii, far exceeded those obtained from furs, and the next year Fort Nisqually itself was transferred to the PSAC with company surgeon and trader William Fraser Tolmie in charge.

---

In the summer of 1841, Canadian emigrants from the Red River colony headed for Oregon. That fall, a line of squealing ox carts brought 116 to

Fort Vancouver, and families settled on plots nearby. But the land was marginal, and farmers received little support, so most moved on to join kindred in the Willamette Valley.[29]

If the violence of Seattle and others in the north and central Sound hampered the fur trade (a fashion change from beaver to silk hats was another factor) and encouraged the British to contemplate settlement, native success blunting raids from the north made settlement in the southern Sound possible. Now the greatest threat came from the Lekwiltok of Vancouver Island, far to the north. Heavily armed by the end of the eighteenth century, this powerful group commenced raiding deep into Coast Salish territory. They turned Johnstone Strait into a gauntlet "like a great mouth," recalled one old informant, "always open to swallow whatever attempted to pass." Slave raids predominated, but the Lekwiltok also went head hunting if a chief died, in order to "let someone else wail." Their 1837 attack on Fort Langley was driven off only with great loss of life. Other versions of their name, "Yougletats" or "Yogoltah," became synonymous with terror on Puget Sound, and it took the Royal Navy to subdue them.[30]

As in Kitsap's day, however, Puget Sounders rallied. After raiders torched houses in Penn Cove, the Skagit, Snohomish, and Lummi allied and made a counterraid. The Leqwiltok responded with a bloody attack on a Whidbey Island S'Klallam village during a wedding celebration. Again, the allies headed north. Smoke rising above an island in the Gulf of Georgia guided them to a potlatch, where the attackers surrounded the unsuspecting gathering, rushed forward, and slaughtered everyone, leaving a row of heads on the beach as a calling card.[31]

But their triumph rang hollow when the Leqwiltok showed up a short time later in their dark canoes unscathed. The allies' victims had been a neighboring group called the S!o'ksun. Kittson may have been describing this fiasco when he noted in late September 1837 that the Skagit had carried out a raid against the "Chooks," "who have been cut up and the survivors made slaves." Again, the allies headed north, but the northerners' guns prevailed; the southerners' canoes ran aground or became entangled in kelp, and their crews were slaughtered. Reprising the aftermath of Kitsap's raid, accounts say only a few reached home, where grieving kin worked to strengthen defenses.[32]

Written descriptions of Old Man House point to the activity of Seattle and other Suquamish during this time period. In May 1841, the ships of the United States Exploring Expedition under the command of Lieutenant Charles Wilkes showed up on Puget Sound. Having left New York in 1838, the flagship USS *Vincennes* had sailed around the world, arriving forty-nine years after Vancouver's visit, to chart its shore and strengthen American claims.

In Discovery Bay, a group of headmen invited on board *Vincennes* asked whose ships they were. By then, they had learned to recognize the political differences between the British "King Georges" and the American "Padsteds," their version of "Bostons," a reference to the hailing port of most American vessels. Sharp trading by the King Georges had kept the Bostons out of the Sound, but the Americans were back in ships bristling with cannon. In one account Challacum is named as the courier Wilkes asked to carry his request for a pilot to Fort Nisqually. When they met, Wilkes, a Catholic, invited him into the *Vincennes*' cabin, where Challacum showed him his cross, repeated prayers, and, for unknown reasons, burst out laughing.[33]

On his way south, Wilkes saw the cross on Whidbey that had been constructed for Blanchet's visit, inspiring him to rename the island as "Holy Cross Island." Warmly welcomed at Fort Nisqually by Alexander Anderson, Kittson's replacement as chief trader, Wilkes sent parties to explore the interior and survey the Sound. Lieutenant Charles Ringgold, commanding the brig *Porpoise*, worked north through Puget Sound, from the present Tacoma Narrows to the Fraser River.

In June, Ringgold and his men followed the western shore, adding inlets, islands, and new names to Vancouver's chart. It was Ringgold's assistant, Lieutenant William Maury, following Port Orchard north, who discovered that its eastern shore belonged to an island he named after the 1812 naval hero William Bainbridge. The narrow northern outlet, named after Alfred T. Agate, an artist in the scientific corps, reached an embayment named after President James Madison, and near the opening they saw what remained of Old Man House and a standing cross, leading passed midshipman Joseph Sanford to think it a temple. On two sides of its sunken floor twenty uprights with "rudely carved uncouth figures" held rafters so immense the Americans could not imagine how even one hundred men could lift them into place without the use of purchases. Challacum's cross beside the remains of Kitsap's masterwork marked its use as a chapel. But the Americans did not credit its construction to the Suquamish, whom George Sinclair, sailing master of the *Porpoise*, judged "a filthy feathered race, as stupid as apes."[34]

Wilkes thought Sneetlum's people on Whidbey more civilized. When the headman welcomed the Americans to his village, he ushered them into his longhouse to show them a Catholic Ladder and a map of North America kept in a chest "carefully preserved in a corner." The Skagit were cultivating potatoes and peas in their gardens, and Wilkes admired their palisaded forts—four hundred feet long on a side, made of stout planks thirty feet high, and built so strongly his officers agreed that only artillery could breach them.[35]

During this time, Seattle moved between residences on Elliott Bay and at Old Man House, where Angeline said he hunted elk with bow and gun. Archaeological work done at Old Man House indicates that its continued use resulted in frequent modification. A map made by anthropologist Warren Snyder during excavations in the 1950s revealed a structure sixty feet wide in an area disturbed by winter storms and an undisturbed adjoining section forty feet wide. The uprights in the wider section had been larger than those in the narrower section, and historical remains, including bricks and part of a clay pipe in the narrower section, indicate that that part had been rebuilt in the 1840s and may have been what Wilkes's officers saw.

Tradition ascribes the original construction of Old Man House to Kitsap or an unnamed brother of Seattle, but one memory has Seattle as its owner and hiring men to build it. This recollection may recall the last *sgwi'gwi* held in Old Man House, hosted by Seattle. At the time of this gathering, the northeast end of the later section, adjacent to the beach bluff, was in ruins, so the *sgwi'gwi* was held in the newer section's western end, rebuilt by Seattle to house his guests.[36]

In preparation for the gathering, Seattle traveled to Fort Victoria with four canoes to barter for blankets, guns, and other gifts. The blankets he traded for were small, but since one headman might receive up to thirty, the total number was prodigious. Seattle had told his people that if they heard thunder, they would know that he was on his way back. And indeed, when he left Fort Victoria, a violent thunderstorm forced a delay for a day, but he made it home safely.

During the *sgwi'gwi*, the weight of blankets piled on the roof of Old Man House caused part of it to collapse, and that image of plenty along with Seattle's novel way of distributing gifts made the event quite memorable. He piled the blankets on a platform floating on two canoes, anchored a short distance offshore, and standing beside them he threw them into the water one by one so that recipients had to swim for them. Many blankets were torn in the process, but since the yarn could be used to weave others, the guests thought this was tremendous fun.[37]

Such stories reveal Seattle's raucous sense of humor. Another recalls a wrestling match between a Suquamish man and a Snoqualmie man that Seattle hosted at Point No Point, at the northern tip of the Kitsap Peninsula. This was part of a *sgwi'gwi* Seattle and his people attended on the lower Sound. The Snoqualmie wrestler was known for his trick of grabbing his opponent by the skin of his sides to throw him down, so Seattle had the Suquamish wrestler rub his body with the face cream Suquamish women made from deer fat. The Snoqualmie was unable to grab his opponent, and the Suquamish won handily.

Despite these festivities, danger was always afoot, and to frustrate surprise attacks, Seattle built an entry maze to his section of Old Man House, complete with a pit, and strengthened one wall with heavy posts separated by narrow slits, like the stockades Wilkes saw on Whidbey Island. If the cross Lieutenant Ringgold's men saw was Challacum's work, fortification of the rebuilt section of Old Man House was Seattle's.[38]

Like Vancouver, Wilkes and his men were more impressed by Puget Sound's strategic value than its folk. When a Makah trader visiting *Vincennes* kept asking, "What for so big ship; What for so many mans?" Wilkes could not imagine that the trader might be questioning the Americans' motives. In their bubble of superiority, the Americans assumed that natives might be useful only if taught agriculture and mechanical arts by missionaries. But although missionaries labored for success, their efforts faltered.[39]

To save Indians' souls and help them survive the crush of civilization, American missionaries had made it their goal to transform them into thrifty, self-reliant farmers who would honor notions of private property. To model a successful farming family, sponsors expended money and effort settling married families at fertile mission stations in the Northwest. When Dr. John Richmond arrived at Fort Nisqually in the spring of 1840, replacing Leslie and Wilson at the Methodist mission, he brought his wife, America, and their four children, including a daughter christened Oregon on the voyage out. But citing domestic affliction, likely the result of isolation and stress, Richmond abandoned the mission two years later without making a single convert.[40]

The struggle to maintain families left missionaries liable to the charge that they labored more for their own welfare than that of the Indians. Nevertheless, the pioneering missionary Jason Lee gained the respect of the Walla Walla chief Peopeomoxmox, "Yellow Bird," and in Lee's mission school in the Willamette Valley baptized his son, Toyannu, Elijah Hedding. Another young Sinkiuse-Columbia nobleman, Kwiltalahun, taught by Henry Spaulding, became a powerful leader known by his Christian name, Moses. Still, missions in the Willamette Valley, at The Dalles of the Columbia, and among the Cayuse, Nez Perce, and Spokanes, yielded barely a handful of converts. When native people seemed to lose interest and revert to traditional practices, the missionaries redirected their efforts toward American settlers, with whom they enjoyed greater success.

In contrast, celibate Catholic missionaries required little and devoted themselves to service, but they also encountered difficulty. In September 1842, Blanchet sent Father Bolduc to Saint Francis Xavier Mission on the Cowlitz to prepare for the move to Whidbey Island. Early in 1843, Bolduc traveled to Fort Nisqually and took the HBC side-wheeler *Beaver* to Vancouver Island on the expedition to build Fort Victoria, the new company headquarters in Oregon. There he bought a large canoe, and in March arrived at Whidbey Island, where the Skagit greeted him warmly. More than 150 camped beside Bolduc's tent under a night sky lit by the tail of a spectacular comet.[41]

The next day, more than one thousand from camps nearby assembled for instruction, roaring hymns in a sunlit gale. After a meager breakfast, Bolduc retired to a glade surrounded by immense firs to escape the wind and baptized 150 children. By day's end, he could barely lift his arm in blessing, and the sun gave him a splitting headache, but native devotion thrilled him. Over the next few days, Sneetlum had his people build

Bolduc a twenty-five-by-thirty-foot log house, lined with mats and shingled with cedar bark, which became the Sacred Heart of Mary chapel.

One group from the mainland, famished after walking four days and nights without food, rejoiced that Bolduc might teach them and baptize their children, saying, "We know there is a Master in Heaven but we do not know how to please Him." The fertile island and its salubrious climate that attracted summertime hundreds showed great promise, and the priest's return to Saint Francis Xavier Mission on April 3 with a hopeful report convinced Blanchet to have Demers establish a permanent mission on Whidbey Island with Bolduc as his assistant.

In May 1844, Demers and Bolduc left Cowlitz Farm at the head of a six-horse packtrain carrying supplies. At Fort Nisqually, they transferred to a canoe, which brought them to Whidbey on May 18. The people were overjoyed to see two priests rather than one, but from that moment, the missionary idyll dissipated like a morning mist. Settled in, Bolduc noticed that the few things he had left behind on his previous trip were gone. Demers questioned the people, and headmen harangued them, but nothing was returned.

When some older people told the priests that the spring near their house dried up in the summer, the search for a better one took them into Suquamish territory on the island, where Challacum had his slaves build the priests a new house by a little lake on the western shore overlooking the Strait of Juan de Fuca. But when Sneetlum heard about the move, he forbade his people from moving the priests' baggage to the new site. In the meantime, six hundred S'Klallam arrived and asked Bolduc to baptize a dying child.

On May 25, the priests celebrated Mass in the flimsy new house and began making furniture and a clay chimney. Six days later, the Skagit raised an alarm: three Lekwiltok canoes had been sighted. Demers and Bolduc hurried to Challacum's longhouse, where he assured them they were safe. Three canoes did not scare him, he said; raiders would have to fight their way through the Skagit and S'Klallam on the beach, and even then it would be difficult to find the priests' house in the dark. To calm them, he posted sentries and put out all campfires.

Despite his assurance, Demers and Bolduc decided to surround their house with a palisade. In June, Bolduc and native men split shingles and planks from magnificent cedars at the mouth of the Snohomish. As the little fort rose, more canoes arrived, this time bearing Makah men armed to the teeth. They stayed the distance of a gunshot away while the priests instructed a group, but Challacum warned that they should not be trusted.

Native religious fervor began to ebb. Gifts of food arrived less frequently, and the priests dined on mussels and biscuits they baked themselves. Then on the morning of June 19, as groups left to go fishing, Challacum's Suquamish left. As the Tyee shared his uneasiness with the priests, Sneetlum's wife arrived to say that the Leqwiltok were attacking a group nearby and planned to kill the priests and seize their baggage. Neighboring headmen said they should leave right away to avoid being enslaved. So on June 22, Demers and Bolduc hurriedly left the island, taking the mission dream with them.

What had happened? Bolduc accused the native people of being "essentially lazy, apathetic, inconstant and insensible to all that one can tell them about religion. They are attached to their superstitions to a point that one doubts whether they will ever be converted." He cited other shortcomings too: their medicine men had great influence; the people practiced polygyny, supported slavery, and nourished an addiction to gambling; and their passions were ephemeral.[42]

It would not be the last time that native failure to reshape their lives along Western lines would be blamed on their lack of character. But other events can explain the change. In 1840, a family brought a critically injured child to the Skagit fort for Demers to baptize, but the child died shortly afterward. And when the S'Klallam brought another child to Bolduc, that child died moments later. Indeed, a rumor was spreading that children on the Fraser River died immediately after being baptized. And if baptism could not save children, what could?[43]

On Whidbey, the Swinomish, the Samish, and Sneetlum's Skagit occupied the north; the Frenchman's island Snohomish, the south. From the west, the S'Klallam menaced Challacum and his Suquamish. The river Snohomish, under their headman Sehalapahan, and the Skykomish pressed in from the east; the Makah intimidated; and the Lekwiltok threatened. In 1839, Challacum had brought the priests onto this turbulent ground to boost his authority, but in 1843 Sneetlum had, for a brief time, kidnapped them. The priests had become hostages to intergroup rivalry.

Some groups decided to skip the priests altogether. Building a church for his Snohomish, Sehalapahan asked Blanchet for a priest. When Blanchet said he had none, Sehalapahan returned and carried out services on his own, earning the nickname "the Priest." When the Oblates of Mary Immaculate later began a mission near his river, upriver groups explained why they did not attend. "If we want to accept the white man's religion," they said, "we can do it ourselves and not have to take orders from Stilacoom or Tulalip missionaries." This suited Blanchet, who had larger ambitions. Intent on building the Church in Oregon from the top down, Blanchet had himself consecrated Bishop of Oregon City west of the Cascades, his brother Augustine Magliore consecrated Bishop of Walla Walla east of the Cascades, and Father Demers Bishop of Vancouver Island north of the border. To assure his control, he had all three dioceses subsumed into an archdiocese embracing about 375,000 square miles with himself as Archbishop, only the second archdiocese organized in the United States. In this vast region, the number of practicing Catholics in it probably did not exceed two hundred. On Whidbey Island, when the native people hesitated and the Lekwiltok threatened, Blanchet removed his priests and left native missions to the religious orders he would invite in that specialized in them.[44]

Bolduc's account yields one of our last glimpses of Challacum. If his effort to invite priests to Whidbey did not pan out, he retained his authority among the Suquamish. His presence is noted in the account books at Fort Nisqually, where in May 1844, he borrowed two beaver traps, returning with a large party in October to barter potatoes, salmon, and land otter and deer hides for blankets, baize, and ammunition. As late as June 1848, he traded many animal hides for more baize, buttons, and ammunition, and in October, in a letter to the War Department, Governor of Oregon Joseph Lane identifies him as "Salcom," chief of the Suquamish. Then, silence. Later writers confused him with a younger man named Steilacoom living near Fort Nisqually in the 1850s, but by then the grand old man was dead. As he passed, the era of British dominance in the region faded, and history shifted its gaze to Seattle.[45]

With fighting largely confined to the northern Sound in 1843, Tolmie moved Fort Nisqually a mile east to a new location, where he did not feel the need to surround it with a wall. More American settlers arrived, and British ships surveyed the maritime border as Great Britain and the United States moved to partition Oregon along the 49th parallel. But when the *Journal of Occurrences* resumed in 1845, Snoqualmie raiders ranging far from their upriver homes dominated the scene.

In February 1846, Tolmie sent armed men to stay with Joseph Heath, the farmer in charge of a sheep ranch six miles north of Fort Nisqually, after the Snoqualmie threatened him and robbed native workers at the tidewater village of Steilacoom. In July, Skykomish warriors threatened surveyors from the forty-six-gun frigate HMS *Fisgard* when they sought to land on Fidalgo Island. James Douglas, chief factor at Fort Vancouver after John McLoughlin's departure, was mystified. "What can have induced them to assume a hostile attitude, at this time, after so many years of friendly intercourse with us," he wrote, "against a force which they must have known would ultimately visit them with fearful retribution?" Unwilling to let the insult pass, he asked the Royal Navy to send the steam paddle sloop HMS *Cormorant* and the brig *Rosalind* into the area to remind locals who had the real power.[46]

But the threat to the British may have been inspired by a stunning reversal of fortune. Since the 1830s, Lekwiltok raiders roaming the lower Sound had been thwarted only by palisades and people's ability to run and hide. By the '40s, their attacks had caused the Cowichan to invite the S'Klallam and groups on the lower Sound to join a new coalition against a hated foe, as had Kitsap.

Once again, an armada headed north, bearing warriors—armed now with muskets. At Kuper Island, the allies learned that raiders in Maple Bay, on Vancouver Island's east shore, were about to attack Cowichan villages. The allies blocked them with their canoes. The Leqwiltok drove their heavier craft forward, and when the allies fired muskets at their approach, the attacking crews leaned to one side, raising the other as a protective shield. But some leaned too far, capsizing their canoes, and crews thrown in the water were butchered while others reaching the shore were hunted down. This time, it was the Lekwiltok who were slaughtered, but the allies were not done. In captured canoes and wearing the war dress of their victims, they surprised a Lekwiltok village and put it to the torch, killing the men and enslaving women and children. When

Lekwiltok emissaries sued for peace, they, too, were killed. Eventually, however, peace was made, sealed through intermarriage.[47]

This smashing victory for the allies may have inspired the Skykomish to taunt the British surveyors. And if British warships made Indians quail at all, the reception traveling Canadian artist Paul Kane received when he visited the lower Sound in May 1847 suggests that the effect was fleeting. As he and his crew approached the beach, hundreds of Indians rushed into the water, seized his canoe, and dragged it ashore, demanding to know what he wanted. After hearing him protest that he wanted only to draw, the anger vanished, and a S'Klallam headman sat happily for his portrait. Traveling next to the fortified village of Toanichum on Whidbey Island, Kane mistook the hail of musket balls splashing around his canoe for a salute, but he soon learned that they were fired "for the purpose of letting us know that they were in possession of firearms."[48]

Still, the allies' victory over the Lekwiltok did not protect the S'Klallam from their neighbors. Two days after his visit to Whidbey, Kane visited the fortified S'Klallam village of Yə'nus, at what is now Port Angeles. The Makah had recently attacked and torched the place, killing many who had fled to the woods. Kane later painted a vivid depiction of the attack as it was described to him. With S'Klallam heads rammed onto poles spiking the prows of their war canoes, the victors returned home with the enslaved. Smarting from this humiliation, the S'Klallam sought revenge, but it took an odd turn.[49]

The S'Klallam had earlier hired a Suquamish shaman to cure one of their sick, but when the patient died before he arrived, the S'Klallam beheaded him. Adding insult to injury, the son of the shaman's assassin kept the head as an object to abuse and defile. This made the Suquamish and Seattle furious, and as a proven war leader, he led a raid against the S'Klallam that killed many. With raids coming from west and east, Skəbiaks, a S'Klallam headman, brokered a peace with Seattle by offering his daughter in marriage to Seattle's son Sa'kw!al. Seattle also got the S'Klallam to help him solve a problem with the Chemakum.[50]

A devastating Makah raid had drastically reduced the Chemakum and left them besieged in a single fortified village. The Chemakum blamed the Suquamish for a decline in their homeland's fertility, and the

Suquamish blamed Chemakum sorcery for the death of Kitsap's brother Təli'but. To further darken the Chemakum name, it was noted that the mother of the son who abused the Shaman's head also happened to be Chemakum. Both the S'Klallam and the Suquamish appear to have concluded that lingering enmity between them could be eliminated if both groups joined forces to destroy the Chemakum. The S'Klallam could expand their range and salve wounded pride, and Seattle could enhance his warrior reputation at a crucial moment when ever-larger numbers of Americans had begun to enter the region.

In fifteen canoes, over one hundred S'Klallam, Suquamish, and Duwamish warriors approached the Chemakum village at the Hadlock portage. Seattle is credited with leading the raid, but a Twana account claims that Sa'kw!al carried out the actual attack. Since beating up Lahalet at Fort Nisqually, he had developed a reputation as frightening as his father's. His guardian power was described as old driftwood eaten out by sea worms—bringing to mind the stark image of a heart void of remorse during battle fury. In an earlier attack, he had shot a Chemakum man. The ball that had passed through the victim had been found lodged in a wall plank, and the Chemakum had dug it out, hammered it back into shape, and vowed its return.

Arriving at night, Seattle and Sa'kw!al's war party hid in the woods. A Duwamish account said they formed a circle around the stockade, keeping close enough to touch fingers. A grandson of Təli'but said the shaman who had hexed his grandfather walked out early in the morning to go clamming, unaware of the trap. Hidden warriors shot him down, and awakened by the noise, Chemakum men grabbed their muskets and poured out of the stockade, only to be cut down in a murderous cross fire. The attackers raced inside, killing many other men, at least one with an ax, and capturing screaming women and children. Near the end of the slaughter, a Chemakum man loaded the fateful ball into his musket, took aim, and fired it into Sa'kw!al, shattering his backbone. Seeing him crumple to the ground, Seattle cried out, "Oh! My son! My son! He is down!"[51]

Many strands of memory were woven into the account of this important raid. A Suquamish account says women and children were captured. Although they were not involved in the raid, the most detailed account comes from the Twana, probably because the Chemakum headman and several other survivors who escaped took shelter with them. In that account virtually all the Chemakum were killed. The few survivors who did not flee to Hood Canal moved north to Kah-tai Lagoon at Port Townsend, but they were a broken people. If the Twana account draws some of the blame from Seattle, there is no doubt that he was present at the slaughter; indeed, it bears all the hallmarks of his earlier work: a surprise attack carefully planned, well executed, and brutally effective. In the years during which Challacum and Seattle pursued their different agendas, Challacum's way held great promise, but Seattle did not buy into it, believing the way of Thunder and blood was more decisive.

# CHAPTER FOUR

*"I am glad to have you come to our country."*

Of Americans, French political writer Alexis de Tocqueville observed, "Fortune has been promised to them somewhere in the West, and to the West they go to find it." Royalists, Puritans, Quakers, and Gaelic Borderers crossed the sea to found colonies, and beyond the Appalachians, the Watauga Association and proponents of the state of Franklin continued the process. "Emigration was at first necessary to them," de Tocqueville said. "And it soon becomes a sort of game of chance, which they pursue for the emotions it excites as much as for the gain it procures." The Republic of West Florida in 1810 and the more consequential Republic of Texas in 1836 preceded national expansion, and by the 1840s American settlers were entering Oregon.[1]

If the Chemakums' destruction enhanced Seattle's fearful reputation among native groups, it did him no favors with the Hudson's Bay Company. However decimated Native Americans were by disease, they still vastly outnumbered whites in the region. Fearful of losing its identity in the polyglot population, the small American colony growing around the Methodist mission in the Willamette Valley petitioned the United States government in 1838 to take possession of the country, but the request was premature.[2]

A bill offered by US senator Lewis Linn of Missouri to counter the British presence and encourage emigration to Oregon by promising a husband and wife free land seemed assured of passage, and in 1843 over eight hundred pioneers left Independence, Missouri, in nearly a hundred wagons with a vast herd of cattle to be on the ground for the claiming. As the "Great Migration" headed west, American settlers' efforts to create a government in the Oregon Country finally bore fruit. At the Willamette Valley settlement of Champoeg, French Canadians, English, Scots, and Orkneymen joined Americans to vote sovereignty for Oregon in early May. Prevailing 52 to 50, the settlers organized a provisional government.

The idea that a people acting collectively had sovereign power to govern themselves and enact laws had less to do with liberty than land, and among the provisional government's first acts was its affirmation of existing land claims of 640 acres for a white husband and his wife, as had been suggested by Linn. In Oregon, it was understood that a provisional government would be temporary until a national government providing legal protections would take charge. Even though Linn's bill failed, supporters of western expansion were determined to reintroduce it.

In the American mind, the Oregon Country was the crucial area in the Northwest on the lower Columbia, and accounts of the time regard happenings on Puget Sound as peripheral. Seattle himself does not show up unequivocally in American accounts until 1851, but a cast of characters with whom he would play an important part made themselves known during these years. Arriving on a wagon train in 1844, sixty-four-year-old George Washington Bush arrived in Oregon as a free man of color. He had left the slave state of Missouri with his German American wife, Isabella, their five children, and many of his white neighbors. Among these were Michael Simmons, a thirty-year-old miller, his wife, Charlotte, and their family, and James and Charlotte McAllister and theirs. When Bush learned that the provisional government sought to keep out slaveholders by forbidding African Americans entry, the Bush-Simmons party crossed to the Columbia's north bank, where more liberal British attitudes prevailed. John McLoughlin let them winter near Fort Vancouver, accepting shingles and saw logs in return for supplies.

In early 1845, the party looked for suitable homesteads along the Cowlitz River. Finding none, in July they hired Peter Borcier, a retired engagé who had guided Wilkes, to lead Simmons and eight men north from Cowlitz Landing to the Deschutes River, at the southernmost reach of Puget Sound.

Here they met the *sia'b* named Gray Head, who lived at a village called St!əch!a's, and who earlier with Steilacoom and Seattle in 1832 likely sparked chief trader Heron's interest in a new site for Fort Nisqually. When he was young, Gray Head's hair turned prematurely gray, earning him his first nickname: Snew-kude-dupe-tum, which means "It Was All Changed into Something Else." With a straight face, Gray Head warned Simmons that without guides an invisible beaked monster with fiery eyes and fierce claws would devour them if they went astray. Undeterred Simmons paid him for canoes and guides, who took them down Sound—past Whidbey Island, through Deception Pass, and back through Saratoga Passage—before returning safely back to the south Sound and a place called Tumwater ("Strong Water" in the Jargon), where falls on the Deschutes promised a good mill site. Staking his claim, Simmons told Gray Head that he had killed the monster with a golden bullet, a tale so delighting the headman that he invited the Americans to a feast.[3]

In late September, the Americans brought their cattle north, and in October they floated their belongings down the Columbia in flatboats and up the Cowlitz River in canoes to Cowlitz Farm. Simmons carried letters of introduction from McLoughlin to the farmer in charge, James Forrest, and to Tolmie at Fort Nisqually, asking them to provide for the settlers' needs. At Cowlitz Landing, where the portage to Puget Sound left the farm, the men built sledges and a wagon for the fifty-eight-mile trip to Simmons's claim, optimistically named New Market. They arrived in October, too late to put in a crop, relying on the generosity of the company and local Indians to see them through that rainy fall and winter, splitting shingles to pay down their debt.

At some point on the journey, they were met by Lə'shai—Leschi—a Nisqually *sia'b*, who, the McAllisters's middle daughter, Mary Jane, wrote, "welcomed them to his country, making each family a present and inviting them to join his tribe, saying we might be annoyed by rov-ing Indians, and if we did not belong to his tribe, he could not protect us." Contemporaries described him as five and a half feet tall, weighing about 175 pounds, with the flattened head of a *sia'b* and "a benevolent countenance that unmistakably stamped him as a good man." On his father's side, he descended from nobility living on Carr Inlet. His mother, remembered as a singer, possibly a ceremonialist, was the daughter of We-ow-wicht, a leader of the Pshwanwapam band on the upper Yakima River and the brother-in-law of Owhi. Born and raised at a village of mixed Salish- and Shahaptin-speaking peoples on the Marshel River, a Nisqually tributary, Leschi spoke the languages of both fluently. He was in his early forties when the McAllisters met him, a wealthy man living with several wives, where he pastured many horses at Yelm Prairie, and enjoyed a reputation for intelligence, oratory, and generosity. After a forest fire drove deer from a neighboring group's hunting range, he invited them to spend the winter hunting on his. His claim to have visited the land of the dead and to have shot a Tsiatko, a hairy wild creature—a Sasquatch—reveals a flair for the dramatic.[4]

With the generosity he lavished on his own people, Leschi invited the settlers to stay. James McAllister settled near the mouth of the Nisqually, on rich ground beside a stream called Sxuda'dap, "Where There Is a xuda'b" (a shamanic power), later renamed Medicine Creek. "We were in the Indian country indeed," Mary Jane recalled. "There were twenty Indians in the valley to one on the prairie." The settlers traded for bear meat, venison, and waterfowl. The Nisqually people taught them how to dig clams, how to cook food by steaming it wrapped in leaves over hot coals, how to dry fruit without sugar, and how to make bread from fern roots. Determined to flourish in this new world, the settlers were eager to learn, and their vulnerability promoted trust.[5]

Bachelors took native wives, which gave them a voice at council meetings. To the settlers, Indians seemed more like them than the mercenary Hudson's Bay Company men. To the Indians, the Americans, if odd, were energetic and resourceful, and, more importantly, they had items to trade that challenged the HBC monopoly. That summer, Simmons cut millstones from beach boulders, built a water-powered mill at the falls, and ground the area's first flour from wheat that Bush grew on an upland prairie.

Oregon had loomed large in the presidential election of 1844. During the campaign, James Polk's supporters threatened war unless Great Britain relinquished claims up to latitude N 54°40', and for a brief period, American and British naval squadrons maneuvered ominously off the coast. But the Oregon Treaty, signed in June 1846, accepted the 49th parallel as the boundary, gaining Puget Sound to the United States and ensuring peace with Great Britain while American armies invaded Mexico. The news cheered Americans in Oregon, already numbering six thousand, who were pleased to learn that their nation had acquired another quarter million square miles of land.

That year, pioneers Levi Lathrop Smith and Edmund Sylvester each claimed a half section of land on tidewater two miles below New Market and Gray Head's village. Smith named his section Smithfield, and the next year a trail that he blazed from New Market to Smithfield extended the trading link from the Columbia to Puget Sound. Financed by Bush, settlers purchased unused sawmill machinery from the PSAC, powered it by an overshot waterwheel at the falls, and formed the Puget Sound Milling Company.[6]

The mill's manager, Antonio Rabbeson, who had, with twenty-seven-year-old Virginia emigrant Samuel Hancock, fired the first kiln of bricks north of the Columbia, invited native people to see the operation. They watched the mill's rocker arm lift and lower the saw blade, commanded, it seemed, by Rabbeson's gaze. After sawing the first log, he asked his audience to roll another onto the carriage. When they could not, he amazed them further by levering it easily into place with a cant hook, with which, he offered jokingly, to toss them over the river.

Despite their abilities, the American settlers were still very few, the Indians very many, and the potential for discord very great. Delaware and Shawnee Indians in Oregon told how Americans had driven their peoples from their eastern homelands. The prominent Walla Walla chief Yellow Bird experienced settler violence when his son Elijah Hedding was murdered by an American near Sutter's Mill, California, during an argument over horses.

On Puget Sound, the native people likened the Americans to birds, rootless and ever on the move. Farther south, the term applied to them was "moving people," which historian Gray H. Whaley suggests was "a derisive comment on their paternity and lack of social commitment." As more arrived, they claimed land relentlessly, ignoring native customs as they consumed resources. Blamed for outbreaks of disease ever since the chief trader at Fort Astoria threatened to release smallpox, new epidemics were blamed on their use of iron plows and rumored to be part of an effort to exterminate Indians. As American armies plunged into Mexico, drawing men and supplies away from the Northwest, settlers feeling even more vulnerable were quick to point guns at any perceived threat.[7]

The winter of 1846–47 blew in cold, killing stock and weakening the health of the native people, already prey to contagion. In July, the artist Paul Kane witnessed the return to Fort Walla Walla of a party of Cayuse and Walla Walla from California after the unsuccessful attempt to bring

Elijah Hedding's murderer to justice. Many had died of measles, and as the names of the dead were announced, "a terrific howl ensued," according to Kane, with "the women loosening their hair and gesticulating in a most violent manner." The HBC men feared for their lives, but, Kane observed, "this fear . . . was groundless, as the Indians knew the distinction between the Hudson's Bay Company and the Americans."[8]

The Indians had brought the measles with them, and by November over half the Cayuse were dead. Many believed this was the missionaries' doing. After watching his child die on November 26, the Cayuse chief Tiloukaikt led his brother Tomahas and others to missionary Marcus Whitman's house the next morning. They knocked. Whitman opened the door. Tiloukaikt demanded medicine, and as Whitman turned to get it, Tomahas sank a tomahawk into the doctor's skull, setting in motion the bloody rampage that took the lives of Marcus's wife, Narcissa, and many others.

As panicked Americans fled down the Columbia, the provisional government sent two companies of hastily enrolled volunteers east to apprehend the killers. The Cayuse sought allies in their fight, and in January the Walla Wallas, Nez Perce, and Yakamas were rumored to have joined them. This was not true, but the conflict marked a fatal watershed in native-settler relations and heightened divisions among native groups as factions debated what to do.

Brought downriver by its victims, the measles spread north to Cowlitz Farm and Fort Nisqually. It peaked in February 1848 and subsided by March, leaving the inevitable residue of anger and grief. Nevertheless, that spring, pioneer Thomas Glasgow blithely hired a native crew at New Market to take him exploring down Sound. Attracted by Whidbey Island's verdant gardens, he built a cabin near Challacum's old camp, planted wheat and potatoes, and married a native woman, Julia Patkanim. In Elizabeth McAllister's words, he had "joined the tribes."[9]

Returning to New Market, Glasgow convinced Rabbeson and another newcomer, George Carnefix, to join him on the island. Waiilat was more than two hundred miles from New Market, a week's hard travel over the mountains.

While the tall equestrian Indians east of the mountains fit the American image of romantic warriors worthy of respect, coastal fish-eaters wintering near noisome tideflats in plank villages amid bark-ing dogs, seemed less threatening. Americans called them "Siwash," from the Jargon "Sow-wash," from the French *sauvage*. It became a blatantly racist term for local native people in general, comparable to the baleful corruption of Negro for African Americans, and used in the same casually derisive manner. But settlers would find that the people west of the mountains could be just as dangerous as their eastern kin.[10]

While Carnefix, Rabbeson, and Glasgow were camping near the Skokomish River, it was Carnefix's turn to cook supper, but when a visiting headman mistook him for the group's slave and offered to buy him, the ensuing laughter so incensed Carnefix that he returned to New Market in a huff, leaving Glasgow and Rabbeson to go on without him. They reached Whidbey in July, when groups traditionally arrived to work their gardens, and found a vast crowd gathered in raucous debate. With Glasgow's wife, Julia, translating, the two concluded that they were in grave danger, so they all returned to New Market with a sen-sational account of a grand war council and their hairbreadth escape from certain death.

In their telling, those calling the council were Snoqualmie, the "rov-ing Indians" Leschi probably had in mind when he offered protection to the Bush-Simmons party. An account of a Snoqualmie raid against Yəla'kwo, at the confluence of the Green and White Rivers, led by the headman Xotik!edəb, sounds so like the one led by Seattle and Curley in the early 1840s that it would appear to be one and the same attack. The Snoqualmie were once again on the move.[11]

In the fall of 1847, Joseph Heath's Indian neighbors had warned that the Snoqualmie planned to kill him and all the whites at Fort Nisqually. Suffering from a lingering illness, Heath had said, "They would find me very tough, adding that I was getting very old and little more than skin and bone." That winter, a Snohomish man warned Tolmie that those who believed whites were spreading disease planned to attack the fort at night, set fire to its bark roofs, and shoot those running from the burning buildings, very much like Seattle's raid on the Chemakum. In light of the Whitman Massacre, Tolmie took the threat seriously and sent warning to James Douglas at Fort Vancouver, who directed him to surround the fort with a palisade. This provoked anger during the spring and summer of 1848, as the earlier wall had in '33.[12]

PAT KANIM-

-PUGET SOUND INDIAN

Snoqualmie Chief Patkanim initially resisted white immigration but later came to support the Americans.

Many native people on the northern Sound had relatives east of the mountains who were afflicted by the disease moving up tributaries of the Columbia, and local opinion swayed in support of war events in the interior. According to Glasgow and Rabbeson, the person at the "war council" on Whidbey who had been arguing most forcefully for war was the father of Glasgow's native wife, a Snoqualmie nobleman of medium build named Patkinəm, known today as Patkanim.[13]

Probably in his late thirties at the time, Patkanim was brother to Xotikʔeʹdib and six other sons of a Snoqualmie mother and a Stillaguamish father, the latter living along that river emptying into Skagit Bay. During his spirit quest, Patkanim was said to have encountered the guardian power Marmot, who gave him wealth and charisma. "Look at me, boy," the power told the young supplicant. "I am watching the people. I am higher than all the others. You will be like me. You will be a high man."[14]

By the late 1840s, Patkanim was headman of a major Snoqualmie village. Historian Frederick Grant's mention of his "bright, intelligent face, which was broad and full, eyes large and lustrous set straight in his head, a straight Greek nose, delicate mouth with thin lips and graceful curves at the corners and at the 'cupids bow'" drew from a daguerreotype taken in the 1850s, but his judgment that Patkanim "was ambitious and knew how to gain ascendency over others," came from living memory. "Shrewd" was the word most used to describe him, and like Kitsap, he was determined to repel new invaders.[15]

Accounts of Glasgow and Rabbeson's experience on Whidbey differ in detail but generally agree. The three-day council they had witnessed opened with a feast hosted by Patkanim, who declared that the Hudson's Bay Company must go. A Snohomish man, whose English name was John Taylor, added that the Americans should go, too. He had visited their settlements in the Willamette Valley, he said, and had heard that in their own country they were as numerous as sand on the beach. Patkanim warned his audience that the Americans would seize their lands and exile them to a distant, dark region, where they would perish. If the settlers were driven out now, he said, when their numbers were few, the native people could divide the spoils left behind. But Michael Simmons's friend Gray Head reminded the council that until the Americans showed up, his people were often the target of raiders, lately the Snoqualmie, and that the settlers' armed presence discouraged raiding. Then a Duwamish chief rose and announced that his people would protect those at the head of the Sound from raiders. Gray Head replied sarcastically that he preferred one American with a rifle to all the Duwamish. Glasgow and Rabbeson said that as the council broke up in discord, they heard that Patkanim planned to murder them and tell Americans that Gray Head was involved, reasoning that if the settlers sought revenge, Gray Head would have to support his and John Taylor's plan. To save themselves the two fled.[16]

Did a council actually debate starting a war against the whites? The warnings recorded by Heath and Tolmie indicate that something like that was in the air. If the wall rising around Fort Nisqually suggested to the native people that HBC and the Americans were in cahoots, its construction may have precipitated the council. The unnamed Duwamish chief did not protest Patkanim and John Taylor's plan, but his offer of protection to Gray Head targeted the Snoqualmie and contributed to the council's rancorous end.

Who was this Duwamish chief? Territorial Governor Isaac Stevens's assistant, the naturalist George Gibbs, identified Seattle as chief of the Duwamish at that time, and Gray Head's insult adumbrates the disparaging references to Seattle's slave ancestry heard later by Indian agent Edmund A. Starling. Given his notoriety following the destruction of the Chemakum, I believe Seattle, still wearing the mantle of war leader, was the Duwamish chief at the council.

Spurred by the Cayuse War, Congress established Oregon Territory in August 1848, which, with the annexation of northern Mexico, rounded out the shape of the continental United States. Once Fort Nisqually's new palisade was completed in September, demonstrations subsided, but tensions remained high, and the Indians did not hide their displeasure. Years later, Tolmie recalled that they played on the whites' timidity, saying that the Indians "[know] white men better than white men know them, because white men do not take the same trouble to study Indians that they take to study us."[17]

The Snoqualmie also had issues with the Nisqually, specifically with their headman, Lahalet. Earlier, the father of the Sinkiuse-Columbia nobleman Moses had murdered a Snoqualmie man west of the mountains. Kin planned to kill Moses's father near Snoqualmie Pass as he traveled home, but during an ambush near Snoqualmie Falls, he escaped. The Snoqualmie, however, captured the bodyguard, and when they threatened to kill him, Lahalet negotiated a peaceful settlement sealed by the marriage of his son Wyamooch to a Snoqualmie headman's daughter. Shortly after the marriage, however, the Snoqualmie heard that Wyamooch was mistreating his bride. That winter, a father-in-law's murder of a Nisqually headman who had also mistreated his wife suggested that Wyamooch should worry.[18]

There is another strand in this story. Recall that Julia Patkanim—Patkanim's daughter—had married the American, Thomas Glasgow. Years later, Glasgow was depicted in news stories as a "tyrant" and a "monster" for the alleged persistent abuse of his native wife from Whidbey. Patkanim likely had others besides Wyamooch to give him cause for anger, and as news of the California gold rush drew pioneer men south, he acted.

April 1849 brought cloudy weather and rain. At Fort Nisqually, frogs sang as native workers sowed oats, peas, and potatoes in the fields. On April 5, a large group of Snoqualmie and Skykomish arrived and camped on the beach, joined a few days later by a large party of Suquamish coming to trade, who stirred the sultry tedium by killing a whale. On April 28 came news that Sneetlum, normally a friendly headman, and a party of Skagits had robbed a Victoria-bound express of a gun, an ax, and all its provisions. On May 1, as Fort Nisqually officers and employees headed to the dining hall for the noon meal, the approach of about one hundred armed Snoqualmie and Skykomish sent local natives fleeing into the stockade. Led by Patkanim, the group divided, some going to Lahalet's lodge and others congregating near the fort's waterside gate. When asked why the armed group was acting in such a warlike manner, the Indians said they had issues with Lahalet's son beating his wife, but had no intention of harming whites.[19]

As Patkanim went into the fort to parley, tobacco was given to those outside. But inside the fort, a gun fired. The Snoqualmie charged as the gate was closed, leaving an American, Leander Wallace, outside. In the ensuing hail of bullets, Patkanim escaped; Wallace and a Skykomish shaman were killed, and two other settlers were wounded, along with a native man and child who would die from their injuries. Near the end of the affray, when a native man leveled his gun at HBC clerk Walter Ross, the Snohomish headman Sehalapahan, "the Priest," knocked it aside, saying, "Enough trouble for one day."

Trouble indeed. Had Patkanim planned to seize the fort? The gun-shot turned out to be accidental. With tensions high, the bodyguard's rush to the gate to rescue their chief was not surprising. That Patkanim's escape was helped by Lahalet suggests that the two were negotiating the problem. The Hudson's Bay Company men concluded that the Snoqualmie had planned "to kick up a row at the fort and then kidnap as many of the women and children as they could catch." Sneetlum's behavior and Sehalapahan's presence in the attacking party suggest that groups on the lower Sound had issues other than Wyamooch's spousal abuse, but what these were can only be guessed at now.

What is certain is that because they felt vulnerable and believed Glasgow and Rabbeson's story, the Americans took seriously the threats Patkanim was said to have made as he retreated, warning them to abandon their property and leave. Two weeks later, clerk Walter Ross recorded Simmons's request for ammunition and noted that Americans appeared to be "giving credence to the Indian rumors of invasion on the part of the Snoqualmies."[20]

In reaction, settlers erected blockhouses at New Market and Cowlitz Prairie, and, in the excitement, George Bush announced that he would sink any hostile canoe approaching New Market with a "terrible great gun" that only he could fire. Simmons wrote immediately to Oregon's new territorial governor, Joseph Lane, describing the settlers' peril. An ambitious Southern appointee who had led troops during the Mexican-American War, Lane was at The Dalles on the Columbia River conferring with native leaders about the Cayuse War when word of the attack and Leander Wallace's death reached him.[21]

Lane left immediately with arms and ammunition for New Market, where he received word that the steam frigate USS *Massachusetts* was on the Columbia with two companies of artillery. Additionally, a regiment of mounted riflemen organized by the War Department to protect Oregon Trail emigrants would soon enter the territory. Satisfied that he had sufficient force, Lane asked Tolmie to withhold powder and shot from the hostile Indians and inform them that "any repetition of the like conduct will be visited promptly with their complete destruction."[22]

Whatever his intentions, Patkanim had put himself and his people on a collision course with the Americans, who would not ignore what they considered a direct threat. By mid-May, other Indians were distancing themselves from him. Sneetlum and another Skagit chief apologized to officials for their treatment of the courier, and Xotikʔeʹdəb arrived at the fort to express his regret over "the foolish conduct of the creators of the disturbance of the 1st and his resolve to have no part or lot with the guilty Snoqualmie." When Patkanim and his retinue landed at Ketron Island, four miles north of the fort landing, in June, Tolmie sent for him. After hearing Lane's order, Patkanim expressed his regret, and the hope that whites would not harm his people. Tolmie said that was up to the governor.[23]

In late July, J. Quinn Thornton, the Indian agent appointed for the territory north of the Columbia, arrived at Fort Nisqually to confer with Tolmie. Exceeding his mandate, Thornton investigated Wallace's death, ordering Xotikʔeʹdəb, identified now as the Snoqualmie head chief, to surrender the Indians accused of the murder to Captain Bennett J. Hill, commander of Company M of the First Regiment of Artillery. Dangling a carrot from the stick, he offered eighty blankets if this were done in three weeks. Four months after abusing Tolmie's men but eager now to cooperate, Sneetlum guided US Army brevet major John S. Hatheway on a tour from the Sound's eastern shore to Joseph Heath's farm, which had been abandoned after the farmer's death in March, where Hill's unit entered winter quarters in buildings leased from the PSAC and renamed Steilacoom Barracks.[24]

Thornton asked Tolmie the names, populations, and habits of groups on the sound and their disposition toward whites. The "Shoquamish" on Port Orchard and the west side of Whidbey Island, "about 500," were "friendly and well-disposed," as were the Sineramish (Snohomish) who, with the Nisqually and Puyallup, numbered 550. The Journal of Occurrences notes that on August 21, Thornton addressed "representations of the Scadjet, Sinahomish, Soquamish, Stichasamish and Nisqually Tribes to make presents to the chiefs and principal men" at the fort. To honor chiefs Thornton gave each two three-point HBC blankets, the highest grade, with three narrow marks woven on their edge to indicate relative value.[25]

Although Thornton does not name the chiefs, they are likely those Lane listed a year earlier in a letter to the War Department: Sneetlum of the Skagit, the Frenchman of the Snohomish, Lahalet of the Nisqually, and Salcom—Challacum—of the Suquamish. Although neither mentioned nor listed, Gray Head was chief of the St!əch!a'sabsh, the Stichasamish in the Journal, and well known for his friendship with the Americans. The Duwamish are nowhere mentioned, and Seattle's reputation as a war leader appears to have been too fresh in company minds to warrant his inclusion among pacific leaders.

This is our last glimpse of Challacum; his name does not appear on the 1855 Treaty of Point Elliott where Seattle is identified as the Suquamish chief. The complete lack of comment regarding Seattle's remarkable rise in American perception from nonentity to the paramount chief of the lower Puget Sound groups requires our close examination of what little information exists about his movements during these crucial years. A helpful clue may come from an interview anthropologist Warren Snyder carried out in the 1950s with Wilson George, a native man living at the Tulalip Reservation. George recalled that a man named Walak served as head chief of the Suquamish some time after Kitsap. He was a wealthy noble and a fine speaker who George claimed served as an interpreter at the Point Elliott Treaty Council. George Gibbs included a man named Wilak as a subchief among those he listed for the Duwamish and Suquamish in March 1854, but the

Suquamish today do not recognize any other head chief from Kitsap until treaty times but Challacum and Seattle.[26]

Kitsap had strong connections with the Green River, Challacum with the Ch'teelqwubsh of Steilacoom Creek, and Seattle with the Duwamish. Elsewhere on the Sound, other groups are known to have chosen people from outside their group as head chief. This made sense by reducing conflict that might otherwise arise from rivalries between related noble families. We recall that the Romans, during their regal period, never selected a king from their own patrician families for the same reason. The period between kings, when a new selection was made, was called an *interregnum*, and it seems to me that Wilson George may have remembered an advisory role Walak played during the Suquamish interregnum between Challacum and Seattle. In this context we may better understand Seattle's actions after 1849 when we return to him.

On September 3, Patkanim and other Snoqualmie headmen arrived at Steilacoom village to receive the eighty blankets and other gifts in exchange for the surrender of Patkanim's brother Quallahworst, along with Kussus, a Skykomish headman, and four others: Stuharrai, Tatalum, Whyeek, and Quailthlumkyne, who were arrested and taken to Steilacoom Barracks in chains. Thornton's payment to the instigators of the raid angered Governor Lane and others, who learned of it after the fact, and gave native people like Seattle grounds to question American judgement.[27]

On October 1, 1849, the first US District Court for Lewis County, in Oregon Territory north of the Columbia, Judge William P. Bryant presiding, opened in a crowded frame building at Steilacoom Barracks. To show judicial power striding swiftly and effectively to points of conflict, Lane spent more than $2,000 of the fund Congress had allotted for Indian gifts to pay the court's and jurors' expenses. Joe Meek, a famous mountain man turned territorial marshal, called the court into session, and Bryant swore in a grand jury of fifteen white men to consider charges against the defendants. Alonzo Skinner, a thirty-five-year-old Ohio lawyer who had arrived in Oregon in 1845, was appointed prosecuting attorney, and attorney David Stone, a pioneer of 1843, served as counsel for the accused. A bona fide American court of law was on extravagant display.

It met at ten o'clock the next morning to hear the grand jury return indictments for murder. On October 3, the accused were arraigned and pleaded not guilty. A petit jury of twelve men, all Americans except Simon Plomondon's mixed-blood son, Lewis, was called, and the trial began. No record of testimony survives, but Quallahworst and Kussus were swiftly found guilty and the others acquitted. Quailthlumkyne could not be identified as having been at the crime scene, and it was supposed he was a Snoqualmie slave sent to court in hopes of satisfying the blood debt and saving the condemned. But there was no saving them. Bryant ordered their deaths by hanging.

At four o'clock the next afternoon, troops guarding the place of execution came to attention as the prisoners were led from the barracks to a platform built beneath a cluster of oak trees, where they climbed its stairs. The crew of a ship anchored nearby had supplied the rope that hung in nooses from low limbs. Among a "vast gathering of Indians from other tribes on the sound" were, as Bryant reported to Lane, several hundred Snoqualmie ordered to witness the fate of murderers condemned in an American court of law and to understand "that our laws would punish them promptly . . . and that we would have no satisfaction short of all who acted in the murder of our citizens." How their headmen were to take this, being made eighty blankets richer, is left to conjecture.

The only sounds breaking the silence as Meek tied the men's legs, tightened the nooses around their necks, and blindfolded them were heartrending appeals made by the wife of one of the condemned men. Pushed off the platform, their bodies jerked in the afternoon light. If the missionaries had failed to teach the Indians to fear the white man's God, a determined Governor Lane would teach them to fear the Americans.[28]

The momentary pause of American settlement around Puget Sound caused by the California gold rush ended quickly once those who had gone south understood they could do better supplying the needs of others flocking to the diggings. Patkanim took the time to rethink his attitude toward the Americans, as did Seattle and other headmen on the Sound. In later life, Angeline recalled that her father "thought it was right that the two Snoqualmies were executed." Even at this remove, the words have the sound of an opinion arrived at after long consideration, and we may also hear a hint of his distrust of Patkanim that ripened over time. Seattle was in his sixties at the time of the trial, an old war leader still feared but in danger of becoming an anachronism. But the skills of a successful war leader—effective tactics and strategic vision—are, as those who have read Sun Tzu's *The Art of War* know, applicable in other situations.[29]

---

Toward the end of 1849, several who had left claims north of the Columbia for California pooled their resources to purchase the brig *Orbit* and a cargo of merchandise for the return home. Reaching the freezing mudflats of Budd Inlet on January 1, 1850, *Orbit* became the first American vessel to trade with settlers there, and Michael Simmons, who had sold his New Market claim and sought other investments, purchased controlling interest in the brig, intending to ship lumber to San Francisco. He and another part owner, thirty-two-year-old Isaac Neff Ebey, looked for a town site and noted Smithfield's rough clearing. Levi Lathrop Smith had died, and the claim had passed to Edmund Sylvester, who offered Simmons two lots if he would build there.[30]

Joining the Americans cutting lumber in the woods were native people eager to work. Standing in deep snow, the settlers shivered to watch them in breechcloths rafting pilings, squared timbers, and planks through icy water to the vessel. When *Orbit* returned in July with more merchandise, Simmons and partner Charles Hart Smith were ready to sell goods from a two-story frame house in the town, renamed Olympia. Many of the customers would have been Gray Head's people, but the Duwamish also showed up below the old village site, forming a new community on the beach below the town that came to be called Chinook Street. That Seattle and his people came here we know; how this came about we can only speculate, but it is likely that Gray Head played a role. It appears he and Seattle got beyond the insults traded earlier at Whidbey Island, and Gray Head convinced him that the Americans could be useful. It was time for him to put away his weapons and play a different game.[31]

Disembarking from *Orbit* was Samuel Hancock, returning from San Francisco to his claim on Budd Inlet with his own stock of trade goods. Outfitting himself as a "mahkook man," the Jargon word for "merchant," he hired Indians to paddle him down Sound in search of coal. In the first year of the gold rush, San Francisco's population had mushroomed from two thousand to twenty thousand, and steamships furrowed the bay. But when local coal and timber could no longer satisfy demand, entrepreneurs searched for more distant sources. Hancock stopped briefly near Elliott Bay, where an eager native crowd greeted him on the beach. If his flaming-red hair caught their eye, the pipes, tobacco, mirrors, and brass rings packed in his bulging valise caught their attention, and as he distributed gifts, the people prepared a feast of clams and salmon. Afterward, he reached once more into his bag, held up a piece of coal, and announced that if they knew where they could find similar rocks that burned like wood, he would pay them well.[32]

Hancock found burning peat beds on Whidbey but no coal. On the lower Sound, outsiders still excited suspicion, and he heard that several traders preceding him had been murdered, but his trinkets, good nature, and courage won him friends who spread the word that Americans had arrived to trade. Gray Head had welcomed them to his homeland and Leschi to his, but from this point on, a pattern emerges in which many pioneers arriving at Olympia looking for good locations were taken north by native crews and guided to Elliott Bay. From later sources, it becomes clear that Seattle directed this effort, advertising his homeland and bringing Americans north to settle among his people—not at Old Man House, but among his Duwamish on the eastern shore.

It was a remarkable turnabout for a man in his elder years. From our perspective today, in the thriving city bearing his name, his decision to court the Americans appears uniquely farsighted. What is genuinely remarkable about Seattle's decision is the single-minded energy he brought to it, how he followed it up, and how he dealt with the enormous challenges the Americans imposed on him.

One of Seattle's most significant catches was Robert Fay, a thirty-year-old whaler from Vermont, who captained vessels trading between San Francisco and Puget Sound and brought the *Orbit* back to Olympia in the summer of 1850. In San Francisco, Fay and partners

Robert Fay—whaler, captain, and businessman—was Chief Seattle's partner in the Elliott Bay salmon-fishing venture.

advertised themselves as commission merchants with an office near the corner of Battery and Pine Streets. The HBC had sold barreled salmon to California and Hawaii, and Fay sought to supply the same to Bay Area retailers for a percentage of profit. Promising advantages, Seattle convinced him to move north, and Fay made plans to operate a fishery on Elliott Bay.[33]

In August, twenty-two-year-old Ohioan John C. Holgate, in Oregon two years, headed north to explore the Sound, and a native crew took him to the Duwamish River, to Txwkwiltəd, village of the K!elka'kubiu, described as a proud and confident people. There, Holgate saw fine, hand-hewn cedar house planks, which he described in a letter home as "40 feet long, 2½ feet wide and not more than 2½ inches thick." Welcomed by the people and impressed by their gardens, he staked a claim but returned to Ohio to marry, unaware that the Donation Land Claim Act enacted by Congress would require that a claim's location be filed at a territorial land office.[34]

In September, President Millard Fillmore signed this long-awaited act into law, reaffirming grants of 320 acres of free land to each white male citizen twenty-one years or older who arrived in Oregon before December 1, 1850, and the same for each man's wife—a square mile free if they lived on it for four years and made improvements. The amount of land would be halved in 1851, but the law's passage opened the floodgates of emigration and precipitated a mental change: those coming west were pioneers no longer but proprietors coming to get what was theirs.

Early that fall, Ebey joined another of *Orbit*'s part owners, Benjamin Franklin Shaw, and settler Daniel Kinsey loading trade goods in a longboat to explore Whidbey Island and the eastern shore to the British line. A strong wind and native directions brought them to Elliott Bay where a celebration happened to be in progress. As the boat grounded, hundreds of shouting Indians poured out of a large house and surrounded them, jumping stiff-legged into the air, waving blankets and knives, and shooting guns. A half century later, Shaw could still clearly recall this unnerving reception and the large old Indian "with a very wide head" who came out of a longhouse, stood on a log, and, through an interpreter using the Jargon, welcomed the Americans to his home, saying:

My name is Sealt, and this great swarm of people that you see here are my people; they have come down here to celebrate the coming of the first run of good salmon. As the salmon are our chief food we always rejoice to see them coming early and in abundance, for that insures us a plentiful quantity of food for the coming winter. This is the reason our hearts are glad today, and so you do not want to take this wild demonstration as warlike. It is meant in the nature of a salute in imitation of the Hudson's Bay Company's salute to their chiefs when they arrive at Victoria. I am glad to have you come to our country, for we Indians know but little and you Boston and King George men [know] how to do everything. We want your blankets, your guns, axes, clothing and tobacco, and all other things that you make. We need all these things that you make as we do not know how to make them, and so we welcome you to our country to make flour, sugar and other things that we can trade for. We wonder why three Boston men should wander so far away from home and come among so many Indians. Why are you not afraid?[35]

Reprinted fifty years later, the speech had doubtless been edited by Shaw, but it has the simple diction of Chinook Jargon, and having emigrated from Missouri in 1844, Shaw knew the Jargon well enough to catch the adroit comparison of the chief factor's grand entrance at Fort Victoria with the arrival of the salmon chief to their river. It is very likely that Seattle witnessed George Simpson's grand arrival at Fort Victoria in 1842, and the allusion in the speech argues for its general authenticity.

To answer Seattle's question, Shaw stood in the longboat's bow and proclaimed that he and his friends had no fear because they came in peace from a great people across the mountains, whose factories and mills would satisfy all the Indians' needs. This was well received, and after Ebey, Shaw, and Kinsey ate supper on the beach, Seattle invited them into the ceremonial house to witness a secret-society initiation.

The trio spent the night there, and early the next morning Seattle arranged to have them taken up the Duwamish. In words reminiscent of

Vancouver, Ebey described the river meandering "through rich bottom land, not heavily timbered, with here and there a beautiful plain of unrivaled fertility, peeping out through a fringe of vine maple, alder and ash, or baldly presenting a full view of their native richness." Paddling up Black River, they entered a magnificent sheet of water Ebey dubbed Lake Geneva, which settlers would call Dwamish Lake and rename Lake Washington. Ten miles up its eastern shore, they were shown a trail the guides said crossed the mountains. On White River, they saw prairies of tall grass and nodding clover. Seattle had delivered them to the world where his mother's bones rested, a rich country whose bounty he hoped his people and the Americans could share. That he had left Chinook Street in Olympia to be on hand when the trio arrived *and* direct a ceremony to welcome them reveals a considerable amount of forethought and planning. Shaw returned to Olympia, and Ebey took a claim on Whidbey near Thomas Glasgow's, but a vivid description of Seattle's homeland that Shaw sent to Michael Simmons appeared that fall in the *Oregon Spectator*.[36]

Farther north, the Stillaguamish showed Samuel Hancock beds of lignite banding a cliff above their river. When his Indian crew told the Snoqualmie that he might settle nearby, "some would approach my tent entirely naked and others with only an old blanket and laying down some present for me outside, walk away without saying a word, but taking care that I should see their gifts."[37]

Still under a cloud but determined to find a trader of his own, Patkanim accompanied Hancock back to Olympia in November and convinced the recently arrived doctor from Vermont, David Maynard, then forty-two years old, to return with him and view the seam. On their way back, they put in briefly at Elliott Bay, Patkanim letting Seattle know that he was not the only tyee shopping for Americans.[38]

In April 1851, Olympia was made port of entry on the Sound, and the upper floor of Simmons's house became the customs office. There were no more than three other American houses there, but along Chinook Street during the rainy season, Seattle and the Duwamish occupied "some 20 or more Indian huts at a short distance from the Custom House," where Seattle advertised himself and hired his people out to provide tours and labor. A diarist described "his stately walk and dignified carriage," adding that "he is very friendly to the whites . . .

and while he considers it beneath his dignity to use the jargon of the country, he will show you by friendly shake of the hand and a grunt that he expects to be noticed by the newcomer." Another early pioneer, John M. Swan, founder of the Swantown neighborhood, remembered Seattle as "good dispositioned . . . a large, portly old man with good features." Several hundred Indians and their barking dogs had gathered near the customs office and supplied white settlers with fish, ducks, venison, oysters, and berries.[39]

Another new settler directed to the Duwamish River was Luther Collins, a thirty-six-year-old New York farmer who had arrived in Oregon in '47, tried his luck in California, and returned in 1850 to explore Puget Sound. He, too, was taken up the Duwamish and liked what he saw, but fearful of so many Indians, he staked a claim on the Nisqually River to be nearer other Americans. In the spring of 1851, he convinced Samuel Mapel (subsequently written Maple), his son John, and Dutch immigrant Henry Van Asselt to join him, but the sandy Nisqually bottom did not impress. Hoping to retain their company, he described what he had seen along the Duwamish, promising that its rich soil would yield a good life as long as they didn't mind living with many savages.[40]

Native paddlers brought them up the Duwamish to the proud people's fertile gardens, which they liked very much. Collins unknowingly staked his claim on Ohioan John Holgate's, downstream from the rest, and sold his Nisqually property. In September, they rafted supplies and cattle north to Duwamish Head, where Indian workers whom Robert Fay and Seattle were assembling for the fishery helped tow the raft upstream. Seattle's role reveals itself in a later recollection that as the party rounded a bend, the old chief stood on the bank with his arm raised in greeting.

Another group invited in was the Denny-Low party. In April 1851, four wagons bearing Arthur Denny, along with his wife, Mary Ann, their children, their parents, and his unmarried brothers, and the family of Carson Boren, left the little hamlet of Cherry Grove, in northern Illinois, for Oregon. Three months later, on the Snake River, they joined the wagons of John Low of Ohio and his family. The party arrived in Portland in late August. They were looking for town sites rather than farmland, and in September, Arthur Denny's brother David and Low pastured their cattle north of the Columbia and went on to explore Puget Sound. At

Olympia, they met Leander Terry, a New Yorker, and Fay, who brought them in an open boat, likely a native-crewed canoe, to the fishery that he, Seattle, and a Swedish sailor, George Martin, were operating at the mouth of the Duwamish.[41]

On September 25, they arrived at Skwədks, a busy camp at Duwamish Head, where, under Seattle's direction, between fifty and one hundred Indians were out on the bay fishing from canoes. Seven hundred Indians gathered there that summer, trolling for the big Chinook salmon and bringing the catch to the shore, where women cleaned, cut up, and salted the fish, then packed them in barrels Martin coopered from fir staves hooped with hazel withes. Boiling brine, ladled into each barrel through a hole in its waist, filled it to the rim of a wide clay collar built around it. As the salmon flesh absorbed brine, rising blood and oil were skimmed off and the hole was sealed with a wooden bung.[42]

No business records survive, but Fay would have bartered goods that Seattle used to secure a workforce. The chief's ability to organize his people, attract Americans, and do business with Fay underscored his successful turn from a war leader with a bloody reputation of repelling invaders to a power broker actively directing Americans to live and prosper with his people. Long before the tech industry, before aircraft, coal, or lumber, the fishery was the first commercial enterprise Americans entered into on Elliott Bay, and they did it in concert with Seattle and his people. Despite his old age, a powerful vitality still drove the man, and David Denny never forgot his first impression of him as a "man of more than ordinary ability both physically and mentally."[43]

The night they arrived at Skwədks, the Americans camped under an immense cedar. At dawn, Fay left to oversee the work, and Seattle had guides take the three upriver to the now-famous gardens at Txwkwi'ltəd. Low and Terry disappeared down a trail, and Denny waited anxiously until he was brought back to Seattle's camp that evening. Returning to where he had left them the next morning, he was relieved to see them coming downstream in an Indian canoe. They had gotten lost and spent the night at Skoa'lko, a village farther upstream at the confluence of the Black and White Rivers, whose people were bringing them back down to the bay. The Americans had been introduced to Seattle's upriver kin, and, thanks to him, were about to meet more of their own.

That evening, Fay and the others heard voices at Skwədks, and when they walked down the beach, they saw Luther Collins rounding Duwamish Head, poling a scow bearing his ample wife, Diana, their thirteen-year-old daughter, Lucinda, and more supplies. While the women practiced the Jargon with Fay, Collins described the settlement taking shape upriver in glowing terms. The next day, Low and Terry laid out a town site on Prairie Point, a spot able to be seen by passing ships, which would supply the fishery and settlers upriver in the fertile valley. Terry named it New York.

Fay sounded a note of caution when campfire talk addressed the virtues of Indian plank houses. A stout log cabin, he said with a wink, would give better protection from "stray bullets" when the Indians were out "hunting." Despite Fay's concern, Seattle's optimistic view prevailed—that both the land *and* its people had promise—a different view than that of earlier explorers. When Fay and Seattle returned to Olympia, Low went with them, hiring Denny and Terry to build a cabin while he went on to Portland to fetch his family and deliver David's fateful note to Arthur saying that he and his companions had found a valley with room for one thousand settlers; "Come at once."[44]

———————

Many streams flowed into Puget Sound. In the 1830s, the Hudson's Bay Company had anchored a western trade network at Fort Nisqually. In the '40s, Americans cultivated farms nearby and started a town. And during the summer and fall of 1851, the Duwamish River witnessed a remarkable burst of activity. Like Leschi and Gray Head, Seattle had invited Americans to join his people, as any *sia'b* would who sought to benefit by introducing powerful and wealthy newcomers into his group. But no other native leader was so aggressive or as successful a recruiter as Seattle. He had taken the Americans' measure as restless and not especially wise, but capable and wealthy. He became an "impresario" as the Spanish used the term: one who brought a new community into being and managed affairs to ensure its prosperity. And while they were still very few among large crowds of native people, American settlers were willing to be managed.

As luminous summer gave way to rainy fall, groups arrived to observe Seattle's experiment at Skwədks. His half brother Curley, headman at the village of Dzidzəla'ləch, the "Little Crossing Place," across the bay, politely requested that he and his retinue be allowed to camp near the brushed-out site. Struggling to master Indian pronunciation, the Americans gave him his easier nickname and would later describe him, like his halfbrother, as a man of subtle intelligence and tact. Locally, there were actually several Curleys: Cultus Curley, "Less Important Curley," a headman at Baba'kwəb, "prairies" a village north of Dzidzəla'ləch; Hu-hu-bate-sute, nicknamed Salmon Bay Curley, an impressively large man; and a Curley at Quilcene, on Hood Canal. Tolmie described Seattle's hair as curly, and if the Curleys were kin, the nickname may describe an inherited trait. Curley laughingly recalled that first meeting when he had offered the new neighbors a choice portion of roast duck. Unsure of native cooking practices, they had squeamishly declined.[45]

Unable to lift the heavy logs for cabin walls, Denny and Terry paid Indians with ship's bread to help. Less agreeable were a party of Skagit men led by an imposing bearded figure, whose canoe loomed out of the fog one morning. The Americans resisted the Skagit attempt to push into their tent, and eventually they departed, but the experience left the Americans shaken. These were not the defeated Indians of folklore, or the timorous Siwash described by the ignorant, but a numerous people strong in their own country.

Then Fay left for San Francisco with his barreled salmon, and Terry went with Collins to Olympia to get a shingle froe, leaving David Denny alone for three weeks. On the drizzly shore, he cut his foot with an ax and caught cold. Skunks ate his food. The native people put their paddles away and roared power songs in the longhouses in the cold November drizzle.

On November 13, the schooner *Exact* let go her anchor with a rattle of chain, and the seven men, five women, and twelve children of the Denny-Low party were rowed ashore in a pelting downpour to a dripping forest. Ill and forlorn, David stood before a roofless cabin, watched by his many Indian neighbors. The future he sought had become larger and wilder than he had imagined, and peopled by an unfamiliar and intimidating race. He limped across the seaweed-slick cobbles and blurted out to Arthur, "I wish you hadn't come."[46]

David's anxiety had grown in Seattle's absence. When the barreled salmon had rotted on his voyage south, Fay returned to the quarterdeck as captain of the schooner *Albion*. Undeterred, Seattle returned to Olympia to find his replacement.

Meanwhile, the trade goods Leander Terry's brother Charles brought up with him from Portland realized the dream that native people had nurtured since Vancouver's time. The Duwamish and other groups poured in, eager to barter goods and labor. Headmen were all elbows striving for advantage as they had at Fort Nisqually, and Arthur Denny recalled that more than one thousand gathered there.[47]

Planks for their shelters came from the building Shaw had seen at the Little Crossing Place, ferried to the site. After building Low's log cabin and another for Arthur Denny, all the timber that could be gotten along the shore without draft animals was used up, and, disregarding Fay's caution, pioneers began splitting planks Indian-fashion for William Bell's and Carson Boren's houses.

At times, the excited throng seemed about to explode. One day, White River men led by Pialchəd, a headman whose name became Nelson on the settlers' tongues, confronted several Snoqualmie led by John Kanim, a brother of Patkanim, on the beach in front of Low's cabin. When they seemed about to fire their guns point-blank at each other, Arthur Denny grabbed Nelson and hid him behind Low's cabin until the Snoqualmie left. It was, he was told, just a show. But one man who leveled his gun at Mary Ann Denny had something else to show. There had been trouble up at Luther Collins's place, and he was letting Mary Ann know that her family's fate rested entirely in native hands.[48]

It is around this time that we have one of our last glimpses of Seattle on Chinook Street in Olympia. The schooner, *Exact*, that had carried the Denny party to Elliott Bay also brought Irish immigrants John Alexander and his wife, Frances, who had arrived over land via wagon train to Oregon, to Olympia, where they lived briefly in a cabin next to Chinook Street. When Frances's clothesline came up missing, John said he knew who had it and told her to see Seattle. She found him sitting in a tent "in his skin mending his pants" and told him that someone had stolen her clothesline. He grunted, got up, walked to the tent flap, "and then," she said, "I never in my life heard anything like the screech he gave." Everyone—old men crawling, young men "running like horses," old women and young women with their babies, children, and even the

dogs—gathered to hear him speak a few words, and then they left as quickly as they had come. Trembling, Frances was about to reenter her house when an Indian ran up and silently handed her the clothesline, the last thing Frances ever had stolen there.[49]

When Seattle returned to Elliott Bay, he reined in the turbulent native crowd. To remind them who was in charge, he organized a show, as he had for Shaw and his colleagues, during which his retinue drama-tized the slaughter of the Chemakum. It worked. After John Low's wife, Lydia, complained that a shirt had been stolen from her clothesline, it was returned along with several pieces of clothing she had not yet missed.[50]

The settlers' eagerness to return favors sometimes had macabre results. When Seattle's second wife, Owiyahl, Angeline's stepmother, died that winter, William Bell and Arthur Denny made a coffin, but it was too small. The Indians solved the problem by removing several blankets wrapping the corpse, leaving them atop the coffin when it was buried at Prairie Point. Her interment reminds us that she came from the wealthy village of Herring House, whose headman had married Seattle's halfsister. The fact that she was buried in a coffin in the manner of a Christian sug-gests that she had been baptized, and some recall that her Christian name was Mary. This man, Tsutsa'lptəd, may have been the Duwamish chief who legend says invited competing shamans to cure his daughter during

A rendering of Herring House, a noted native village on the western shore of Elliott Bay, as it looked in the 1890s in what is now the West Seattle neighborhood. Clifton A. Faron created the sketch at the turn of the twentieth century.

a *sgwi'gwi*, but when the settlers met him, he was a devout Catholic. His people helped cut and haul pilings to the bark *Leonessa* that December, establishing direct trade with San Francisco.[51]

While Leander Terry returned to the East Coast that spring, his brother Charles imported more trade goods, and people arriving from as far as Whidbey Island and the Nisqually River haggled and threatened one another in front of his store, the "New York Markook House," a variant of "Mahkook," while wearing his tin cups around their necks. Around this time, a visiting ship captain asked the settlement's name. Hearing "New York," he laughed, and said, "Yes, New York alki, I reckon." In the Jargon, *alki*, pronounced "AL-kay" meant "by and by." Eventually, as New York Alki's success waned in the manner of most start-ups, the name New York was dropped, and Prairie Point became Alki Point.[52]

In league with Old Dick, Seattle kept things humming, and when dealings in Olympia required his presence, he put others in charge. After Leander Terry and John Low had platted New York, Curley directed the other settlers' attentions eastward. Eager for *mahkook* men of their own to trade with, the Duwamish across the bay pointed out that a spur of the transmountain horse trail that Ebey had seen from the lake reached tidewater beside their houses. The shore south to the Puyallup River did not impress the settlers, so in February 1852, they borrowed a canoe, tied horseshoes to Mary Denny's clothesline, and sounded the bay's deep eastern shore.

To strengthen relations between the settlers and the Duwamish, Seattle's mother's people, Seattle brought his cousin Kwia'xtəd, the old headman of the main Duwamish village, and his three adult sons to Arthur Denny to be given "Boston" names. Regarded by the Indians as the settlers' tyee, Denny found the request amusing, but he complied, naming two after famous midwestern Indians. The oldest, Kwilsk!edub, he named Tecumseh, and the middle son, Xasidut, Keokuck. Unable to think of another midwestern Indian name, he called the youngest, Stoda', William, presumably after the leader of the Creek Nation. Traditionally, the rite of naming gave native people status, and sharing honorific names bound families and peoples together. Although tested by war, the ties between these native families and the Americans were never sundered.[53]

On February 15, the settlers staked claims on the east shore: Bell in the north, near Baba'kwəb, Boren south at Dzidzəla'ləch, and Arthur Denny in the middle. Aided by Seattle's cousin (or granddaughter) Mary Sam Seattle, pioneer women were paddled over to lay cabin foundation logs, but the families did not leave New York until March, when Seattle returned from Olympia with the man who would take Robert Fay's place.[54]

A depiction of the "Little Crossing Place," the Duwamish village on the east shore of Elliott Bay in what is now the Pioneer Square neighborhood, as it might have looked when the Americans arrived.

# CHAPTER FIVE

*"How then can we become brothers?"*

In 1850, California entered the United States as a free state, where slavery was banned. It was a positive step in the national narrative, surely, but California statehood was part of the Compromise of 1850, an act passed to appease the anger over slavery already dividing the nation. Since much of California was south of the 1820 Missouri Compromise line of N 36°30′, Congress invoked popular sovereignty to allow a choice on slavery by voters in the new Kansas and Nebraska Territories. Settlement of the central Great Plains was expected to increase land value, enabling the federal government to offer land grants to railroad corporations to help build a transcontinental line to the Pacific. The commoditization of land drove the nation's economy, even in its farthest northwestern reach.

The man Seattle brought back to replace Robert Fay was Dr. David Maynard. According to his biographer, Thomas Prosch, Maynard left California for Olympia in the fall of 1851 with a cargo of damaged goods to sell at reduced prices, delighting customers but infuriating other merchants, who suggested he leave town. Another problem Maynard, a married man, faced was his affection for the recently widowed Catherine Broshears, née Simmons, whom he had met on the Oregon Trail. She was a sister of pioneer Michael Simmons, who did not approve of her involvement with Maynard.[1]

In Olympia Seattle shook Maynard's hand and suggested he could do better elsewhere. He gave his practiced spiel listing the virtues of the Duwamish country: a big river and lake, a trail over the mountains, good soil, lots of game, friendly people, and now, a commercial fishery. His people would supply the labor, and eager to trade, they would make Maynard rich. Despite the limitations of speaking in the Jargon, the two men got along well. Like David Denny, David Maynard found much to admire in the chief.

Shortly after they met, someone tried to shoot Seattle. Noting the hole in the old man's tent, the doctor watched him finger a weapon while calmly discussing the move north. Inquiring into Maynard's personal life, Seattle offered the frustrated suitor Angeline's daughter, Chewatum, known later as Betsy, part of his plan to marry his people's future with the Americans', as native people always had with vigorous newcomers. Maynard did not object.[2]

In late March 1852, Seattle's retinue helped Maynard load his goods into the chief's large canoe, then he, Maynard, Betsy, and the chief's retinue departed for New York. It was beautiful weather, and with a spring breeze, the trip from Olympia would normally have taken only a day, but the four they spent suggest that Seattle was negotiating the resumption of the fishery along the way and announcing the arrival of another *mahkook* man.

Seattle traveled large. He owned a *stiwəl*, a freight canoe, paddled by four to six young men, and a great canoe carved in the northern style with a high prow, painted and bedecked with furs and said to have been powered by fifty paddlers. Family members paddling their canoes also typically accompanied him on his trips. When encountering passersby, he hailed them in his booming voice, announcing regally, "*Ətsa' Si²a'ł!*" (Uh-tsah Si-AH-hl)—"It is I, Seattle!"—to reassure them that he meant no harm.[3]

Arriving at New York on March 31, Seattle pointed out the old fishing camp but took Maynard over to Dzidzəla'ləch, "Little Crossing Place," a low gravelly neck that at low tide joined a forested islet to the shore. Seattle had entertained Shaw, Ebey, and Kinsey at a large ceremonial house near the islet's elevated south end, but villagers had since carried off its planks to New York, and Arthur Denny thought that the uprights he saw overgrown with wild roses marked an abandoned fishing camp. East of it, spring water meeting the river's surge built a narrow spit that enclosed a swampy lagoon where flounder were speared by torchlight. Believing that history began with their arrival, the settlers had ignored the site's antiquity, and now Carson Boren's claim encompassed it.

This was embarrassing. Land that Seattle had planned to offer Maynard had already been claimed. Wanting the doctor to stay, however, the settlers agreed to move their claims north to give him the island. Maynard deferred, saying that he wanted only a place to pack salmon.

But the agreement allowed Seattle to offer Maynard unclaimed land, and its advantages overcame any lingering scruples. Seattle had Carson Boren's and William Bell's families ferried over to the eastern shore and put David Maynard near the islet's southwest point, at a bluff settlers soon called "the Nose," which today is four blocks south of Pioneer Square. They split planks for houses, and within a week the doctor was selling his goods out of a store measuring eighteen by twenty-six feet, treating the occasional patient, and sharing the cramped attic with Betsy.[4]

Fay also returned that spring. With much of the shore claimed, he would settle on Whidbey Island, but his ship, the *Albion*, remained a crucial link in the salmon business. As they had flocked to New York to be close to the merchants there, the Duwamish returned to trade with Seattle and the settlers across the bay. That winter, several hundred Duwamish rebuilt houses at the Nose and a mile north at the village site of Baba'kwəb. Because the Donation Land Claim Act required settlers to live on their claims, pioneer homes were necessarily distant from one another, and the desire to locate near native villages to access labor scattered them among a dense population of Indians. Collins and his white neighbors established homesteads next to the K!elka'kubiu, New York was near Herring's House, Seattle put Maynard at Dzidzəla'ləch, and Boren and Bell staked claims near Baba'kwəb. Having been bedridden with malaria at New York Alki, Arthur and Mary Ann Denny did not arrive at their claim between Baba'kwəb and Dzidzəla'ləch until May. Finding no water there, Arthur Denny acquired the western part of Boren's claim and built another house beside a spring nearer Dzidzəla'ləch. On the east side of the bay, fifteen whites—eight of them children—scattered themselves among hundreds of Indians, hoping that Seattle and at least two Curleys would keep them safe.

Required to trust native leaders they barely knew, the isolated settlers felt acutely vulnerable, especially the women. Uprooted from secure homes and neighbors and left alone for days while their men worked in the woods, they found themselves among a race that had always been described to them as murdering savages. Huddled with her children in a tiny cabin, Lydia Low feared that Indians would seize the keg of whiskey her husband kept in the back room, get drunk, and kill them all. To warn them off, she practiced firing his Colt revolver at a target on a nearby tree.

Male settlers also tasted fear. "I thought they was a savage look-ing set as I ever had seen," recalled the twenty-one-year-old brother of Samuel Maple, Eli, who traveled upriver to join his family at their claims. "We come in sight of a great many Indian houses," he wrote. "The Indians steered the canoe a shore; I thought they was a going to kill me."[5]

The settlers' vulnerability so concerned Captain William Hudson of the USS *Vincennes*, Wilkes's old flagship, on a February 1852 visit, that he made a point of holding gunnery practice off Alki Point. Settlers thought it "music of a delightful character," but pioneer cabins scattered among native winter villages remained cause for anxiety. When Ohio pioneer Henry Smith arrived on Elliott Bay in November, he could see no white settlement along the eastern shore.

Even though Maynard and the rest of the settlers were where Seattle wanted them, the sight lines Arthur Denny surveyed, marked by blazes and boundary stakes, caused native concern. Precise land holdings were not part of traditional culture, although proprietary rights to resources were. Native people understood that crops and cattle required Americans to fence off land, but the idea of land as a commodity to be bought or sold was unfamiliar. The practice would eventually dispossess them, but at the time, the Indians, like the Americans, were anxious to get along.

The settlers learned native names for local house sites, rendering them as "Zedhalalitch" and "Mukmukum," and identifying Alki Point as "Soquampsh." This last name, actually an ethnic term rather than a place name, is interesting. Herring House, the large winter village on the bay's west shore, was Duwamish, not Suquamish, but although groups from throughout the Sound went to New York to trade, apparently enough Suquamish gathered there to be memorable. Still, when Seattle returned to the area with Maynard, he took him to the place where he had first met Ebey, Shaw, and Kinsey. For the Duwamish, two trading outlets in their homeland were better than one.[6]

The town grew in part because of its central location on the Sound, but it also depended upon the cooperation of Seattle and his people. To ensure success, Seattle worked as hard as any pioneer. Writing of events in 1852, Edward Huggins, Tolmie's successor as head of the Puget Sound Agricultural Company, noted that Seattle resided "at or near Alki Point." But Seattle also interacted with Americans at Olympia and at

Dzidzəla'ləch. Overseeing these separate sites required constant travel, but his actions were freighted with greater consequence than a *sia'b*'s visits to kin in multiple places. Seattle's efforts were far more ambitious than Steilacoom's on Whidbey. On Elliott Bay, he created what he hoped would be hybrid-racial communities to expand trade in central Puget Sound, the goal since Tolmie's 1833 visit. The outlets established at Soquampsh—Alki—and on the eastern shore, known by the settlers as as Duwamps, identified their markets.[7]

The settlers' arrival at the new site excited rivalry among headmen anxious to gain advantage, as it had at Alki. Upriver Duwamish continued to honor Arthur Denny with acts of generosity, and even Patkanim paid court, establishing a rapport with him that proved crucial to the settlement's survival. If relations between native people and white people could be jarring and intense, they were also often friendly and productive. With Seattle's help, settlers hired native men to clear claims, build houses, and cut timber for the California market. Native women bartered cranberries, clams, duck down, and pitch wood for trade goods and hired themselves and their children out as household servants. Some native women shared white men's beds.

Several native men expressed interest in Louisa Boren, in her early twenties and the Denny party's only unmarried white woman, but when she learned that the punt poles they left leaning against her family's cabin signaled their desire to wed, she was careful not to touch any, lest it signal a choice. Twice pretending ignorance, her fiancé, David Denny, chopped them up for firewood. In its desire to share a common future, the native community offered its women in marriage. American bachelors happily accepted, but American families held on to their daughters.[8]

Because white women were rare, native people observed them keenly, often to their intense discomfort. At first, upper cabin doors opening separately from the bottom kept native people out, but once they learned to trip the bottom lock, they entered as freely as they did their own houses. It is a telling detail: settlers trying to keep Indians out; Indians finding ways to let themselves in.

Inside a settler family's home, however, they ran afoul of American women determined to preserve domestic order. Mary Ann Denny once rapped a man's knuckles when he tried to snatch a fish frying in her pan. Lydia Low slapped another's bare buttocks with a spoon coated with boiling mush as he reached for a ham hanging on her wall. Another woman threatened Curley with a butcher knife. Such acts sparked uproar among native people accustomed to open hospitality, but as Seattle would explain, American largesse came in different forms.[9]

Overcoming fear, some settlers saw native people as individuals much like themselves. The revelation came to pioneer Ezra Meeker during a tour on the Sound in 1852, watching as a mother prepared a meal for his party and coaxed her shy children out to meet their guests. "We took it for granted that the Indians were our enemies . . . ," he recalled, "but here seemed to be disposition manifested to be neighborly and helpful."[10]

---

In late August of that year, Modeste Demers, newly appointed bishop of Vancouver Island and New Caledonia (part of present-day British Columbia), visited Elliott Bay on his way north, accompanied by Father Louis Lootens, a Belgian priest Demers had recruited on his *ad limina* trip to Rome. They spent a Saturday night in Arthur Denny's cabin, charming the family with genial kindness, and the next morning, historical records say that the settlement celebrated its first church service—in the cookhouse at Henry Yesler's sawmill, with Arthur Denny preparing the altar and Seattle assisting at Mass.[11]

But it did not happen that way. Yesler did not arrive until October 1852, and Seattle was not baptized, so what the priests held on August 22 was prayer service, not a Mass. Settlers had already crowded the room, but it was a lovely day and they soon were joined by others outside the open door and window. Seattle's remembered presence suggests that he and his retinue brought Demers and Lootens up from Fort Nisqually on their way to Victoria and visited the town in the spirit of fraternity. Demers would have worn a dark soutane and a small black skullcap as he recited Latin prayers from a worn lectionary.

That Methodists and Baptists from Illinois would attend a Latin service led by a Catholic bishop in the company of Indians underscored the extraordinary flux of pioneer life, where people shed old biases and adopted new behaviors to get along and prosper. In the eastern United

States, the massive influx of Irish Catholic and German immigrants had excited nativist reaction. As this spread westward with emigration, and old habits of bias and exclusion took hold, the memory of heartfelt participation in a Catholic rite was transferred to the less church-like setting of Yesler's cookhouse, built later that fall. Likewise, later Catholic enthusiasts have tried to make the gathering more Catholic than it was.

However, the unalloyed sweetness of that morning stayed in the memory of Arthur and Mary Ann Denny's daughter Lenora, who later recalled Demers's sermon when she was five years old as being the first she had ever heard. She also remembered the appeal he made in his sonorous Quebecois accent: "Charity, my friends, charity." Demers knew native leaders east and west of the Cascades, and having been present during the Cayuse War, he knew how easily fear and anger could lead to bloodshed, so sensing the goodwill of his American hosts at Elliott Bay, he encouraged them to open their hearts to one another and to native people as well, believing that if the fragile edifice built of shared hopes was to survive, it must shelter both communities.[12]

In the accommodation taking shape that summer, the learning curve was steep, and both peoples ascended its slope with difficulty. Just as earlier native leaders had hoped for good when cooperating with Hudson's Bay Company men, Seattle hoped his people and the settlers would prosper together, and he labored to mitigate conflicts. He and David Maynard resumed the fishery, with Maynard hiring settlers to make barrels and Seattle keeping his people busy catching and preparing fish. And in the weeks following Demers's departure, in the elevated mood the bishop had inspired, the settlers acknowledged their continuing need of Seattle's support by unanimously naming the settlement after him.[13]

It was no new thing for Midwesterners to name a town after a Native American. Around the Denny and Boren families' hometown of Cherry Grove, Illinois, the towns of Osceola, Prophetstown, and Keokuk (in Iowa) recalled famous native leaders. On the Sound, Port Steilacoom, established in 1850, recalled the Suquamish chief, and Sehome on Bellingham Bay, honored friendly Samish headmen. So settlers were surprised when Seattle showed displeasure. "Se-alth was quite disturbed," wrote Ezra Meeker, "to have his name trifled with and appropriated by the whites, and was quite willing to levy a tribute by persuasion upon the good people of the embryo city." According to historian Clarence Bagley, Angeline claimed he feared that after death, "he would have no rest, for he would be turning over all the time." Pioneer author Hezekiah Butterworth had him answering a pioneer's question about his demand this way: "The name of the town will call me back after I am dead, and make me unhappy. I want my pay for what I shall then suffer now."[14]

But there may be more to it: leaders of Seattle's stature led by consensus, and fixing his name to a native community may have appeared presumptuous to them. His protest pointed out that the naming was the settlers' idea, not his. For whatever reason, he objected, and anxious to retain his goodwill, the settlers paid him an unnamed sum, probably in goods.

If the learning curve proved costly, indifference was unaffordable. That Seattle is the largest city in the world named after a Native American is due to many things, but the name is best understood as an artifact from this short, crucial period of cooperation. Responding to later critics, pioneers focused on their own role in creating the town, ignoring many native contributions, just as they altered memory of the town's first church service. They went so far as to say that they named it Seattle because it sounded nice, when, in fact, the name was difficult to pronounce. Nonetheless, the fact remains that the town's growth and survival depended as much on Seattle as it did on anyone else. For the settlers, he had become the indispensable man.

To their credit, some pioneers remembered Seattle's contributions. Echoing his brother David's sentiments, Arthur Denny described him as a firm and courageous leader, "not of the turbulent and aggressive kind, but . . . the mildest and most generous type . . . with more than ordinary intelligence." This follows closely what anthropologist June Collins would describe in her study of native class distinctions and political authority. Her informants told her that a *sia'b* was expected to be "slow to take offense personally . . . [and] tries to maintain peace in the family. He is lacking in aggressive behavior in his ordinary personal relationships and is said to 'talk good' to others." That these words describe the Seattle of David and Arthur Denny's experience rather than the truculent figure depicted in the *Journal of Occurrences* underscores his successful transformation from bellicose war leader to an advocate of cooperation. For generations, native and white had been in storied conflict, and in Oregon Territory blood had been shed east and west of the Cascades, but on Elliott Bay, Seattle, Curley, Old Dick, the Dennys, the Terrys, Maynard, and others worked to avoid that fate, and in those early days when individual acts augured several possible futures, peace and prosperity seemed possible.[15]

Not all were so disposed. Many settlers hunted game on native ranges without permission, plowed up native gardens, or pastured stock in them without care, but when native people helped themselves to what settlers raised in their fields, they were branded thieves. "We adopted a rule," wrote Eli Maple, "when an Indian stole anything or done anything bad we tyed [sic] him up and whipped him. If that did not settle him we would threaten them with the soldiers." Few Indians spoke English, and fewer settlers spoke native languages, leaving the Jargon as the lingua franca. It enabled barter, but its spare diction trivialized discourse, and many settlers' assumption that it *was* the native language only reinforced their dim view of Native Americans' capacity.[16]

Wealth itself caused trouble. Americans ransacking forests alerted native people to the monetary value of resources. "The Whites pay a great deal for a small piece [of land]," the Skokomish head chief Nah-whil-luk would say, "and they get money by selling the sticks. Formerly the Indians slept, but the Whites came along and woke them up and we now know that the lands are worth much." On one trip in 1852, the brig *Franklin Adams* took on twelve thousand feet of squared timber, eight thousand feet of piling, ten thousand shingles, and thirty cords of wood. Native people eagerly bartered their labor in the woods, but they resented the fact that whites rarely paid them for the timber.[17]

Native resentment of the settlers' arrogance and envy of their wealth led to unsettling incidents. The same summer that Father Demers preached at Elliott Bay, Indians drove a man named Loomis off his claim near the mouth of the Duwamish and seized his cabin. Tom Pepper, a mixed-blood Duwamish man, and several accomplices robbed another house. But most native people condemned such acts, and when Luther Collins and others pursued the plunderers of Samuel Maple's cabin, native men helped recover the stolen property.[18]

Headmen counseled forbearance and underscored the benefits that came from the influx of rich and powerful newcomers. If baptism did not prevent smallpox, inoculations given at Forts Nisqually and Steilacoom did. In addition, headmen believed that the newcomers' wealth would enhance the natives' way of life, and knowledgeable headmen knew that the vaunted numbers of Americans were real. In 1851, Port Townsend settlers sent Tsitz-a-mah-han, a S'Klallam leader, whose name they rendered as Chetzemoka but called Duke of York, on the *Franklin Adams* to San Francisco for a guided tour, and in 1852 Patkanim followed. Both were stunned by the roaring hive of twenty thousand, and they brooded on its implications. Coming back, Patkanim said that his heart had changed toward the Americans; they were too many to resist. Seattle reached the same conclusion on his own. The Americans were like the long rivers of migrating birds filling seasonal skies with noise. He sought to marry his people's future to theirs because doing otherwise invited disaster. Prosperity would come to both, he believed, if they worked the land together as a garden. What he and others did not yet understand was that prosperity itself would be the serpent in the garden.[19]

In October 1852, Henry Yesler arrived. Born in Maryland, he had worked as a carpenter in Ohio and New York, and his travels let him see how commerce flourished with industrial expansion. He was looking for a place to erect a steam sawmill to cash in on San Francisco's appetite for lumber, and eager to keep him, Denny, Boren, and Bell offered to move their claim boundaries, as they had for Maynard, to give Yesler what he wanted: access to the harbor and a narrow strip down which logs could be skidded from the timbered hills. As Seattle had done with Maynard, Curley offered the potential new settler a daughter—Susan—although Yesler, like Maynard, had a wife back east. Yesler was also given access to the labor pool at Dzidzəla'ləch. Following Maynard's lead, he stayed and welcomed Susan into the cabin erected for him near the beach.[20]

The mill would become the town's ticket to success. But the intimate scale of its beginnings—the conversations leading to settlement, the understanding and trust necessitated by cooperation—were quickly overshadowed by the enormity of industrial development and the wealth it generated. The same month the town got the mill, Maynard advertised for a blacksmith "at the town of Seattle" in the *Columbian*, Olympia's first newspaper. But if settlers' hopes soared, Seattle's diminished. His stake in the salmon trade vanished when most of the nine hundred barrels of salmon he and Maynard had sent to San Francisco had, like Fay's, rotted on the voyage. Oh, for a competent cooper! Maynard's loss was cushioned by income from his store and real estate, but Seattle was out. And his dream of marrying his people's future to the Americans withered further when Maynard turned out his granddaughter Betsy.

Although Seattle's offer of Betsy may have influenced Maynard's decision to leave Olympia for Elliott Bay, his affection for Catherine Broshears back in Olympia did not wane. Opportunity to gain a divorce from his first wife came with Maynard's involvement in politics. As Indians returned to their winter villages and renewed communal ties in ceremonial dances, settlers north of the Columbia, feeling neglected, joined in a dance of their own, seeking the creation of a new territory called Columbia, north of the great river. The idea was well received south of it as well, where many hoped it would speed Oregon's progress toward statehood, and Maynard's involvement in the effort made him popular. At a December 1852 convention in a place called Monticello (now Longview, Washington), he helped draft a memorial to Congress seeking establishment of the new territory.

Continuing south to Salem, he submitted an application for divorce to the Oregon territorial legislature, where he had many friends. Legislators had earlier appointed him justice of the peace, and upon granting his divorce on December 21, they appointed him notary public, made the gaggle of longhouses and cabins called Seattle the seat of newly organized King County, and named his store, the Seattle Exchange, its voting station. After returning north on January 15, 1853, the now-respectable suitor and Catherine were married at Bush Prairie by the Reverend Benjamin Close.[21]

Having arranged for Joe Foster, the brother of a prominent Black River pioneer, to marry Betsy, Maynard, in his role as JP, married them, and the couple moved to Foster's claim near Skoa'lko, where Terry and Low had spent the night. If Betsy grieved over her dismissal, we have no record of it. But, recalling Angeline's first husband's fate, one wonders whether Maynard put forward Seattle's name for the town to placate him over his granddaughter's treatment. In any case, Seattle maintained the equanimity expected of a *sia'b* and did not embarrass Maynard, a person of growing consequence in the community. The doctor had the skills needed to make the community grow, and unlike Fay, he intended to stay. Perhaps for similar reasons, Curley is not known to have objected when Yesler later turned out Susan and their four-year-old daughter, Julia, when his wife, Sarah, arrived from Ohio. Following Maynard's lead again, Yesler arranged with Jeremiah Benson, a logger and cook hailing from Michigan, to marry Susan and take custody of their daughter.[22]

Although these attempts by Seattle at matchmaking had not panned out, settler memory suggests that he enjoyed engineering marriages. In 1853, Charles Terry, a non-Catholic, married Mary J. Russell, over the objections of her Catholic parents. Their descendants claim that Seattle loaned Terry a canoe to elope with his intended. Another account describes the couple leaving Alki Point in two canoes manned by braves en route to Port Madison, where Edward Lander, later chief justice of the territorial supreme court, performed the ceremony, with Seattle attending as a "distinguished guest."[23]

Stormy winter weather reminded settlers how much they still depended on native generosity. When local pastures proved insufficient, Salmon Bay Curley told settlers they would find grass near his place. William Bell and the Denny brothers slogged through a rain-soaked forest and found excellent pasture near Salmon Bay, eliminating the need to slaughter stock. When settlers ran out of potatoes, the Duwamish took John Low and Arthur Denny in canoes to purchase fifty bushels from Black River villagers, enough to keep them going until a trading vessel arrived. The land nourished all, and many Indians called white children born here *tilikums*, Jargon for "friendly relations." "You were born in our country," they said, "and you are our people. You eat the same food, will grow up here and belong to us." But the Americans nurtured other plans.[24]

On March 2, 1853, Congress established Washington Territory, and President Franklin Pierce appointed Isaac Ingalls Stevens, a fellow officer in the Mexican War, as territorial governor and superintendent of Indian affairs, with the power to conduct treaty councils within its bounds.

Crafting territories had gone on for three generations, and settlers raised the edifice of self-government as handily as they would a barn. They organized a council and an assembly modeled after Congress. White male residents over twenty-one who were citizens or declared their intention to become so could vote and hold office, excepting military personnel who were not permanent residents. Judicial power rested in a supreme court, district and probate courts, and justices of the peace. To prepare for legislative elections, a census carried out that summer counted 3,965 settlers in the territory, which reached from the Pacific Ocean to the Continental Divide and from the Columbia River and N 46° to N 49°. Surely, they believed, the future belonged to them.

Of 170 whites in King County (most in Seattle), 111 were men eligible to vote. Stevens hired George Gibbs, an educated New Yorker and Oregon pioneer, to carry out a native census, and in King County, which then spanned the Sound, he counted 485 Suquamish and 351 Duwamish. Broader counts yielded 7,559 native people west of the Cascades, and he doubled that for the territory. A later count yielded a somewhat larger number of native people, four times the Americans' number, but because they were not citizens they were not counted as part of the emerging civil and political community. Despite Seattle's hope and Father Demers's prayer, a political basis for decrees separating white people from native people was set in place, and white racism supplied mortar for the rising wall.[25]

Influential headmen like Seattle encouraged cooperation, but in the early 1850s Seattle was nearing his seventies, and one by one, the older headmen who had pioneered relationships with the Hudson's Bay Company and early settlers passed away. On December 16, 1852, Sneetlum died. His grieving Skagit people called upon the S'Klallam to join in mourning, and they erected a wooden statue of him on Whidbey Island's east shore. "They all seem to take it very hard," Rebecca Ebey, Isaac's wife, wrote in her journal after inviting several headmen out of the snowy cold to warm themselves at her fireside. Absent these older leaders' caution, others not as enamored of the newcomers felt less restraint showing displeasure.[26]

After Louisa Boren and David Denny married and moved to their cabin on a claim north of William Bell's in January 1853, Louisa enjoyed a social call from Bell's wife, Sarah, while David was away. Later, Patkanim's brother, John Kanim, told David that two native men the women had noticed watching them over the half door were dissuaded from murdering Louisa and looting the cabin only after seeing another woman with her, thinking that their men might be close. On Whidbey Island, native boys threatened Rebecca Ebey with a rifle while her husband was away, expressing a growing discontent.

The perennial questions regarding Americans' intentions dogged native communities: Why were they coming in such great numbers? What did they want? Did they intend to steal the land and exile the people or worse? That winter ships brought smallpox to the Columbia, and it spread, via the Chehalis River, to Puget Sound. Inoculations at Forts Nisqually and Steilacoom moderated its effects, but in March an American ship carried the disease to Neah Bay, where it wiped out nearly half the Makah and spread to the northern Sound and as far east as Sauk Prairie, near the headwaters of the Stillaguamish.[27]

Convinced that settler Samuel Hancock had loosed the disease, the Makah threatened to kill him, and he fled to Whidbey, where grief over Sneetlum's death and fear of disease rekindled old paranoia. When a S'Klallam headman died shortly after Snaetlum, those who had mourned together began accusing one another of sorcery. Weeks later, Tsitz-a-mah-han's older brother, S-hai-ak, a S'Klallam headman settlers called "King George," killed a Skagit man suspected of casting spells. The Skagits in turn killed four S'Klallam, prompting the latter to plan a raid. Property was sold to purchase powder and shot. The *Columbian* flippantly likened the dispute to a "War of Extermination."[28]

Indians killing Indians was not thought unusual, and American opinion about native people was often as divided as native opinions about Americans. The *Columbian*'s young editor from Illinois, Thornton M. McElroy, reassured readers that "our Indians are perfectly docile and of great service to the community as boatmen on the Sound, and laborers on land." But he also looked forward to a future when Americans would no longer need to maintain good relationships with the native people, who still outnumbered them. He anticipated a day when they would be removed to "some obscure locality," where they would "ultimately succeed in dragging out to the bitter end their wretched existence." As

Governor Lane had shown, their removal and disappearance could be done legally by executive action, legislative statute, and in courts of law backed by the military.[29]

On the frontier, racial peace had always been strained. Early in 1854, a drunken American liquor peddler named Spencer who killed an Indian with an ax near New Dungeness (now Port Angeles) was arrested and sent to Port Townsend to face charges. The victim's kin showed up to see justice done, but they were bought off with twenty blankets and a promise that Spencer would be sent to Fort Steilacoom to await trial. His arraignment made news, and settlers passing through paused to watch the rare spectacle of one of their own being charged for the murder of an Indian. Meanwhile, on the northern Sound, warrants were issued for the arrest of Indians accused of killing Americans, and soldiers were sent to apprehend them.[30]

As sawmills mushroomed along Puget Sound to feed the California market, both races shared in the boom. Many Indians departing villages that spring showed up at Yesler's mill to earn cash from dropping the ancient trees shading the shore and bringing logs to the saws. That summer alone, twenty ships arrived in Elliott Bay to load lumber and debark immigrants, who no longer had to squint to see houses above the beach.

Some new settlers continued up the Duwamish to the country Seattle had shown Isaac Ebey. John Thomas and Ephraim McFarland found land they liked at a White River village midway between Flea's House and Yəla'kwo. Unnerved by so many Indians, McFarland left, but Thomas built a cabin and, helped by the White River headman Nelson, moved onto his claim a few months later with his young wife, Nancy. Near the head of Black River, another Vermont doctor, R. M. Bigelow, found a coal seam angling up a sandstone bluff. A sample tested well in a Seattle forge, and in October 1853, he and several neighbors formed the Duwamish Coal Company. This was a major discovery, and Seattle citizens hoped for commercial success. Yesler's mill offered steady work, but the discovery of coal fourteen miles upriver promised an industrial bonanza. The prospect also excited the Duwamish, because, after all, the mine was on their land.

Indeed, the settlers did not yet own the land, even as the government encouraged them to claim it. By passing the Indian Appropriations

Act of 1851, Congress authorized funds to move Western tribes onto reservations, but as yet no treaties had been negotiated north of the Columbia. The issue over land claims was described to Governor Stevens by Edmund Starling, an educated New York immigrant hired by Oregon commissioners in 1851 to gather information about Indian bands scattered throughout the western Oregon Territory. With the creation of Washington Territory, Starling compiled a report describing the groups in Stevens's jurisdiction as a courtesy. Regarding land claims, he wrote, "As the white population increases—which it has done quite rapidly in the last year—and they encroach upon the Indians, they become more restless and troublesome."[31]

Many single settlers happily made homes with native women, but back east, old racial fears that English settlers brought to the New World evolved into harsher views of nonwhites as the issue of slavery threatened disunion, particularly among the urban middle class. On Puget Sound, we can read it in the letters of Methodist Episcopal minister David Blaine, Seattle's first resident pastor, and his wife, Catharine, a signatory of the 1848 Seneca Falls petition calling for women's suffrage. This intelligent, literate couple arrived from New York State via Panama in late November 1853, and their letters back home provide a mine of information about early settlement. But these same letters distress modern sensibilities with their derisive depictions of native people as "coarse, filthy and debased." "You talk about the stupidity of the Irish," wrote Catharine after dismissing a native servant. "You ought to have to work with one of our Indians and then you would know what these words mean." Such opinion was not universal among the Blaines' peers, but it was common enough to color the view of an emerging professional elite.[32]

Even American idealism could cause problems. Seattle complained to Territorial Secretary Charles Mason that Dr. Bigelow had hired a slave but refused to return him to the Suquamish, who owned him. Mason, serving as acting governor when Stevens was away, instructed Bigelow to assist Seattle by returning the slave. "The policy has been adopted by the Indian Dept. in this territory," he explained, "not to interfere in any of the customs and manners of the Indians peculiar to themselves." But official tolerance of native custom did not extend to use of the land.[33]

Around this time, the S'Klallam headman S-hai-ak, King George, began shopping at a store in Port Townsend, where he pointedly refused to pay for the items he chose. When the owner complained, he told him to subtract their cost from the value of the land the settlers had already taken from him. Settler laments showed up in the *Columbian*: "Our whole territory is alive with Indians, who keep up a most provoking and unceasing broil about the lands which they say the 'Bostons' are holding without a proper and legitimate right and title to the same."[34]

The issue might have been resolved over time through negotiation and compromise, but the rapid influx of Americans shortened the time available, and violence unrestrained by political or legal institutions eroded forbearance. News of Indians fighting settlers in Oregon's Rogue River valley added to tensions, and in the White River valley, with its own troubled history, violence undercut Seattle's hopes for peaceful prosperity. In the summer of 1853, a local Indian nicknamed Messachie Jim, "Bad Jim," beat his wife to death after accusing her of adultery and threatened the white neighbors whom he accused of enjoying her favors. They lynched him. His nickname limned an evil reputation, but angry relatives still exacted retribution, and local whites began disappearing as settlers were down Sound.

Later that summer, an Olympia resident, James McCormick, went missing during a visit to Seattle, and opinions over what to do were divided. Of those involved in Messachie Jim's lynching, Luther Collins, now a popular King County commissioner, was an ardent proponent of vigilante justice, but Yesler and others condemned such action as needless interference. Some settlers were ready to accept a retaliatory murder or two, as they had after the hangings at Fort Steilacoom. No one wanted to poke a hornet's nest on the eve of Governor Stevens's arrival, but the toll kept rising.

Many settlers approved of firm action but blamed the violence on a growing liquor trade. "It is high time that not only the Indians be made to behave themselves," the *Columbian* declared, "but that certain nefarious practices, which in nine cases out of ten are the sole causes of these troubles, should be stopped." If drunken whites scandalized settlers, drunken Indians terrified them. "Could the Indians and alcohol be removed," wrote David Blaine wistfully, "this would be in most respects one of the most delightful regions of the country."[35]

All eyes were on the new governor when he arrived in November. As territorial superintendent of Indian affairs, he quickly appointed settlers to act as Indian agents, selecting Michael Simmons for the Puget Sound region and directing him to visit groups and request that headmen assemble their people for announcements of upcoming treaty councils. To win the support of Seattle, identified by Starling as "one of the most sensible and influential chiefs on the Sound," Simmons worked with Maynard, the old man's friend.

Recognizing his intelligence, sense of justice, oratorical power, and his good relations with the Americans, the Suquamish, "in search of a wise leader," selected Seattle as their head chief "at the time of the treaty." No longer the aggressive war leader, "he was very well-liked," as later native informants recalled, "as he followed the dictates of the majority." Cognizant of his authority among the Duwamish, territorial and federal officials recognized him as chief of both the Duwamish and the Suquamish, but within the native community this recognition had its critics. In Starling's observation that Seattle's slave ancestry could be troublesome, we may hear native voices already asking how he had become so high and mighty.[36]

In addition to Stevens's work as governor and superintendent of Indian Affairs, he was also head of the northern railroad survey, one of five surveys organized by the US government to locate coast-to-coast routes, and had spent the previous four months surveying a path following the route of Lewis and Clark. As a Democrat, Stevens was also the party standard-bearer and expected to drum up support for its candidates. Essential to this goal was making the *Columbian*, nominally a Whig Party paper, into the Democratic Party mouthpiece, which its new editor, J. W. Wiley, accomplished, renaming it the *Washington Pioneer*, then the *Pioneer and Democrat*.

To accommodate these galloping agendas, Stevens combined meetings with multiple native groups that Simmons organized, with a flying tour of the Sound, during which he sought to greet his new constituents, view prospective railroad terminus sites, and campaign for the election of Columbia Lancaster as the Democratic candidate for territorial delegate to Congress. The *Washington Pioneer* noted that

Stevens left snowy Olympia on January 9, 1854, on the sloop *Sarah Stone*. Stopping at the town of Steilacoom, he reached the town of Seattle late on January 10 and dined with its citizens as Lancaster spoke. At dawn, settlers and Indians ferried the governor up the Duwamish to see Bigelow's coal mine, where lumber cut at a nearby mill shored up a shaft dug seventy-five feet into the seam. To power the mill's undershot wheel, a log dam built across the lake outlet raised the lake level and served as an effective fishing weir. Such works delighted the Duwamish, especially the mill, where, Gibbs noted, they "took every visitor through the building to explain its working, and boast of it as if it had been of their own construction."[37]

Back in Seattle, Stevens thrilled citizens with an hour-long address, during which he described the railroad's future route over the Cascades to Puget Sound. In five years, as Henry Smith recalled, he told them, "the echoes of Snoqualmie Pass would be startled by the neigh of the iron horse, whose pantings would be the signal for Seattle to leap forward upon a career of prosperity that would eventually place her among the foremost cities of the world." Over the past two years, a hardscrabble place where settlers hustled dollars pickling salmon, cutting piles, and selling damaged goods out of a store had acquired Puget Sound's first steam sawmill and become the supply base for a mining district. Now the new governor promised the arrival of a transcontinental railroad and a future as a geometropolis. The vision of Seattle as a world-class city crystallized on that cold January evening.[38]

Having described a golden future for the settlers, the next morning, Thursday, January 12, Stevens outlined a very different one for the Indians. Dressed in finery and wrapped in blankets, many gathered around beach fires in front of David Maynard's store, where the governor waited with his retinue. Henry Smith's later written recollection of Indians arriving as a "swaying, writhing, dusky mass of humanity" suggests that a large group of Seattle's people arrived as they would have at the beginning of a *sgwi'gwi*—in canoes approaching the shore in a line, with headmen singing and dancing in the bows. A full moon hanging openmouthed over the Olympics marked a time of danger.

Both Maynard and Seattle had dressed for the occasion: Maynard in a dark suit, a white shirt, and a broad-brimmed straw hat; Seattle in trousers

and a shirt, a frock coat, and a billed military cap. In contrast to these imposing men, Stevens, at barely five feet, strove for a populist image, with woolen
pants stuffed into scuffed boots, a military greatcoat over a red flannel shirt,
and a top hat worn in a vain attempt to create the illusion of height.[39]

It had been Seattle's job to marshal his people to this gathering in
the town named after him, and he had assembled a group many times the
number of Americans present. Seattle's renown and authority had led
him, the heir of Kitsap and Challacum, to this extraordinary moment. If
his people looked to their patriarch to further their hopes, the Americans
saw him as someone who could keep the peace.

Because this meeting was important, Seattle had his Catholic headmen lead their people in prayers and hymns, calling upon the Christian
God as witness. Then he motioned for them all to sit and listen. In the
Jargon, Maynard introduced Stevens as the "Boston hyas tyee," the great
chief of the Bostons, and son of the "hyas tkope tyee kopa Washington,"
the Great White Chief of Washington, a fiction he hoped would appeal
to native regard for family.

Stevens spoke briefly, in short sentences easily translated into
the Jargon, as a father would to children. The Great White Chief of
Washington had sent him in friendship. He would take care of them. If
they had any problems, they should come to him or to those he appointed
to watch over them. At a time to be announced, he would come again to
sign a treaty and seal their brotherhood forever. The Great White Chief
and the other white chiefs in Washington would buy their lands but leave
them enough to live on comfortably. If the Indians agreed to this and
lived in peace with their white neighbors, the Great White Chief would
protect them against their enemies, as he would his white children.

Finished, Stevens sat in a chair. Then Seattle rose to speak and
deftly countered the governor's patronizing tone by placing his powerful
hand on Stevens's surprised head, as a father would a child, speaking
as a *sia'b*, not a supplicant. He greeted Stevens and thanked him for
his visit. A native interpreter, possibly Walak, translated his words into
the Jargon, and a settler, probably Benjamin Shaw, into English. Henry
Smith penciled phrases of the latter into his diary. What Seattle said and
what Smith wrote, a source of debate to our day, would in time become
a national urtext of a change of worlds.

That evening, Stevens left for Whidbey Island. If his promise of a railroad had fired settlers' imaginations, their hopes for a resolution of Indian problems failed to materialize. Indeed, the situation grew worse. In early March, William Young, manager of a sawmill at New York Alki, left to explore Whidbey Island with three Snohomish. When they returned sans Young, one wounded and another wearing Young's watch and clothing, suspicions mounted. While Sheriff Thomas Russell gathered a posse including Dr. Wesley Cherry, the suspects fled back to Whidbey. The posse followed, but late that afternoon Russell and his men returned to Seattle, all wounded, with Dr. Cherry dying that evening.

A shudder passed through the town. "Should their mutual fear of and hatred for the 'Bostons' impel them to unite against us," wrote David Blaine, "the terrible scenes enacted in the Atlantic states, the accounts of which used to chill my blood with horror may be reenacted here." On March 11, Stevens returned with Simmons, Gibbs, and soldiers from Fort Steilacoom commanded by Lieutenant William Slaughter. With Luther Collins interpreting, Stevens called on Indians—including Seattle; his son George, being groomed as a Suquamish leader; his other son, Jim; the Duwamish headman, William; and Patkanim with his Snoqualmie retinue—to hear a lecture. He promised not to punish the innocent but said he would consider guilty all who assisted or concealed the murderers. If whites harmed Indians, he said, they were not to avenge themselves but to come to him for justice. "They were to understand that the whites would all combine to punish all the Indians who were guilty of these crimes. The whites were as many as the trees, and could kill the whole."[40]

Stevens held Patkanim and Seattle responsible for the behavior of their people and had them name others to assist them. Patkanim and Seattle thereupon selected subchiefs that met with Simmons's approval. Seattle's list included twenty-two figures, among them George Seattle, given authority over the Suquamish, and others representing the Duwamish on their river, plus three bands connected with them: the Lake people and those on the White and Green Rivers. Stevens directed Simmons to visit other groups and organize them similarly under chiefs and subchiefs, "taking care that in every case they be persons who, in your opinion, will control them to the best advantage." At a stroke, native people lost an independence they had enjoyed since time immemorial. If they questioned Seattle's role in this, they might have also wondered if he was representing them to the Americans or the Americans to them.[41]

Seattle then spoke up and gave Stevens his understanding of events. Through his contacts, he knew what happened in great detail, a fact that bears remembering in light of subsequent events. Again, liquor was to blame. William Young and his Snohomish guides had gotten drunk, quarreled, and fought. He killed one with a sword and wounded another, whereupon the murdered man's son killed Young. The son went back to Alki with the others, but all fled at the approach of the posse. When Russell and his deputies seized the son at a Snohomish village on Holmes Harbor, on Whidbey's eastern shore, his friends attacked, freeing him after much loss of life. Seattle knew their names but told Stevens they were hiding and would not be found. He finished with what Gibbs described as "a great speech declaring his good disposition toward the whites."[42]

Stevens judged that wrong had been committed on both sides, but reaching Holmes Harbor and finding most village men gone, he repeated his threats against those assisting the murderers to the remaining women. To make his point, he had soldiers destroy the village's canoes and burn its stockade. One at Skagit Head and another on the Snohomish were torched. With their buildings aflame, Stevens called the island's Skagit people together, but headman George Sneetlum, old Sneetlum's son, absented himself out of fear, whereupon Stevens demanded another be selected who would appoint subchiefs whom the Skagit people must obey. The *sia'b* Goliah was thrust forward.

Concluding that "a most salutary impression was made on that and their neighboring tribes," Stevens left the territory on March 26 for Washington, DC, to secure funding for his ambitious goals. Near the same time, soldiers hunting other Indians suspected of murdering other whites on the lower Sound attacked a S'Klallam village at Port Angeles, killing two men and capturing three, whom they humiliated by flogging and by shaving their heads.[43]

In April, David Denny learned from Salmon Bay Curley that James McCormick had been murdered near Lake Union. Suspects were rounded up, and on April 20 a justice court held in Henry Yesler's cookhouse heard testimony from a native witness that led to murder charges being filed against two native men, who were then locked in a cabin to await further judgment. There was not enough evidence to file a complaint against old Petawow, Seattle's interpreter, but a native youth under suspicion was locked in the house of Carson Boren, recently named sheriff, until evidence could be gathered. Courts administered by justices of the peace heard civil complaints in which amounts less than one hundred dollars were involved and referred cases in excess of that amount and criminal cases to a grand jury and a district court.

Urged on by Collins, several settlers broke into the cabin holding the two men who had been charged with murder in the justice court, dragged them to a tall stump south of the mill, and hanged them. Next, they broke into Boren's house and dragged the youth out to hang him, but Boren ran to the site and ordered the mob to drop the rope. "O string him up," came a shout. "He's nothing but a Siwash." But Boren saved the youth, who was sent to Fort Steilacoom for trial and acquitted. Despite these events, the *Pioneer and Democrat* claimed that Snohomish Indians had actually hanged the men, adding, "Everything in that direction between the whites and Indians is quiet, and nothing of a serious character is apprehended from the procedure."[44]

The paper's assertion of calm suggests that editor Wiley did not want news of rampant lynch mobs discouraging immigration or investment. As Starling pointed out, Indian violence often resulted from miscarriages of justice, and since only voting white males over twenty-one could serve on juries and Indians were rarely allowed to testify, objectivity in cases involving interracial disputes was well-nigh impossible. This time, not surprisingly, the vigilantes escaped trial.

In October 1854, the first district courts in Washington Territory were convened. Judges ascended to the bench, often a rough table at a mill or clapboard hotel. Grand juries impaneled to examine evidence selected cases for trial. In criminal cases, the plaintiff—the territory whose laws had been broken—was represented by a prosecuting attorney. The accused were represented by paid counsel or counsel appointed by the court. Ideally, with courts blind to differences between rich and poor, native and white, raids, blood feuds, and wergild would hopefully be supplanted by law, and vigilante outbursts would be made unnecessary.

In the northern Sound district courts, grand juries brought indictments of murder against five Indians. Three were convicted and sentenced to hang, and two had charges against them dropped. Although no evidence indicates that Spencer, the liquor peddler who killed an Indian with an ax, was brought to trial, a rough justice prevailed, but in Seattle the trial of Luther Collins, William Heebner, and David Maurer for the lynching of Messachie Jim devolved into farce.[45]

King County District Court, Judge Edward Lander presiding, convened on October 23 in the Felker House, the town's first frame hotel and a reputed brothel. A grand jury of twenty men brought indictments for murder against the three settlers. Attorneys Frank Clark and Elwood Evans represented the territory and the federal government, the latter anxious that justice be done in the eyes of those with whom it was about to negotiate treaties. But the seriousness of the charge, punishable by hanging, put white jurors in a quandary. Collins had been elected county commissioner, Heebner had been nominated county representative, and Maurer ran a local eatery. All were generally liked and respected, and unquestionably guilty, but how could a jury of their friends and neighbors vote to hang them? A fund was set up to help the accused, "all good Democrats," a later historian wrote, to hire the best lawyers, and the trial began.[46]

William Bell would recall that when Maurer, a German immigrant, was asked to enter a plea and replied, "Guilty; I did hang him," Judge Lander interrupted. "Mr. Maurer," he said, "all I have got to do is to pass sentence on you, and you will be hung; but I will give you another chance for your life," and Maurer changed his plea to not guilty. Decades later, historian Frederick Grant wrote that Maurer said he did not understand the charges read to him, and when the judge asked plainly if he did or did not help hang Messachie Jim, Maurer's heavily accented response, "I suppose I ish guilty Shudge," brought gales of laughter to the courtroom, whereupon, in another's recollection, jury foreman Charles Terry leaned forward and whispered loudly, "Not guilty, you fool! Say not guilty."

The jurors, some of whom also served as witnesses for the defense, solved their dilemma by acquitting Heebner and Maurer, successfully arguing in Maurer's case that the state had not proven that the name on the indictment was actually the name of the victim. At that point, Clark and Evans threw up their hands and dropped the charges against Collins. Ten days after the trial began, the jubilant defendants left the court free men, their attorneys richer. Settlers congratulated themselves on eluding the law, but the native community was left to contemplate a harsh truth: American courts offered native people little beyond severe punishment and let whites get away with murder.

A month later, Seattle's granddaughter Betsy committed suicide. On their isolated claim, it was said that husband Joe Foster had abused her but that after she bore a son he had seemed more attentive and they moved into town that fall. When a second baby died, however, Betsy became depressed and hanged herself in their cabin.

Catharine Blaine wrote to a young cousin that while Betsy's native kin wanted her buried in the traditional way, Foster wanted a Christian burial, but because they were not legally married, Pastor Blaine refused. Grieving native mourners carried her coffin to a nearby burial ground, accompanied by settlers married to native women—"Squaw Men," as Catharine Blaine called them. If Angeline and Seattle attended, she did not say. In her mind, they would have been just two more Indians, but, more importantly to her, the couple's fate underscored the evils of miscegenation. "These squaws," she wrote, "are lower and more degraded than you can imagine, but little better than hogs in human shape, and when men so debase themselves as to live with them they lose all self respect, shun the society of virtuous people, in fact, all white society except it be that of those equally debased."[47]

Some settlers claimed sympathy for Betsy, but native people were constantly reminded that many settlers despised them, and that the Americans they had invited in to share the future had no intention of doing so. There is no mention of Seattle's reaction to the tragedy; the man who murdered a shaman after the death of another grandchild may have hidden his feelings as he grappled with mounting troubles. Nor was Angeline's anguish noted, but her later reputation for anger likely evidenced a deep well of grief and rage.

In December, the three Indians convicted of murder on the northern Sound escaped from Steilacoom with one other. Of these four, one died on the run, and one surrendered, but two headed for Hood Canal.

Soldiers sent on the revenue cutter *Jefferson Davis* to recapture them attacked a S'Klallam fishing camp at the mouth of the Hamma Hamma River. The S'Klallam fled, but six tons of curing salmon they left behind was destroyed, and the cutter lobbed shells into the forest where the people hid, reportedly killing five. The two escapees were eventually captured, and hanged at Port Townsend shortly after Christmas. The Americans had sent soldiers, sailors, and ships to destroy villages, camps, and supplies, killing and wounding a score of native people in the effort to hang three men.[48]

As the territory waged war on its native communities, Governor Stevens returned with his family from an administrative trip to Washington, DC, via Panama and threw himself into preparations for the treaty councils. Amid mounting danger and with his family in mourning, Seattle faced the greatest crisis of his life.

# CHAPTER SIX

*"The Great Chief above who made the country made it for all."*

Prior to the Kansas-Nebraska Act of 1854, the Kansa people lived south of the Ni Braska (the Platte River) in Indian territory west of the Mississippi, organized by Congress as a vast catchment for eastern tribes driven from their homelands. Whatever hopes the exiles had had for respite were dashed in the mid-1850s, when invading pro- and antislavery Americans fought for dominance, prompting Horace Greeley, editor of the *New York Tribune*, to label the region "Bleeding Kansas." As catastrophe engulfed native communities, remnants of the population fled south to Okla Humma, land of the "red people." The bloodshed foreshadowed the American Civil War, and the racial script written in violence defined white-native relations throughout the West. On Puget Sound, the looming chaos shocked those who had hoped for better.

In early December 1854, Governor Isaac Stevens organized a commission to hold treaties with groups living on Puget Sound and the Pacific coast. He reminded his commissioners that Congress expected Indians to be placed on few reservations far from white settlements. But Indian agent Michael Simmons and George Gibbs, named secretary of the treaty commission—both of whom better understood the complexities of native society—argued that more reservations would be necessary, even if only temporarily. A compromise proposed that after the first treaty council at the Nisqually River, the Duwamish, the Suquamish, and the S'Klallam on the Strait of Juan de Fuca would have a reservation set aside for them on the east side of Hood Canal.[1]

On Christmas Eve 1854, Stevens and his entourage met with upper Sound groups at Medicine Creek, a haunt of supernatural powers associated with death in the Nisqually estuary. In two days, negotiating in the crude Jargon, Stevens got these groups to trade their homelands for promises of aid and three small reserves totaling six square miles. Several native leaders, including Leschi, argued in preliminary meetings that the reserves were too small and poor, but at the end, the headmen dutifully signed. In time, the creek's dark reputation colored the memory of what had been agreed to there.[2]

Stevens was pleased. The government acquired two and a half million acres of land for $150,000, a penny less per acre than what President Thomas Jefferson had paid for the Louisiana Purchase. If native compliance at Medicine Creek masked the Indians' trauma, the speed and apparent ease of negotiations heartened settlers. "Next week," enthused David Blaine, "Governor Stevens is to hold a council here to treat with our Indians. When this is done and their lands are purchased it is supposed they will be removed from our midst. What a blessing it will be both to them and the whites, if this can be effected."[3]

As a cold sun rose on 1855, Gibbs surveyed reservation land on Commencement Bay and raffled off presents to council latecomers. On January 3, snow fell, and he boarded a schooner for Seattle, where, on January 5, Maynard and others warned him that "Seattle and the Dwamish Indians had concluded in consequence of advice from cultus [worthless] whites & other Indians not to attend the treaty." Apparently, word of the proposed relegation of the Duwamish to a reservation on Hood Canal's east shore had gotten out. That conditions there were not conducive to village development gives some insight into why the Duwamish had misgivings.[4]

On January 9, Major Hugh Goldsborough off-loaded tents and supplies from the schooner *R. B. Potter* at the council site on Point Elliott, a broad beach near the Snohomish River mouth, named by Wilkes after a junior officer. The point's native name, Bəka'ltiu, "Lots of People Gathered," now Mukilteo, marked where Dukwiba'l, the Changer, began his myth-time journey upriver to transform the world. Goldsborough returned to Seattle to purchase potatoes and other supplies, accompanied by Simmons, who met with Seattle and the balky Duwamish.[5]

Meanwhile, native groups started streaming into Point Elliott. As the Snoqualmie began arriving, Gibbs and their headman Xotik!edəb selected a reservation on nearby land with a good harbor, where settlers had already built a small water-powered sawmill.

On Friday, January 12, Goliah and the Skagit arrived, roaring welcoming songs as their canoes advanced in an impressive line. Ashore, they marched single file past the Snoqualmie, each man doffing his hat and making the sign of the cross. Afterward, they sang hymns and heard preaching "in an exceedingly pious frame of mind," Gibbs observed, adding that they appeared to be "brushing up their religion for a grand display on the Governor's arrival." By January 17, the Lummi were in, led by their chief, Chowitsuit, minus the Nooksack people, who could not descend their frozen river."[6]

That same day, the Duwamish began showing up. Not a word of Simmons's meeting with them was breathed in any official record, but more than half a century later Suquamish informant Wilson George told anthropologist John Peabody Harrington that William, one of the Duwamish subchiefs Seattle had selected in March, "wanted a separate treaty so that they wouldn't have to move away from the Duwamish River." This jibes with Gibbs's observation that "the Duwamish had been influenced to remain at home and insist upon treating upon their own ground." George told Harrington that William was promised two buckets of gold for land from Alki Point to Salmon Bay, including Lake Washington. When William insisted that he wanted land on the Duwamish's west bank to Alki Point, he was told it was too much and would require future negotiations.[7]

Governor Stevens had his agents negotiate with native leaders before he got involved. Likewise, Seattle delegated work to subchiefs who dealt with their counterparts before he intervened. Much of the process was contingent, but despite the promised gold, only three of the twenty-two Duwamish subchiefs Seattle had selected signed the treaty with him, and William was not among them.[8]

The Point Elliott Treaty located reservations on Bellingham Bay, the Skagit River mouth, and the mouth of the Snohomish. By the time the council met, Port Madison on the Kitsap Peninsula had replaced Hood Canal as the location for the Duwamish and Suquamish reserve, but no land was reserved on the Duwamish. The likely reason was that Black River coal was selling for thirty dollars a ton in San Francisco, and later that year three hundred tons would be barged downriver by *Water Lily*, the first American steamer on the Sound. Coal and lumber joined the settlement of Seattle to the booming California market, and residents made sure that if the town was to grow as Stevens promised, land along the Duwamish would remain open for development.

When Stevens arrived on the steamer *Major Tompkins* on the nineteenth, twenty-three hundred Indians had gathered at Point Elliott. On the twenty-second, Seattle, followed by Patkanim, Goliah, and Chowitsuit, formed their peoples into a great semicircle on cleared ground in front of the government tent, and then seated themselves before the subchiefs with the rest of the people massed behind, men separate from women. Six years after the Fort Steilacoom trial, Patkanim's well-advertised "change of heart" and his decision to become Catholic had made him acceptable. But as the oldest of the four leaders, Seattle was the primary native spokesman at the council. At noon, three cheers greeted Governor Stevens and Territorial Secretary Charles Mason as they came ashore and walked among the seated throng.

Commission interpreter Shaw translated Stevens's words into the Jargon, and John Taylor, the Snohomish man of Whidbey Island fame, translated the Jargon into the native tongue. It was a stagy performance, with the audience coached to respond enthusiastically to Stevens's rhetorical questions and cheer at appropriate times. Stevens began by telling them they were like his own children and he would do for them what a man would do for his children. He said that it meant much to him that most were Christians. He had visited the year before, had he not? (He had!) And he did not make any promises then, did he? (He did not!) He had come to learn about their needs, which he shared with the Great Father in Washington. Was he not absent several months on this business? (He was!) He then introduced Charles Mason, the man he had left in his place.

Mason told the crowd that Stevens had come back to tell them what the Americans planned to do for them. (Cheers.) Then Stevens introduced Simmons, who reviewed past events and future plans: The Indians had welcomed the Americans, but some Americans had sold them rum to cheat them and make them poor. Rum was the cause of evil between the races, and they should abstain from its use. If the Great Father approved the treaty, money (the native people thought cash; the Americans, goods) would be sent in payment for their lands. The goods given at the council were gifts. Then he reintroduced Stevens. (Cheers.)

Stevens listed the Great Father's desires: They would have homes and a school where their children would be taught to read, write, farm, and would learn trades. They would be able to continue fishing and hunting, and gathering roots and berries, and they would be happy and prosperous. Was this not what they wanted? (It is!) He wanted a good treaty, as did the Great Father. It would now be read to them, and if they found it good, they would sign. (Shouts.)

Council notes record that after these remarks the Indians sang a Mass and recited a prayer. Since no priest was present, it is likely that this meant they prayed, sang hymns, and recited the Jargon version of the Lord's Prayer. Gibbs assumed this was done to impress the governor, but it may have been done to impress *upon* him the people's sense that dealings this important required the solicitation of divine sanction.

After prayers, as officials labored to add phonetic versions of the headmen's names to the handwritten treaty document, Stevens determined to get the head chiefs to speak for the record, especially Seattle, who he knew had threatened not to attend. "Does anyone object to what I have said?" the governor asked. "Does my venerable friend Seattle object? I want Seattle to give his will to me and to his people."

It would be hard to imagine two more different men—the diminutive graduate of West Point and the tall preliterate chieftain—but they shared important traits. Both were experienced warriors, and both were acutely aware of their own debilities: Stevens, his diminutive size; Seattle, the taint of slave ancestry. Both were driven, but in this contest, Stevens had Seattle at a disadvantage. The absence of all but three Duwamish headmen's names on the treaty reflected old animosities between lower and upriver groups. Seattle had secured a reservation for the Suquamish, but not for the Duwamish, at least not yet. This undercut his authority, but Stevens wanted to bind him and the defiant Duwamish to the treaty's terms. Seattle struggled to find wiggle room in this tight spot, but Stevens gave him none. Through several translations, his tentative response was written into the council minutes.

I look upon you as my father. I and the rest regard you as such. All of the Indians have the same good feeling towards you and will send it on paper to the Great Father. All of them, old men, women and children, rejoice that he has sent you to take care of them. My mind is like yours. I don't want to say more. My heart is very good toward Dr. Maynard. I always want to get medicine from him.

Seattle accepted Stevens's authority and agreed that he and the Great Father should do right by the Indians—in this, his mind was like the governor's. But he introduced a note of reluctance: "I don't want to say more." Knowing how little his words meant without Duwamish support, the chief could not speak for them, and instead mentioned David Maynard, a significant political figure whom the Americans regarded as his friend.

Sensing the shift in tone and anxious to restore the scripted bonhomie, Stevens signaled his intention to respond. Resuming the pose of the caring father, he promised that after the people signed the treaty a doctor would be provided to cure their bodies. "And I trust your souls also," he said. Stevens's last words alluded to what was widely known, that Patkanim, Chowitsuit, and Goliah were receiving religious instruction but Seattle was not. He countered Seattle's friendship with Maynard by reiterating his authority as a patron: "Now my friends, I speak to you as my friends though you are my children."

If Maynard was Seattle's friend, Stevens's favor was greater, because it was given as a gift rather than as a quid pro quo. And to make sure the chief who had patted his head got the point, he reminded Seattle whose hand was on the lever of power. "I want you," he challenged the people, "if Seattle has spoken well, to say so by three cheers." The minutes note that three cheers were given. They record the moves of an old, wary leader trapped in an unfamiliar game with a young and ruthless opponent.

But if Seattle struggled, Patkanim gladly embraced the authority and opportunity presented by Stevens, as evidenced by his words that day.

Today I understood your heart as soon as you spoke. I understand your talk plainly. God made my heart and those of my people good and strong. It is good that we should give you our real feelings today. We want everything as you have said, the Doctor and all. Such is the feeling of the Indians. Our hearts are with the whites. God makes them good towards the Americans.

After Patkanim received his three cheers, the governor called on Chowitsuit, who echoed Seattle's reticence, wanting Stevens to know that he was giving up good ground for the sake of the treaty and that he and Seattle were of similar minds.

> I do not want to say much; my heart is good. God has made it good toward you. I work on the ground and build houses. I have some houses at home. But I will stop building if you wish and will move to Cha-choosen [the site of the Lummi reservation]. Now I have given you my opinion and that of my friends. Their feelings are all good and they will do as you say hereafter. My mind is the same as Seattle's. I love him and send my friends to him if they are sick. I go to Doctor Maynard at Seattle if I am sick.

He wanted Stevens to know that Maynard was his friend, too.

Then it was Goliah's turn. Conscious of how little the authority forced on him at Whidbey Island really meant, he hid behind agreeable phrases.

> My mind is the same as the Governor's. God has made it so. I have no wish to say much. I am happy at heart. I am happy to hear the Governor talk of God. My heart is good and that of all my friends. I give it to the Governor. I shall be glad to have a doctor for the Indians. We are all glad to hear you and be taken care of by you. I do not want to say more.

By then, the treaty was ready, and Shaw translated its fifteen articles into the Jargon, which John Taylor translated for the native audience, his strong voice, Gibbs noted with admiration, lasting "the whole morning without failing."

When Article 6 was read, promising $150,000 paid in installments over twenty years for ceded land, Seattle interrupted to say he did not want his people to have so much money, "that the Great Chief above who made the country made it for all and perhaps he would not be pleased at their taking pay for it." It was the first public objection recorded by any native leader at a treaty council thus far, making it clear that he grasped the Americans' intent. One hundred fifty thousand dollars was a lot, but without land, what could one do with money but spend it, and what then but work for the Americans?

When told that payments would be in kind rather than cash, the minutes note that Seattle appeared satisfied, but he may simply have resigned himself after making his point. Once all the articles were read, the governor asked the headmen if they were satisfied. If they were, he would sign the treaty and they should follow.

How much we wish we knew what they spoke about briefly among themselves, but then they indicated their readiness. Stevens signed the paper. Seattle stepped forward. An official pointed to a diagonal line beside his name. He took the pen offered and drew a crooked line across it. One by one the others stepped up to make their mark. An American flag was raised; *Major Tompkins* broke out pennants and fired a thirty-one-gun salute. For the Americans, it was time to celebrate.

Because it was late, the distribution of gifts was put off until the next morning, when sacks of potatoes, bolts of cloth, hand mirrors, Jew's harps, needles, and kegs of molasses were distributed to the Indians. These were gifts, Stevens reminded them, and there would be more that summer. All eyes now fell on Seattle, who had the last word. Stepping forward with a white flag, he made an impassioned plea.

> Now by this we make friends and put away all bad feelings if we ever had any. We are the friends of the Americans. All the Indians are of the same mind. We look upon you as our father. We will never change our minds, but since you have been to see us we will always be the same. Now! Now, do you send this paper of our hearts to the Great Chief. That is all I have to say.

With "if we ever had any," referencing the recent impasse over the Duwamish reservation, Seattle voiced his determination to continue working with the Americans. Four years earlier, he had brought Maynard north with damaged goods and high hopes. Now he offered a white flag before heaps of bagatelles on that windy day at Point Elliott.

Dutiful compliance had marked Medicine Creek. Seattle's protests before and at Point Elliott had generated council debate. But outright hostility erupted barely three days later on the twenty-fifth at Point No

Point, when twelve hundred S'Klallam, Twana, Skokomish, and remnant Chemakum gathered on a stormy beach. Heavy weather kept Stevens's remarks short but did not mute the headmen's ire. Che-law-ach-tud, an old Twana man, asked Stevens where they would find food if they sold their land. He offered to sell half and keep the rest. "I don't like the place you have shown for us to live on," he said. "I am not ready to sign the paper." Another man spoke up: "I do not want to leave my old home and my burying grounds. I am afraid I shall die if I do."[9]

The Skokomish head chief, Nah-whil-luk, told Stevens that the Americans had awakened the Indians to the real value of their land: "I do not want to sell my land," he argued, "because it is valuable." A S'Klallam headman, Hool-hol-tan, suggested that they sell only half and keep the rest: "Why should we sell all; we may become destitute. Why not let us live together with you?"

Simmons argued that if they owned half, they could not hunt and fish on the other half, but Hool-hol-tan was adamant: "All the Indians here have been afraid to talk," he said, "but I wish to speak and be listened to. I don't want to leave my land. It makes me sick to leave it. I don't want to go from where I was born."

It remained for Tsitz-a-mah-han, the S'Klallam head chief after S-hai-ak's death, to quiet the situation by saying he was satisfied with the governor's promises—that the advantages whites brought outweighed their evil acts, for which he chided Stevens, urging him to "tell the Whites not to abuse the Indians as many are in the habit of doing, or ordering them to go away or knocking them down." The head chief then drew ironic cheers when he acknowledged Stevens and the president as fathers.

Stevens was flustered, but he carried on. "What are you now?" he argued. "What were you formerly? Have you not already been driven from your burial grounds?" The Great Father wanted to give them homes and a school, he said, to protect their fishing rights, and teach them farming. "Was this good or not?" he challenged. "I want an answer!" After this blunt exchange, the headmen signed.

---

In late January, at Neah Bay, the Makah told Stevens they had no intention of becoming farmers or having a single head chief. Nevertheless,

Stevens got them to sign their treaty on the thirty-first. But his luck ran out at the next council, at the Chehalis River, in late February. The aging Chehalis headman, Carcowan, arrived at the council drunk, and his son Tleyuk, recognized as the chief of the Chehalis, strenuously objected to the removal of his people to Quinault lands and refused to sign. When the council reconvened the next morning, Stevens angrily tore up the official document recognizing Tleyuk as chief and abandoned the council, heading east to the Walla Walla River to meet with interior groups.[10]

If native leaders had rediscovered their voice, that most still signed the treaties is difficult to understand. Despite the fact that many Duwamish, many of them Seattle's upriver kin, had refused to participate in the council and that his failure to reserve lands in their homeland infuriated them, he signed. Why? Some argue that the treaty's terms were not explicable in the Jargon, leaving native leaders unsure of details, even when translated by John Taylor. This appears to have been true particularly with Article 3, describing a "central agency general reservation" to which treaty groups would eventually go. Thirty square miles of land on Port Gardner Bay were set aside for this, but many attendees assumed that this area would be roughly contiguous with what is now Snohomish County, about 2,600 square miles. Also confusing was Article 7, allowing the president to change any part of the treaty. The vociferous exchange at later councils suggests that many understood the treaty's shortcomings only too well.[11]

Many believed that the treaties were only a first step in a longer negotiation. Later in the summer of 1855, several headmen who had been at Point Elliott told the Oblate Fathers Eugene Casimir Chirouse and Louis-Joseph d'Herbomez that they had given the government their names but not their land. When the priests told them that the Americans thought otherwise, d'Herbomez wrote, "they all expressed their astonishment. They even seemed irritated."[12]

By signing, Seattle gained a reservation for the Suquamish in their homeland, but did he sell the Duwamish, his mother's people, literally down the river? Or did he assume, as later events suggest, that further negotiations would gain the Duwamish a reservation in their own homeland so that they and the Suquamish could share the future with the Americans as he had envisioned? Amelia Snaetlum, a Suquamish informant of Skagit ancestry, recalled with biting irony what she had been told he said to the people at Point Elliott:

> You folks observe the changers who have come to this land. And our progeny will watch and learn from them now, those who will come after us, our children. And they will become just the same as the changers who have come here to us on this land. You folks observe them well.[13]

The "changer" is Dukwiba'l, the mythic demiurge. Seattle compared what the Americans were doing to what the Changer had begun at Point Elliott, in order to enable his people to grasp the cataclysmic changes they faced. The few examples we have of his ability to stir audiences with vivid analogies bespeak an agile, creative mind. In this, he was not alone. The Skykomish headman Steh-shail later had a photo taken of him before an American flag to admonish his people that they could not live with their American brothers unless they abandoned the old ways. Before he died, Steh-shail told his nephew William Shelton, "You carry that out, Stars and Stripes is our master, instead of eagle feather." It was a warning as well as counsel. To Steh-shail and Seattle, the treaties marked a step in a long walk with Americans toward a common future. But the Americans preferred to walk alone.[14]

Seattle and other headmen had invited Americans into their country to live together and share in prosperity. But the treaty stipulated that upon ratification the people had one year to move away from growing centers of commerce to isolated reservations. As this sank in, anger grew. Nisqually River pioneer James Longmire got an earful from Leschi's kin, who complained that unlike the Hudson's Bay Company men, the Americans "were fencing and stealing the land from the Indians." In Seattle, David and Louisa Denny were visited by an angry shaman who complained that the Indians had been cheated at Point Elliott but that "the white people were few, their doors were thin and the Indians could easily break them in and kill all the 'Bostons.'"[15]

Despite such threats, on the Sound, Americans regarded northern native raiders as a much greater threat than local groups. Kinsmen of a northerner killed by an American in Olympia beheaded two miners on

Bellingham Bay and looted and burned several houses. That summer at Port San Juan on Vancouver Island, an English trader told Captain Isaac S. Sterett of the US sloop of war *Decatur* that two thousand northern raiders were planning a war of extermination in the south. To kill whites or Indians, he did not say, but Sterett extended his stay in northern waters to find out.[16]

From his claim between the Green and White Rivers, settler Allen Porter warned in July that neighboring Indians "were getting saucy." When Patkanim, Sehalapahan, "the Priest," and Chowitsuit arrived for instruction at the Saint Joseph of New Market Oblate Mission near Olympia, they told Father Louis-Joseph d'Herbomez that Kamiakin, a Yakama signatory to the Walla Walla Treaty, was planning an uprising against the whites. On his way to preach to the headmen's people, d'Herbomez stopped with them at Fort Steilacoom on July 22, where, with George Gibbs translating his French, he passed their warning on to Lieutenants William Slaughter and John Nugen that a conspiracy "exists between the Yakama chief [Kamiakin] and the savages of this country from Seattle up to the Cowlitz." He repeated Patkanim's assurances of "the good will and good relations among the three principal chiefs Patkrenim, Sgolaei [Goliah] and Chawidsoud [Chowitsuit] toward the Americans," and that Patkanim wanted "to live as a friend of the Americans."[17]

The astonished officers asked d'Herbomez if he thought Kamiakin capable of conspiring against them after signing the Walla Walla Treaty. "He is haughty and proud," the priest answered, "and if he wants to do something evil, not missionaries nor any others are capable of stopping him." D'Herbomez's naming Patkanim "the 1st Chief of Puget Sound," excluding Seattle from the circle of goodwill, and the mentioned scope of Kamiakin's intrigue, from the town of Seattle south to the Cowlitz, marked the Duwamish as coconspirators, and added up to a growing perception of Seattle's weakness and Duwamish anger after Point Elliott. In August, the *Puget Sound Courier* at Steilacoom printed a settler's warning that the announced intention of the Klikitat, a group closely associated with the Yakama, to visit to trade and race horses masked a plot to kill settlers gathered for the race and go murdering through the territory.[18]

After Medicine Creek, Leschi and his brother-in-law Stahi asked Benjamin Shaw to convey their unhappiness with the treaty to Stevens, and Shaw is remembered to have said the governor "promised to get them other reservations." Apparently mollified, Leschi returned to his home for the remainder of the winter. But the treaty's ratification in March 1855 gave native people one year to leave their homes for the small, isolated reservations. Leschi would lose his horse pastures, and some claimed he traveled to Oregon's Rogue River, where a bloody race war pitted native people against settlers, to seek allies for the coming struggle. But William Fraser Tolmie, who knew him well, argued that his trip was an effort to find an Oregon cousin who understood English well enough to better translate the treaty's terms.[19]

Rumors claimed that the Kamiakin sent his brother Owhi to Hibulb, a village near the mouth of the Snohomish, where leaders heard him speak for war, and that one thousand heard him at Port Madison and others at Baba'kwǝb on Elliott Bay. At Hibulb, Leschi was said to have agreed with Owhi, but Duke of York, Patkanim, Kitsap (a Green River headman with the ancestral name of his older kinsman), and Seattle argued against war. Seattle is recalled to have said, "No, Leschi, don't kill these white people. Yesler and others of them have Indian women. Don't kill them. Take my word." But Henry Moses, a Duwamish great-grandnephew of Seattle, claimed that the chief picked up an arrow stuck in the earth in front of a longhouse, signifying his intent to fight, but that he later warned his white friends, making Seattle, in Moses's opinion, a traitor to his people.[20]

Resentment mounted among those, like Leschi, whose lands settlers coveted. On the White River, where memory and anger ran deep, the headman Kitsap had a change of heart and turned against the Americans, as did Nelson on the White River. Nelson had brought settlers John and Nancy Thomas upriver in his canoe, but his first loyalty was to his own people. Kanasket, an upper Yakima man married into a Green River family with strong Puyallup connections, also opted for war. In hindsight, these moves seem less a conspiracy than a moral quandary to be resolved by taking up arms or not.[21]

To prevent violence, Leschi tried to convince territorial officials to renegotiate the treaty, and, in town, Seattle's half sister Sally poured out her anguish to Abigail Hanford, the sister of John Holgate and wife of pioneer Edward Hanford, saying that her heart was with her people, but as they turned against the whites and the whites against them, "it was all very bad." By query and debate, Kamiakin and others gauged native support for an explosion they saw coming. On Puget Sound, Americans could not imagine local Indians fighting them, but their possible alliance with northern raiders conjured the ultimate nightmare scenario.[22]

At the Walla Walla Council, as troubled Cayuse, Nez Perce, Umatilla, Walla Walla, and Yakama ceded most of their lands, news arrived of a gold strike on the distant Colville River. Jumping the gun, the *Pioneer and Democrat* announced the interior open to settlement, and prospectors headed east, not caring whether the lands they crossed were reserved for the Indians or not. Around Seattle, land office surveyors with compasses and chains began their work mapping section and township lines to aid settlers in locating their donation claims even before the ink on the Treaty of Point Elliott was dry.[23]

If someone had wanted to drive native people to war that fall, they could not have done more than what Americans were already doing. Warnings from Patkanim changed Arthur Denny's initial skepticism into mounting concern. The Snoqualmie chief headed up the Stillaguamish River to hunt mountain goats in order to escape the disaster he saw coming.[24]

---

When several prospectors on their way east came up missing, their friends and families feared the worst. Then men stumbled into Seattle reporting that their companions had been killed by Indians, and the *Courier* and the *Pioneer and Democrat* rumored that groups on both sides of the Cascades were planning attacks on whites. News of more murders came from an Indian identified as "one of Seattle's band." Aware of his recalcitrance regarding Point Elliott and deaf to hearing the news as a warning, the *Pioneer and Democrat* added, "We might mention Seattle, and his band, as suspected among the conspirators."[25]

One September night, after Allen Porter's "saucy" neighbors tried to kill him, he fled downstream, spreading the alarm. All the next day, terrified families abandoned their homesteads and headed for safety in town. Riding through Yakama country in search of the prospectors' killers, Indian agent Andrew Bolon had his throat slit by a group of angry native hunters. Mindful of the Whitmans' murderers' fate, the Yakama refused to surrender his killers and, instead, awaited American vengeance. It was not long in coming.[26]

When word of Bolon's death reached Fort Dalles, army major Gabriel Rains ordered brevet major Granville Haller and 102 troopers north to chastise the Yakama. To support Haller, Captain Maurice Maloney sent Lieutenant William Slaughter and fifty mounted troops from Fort Steilacoom to Naches Pass. Meanwhile, harried Seattle citizens commenced building a blockhouse and organizing a militia. While men hewed logs and drilled, women prayed, and on October 4, 1855, as if in answer, a cannon's boom signaled *Decatur*'s arrival in Elliott Bay.

The ship's sixteen short-range thirty-two-pound carronades fired shells of that weight and grapeshot. It also had two twelve-pounder cannons, a howitzer, and a well-stocked armory. With martial enthusiasm, Wiley, the *Pioneer and Democrat* editor, insisted that treaty-breaking Indians deserved the "extreme measure," italicizing for emphasis that the Yakama should be *"rubbed out—blotted from existence* as a tribe." Countering that bloodlust, the *Puget Sound Courier*'s editor, E. T. Gunn, Wiley's Whig opponent, blamed Stevens's bungling for the attacks, a charge for which Wiley likened Gunn to Benedict Arnold, adumbrating factional strife to come.[27]

On October 6, Haller and his troops met the Yakama on Toppenish Creek and fought a running three-day battle that sent the Americans reeling back to Fort Dalles, with five killed and seventeen wounded. When Slaughter learned this, he ordered his men back to Connell's Prairie, near the White River settlements. Aware that Patkanim was somewhere in the mountains, Slaughter sent a panicky note via express messengers to Territorial Secretary Mason, claiming that the Snoqualmie chief was dogging his every move.[28]

The debacle stunned Americans and galvanized native resistance. Mason asked Captain Sterett to take Patkanim's brothers in town hostage on board his ship. Knowing that Arthur Denny was Patkanim's friend, Sterett asked his advice. Denny believed Slaughter mistaken, saying, "We had enemies enough to look after without attacking our friends," and, via native messenger, sent Patkanim word to hurry back.[29]

Learning of the settler exodus from White River, Mason left Fort Steilacoom, with an armed guard, to query a native fishing camp on the upper White, but those there declared their friendship. In Seattle, the gullible Mason encouraged refugees to return home and told Sterett the townsmen's pleas for protection were only a ruse to augment trade by keeping his ship in harbor. Sterett confronted Arthur Denny, threatening to leave, but Denny argued that Mason had been deceived again, and that if the settlers returned, they would be killed in a fortnight. "How can I tell whom to believe," Sterett fumed. "You seem to be so earnest I will stay and find out for myself."

As the settlers who had been persuaded by Mason returned, neighboring Indians felt threatened. The native grapevine had Slaughter's frightened troops fleeing Naches Pass toward them, soon to be joined by trigger-happy volunteers. An angry Leschi visited his friend James McAllister, declaring that he would fight if forced to leave his home. Worried, McAllister warned Mason that Leschi should be "attended to." On the twenty-second, Leschi himself strode into the territorial secretary's office, warning of war. Mason asked him to return to Olympia until the crisis passed. But Leschi did not, so Mason ordered Eaton's Rangers, a mounted volunteer group, to arrest him. When they reached Leschi's farm, he and his brother Quiemuth had fled, leaving a plow standing forlornly in a furrow.[30]

At this point several native leaders stepped forward to warn settlers that their lives were in danger. We know that Seattle's cousin Salmon Bay Curley told Edward Hanford to leave the bay for town with his family. On the White River, the Thomas and Russell families heeded the warning of Whatcom, another cousin of Seattle, to leave, and on Friday, October 26, 1855, a brooding Nelson visited the White River settlers Harvey and Eliza Jones and their family, muttering grimly that "it would not be very long until Indian be gone and white man have all the land around here." Even seven-year-old Johnny King, Harvey's stepson, and no relation to their neighbors, Mr. and Mrs. George King, sensed the danger. Patkanim had warned Arthur Denny; Leschi warned Mason. But Seattle's voice is not remembered among these. His silence prompted Historian Frederick Grant to later write, "When the Klikitats began the war on the whites he did not manifest the concern of Patkanim for their safety." Why?[31]

Years later, Seattle's Duwamish great-grandnephew, Henry Moses, claimed that Seattle had signaled his intention of joining hostile forces to drive out the settlers, but later warned his white friends, yet no memory survives of him warning anyone directly. At Point Elliott, Seattle claimed he could not say much, and he appears to have made silence a tool as war loomed. Accusations of conspiracy helped him maintain contact with increasingly hostile groups, in the same way that, with ammunition given him by whites, Curley traded for information from fighters pleased to hear "what they were doing to scare the Americans." If he gave warnings as Moses claimed, it was through his kin. As tensions grew, Seattle left for Old Man House.[32]

For days, Eaton's Rangers searched for Leschi. On October 27, McAllister and neighbor Michael Connell, two Indians—Clipwalen, whom the McAllisters had adopted out of slavery, and Leschi's brother-in-law Stahi—headed for a White River fishing camp. On the way McAllister and Connell were ambushed and killed; Clipwalen escaped, and Stahi spurred his horse forward, joining the attack on the Rangers, who were taking cover in an abandoned longhouse.

The next morning, Nelson, Kitsap, and others visited the recently returned White River settlers. They shot Harvey and Eliza Jones to death, smashed in Eliza's face with an ax, and shot hired man Enos Cooper through the lungs. William Brannon fought until his attackers' knives quieted him. His wife, Elizabeth, grabbed their naked infant and fled, but was caught, stabbed repeatedly, and thrown, mother and child, down a well. George King was killed, and his pregnant wife, Mary, dragged screaming from the house by her hair, was stripped, raped, shot, and mutilated. Their infant child, never found, was assumed killed. Yet Nelson saved Johnny King, and his younger sister and brother, and delivered them to safety. King's five-year-old son, George Jr., was also saved by Indians, who treated him well before returning him to white settlers months later, by which time he spoke only Xwəljutsid.[33]

Fleeing survivors warned others, who joined their panicked exodus, the horror they described congealing into a lust for vengeance. In Seattle, nearly all able-bodied white men joined the militia. But the settlers had been driven out from White River. Another bloody chapter in the record of life and death there ended in another explosion of violence. The new actors were much the same as before: upriver people nursing a vendetta against Seattle and his downriver kin, but this time his American friends paid the price. The message was clear: the settlers must go or be killed, and Seattle could not protect them.

Learning that Major Rains was still at Fort Dalles, Captain Maloney halted and sent back word that he would return to Fort Steilacoom. The seven-man express bearing the message blundered into a hostile group at Connell's Prairie celebrating Nelson's bloody deeds. Two were killed near where McAllister and Connell had fallen, and five escaped, sharing details with Maloney as they joined other terrified settlers crowding into the fort.

East and west, as most native people struggled to survive in place, native fighters gathered at isolated redoubts, and settlers fled to safety. On Halloween, Seattle broke his silence to visit *Decatur*. Captain Sterett welcomed him with a show of carronades—firing shot, a bag of one hundred iron balls, each an inch wide, and an exploding shell recently introduced by the navy. Gunners levered the heavy guns forward, a match touched the vent, powder flashed, and recoil from the fiery blast shoved the gun back against a thick hawser run through its breech ring. Ashore, dust and splinters marked where the shot scythed vegetation. Another gun bellowed, the flash igniting a short fuse on the shell, followed immediately by a muffled crump as it penetrated a bluff. Moments later, earth blasted upward as astonished Indians exclaimed, *"Mox pooh!"* ("Two booms!").[34]

But Seattle did not come to be impressed. Through a slave, he announced that the killings on White River had been sparked by the Americans' attempt to seize Leschi, causing his people to "have taken up arms to revenge the insult, and commenced their murderous warfare." Despite translations, one can still hear his angry exasperation. Blundering arrogance had put scores of angry, armed Indians in the field. One of Seattle's sons reported that Fort Colville had been seized and all the whites killed. "It begins to look," observed *Decatur*'s log writer, "very much like a general war with all the Indians occupying the northern portion of the United States."[35]

Seattle had planned his visit to precede one by Patkanim, who showed up the next day at the head of a packtrain, confirming Arthur Denny's trust and presenting Captain Sterett with gifts of venison and hides. In response, Seattle sent two subchiefs on November 3 with more bad news: the Klikitats' three to four thousand warriors and another thousand under Leschi and Owhi would be joined by others in the spring, led by the war leader Squak-lin-sha. Two other fighters, Tus-he-ak and Qui-a-molt, and their men were planning to kill any American they could find. The subchiefs added that Nelson, Kanasket, and forty others carried out the White River killings, along with a "great medicine man," Cli-am-hum, covered with bullet and knife wounds that marked him as invulnerable—"at least so it seems," added the log writer. The subchiefs finished by offering Seattle's view that hostilities were the result of Stevens's taking Indian lands in exchange for trifles, and that these often were given to the wrong people, a likely reference to Patkanim's eighty blankets. The Snoqualmie chief might have proffered loyalty and gifts, but, at no little risk, Seattle had demonstrated that he had information the Americans might find useful if they cared to listen. Having invited them into his country, he would stand with them despite their defeats and blunders.

That same day, Captain Maloney had sent Lieutenant Slaughter's men and volunteers to press Leschi's fighters, covering their own people's retreat to the White River. One soldier was killed while dropping a tree across the river, but after a daylong skirmish with much ammunition fired at long range, Maloney believed his men had killed at least thirty Indians. The real story was that Leschi's men had raised hats on sticks above logs to draw fire, a trick bringing what they called *hiyu hee hee* (lots of laughs). The next day, Maloney moved north to Green River, but after two more soldiers were wounded, he decided to retreat. When word of the American "victory" reached town, elation replaced gloom.[36]

To counter Seattle's allusion to him as one of "the wrong people," Patkanim returned to *Decatur* as the good news arrived and had Indian agents David Maynard and Michael Simmons, along with Lieutenant A. J. Drake, craft a bombastic letter to Territorial Secretary Charles Mason, "his closhe tumtum [good friend]," protesting "slanderous reports . . . regarding my actions + tumtum [heart]" and offering one hundred good men "to fight anywhere this side of the Cascades" and "arrest any and all such as I can find within my jurisdiction who may appear as enemies to the Bostons." Next to "Respectfully yours to serve, Patrick Canam, Chief of the Snoqualmy Tribe," he inked his mark. Comic opera aside, Patkanim was determined to outshine Seattle.[37]

The feared Indian uprising was a fact. To counter it, Mason and Simmons cobbled together a strategy, sending regulars and militia to forestall movement over the passes while rounding up and concentrating Indians living in what was designated the war ground—virtually the entire east side of Puget Sound—at island camps and on the Sound's west shore, where they could not give support to "hostiles." In Seattle, David Maynard and Henry Yesler expected to house one thousand Indians at the Nose, in huts built from mill refuse. Simmons had appointed Maynard special Indian agent to herd "friendlies" to the camp, but Yesler requested that Curley's people be allowed to remain next to the mill so he would not have to walk the quarter mile to hire them as needed. Remarkably, as townsmen trained for war, native labor kept the mill running. Supporting Yesler were Arthur Denny and others who saw the mill's continued operation essential to the town's economic survival.[38]

East of the mountains, Major Rains led seven hundred regulars toward the Yakima River. ("Yakima" is the older place-name form of "Yakama.") Although unable to defeat Kamiakin's force during a skirmish at Union Gap on the Yakima River in November, he was able to drive native fighters from the field and returned to Fort Dalles, leaving a final reckoning for another day. East of Lake Washington, Maynard found that friendly Indians were unimpressed by the American offer of protection, and by mid-November the doctor had convinced only 225 to gather at the Nose. Of these, 75 were Suquamish, whom Yesler had also persuaded to move next to his mill. The rest refused to leave their well-stocked winter villages, claiming that Curley and Yesler said they would be fools to do so and that Maynard and Simmons were liars.

To Maynard, Chief Seattle and the subchief Now-a-chais "appeared considerably disturbed in their minds since, by their actions, the Americans had made it virtually impossible for the two to maintain authority over their people as they had been enjoined. Maynard sent them to talk with Simmons and Mason in Olympia about moving their people across the Sound, and they returned with instructions for Maynard to use his own judgment. But then, on November 21, Simmons arrived with orders to remove everyone to the western shore, instructions that created a huge row.[39]

An anonymous writer sent the *Courier* an account of a stormy meeting at which a majority of settlers and Indians opposed the move, the

Duwamish protesting that they "would sooner be killed than go." Yesler and others warned that removing the Duwamish was "tantamount to a declaration of war against them" and asked for Maynard's removal as subagent, arguing that he consulted only with Seattle, while "a large majority of the Indians here are not his people and do not acknowledge him as their chief." Mason's response that Seattle was the recognized head chief of the Duwamish ignored the fact that, thanks to the Americans, many of Seattle's own people had turned against him.[40]

Many settlers tellingly observed that it had been an oversight not to offer the Duwamish reserved lands in their own country, and that they must have little thought of hostility "or they would have been driven to it, ere this." Seattle's hybrid community had become an economic reality, and its practical residents refused Simmons's order. Even Christopher Hewitt, commanding the recently organized volunteer Company H, and about to lead volunteers up the White River, opposed removal, writing Mason that he would postpone the move if he could not get native transport. "It is the wrong time," he warned, "to have trouble at home."

Nevertheless, Commander Samuel Swartwout, in charge of naval forces on Puget Sound, advised Sterett to arrest those who interfered with the government's Indian policy, but Sterett wisely chose to let well enough alone. Denny's trust in Patkanim's word in a matter of life and death reveals how much settlers had shed their view of Indians as fickle savages.[41]

As native children crowded into drafty huts at the Nose sickened, families agreed to move across the Sound, and Maynard obtained a sloop and scow for transport. On December 20, wind and rain caused many to reconsider, and barely eighty left, essentially Seattle, his household, and the Suquamish in many canoes. Nightfall saw them on a bleak spit at Point Monroe as the wind flattened their tents and snuffed out their campfires. Maynard would recall wryly, "From the complaints I judged that they were becoming unfavorably impressed with the idea of migration and colonization at this season of the year." Dawn came; the storm blew. The refugees broke camp and moved toward what the treaty said was their land.[42]

Meanwhile, northern Indians traveled unhindered in their dark canoes. When a group landed near Steilacoom, a delegation of anxious citizens demanded that they leave or face consequences. Sizing up their antagonists, the Indians opted to stay, whereupon the townsmen appealed to Sterett, who sent a lieutenant and a boat crew to the northerners' camp on Christmas Day. When a northern man leveled his gun at the sailors, a native woman in the group struck it down, and after discussion they left peaceably. Meanwhile, Sterett sailed on to Port Orchard, keeping a weather eye open for trouble and leaving Lieutenant Drake and eight marines to guard the town.[43]

Fresh from San Francisco's Presidio, US Army captain Erasmus Keyes and his company reinforced Lieutenant Slaughter, as soldiers returned to the war ground. But spooked in the dripping forest, the Bay Area soldiers shot at sounds and shadows. Occasionally, shadows shot back. On December 2, one soldier was killed fetching water, and that night most of Keyes's mounts were driven off. Two days later, Slaughter and sixty-five men pushed north up the Puyallup River to the Stuck to join Hewitt's volunteers, who were moving south on the White River to its confluence with the Green.

Earlier, Hewitt had led volunteers and native scouts to the charred White River homesteads, burying the corpses they found. He noted that Mary King's left breast had been cut off and feral hogs had pulled out her intestines. Soldiers cracking jokes during their grisly errand disgusted the scouts. "Boston men are fools," said one. "They do nothing but eat and laugh." But dark humor masked the Americans' terror. A third of the volunteers' guns were useless, and a black settler warned that 150 hostiles lurked across the river.[44]

On the evening of December 4, with his men secure at the confluence, Hewitt reached Slaughter and urged him to continue the short distance to his encampment, but Slaughter's exhausted men were already making camp. Cooking fires smoldered in the rain, and officers gathered in a log storehouse, silhouetted in the firelight. Shots rang out. A bullet pierced Slaughter's heart. Fires were frantically stamped out.

Amid scattered gunfire, Keyes took Slaughter's body and led his terrified men to Hewitt's camp as whooping attackers overran the bloody ground. A dawn party sent to bury the dead found them robbed and scalped. As canoes floated the men down the rain-swollen current to Elliott Bay, one of the wounded died. Coming after Haller's retreat and the White River killings, the death of Slaughter, a capable officer who had enlivened local society with his attractive wife, Mary, broke the resolve of many settlers.

Victorious, Leschi and others wished to negotiate, but American brutality gave those less inclined more reasons to fight. In December, volunteers in the Walla Walla valley took the Walla Walla chief Yellow Bird and others prisoner during a parley under a flag of truce. A running battle ensued, and during the evening of December 6, the volunteers killed their hostages, scalping and skinning the chief's body and pickling his ears in alcohol. Later, they dug up his corpse to collect more souvenirs. In Portland, the volunteers were said to have toasted their victory by sipping the alcohol.[45]

On Puget Sound, native fighters planned a bold stroke. The arguments of those counseling peace or declaring the Americans too strong to resist rang hollow. The regular army had been defeated. Settlers had been driven out, and soldiers riding out from Fort Steilacoom to chastise Leschi were in retreat, taking their dead commander with them. A handful of volunteers and marines defended the town of Seattle. If it could be wiped out, the soldiers would have little left to defend and might yield altogether if pressed by fighters resupplied from captured stores. Calls for outside help bore fruit later in December, when fighters led by Qwalchan, the Yakama father-in-law of the Green River headman Kitsap, crossed the mountains on snowshoes to join with upriver Duwamish, Sammamish, and other resolute allies on Lake Washington.[46]

As this force grew, Leschi and Kanaskat tried to negotiate with territorial officials through Indian agent John Swan on Fox Island, where more than eight hundred Puyallup and Nisqually were concentrated. Rivalry between army and navy personnel flummoxed the effort to capture the Indian leaders, and in late January 1856 the two slipped away before a trap could be sprung. Momentum shifted to native leaders with a different agenda.[47]

On January 19, Governor Stevens returned to Olympia from treaty-making east of the Rockies. Citizens welcomed him with a thirty-eight-gun salute and filled the legislative hall with cheers as he promised to prosecute the war "until the last hostile Indian is exterminated." With whirlwind energy, he rallied citizen support and pressured the army into an early campaign. He reorganized northern, central, and southern vol-unteer battalions for six-month terms; requested James Douglas, now governor of the Crown Colony of Vancouver Island, to send arms; and ordered reinforcements and supplies up from California. Natives who asked if the Hudson's Bay Company would support them in their war with the Americans were told "in a war of races they had a war with all white men."[48]

But an event favoring an attack on Seattle happened while Qwalchan's fighters crossed the mountains. On December 7, with look-outs scanning the horizon, *Decatur* slammed into a reef near Restoration Point, punching a hole in its hull and shattering internal timbers. At Yesler's wharf, sailors removed topmasts, off-loaded guns, and beached the vessel for temporary repairs. The news excited the hostiles: stripped of cannons, *Decatur* beckoned as a storehouse of arms, powder, and lead.

Chief Seattle and David Maynard had also been kept busy since their November exodus. With lumber sourced from George Anson Meigs's mill in Port Madison, Maynard had houses built near Old Man House, roofless now and sprouting ferns from its remaining rafters. Named Fort Kitsap, the village became home for Seattle's people in a changed world, marking it year one on the reservation as wards of a distant, alien government.

In Seattle, Henry Tobin, a Black River settler Maynard was appointed to help, reported that some Indians awaiting transfer from the Nose had opted to stay. Having been ordered by Stevens to supply Indians to the militia and requested by Guert Gansevoort, Sterett's replacement as commander of *Decatur*, to let Curley's people remain, Maynard concluded that he was no longer responsible for them and focused his energy on Fort Kitsap, where he had trouble enough. On Christmas Eve, Seattle told Maynard that hostiles lurking about were intent on killing the doctor and his wife, Catherine, and advised Maynard to keep his room dark and his door shut. If he went out at night, he should wear a blanket like an Indian. Catherine recalled "dressing like a squaw for weeks."[49]

In the midst of all of this, remarkably enough, Seattle found time to marry a third wife, whose name is lost to us. She had been digging pota-toes in a garden on the Green River when the settlers were killed on the

White River. Foreseeing the conflict, Seattle had developed a plan with kin and others that enabled them to escape safely to Port Madison, where she and Seattle were married near the beginning of the year. The garden that marked her as a Green River woman suggests that the chief, ever resourceful, was seeking to strengthen his ties to the upriver Duwamish at this crucial time.[50]

By January 1856, Maynard counted 250 people in his care. While many scoured winter beaches for food, Meigs put others to work at his mill. On January 5, when boys said they saw raiders in the woods, Seattle warned Maynard and sent men to search. That night, there was shouting. Seattle's wife, Angeline, and H. Haley, another assistant, saw someone aim a gun into Maynard's empty cabin. The assassin fled, but three days later other putative assassins returned. Seattle once again told Maynard to stay inside and light no lamp—it was clear that they were after him.[51]

Nothing happened that rainy night, but at first light, a call sounded in the dripping woods. Seattle met Maynard at the door: they would soon know how many there were. He left and then came back. The call had been for retreat. His blood up, Maynard offered one hundred dollars per scalp. Seattle assured his friend; they would scour the woods but would find no one.

On January 24, Seattle's spy, Te-at-te-bash, brought word that Leschi and a large force were about to attack the town. Seattle pressed Maynard to warn Commander Gansevoort, and accompanied by other subchiefs, they paddled over to *Decatur* that evening.

The attacking Indian force had gathered along the lake's east shore with Owhi's men at Sa'tsakal, a village near the head of Mercer Slough, hidden from open water by an immense swamp. It was a storied place, where Mink is said to have invented a trap to capture Ruffled Grouse, a supernatural being connected to the land of the dead. Dining on kokanee and settlers' cattle, the native war leaders were planning a trap of their own.[52]

Where the lake outlet joined the Cedar River, stood Txwxudaw, the main Duwamish village. Downstream, Hewitt's volunteers had erected a log fortification, Fort Lander. Since this route to the bay was barred, Kitsap, Kanaskat, and Owhi directed the Yakama-Duwamish headman

Klakum to ferry their fighters in canoes across the lake. With volunteers on their flank, the move was risky, but the Americans helped them out. On January 22, three days before mustering out, the volunteers packed up and headed downriver.

Just as Slaughter's march to Naches Pass had left White River settlers open to attack, the Americans were again letting hostile forces move unhindered against a settlement. But when Maynard and Seattle warned Gansevoort, he seemed unconcerned. As they left that morning, Maynard observed Seattle's deep frustration. The Americans seemed blind to what confronted them. In his repaired and rearmed ship, Gansevoort believed he had matters under control.[53]

On January 25, Kwia'xtəd's son, whom Arthur Denny named Tecumseh, and 125 Duwamish fled downriver, with Curley reporting that "hiyu [many] Klikitats" were on the lake's west shore. As citizens directed the Duwamish to the Nose, Stevens arrived on board *Active*, a US steamer, returning from visiting Governor Douglas in Victoria. After citizens shared their fears, Stevens blithely assured them that New York and San Francisco were in greater danger of attack than Seattle. Once *Active* departed, however, Yesler and others told Gansevoort that the large number of Indians east of town might attack that evening.

The crew from *Decatur*, along with about 270 Indians and 250 white residents and refugees, crowded into Seattle. Rough cabins and frame buildings were clustered on muddy paths near the Nose, where Tecumseh's people had to make do in the earlier shelters. Sawdust and trash filled part of the old lagoon, and north of Yesler's mill Curley's people occupied dwellings below the blockhouse, whose two corner bastions each housed a nine-pounder cannon. North of it stood David Blaine's white-painted Methodist Episcopal church and several family homes bordered by picket fences. Near slopes had been logged, but stumps and brush reached to the untouched forest. The settlement occupied a triangle eight blocks long and four blocks wide at its southern base, sandwiched between mudflats, a gravel beach, and steep hills.

Gansevoort deployed three groups of sailors and marines near the lagoon, and a fourth east of the mill, and mounted the howitzer in a longboat. He posted marines in the blockhouse and kept sentries alert through the night. Owl hoots, interpreted as hostile signals, broke the quiet. Around four in the morning, Lieutenant Thomas Phelps saw Indians loading canoes. When he asked an old woman why, she replied calmly, *"Oh, hiyu Klikitats chico memaloose conaway Bostons."* ("Lots of Klikitats have come to kill all the Americans.")[54]

At seven fifteen, Gansevoort ordered his men to mess in *Decatur* while settlers in the blockhouse went home to prepare breakfast. By then, attackers were at timber's edge and creeping through underbrush. Alerted by Curley's sister's son, Yarkekeeman, Indian Jim, Yesler hurried to *Decatur* to tell Gansevoort, who sent his men back onshore and ordered the howitzer to be fired at movement in a cabin across the lagoon. The ball smashed a wall. A carronade thundered, and an exploding shell blew the cabin to smithereens. A terrific shout rose from the woods, followed by an explosion of gunfire from both sides.

Terrified settlers raced back to the blockhouse as combatants reloaded and commenced an intense, continuous fire, punctuated by loud reports of the howitzer and the thunder of *Decatur*'s broadsides. As shot and shell screamed ashore, the hostiles moved north between geysers of earth and fired into town, their roaring volleys returned by sailors, marines, and settlers firing from barricades.

The Battle of Seattle lasted much of that cold day but produced few American casualties. Fifteen-year-old Milton Holgate and a visitor from Steilacoom, Robert Wilson, were killed as they stepped out from shelter to have a look. A source told Curley that sixteen native fighters had been killed. Native residents rode out the battle offshore, safe in their canoes, but settlers, who had never been in a battle or imagined Indians capable of such a thing, were terrified. Despite exploding ordnance, native fighters held their ground and retired in good order at the end of the day, when it became obvious the Americans would not be dislodged. After dining on livestock, the Indians used the supplies of pitch they had brought to set fire to the town, torching outlying homesteads instead. On board *Decatur*, Gansevoort needed a drink.[55]

At Fort Kitsap during the battle, booming cannons could be heard all day. At night, red light trembled in the east. Catherine Maynard remembered that, during the attack, Chief Seattle, seventy years old, exhausted, and sick at heart, "was in great distress and made pitiful demonstrations of the anguish he was in." All his efforts were going up in flames.

In Olympia, a shocked J. W. Wiley underlined the impact of the disaster in the *Pioneer and Democrat*: "The whole country may be said to be literally used up and rubbed out." In response, a chastened Governor Stevens returned to Seattle and pleaded with settlers not to leave. "The Governor and others," wrote David Blaine, "say that Seattle must not be given up, else ten thousand men could not subdue the Indians."[56]

# CHAPTER SEVEN

*"I want you to understand what I say."*

The "Battle at Seattle" headlined San Francisco's *Alta California* on February 6, 1856. On February 28, the *New York Herald* covered it on the front page of its morning edition, where Seattle, identified as chief at the reservation, was quoted saying of the attackers, "They are determined to destroy the town." Having sown the wind by imposing impractical treaties and stupidly ignoring native protests, the Americans reaped the whirlwind. Native communities were displaced, scores of Indians had been killed, and their societies smashed. Whites were slaughtered; their homesteads, buildings, and businesses destroyed, and many left the territory for good.[1]

The war in Washington Territory was only one of many maelstroms roiling the cauldron of national rage. As Kansas bled, American filibustering expeditions imposed short-lived but slaughterous slave regimes in Baja California, Sonora, and Nicaragua until enraged locals drove them out. All the while, the United States moved inexorably toward a horrific civil war. If it was a time for picking up stones, what balm was there in Gilead?

In a way, the Battle at Seattle mirrored what Kitsap had accomplished with his earlier raid against the Cowichans: both were tactical failures. But Kitsap had halted Cowichan raids, and the battle halted white immigration to the town for a decade, allowing the hybrid community, however challenged, to survive. In histories written at the end of the nineteenth and early twentieth centuries, this period is depicted as a morality tale of heroism, civilization, and law overcoming savage lawlessness, primitive and proletarian. Deeper and more telling descriptions are provided by recent historians like Coll Thrush, who in his book *Native Seattle* describes how the fabric of native-white relations continued to be woven by native people determined to remain in Seattle despite the equally determined effort of many whites to drive them out.

The result, after more than a century, is a place far more conscious of a native past than any other modern American city, and where Seattle, its eponym, weighs heavily on the collective mind.

In *Warship under Sail*, a study of life on board *Decatur*, historian Lorraine McConaghy examines the interplay between groups often dismissed as criminal or uncivilized: insubordinate and drunken crewmen, settlers and merchants selling liquor to all comers, and a "floating population" of transients and Indians, all producing, consuming, and surviving. If the criminal and uncivilized were the despair of those who valued order, they were also the majority. Most who left a written record typically ignored this protean mass or defined it as antagonistic to the town's progress. But Seattle, the head chief of divided and often violently antagonistic groups, a leader who avoided condemnation to retain an effective voice, who wrote nothing, left a profound and lasting mark.

While Seattle brooded at Fort Kitsap, local Duwamish joined *Decatur*'s crew and settlers building a second blockhouse and a palisade. Hostiles were rumored to be up at Luther Collins's place readying another attack, and on February 2, several were fired on as they tried to torch outlying buildings. But in the native camps on Whidbey Island, headmen told Indian Agent Nathan Hill that they had a plan to defeat the enemy. He sent them to Olympia to make their case, and Governor Isaac Stevens approved formation of an Indian force led by Patkanim to join the northern battalion of volunteers on the war ground.[2]

Leading more than seventy warriors up the Snohomish River in canoes, accompanied by Michael Simmons and two other white observers, Patkanim planned to attack Leschi, link up with troops to defeat hostile forces, and prevent others from crossing the mountains. Prior to their attack, they took shelter at Fort Ebey, a base of operations at the head of the Snohomish delta named after Isaac Ebey, the commander of the Northern Battalion. The exploits of "Pat and his Snoqualmie soldiers" riveted readers as reports from the war ground traced their bloody progress in territorial papers.

Regaining a measure of sangfroid at Fort Kitsap, Seattle also volunteered to lead warriors, who would drive hostiles toward Patkanim. David Maynard passed this on to Stevens, along with the old chief's warning that the enemy was gaining strength as more fighters crossed the passes. Stevens ordered Judge Edward Lander's recently organized volunteer Company A to ally with Seattle's men, but when Maynard told his charges of this plan, they balked, fearing that Lander's volunteers didn't care whether the Indians they shot were friendly or hostile as long as they were dead.[3] Seattle then sent a trusted warrior, Wyab, to help guide American soldiers to Leschi's camp on the Green River. He also passed on some advice. "Put away those drums," he told Wyab, referring to a traditional battlefield ritual. "Go quiet." Results mattered more than show.[4]

Patkanim convinced Stevens to let him lead an exclusively native force. When this independence was not offered to Seattle, his men complained that they wanted rations and pay before serving and that they had lost most of their weapons in a bad run of gambling luck. Maynard enrolled only twenty-three willing to defend Fort Kitsap. Some offered to patrol east of town, but Maynard cautioned Stevens that he could not vouch for their fidelity.

In mid-February, the *Pioneer and Democrat* reported an attack on hostiles below Snoqualmie Falls, and Patkanim's capture of three Klikitat spies. One turning "state's evidence" incriminated two others, who were hanged. With ax and knife, newspaperman Thomas Prosch would later recall, Patkanim "cut off their heads, which he threw into a sack, as a farmer would throw in rutabaga turnips." Simmons had to request that the old people and children who had been rounded up with those who surrendered not be murdered. Swiftly and brutally, Patkanim regained power among his people and settled old scores.[5]

The expedition headed west to deserted Sa'tsakal and south to Leschi's fortified camp on the Green River, where John Swan continued trying to negotiate peace. He estimated that 150 fighters, women, and children were in twenty longhouses at the base of a steep hill, protected by a large slough. Ammunition was low, Leschi faced growing dissension, and departing Duwamish had stolen many of his horses. As evening approached, Swan left.[6]

After dark, Patkanim's men moved silently down the hill, but barking dogs gave them away. Regrouping at dawn, they directed intense fire at Leschi's house, driving him and his followers into another. They were trapped inside by a hail of bullets, and shouts and screams suggested that many were killed and wounded, but at last Leschi and his men broke through the slough and crossed the river, at which point Patkanim's men ran out of ammunition. Turning to taunt his foe, Leschi shouted, "Come on, Bostons! Come on!"[7]

Once again, Leschi had eluded his captors. With several of his fighters dead and himself wounded, Patkanim returned to Fort Ebey at the mouth of the Snohomish, where he impaled his severed heads on stakes and staged a war dance to entertain the garrison. He told Simmons that Leschi had many men and the promise of more, as "many of those Indians who lately left [the town of] Seattle have gone with him and some from Puyallup." In the *Courier*, Maynard reminded readers that they had enemies other than Leschi, and that Seattle and his men were ready to fight if they could get arms and ammunition.[8]

Patkanim's noisome sacks of heads were taken to Olympia for payment. In the battle of the sons of light against the children of darkness, the sons, in this case the territory, paid twenty dollars for a common head and eighty dollars for a chief's. Flush with his reward, the chief bought new clothes and sat for a photo, returning to Seattle "arrayed in citizen's garb including Congress gaiters, white kid gloves, and a white shirt, with standing collar reaching half-way up to his ears, and the whole . . . finished off with a flaming red tie." Such a garish reminder of their role in the carnage dampened what elation the settlers might otherwise have felt.[9]

Canoes traveling up the Duwamish roused suspicion, and on the evening of February 28, volunteers fired on one, killing at least two men and wounded more. Furious Duwamish said the men had been fishing and asked how they could survive if they could not fish. Unsure of their loyalty, Maynard wrote Stevens that Tecumseh, William, and Curley needed watching.[10]

Another attack seemed imminent, and a native spy told Maynard that hostiles were rebuilding volunteer forts on the Black River and Lake Washington, and massing again on the lakeshore. Near Three Tree Point, an Indian who had been killed turned out to be Seattle's spy Te-at-te-bash, whose wife was later murdered near the Puyallup, along with another woman.

Fear of vengeful volunteers silenced native offers to fight, and even Judge Lander doubted they would be safe. To get out of harm's way,

Tecumseh and nearly 150 Duwamish left Elliott Bay for Bainbridge Island, where Maynard and Seattle took charge of them.

By then, regulars from Fort Steilacoom, under Colonel Silas Casey and Captain Erasmus Keyes, were advancing across the Puyallup toward the White River. Early on February 29, a sentry fired at dim figures descending a hill and dragged a wounded man into camp. This was Kanaskat, who, with Leschi, had sought peace with the Americans but had become their implacable foe.

His face contorted with pain and hatred, Kanaskat shouted in the Jargon, "My heart is wicked toward the whites, and always will be, so you had better kill me!" As Keyes's men readied a noose, Kanaskat shouted to compatriots in the woods. Gunfire erupted from the dark; a soldier put his rifle to the warrior's head and blew his brains across the grass. The memory of "the massive jaw, fixed scowl and bronzed skin of the monster's visage" would haunt Keyes for the rest of his life.[11]

The next day, the army drove the Indians from the White River in a fight leaving two soldiers dead and eight wounded. On March 5, they set Leschi's encampment ablaze. Reinforced by the Yakama, Leschi planned to ambush the soldiers as they crossed Connell's Prairie, but on the morning of March 10, the Americans halted just before entering the trap. After a furious daylong battle, Leschi was driven from the field. Accompanied by twenty warriors with their wives and children, he retreated across Naches Pass in bitter weather, burying his dead in the snow.[12]

With this, organized native resistance west of the Cascades ended but not the war. South of the Nisqually, native fighters had murdered settlers returning to their homes. In retaliation, volunteers surprised native men on the Carbon River, and those not killed in the firefight were lined up and shot. Inhabitants in at least three longhouses, including one in Leschi's birth village, were slaughtered.[13]

Springtime signaled the breakup of winter villages, but on Bainbridge Island and in other camps, no one was permitted to leave without a pass from an Indian agent. The Duwamish left anyway. In a letter to Simmons, Maynard blamed their departure on whites determined to keep native laborers and their families in town. Stevens sent Lieutenant Colonel Henry Crosbie to investigate. The Duwamish complained that Maynard allowed one thing one day but not the next. Curley said his people had not been paid for their services, denied that Maynard had authority over them, and refused to accept provisions from him. Crosbie concluded that Maynard was the problem and proposed his replacement by Yesler.[14]

On a gray March day, Seattle and Now-a-chais, a Duwamish head-man at Fort Kitsap, went to Maynard with complaints about three trouble-some characters: Stuttering George, Enoc-a-lid, and One-Eyed Tom. In his monthly report to Stevens, Seattle repeated the charges: that on two occasions, they had been prevented by Chill-whale-ton, a treaty signa-tory, from stabbing Maynard, and that they were "dangerous tamanous [spell-casting] workers + are about to cause them all to sicken + die." This was the old fear of sorcery, heightened by chaotic life on the reservations.[15]

Seattle and Now-a-chais wanted them put to death, or at least removed and confined, but Maynard had tired of it all. With his wife, Catherine, ailing, and wounded by mounting criticism, he sent Stevens his resignation, suggesting that his assistant Haley replace him. Stevens agreed, but Haley had no more luck with the Duwamish than Maynard had. When he told them they could not leave without his permission, they told him they would go where they pleased.

Even Americans were at each other's throats. In an argument over orders, Lander's replacement in charge of Company A, Arthur Denny, was relieved of command. When Denny's men signed resolutions demanding his reinstatement, territorial adjutant general James Tilton refused them honorable discharges, which meant they received no pay. Suspicions that some whites married to Indians had aided the enemy led Stevens to order their removal from their farms to Fort Steilacoom. When some moved back after the battle at Connell's Prairie, they were arrested for violating orders and held for trial in a military court. When critics sought to have them tried in civil court, Stevens placed Pierce and Thurston Counties under martial law, beginning a shrill legal and political row, as partisans blamed one another for the conflict, now in its final stage. George Gibbs, once Stevens's trusted assistant, became his political enemy. Tensions between the regulars and volunteers, and outright animosity between Stevens and General John Wool, commander of the US Army's Department of the Pacific, led factions to slug it out in the newspapers.

In Seattle, Tilton convened a military commission to try Indians accused of murders during the war. Klakum, whom Yesler believed led the attack on Seattle, stood trial with others on May 16, but conflicting testimony and the belief of military commissioners, regular officers who were unimpressed by Stevens's leadership, that the accused were engaged in legitimate acts of warfare led to their acquittal, leaving Seattle and those who counseled peace and cooperation looking like dupes. In June on the Naches River, Leschi, Kitsap, and Nelson surrendered to army colonel George Wright, who treated them with the respect normally granted militant opponents.[16]

At Fort Kitsap, Haley sought money for supplies by having Indians log land and plant potatoes, but the effort stalled when a settler claimed that the land was his. In early July, two armed deserters from the navy screw steamer USS *Massachusetts* commanded by Samuel Swartwout showed up at Haley's door, followed by an angry native crowd. The Indians clearly wanted to get their hands on the sailors, for reasons never recorded, and Haley did not trust them to return the men safely to their ship. But when he asked Seattle to take a letter to Swartwout requesting aid, Seattle refused. When he then asked for a canoe to deliver the letter himself, Seattle refused again. Afterward, Haley wrote that "some time during the day he sent Indians himself contrary to my orders and without a pass. I told him Gov. Stevens had ordered me to allow no Indians to leave the reservation without a pass and that he must not do the like again. He was very angry and we had hard words."[17]

As the recognized chief of the Duwamish and Suquamish, Seattle was held accountable by American authorities for both, but the defection of the Duwamish, aided and abetted by the Americans, and the participation of many of them in the war were a blow to his authority, as well as a personal affront. He had enough problems without Haley insisting that he go through proper channels. Unfortunately, Stevens was about to make his situation even worse.

In mid-July, a reported defeat of Walla Walla, Cayuse, and Umatilla Indians by volunteers east on the Grande Ronde River appeared to justify Stevens's wartime actions. Buoyed by the news, he decided to renegotiate the Medicine Creek Treaty and settle issues at the root of conflict west of the mountains: First were the small sizes and poor locations of reserved lands. Another was the failure to address the needs of the White, Green, and Stuck River groups, whose headmen had refused to attend the Point Elliott Council.

In early August, Governor Stevens, Michael Simmons, and Colonel Casey arrived at the Fox Island reserve, where a recent influx of refugees had boosted native population to more than a thousand. Seattle, under whose authority these bands had originally been placed, was not invited to participate. Swan's replacement, Indian agent Sydney Ford, enjoyed the headmen's respect, and with the much-admired William Tolmie interpreting, the people gathered to hear the governor out. He began by baldly rewriting recent history, saying that the Nisqually and Puyallup reservations, "suggested by yourselves," had been surveyed and found wanting. Stevens said he told Leschi that the reserves were not good, and that Simmons told the Nisqually they should be changed. He said that Leschi had led half his people into poverty and hunger, but Stevens had seen to it that these were fed and made comfortable. "I do not say Leschi was wrong," the governor said. "I say he did not know what was for his own interest." He went on to say that the government would choose better and larger reservations with "ground enough for horses," and that he would set aside land between the Green and White Rivers for the "horse Indians . . . so that you will be satisfied." His shameless spin did not impress the headmen, and they insisted that he hear what they had to say. They were determined, if need be, to die in their homelands; even if the Indians were few, they loved their own land best.[18]

Had Stevens agreed to reserve larger and better lands for the Nisqually and the Puyallup, if the Duwamish and related groups in their watershed had had land reserved for them at the Point Elliott Council, there probably would have been no war west of the Cascades, and Seattle's authority over those over which he had been made head chief would have been enhanced. If Stevens's conciliatory attitude toward Leschi had persisted, the later history of native-white relations might have been more like that envisioned by Seattle. But creating a new reservation for the upriver Duwamish, who fought the Americans, effectively detached them from their downriver kin, who got nothing for their support of the Americans except more reasons to ignore and despise Seattle.

That summer, George Paige replaced Haley as Indian agent at Fort Kitsap, the third in less than six months. In his first annual report to James W. Nesmith, Stevens's replacement as territorial superintendent of Indian affairs, Paige described the "most unamiable feelings" that divided the Suquamish at Fort Kitsap from their uprooted Duwamish kin, who, he said, regarded them "with feelings of hatred." Aware of the ties to their homelands and their social connections, he wrote, "These two tribes are not actually hostile; on the contrary they are intermarried and frequently visit each other. The feeling of animosity was caused by a former feud and will prevent their living peaceably together on the reservation." The feud harked back to upriver conflict with downriver groups, over trade, the treaty, and with the fact that the Suquamish had a reservation while the Duwamish did not.[19]

Paige sought a remedy. After failing to move several hundred Duwamish back to Fort Kitsap, he received permission from Governor Stevens to create a subagency at Holderness Point, today's Duwamish Head, on Elliott Bay, where he placed a number of Duwamish in the care of subagent James Goudy. Reassured, Curley and his people joined them there. Paige had orders to keep them off the river, and since they were home and the salmon had yet to run, they obeyed.

Bolstered by the successful negotiation at Fox Island and believing that the volunteers had won a victory on the Grande Ronde, Stevens summoned interior groups to meet him in September for a second Walla Walla Council, where he expected to solidify a peace and force the surrender of those he branded guilty of starting the war. But the volunteers' "victory" had actually been a massacre of women, children, and old men, which shocked and enraged native groups who had put themselves at risk supporting the Americans, and at Walla Walla the native leaders Stevens had assumed would be compliant were furious. They would surrender no one, and after the council's angry conclusion, Stevens and his party were attacked and driven to seek protection from regular army troops encamped nearby under the command of Major Edward Steptoe, who had no love for the governor. Shocked and humiliated, Stevens returned to Olympia in no mood to be merciful to those he regarded as enemies.

Leschi headed his short list. Destitute and nearly naked, the Nisqually war leader showed up at Fort Nisqually in October 1856, asking Tolmie and Tolmie's assistant, Edward Huggins, for powder and shot to hunt in order to survive. He also offered to cut off his right hand as a sign of peace. They refused his offer and did not give him supplies but, moved by his plight, advised him to remain hidden until tempers cooled.

Leschi traveled past the charred ruins of his birth village to a distant fishing camp on the upper Nisqually, where traumatized kin were gathering salmon, but he found no solace there. In anger, his nephew Sluggia and another man seized him and handed him over to Sydney Ford for a reward of fifty blankets.[20]

At the confluence of the White and Black Rivers, soldiers tired of short rations invited the Duwamish at Holderness Point to build weirs and catch fish for them. Paige complained, but when Goudy visited the Duwamish subchief at William's camp and ordered the Indians who had returned there back to the subagency, William told him he would see Governor Stevens and all his agents in hell before they would move. As he had told Simmons before, he wanted to meet with the governor to tell him that this was their country. If the Americans wanted peace, they must not try to make them leave.[21]

On the Sound, roving groups of northern Indians continued to unnerve residents. As part of the normal rotation of ships and commanders, the *Decatur* departed Puget Sound in February, replaced by Swartwout on the *Massachusetts*, armed with nine guns. Learning that Port Townsend businesses encouraged the northerners to trade at their town, he suggested to Stevens that the prospect of being arrested and tried for obstructing federal policy might cause the merchants to reconsider. But some northern rovers had not come to trade. In June, two northern canoes stopping briefly at Fort Kitsap kept tensions high until they departed. Sensing trouble, Seattle asked Paige to bring his people in from Port Gamble and Port Ludlow. All was quiet until October, when a native band from Russian Alaska seized a small schooner near Seattle, killing a crewman and wounding another. Settlers' cabins north of Olympia were looted, and sixty northerners plundered the Nisqually reserve on Fox Island.[22]

Having pursued a group of raiders into Port Gamble near the tip of Kitsap Peninsula, where Maine lumbermen George Pope and Frederick

Talbot operated the Puget Mill Co., Swartwout made several attempts to parley, but the northerners were in no mood to talk. The next morning, November 21, Swartwout moved *Massachusetts* and the steamer *Traveler* nearer their camp, across from the mill. As workers watched from a blockhouse, he ran out his guns and put marines and a howitzer ashore. The northerners hid behind logs and trees, taking aim with their muskets. A cannon on *Traveler* boomed, the shore erupted in fire, and *Massachusetts* ripped the camp with round shot and grapeshot. The attack was over in twenty minutes. As native survivors fled to the woods, marines torched their huts and smashed their canoes.[23]

One crewman was wounded, but Gustavus Engelbrecht, who had peeked over a log to see whom he had shot, became the first member of the US Navy killed in action in the Pacific. With twenty-seven Indians killed and many wounded, the northerners were defiant, but hunger forced their surrender. Swartwout ferried eighty-seven to Lasqueti Island, near to Russian Alaska from which they had originally come, in the Gulf of Georgia and then sent them north in six provisioned canoes with a warning never to return. The Indians said they bore no grudge, had behaved badly, and would go home and stay there. Americans cheered the drubbing, but Seattle and others were less sanguine.

Other problems assailed the native people concentrated in the camps. With winter's approach, restrictions on fishing, hunting, and gathering threatened famine. William's defiance voiced the question the military could not answer: If the Great White Father would not care for his children, why should they obey?

In December, Simmons boarded the schooner *Eclipse* with a cargo of flour, bread, beef, coffee, and molasses for the natives at Fort Kitsap. Seattle and Nowachise oversaw the distribution and, at a public meeting, expressed gratitude and concern. As before, Seattle let others speak for him. They wanted to know when the treaty would be ratified and the schoolhouse erected for their grandchildren. Nowachise wanted a church built, and when the meeting ended, he asked everyone to stay as he knelt to ask the Great Spirit to foster the feelings of friendship and kindness.[24]

Beyond Fort Kitsap, desperation gave way to anger. Traders and whiskey sellers told native people that Simmons's presents were actually payment for land. At Penn Cove, Goliah, George Snaetlum, and other

Skagit headmen argued that "they could not understand why the whites should commence the survey and division of their land before it was known whether the Treaty for the sale of their land had been approved by the government." At Skagit Head, Snohomish headmen voiced the same complaints. At Port Gamble, Tsitz-a-mah-han told Simmons, a tad sarcastically, that while he personally did not believe the stories he heard, he had trouble persuading his people otherwise, "many of whom had not the same confidence in the white man's faith which he had." Shaken, Simmons warned Stevens that "unless the Treaties are ratified and we enter upon the performance of their stipulations within eighteen months it will not be safe for a white family to live within the limits of the Puget Sound District."[25]

For the Duwamish and the Suquamish, a straitened life beholden to government agents was nothing like the broad autonomy they had known, and the move to separate them from towns left them prey to poverty and despair. In her book *Indians in the Making*, historian Alexandra Harmon writes that the designation of native people as "Indians" was and remains a long, fraught process, and that, through their abundant interactions, native and nonnative people "were continually defining and redefining themselves in contradistinction to each other." The challenge facing Seattle's people was finding a way to survive in an increasingly American world. They had to change, to redefine themselves, but how? Remembering Challacum, Seattle approached the priests.[26]

On Puget Sound, these were the Oblates of Mary Immaculate, a French missionary order founded in 1816, whom Francis Norbert Blanchet and his brother Augustin invited to minister to the Indians after the failure of the Whidbey Island mission. Led by Father Pascal Ricard, forty-two years old and in poor health, a little band of five priests departed Le Havre, France, in January 1847 for New York, traveled overland to the Columbia Basin on the eve of the Whitman Massacre, and founded several missions, most of which were destroyed in the wars. They had better luck west of the Cascades, where Father Ricard purchased land on Budd Inlet, north of Smithfield, and founded the Saint Joseph of New Market Mission.

Joined by Fathers Louis-Joseph d'Herbomez and Eugene Casimir Chirouse, the missionaries gradually established a rapport with native people, which deepened over time. As word of the mission spread, people traveled great distances for religious instruction, and by the early

1850s, as many as forty boys were studying in a frame schoolhouse with high windows, which served as a chapel. Those who died there were buried in a nearby hillside cemetery. All of this the Oblates detailed in letters to their superiors.[27]

After receiving instruction at the mission in 1855, Patkanim, Sehalapahan, and Chowitsuit were given Catholic ladders—the pictorial catechisms—and sent back as catechists to prepare their people for d'Herbomez's July visit. In the depths of war, the people were receptive when he arrived, and on the Swinomish reserve, a number of people confessing their sinfulness publicly whipped themselves "to show the sincerity of their repentance." At Bellingham Bay, d'Herbomez visited more than three hundred Lummi assembled by Chowitsuit to pray and sing.[28]

Joined by Chirouse on a second tour, late in the summer of 1856, d'Herbomez enjoyed even greater success. The priests spent six weeks on the lower Sound preaching to native groups that crowded into the camps and baptizing 150 infants on Whidbey Island. Joining them was Patkanim, whose newfound piety was not without its critics. A Snoqualmie man, Peter, upbraided him, arguing that if he prayed he could not fight and if he fought he could not pray. Having killed and beheaded many, Peter said, Patkanim must give up the ladders.

D'Herbomez praised the faith of the Indian converts who fought beside the Americans and recommended their captives to God before killing them. But if he applauded Peter's zeal, he lamented that simple souls like him were unable yet to distinguish between "an unjust war and a just one," a sophistry not lost on Patkanim, who kept the ladders.[29]

Seattle had escaped notice during the first tour but appeared in the Oblate's letters near the end of the second, when he invited the priests to visit his people at Fort Kitsap. This was sensational news, and d'Herbomez and Chirouse enthusiastically undertook a third tour in October to the "Reserve de Seatle," where the old chief and Indian agent Paige greeted them warmly. "They now have houses of planks," d'Herbomez wrote to Ricard, "which they have built themselves or which were made by the whites so their camp looks like a small village."[30]

The generosity of Seattle and his wife impressed the priests, who were put up in a neat frame dwelling in sight of Old Man House. After sixty years, only a few uprights held rafters, but d'Herbomez could still marvel at its construction. Carved on posts facing the interior were "the figures of men and women (au naturel)," but, he noted warmly, "the chief and his wife are the best images."

The seventy-year-old chief began his rigorous preparation for baptism into the Church. Morning prayers were followed by lessons from the Catholic ladder and a follow-up catechism taught by Chirouse in the Yakama language he had learned east of the mountains, translated into Xwəljutsid by locals. After a noon break, lessons resumed until after dinner, when neophytes practiced prayers and hymns in the Jargon. For these, d'Herbomez noted that "they have a very great hunger," and Paige observed that the preaching and baptism of infants "had a good effect on the Indians."[31]

Eventually the Oblates returned to the Saint Joseph Mission, where Seattle and his retinue presumably visited to continue their instruction, as had Patkanim, Chowitsuit, and Sehalapahan. That fall and winter, many native people arrived at the Saint Joseph Mission for instruction. To aid in the memorization of prayers and hymns, pictures, religious medals, and crosses were given to children as prizes, and, according to the priests, the parents' enthusiasm rivaled that of the children. "Despite the cold," wrote d'Herbomez, "despite the rain, despite the wind, nothing stops them." One group marched two days in snow up to their hips and traveled another two in canoes, through cold so intense that one of their babies died in camp. "If we were able to continue despite the perils," a survivor told the Oblates, "it was because we knew the priests loved us; they think of us as their children and they want our true happiness, because they came here for nothing except to teach us the true road that leads to heaven."[32]

By establishing catechists in each group to teach and to baptize infants born dead, the Oblates hoped to create core Catholic communities. Spiritual salvation was paramount, but like earlier counterparts, the priests also believed that by practicing Christian virtues converts could better survive change in an often-chaotic world. This agreed with Seattle's exhortation to his people at Point Elliott to "watch and learn" from the Changers.

Kitsap's way of the destroying raid no longer worked. The way of Leschi forced Americans to compromise, but the battle could not be sustained. In this new dispensation, headmen had to offer their people a way of living that Americans would tolerate. Steilacoom and the Snohomish headman Sehalapahan, "the Priest," became religious leaders in their communities, and Patkanim, Chowitsuit, and Goliah followed suit. It may be too easy to see Patkanim's conversion as a means to erase American distrust, but wealthy Chowitsuit was a savvy political leader, and Goliah's sincerity was heartfelt. That they began their instruction at the time of the treaty councils suggests a conscious effort to garner priests, and even the Hudson's Bay Company, as allies at a crucial time, to better navigate the currents assailing native communities. That it took Seattle more than a year to join them suggests that he was slow off the mark, but his reticence may also have reflected his determination to see how they fared before making his own decision.

D'Herbomez's mention of Fort Kitsap as Seattle's reservation and Paige's calling its residents "Seattle's tribe" highlighted a new type of native community, where leaders, backed by American authority, exercised far greater power than before. Fort Kitsap adjoined the ancient village at Agate Passage, but as the new name suggested, the community was organized along more martial lines. Where earlier breaches of custom had been mediated by exchanges of property, expulsion, or murder, American punishments—flogging and hanging—enforced social and moral codes. Seattle and his subchiefs enforced a severe moral regime. Back in March, he and Now-a-chais had wanted three troublemakers killed, and in June, he and his subchiefs had two men and three women held because of "bad conduct" until they promised to reform. The Oblates reported that among Catholic groups, moral lapses were enforced by flogging: ten lashes for brawling and twenty for sexual infractions and drunkenness.[33]

The power of reservation chiefs was backed by the agent in charge, who had recourse to courts and the military. Agents manipulated behavior by withholding or dispensing goods. To reduce indolence, Paige cut the food allowance. When an agent had chiefs distribute bushels of potatoes, bags of flour, kegs of molasses, and tobacco twists, it was a gift-giving few could match. In the earlier tug-of-war over the Duwamish, Curley's refusal to accept supplies from Maynard had underscored Maynard's power to co-opt his authority. This was the American strategy: if agents could control the chiefs, and the chiefs could control the people, the

Indian problem was manageable. Freedom of maneuver was permitted if agent and chief understood one another.

Paige and Seattle got along well: on Seattle's advice, he did not intervene when a native man was killed to settle a blood feud, and Paige was confident that in the event of an outbreak, Seattle would provide intelligence and keep his people friendly. As his friend, Paige made Seattle a wooden high-backed rocking chair to satisfy the old man's desire to ease his tired frame and to live in a more American manner.[34]

As the weather improved, families from the Snohomish River and Hood Canal went to the Saint Joseph Mission. In mid-February 1857, twenty canoes arrived from Fort Kitsap, the small flags fluttering from their gunwales presenting "the image of a small flotilla." This was Seattle, described by d'Herbomez in a March 30 letter to his French superiors, "one of the grand chiefs of the Bay who had come with most of his people to finish his instruction and be baptized!"[35]

In a June 30 semiannual report to Simmons, however, Paige wrote that "nothing of any moment" had happened at Fort Kitsap, suggesting that d'Herbomez's mention of "his people" referred to Seattle's family and other catechumens. We do not know their percentage among the 650 people at Fort Kitsap, but despite the spiritual divide, d'Herbomez considered it a good beginning.

For Seattle, it was momentous, but since the Oblates baptized people on a regular basis, they did not describe this single occasion in their letters. However, because the rite followed a printed rubric, it can be reconstructed. Although Seattle's responses in the Jargon were scripted, the dialog puts us at his side during the event and helps convey the rites' august, collaborative tone.[36]

It was held at the school chapel. Father Ricard had been in poor health, aggravated by the difficulty of dealing with the prickly bishop of Nisqually, and in January 1857, d'Herbomez was appointed temporary administrator. Ricard left for France in early March, leaving d'Herbomez and Chirouse to carry out the baptisms. Because Seattle was an important figure, d'Herbomez was probably the one who baptized him. He wore a white stole over his black soutane. Chirouse, assisting, wore a white alb. Seattle was dressed in trousers and a loose-fitting white shirt that could be opened so his chest could be anointed with oil.

As baptismal candidates and their sponsors assembled in the chapel, d'Herbomez read, in Latin, from Psalm 8, "Oh Lord, our Lord, how glorious is your name over all the earth"; from Psalm 29, "Give to the Lord, you sons of God, give to the Lord glory and praise"; and from Psalm 42, "As the hind longs for the running waters, so my soul longs for you, oh God," followed by antiphonal prayers. Then, with clove-scented breath, he addressed the candidate. *"Quo nomine vocaris?"* he said. ("What is your name?")

Seattle's sponsor, his baptized godparent, placed his hand on Seattle's shoulder, and if he did not translate the Latin into the Jargon, Chirouse did. We do not know who his sponsor was; canon law forbid members of religious orders from taking the role, but Seattle answered d'Herbomez directly, giving his chosen baptismal name, Noah, which appears as Noe′ Siatle in the Oblates' earliest surviving sacramental register from Puget Sound, dating from October 1857.[37]

D'Herbomez continued: "Noah, what do you ask of the Church of God?"

Having been taught the questions and responses beforehand, Seattle likely responded in the Jargon, *"Mitlite kopa Saghalie Tyee."* ("Life with God," or "Faith.") The following Jargon words and phrases closely approximate the rite's wording.

"What does faith offer you?"

*"Mitlite kwanesum."* ("Life always," or "Eternal life.")

D'Herbomez enjoined Seattle to keep God's word and to love [*tikegh*] people, and he professed that there was one God but three God-people: the Father, the Son, and the Holy Spirit (the breath of God), but all three were one God. Then he asked Seattle to make baptismal promises similar to those Demers had the people agree to on Whidbey Island.

"Noah, do you renounce Satan?" d'Herbomez said.

*"Nawitka,"* Seattle responded. ("Indeed, yes.")

"And all his works?"

*"Yes."*

"And all his allurements?"

*"Yes."*

"Do you believe in God, the Father Almighty, creator of heaven and earth?"

*"Yes."*

"Do you believe in Jesus Christ, his only son, our Lord, who was born into this world and who suffered?"

*"Yes."*

"Do you believe also in the Holy Spirit, the Holy Catholic Church, the communion of saints, the forgiveness of sins, the resurrection of the body, and life everlasting?"

*"Yes."*

D'Herbomez breathed three times on Seattle's face, saying: "Depart from him, unclean spirit, and give place to the Holy Spirit, the Consoler." Breathing in the form of a cross again on Seattle's face, he said, "Noah, through this rite of breathing upon you, receive the good spirit and the blessing of God. Peace be with you."

*"Weght mika,"* Seattle said. ("Also you.")

With his thumb, d'Herbomez made the sign of the cross on Seattle's forehead and on his broad chest, praying aloud as he did so that Noah would live a good life, turn away from evil spirits and their images, and worship only the one true God, the Father and the Son "who will come to judge the living and the dead and the world by fire."

To this, Seattle responded, *"Kloshe kahkwa."* ("Good thought," or "Amen.")

D'Herbomez asked God's mercy and marked Seattle again with his thumb. "I sign you on the forehead that you may take up the Lord's cross. I sign you on the ears that you may listen attentively to God's commands. I sign you on the eyes that you may see God's glory. I sign you on the nostrils that you may perceive the sweet fragrance of Christ. I sign you on the breast that you may believe in God. I sign you on the shoulders that you may take upon yourself the yoke of his service."

So it went. Praying again for divine protection and mercy, the priest placed his hand on Seattle's head, praying that he be seasoned by divine wisdom, and taking a pinch of salt from a plate, he touched it to Seattle's lips with another prayer. Commanding him to kneel, he undertook a triple exorcism, having Seattle repeat the Lord's Prayer as far as "deliver us from evil" (*"mamuk tlac nsayea copa mashatshi"*), at which point he had Seattle and his sponsor make the sign of the cross. Then, laying his hands on Seattle's forehead, d'Herbomez prayed that God would send his angels to lead him to grace, and commanded the devil to depart. This was done three times.

The priest then led candidates and sponsors inside the church to the baptismal font, likely a basin on a table, where he had them prostrate themselves on the plank floor and then rise to recite with him the complete Lord's Prayer and the Apostles' Creed. After moistening the end of his finger with his tongue, d'Herbomez touched Seattle's ears and nostrils, and prayed again, recalling Christ's healing the deaf man at Bethany. Again, the priest asked Seattle to state his name, and to renounce Satan, his works, and his allurements.

Then he anointed the old chief with the oil of catechumens (olive oil that had been blessed on Maundy Thursday—the Thursday in Holy Week marking the Last Supper). Making the sign of the cross on his breast and between his shoulders, d'Herbomez thrice commanded the devil to depart. He asked Seattle a third time to give his name and asked again, "Noah, what is it that you are seeking?"

"Baptism."

"Noah, do you wish to be baptized?"

*"Yes."*

D'Herbomez had Seattle lean over the basin. Taking a pitcher of holy water, the priest poured some on Seattle's head in the form of a cross, saying, "Noah, I baptize you in the name of the Father" (he pours a second time) "and of the Son" (he pours the third time) "and of the Holy Spirit." Then, dipping his thumb in a vial of holy chrism (a mixture of olive oil and fragrant balsam resin), he signed the cross on Seattle's head, saying, "May Almighty God, the Father of our Lord Jesus Christ, who has given you a new birth by means of water and the Holy Spirit and forgiven all your sins anoint you with the chrism of salvation in the same Christ Jesus our Lord so that you may have everlasting life." Placing a white cloth on Seattle's head, he said, "Receive this white garment. Never let it become stained, so that when you stand before the judgment seat of our Lord Jesus Christ, you may have life everlasting."

The baptized were traditionally given a lit candle, a symbol of the spiritual light in which they would meet the Lord and saints in heaven. But the Oblates were poor, and their purchases did not include tapers, so the ceremony probably ended with a farewell: "Noah [and sponsor], go in peace, and the Lord be with you."

*"Kloshe Kahkwa."*

Few things were more important in Puget Salish society than a person's name. A supernatural guardian might give someone a name in a vision, and this was so personal that it was rarely revealed. Seattle had received his ancestral name at a *sgwi'gwi*. His Hudson's Bay Company nickname, Le Gros, described his powerful frame. Because a baptismal name marked one's new identity as a follower of Christ, the baptisms of native leaders were important religiously and politically, and the names chosen by them were often those of biblical patriarchs, such as Noah and Jacob, or figures like Joseph and Moses, who had led their peoples at critical times and enjoyed God's favor. Candidates sometimes chose names for reasons other than what the priests preferred. During the 1838 mission at Fort Vancouver, Challacum noted that "that man Noah had more children than the first man, Adam." Seattle appears to have chosen the name Noah as the ultimate survivor, one who trusted in God and preserved his people after their old world was drowned in a great flood.[38]

We have noted earlier that one of Seattle's brothers was baptized David; another, John. Surviving sons were baptized James and George, the Christian names of HBC officers James Douglas and George Simpson, associating them with the powers of their namesakes. We don't know if Curley was baptized. Angeline's baptismal name is not known, but we know she was a baptized Catholic. She named her daughters Mary and Elizabeth (called Betsy) for Jesus's mother and the mother of John the Baptist. Given the number of canoes that accompanied Seattle on the occasion of his baptism, we can imagine his family participated in the sacrament with him, underscoring the importance he placed on it.

It has been fashionable to suppose native people had little idea of what baptism was about, but this ignores their rigorous preparation for the sacrament and its collaborative nature. Most baptized Indians remained loyal to their faith, and some, like Seattle, renewed it later by receiving the sacrament of Confirmation. Seattle became a Catholic despite being aware that American Protestants regarded Catholics with suspicion. In fact, the social distance between American Protestants and native Catholics likely appealed to Seattle's sense of native dignity, as a person belonging to a people who knew who they were and intended on navigating the evangelical American tide in their own canoe.

A story about Seattle that native informants told pioneer Samuel Coombs may refer to this effort. Seattle was said to have developed a common language, spoken from the Snohomish River to the head of Puget Sound, the dialect range of Xwəljutsid. Linguists accept that the dialect evolved over a period far longer than the life of one man, so what could the story have meant? According to anthropologist Nile Thompson, Puget Sound Salish underwent a change at the time of settlement, when, for example, consonants such as *m* became *b*, so that what was heard as "muck-muck-wum" became Ba'qbaqʷab. Other informants have said that the Jargon became more widespread after settlement. It is true that the way the people spoke after the Americans came was different than before, and given Seattle's pivotal role during this transformative period, some may have attributed the change to him.[39]

As groups dispersed during the spring of 1857, fear of northerners returning to avenge those killed at Port Gamble deepened, and Seattle, Patkanim, and other chiefs relayed what they heard to Governor Stevens, who passed it on to Commander Swartwout on board the *Massachusetts*. On the lower Sound, settlers built blockhouses, and Whidbey Island Skagits, whose stockade the Americans had burned in 1854, asked Simmons for tools to build another. Settlers petitioned Swartwout to stay until the *Massachusetts* was relieved by the navy surveying steamer *John Hancock*, but citing his vessel's need for maintenance, Swartwout and his ship left for San Francisco on April 1, repeating the stupefying American penchant for leaving threatened people unprotected.

No American official bothered to ask native people to help defend the region. Patkanim had done so; Seattle had offered to do so, and as Kitsap's heir, his would have been a powerful voice. Alliance with an armed native force, similar to Patkanim's, could have inspired fraternity, but when it came to dealing with native people, neither sense nor imagination were the strong suits of American officials.

In the vacuum, Chowitsuit invited lower Sound, Fraser River, and southeastern Vancouver Island groups to a great *sgwi'gwi* held at Gooseberry Point, across from Lummi Island, to discuss the threat posed by northern raiders. These were largely the Lekwiltok that the Cowichan and their lower Sound allies fought in the early 1840s, but by the 1850s, groups from the Stickeen River in northern British Columbia and from the Alaskan coast also threatened.

Edmund Fitzhugh, Indian agent on Bellingham Bay, and US Army captain George Pickett, posted to the settlement of Whatcom to protect settlers, requested a canoe to visit the gathering, but the Indians removed themselves and their canoes from the bay's eastern shore. When Fitzhugh and Pickett finally arrived, they found the headmen drunk and Patkanim supposedly so hungover that he was unable to meet with them. They knew that something was amiss, and their suspicion turned to alarm when they learned that the Indians had made peace with the northerners.[40]

The old hobgoblin of a local alliance with the northern raiders stared Americans in the face, and Michael Simmons spent several days arguing fruitlessly that the native people should not trust the northerners. Seattle's involvement in the accord sounds in Simmons's report to Stevens: "My opinion is that in the event of an attack of the Northern Indians we could not expect nor could we receive the slightest assistance from any Indians on the Sound."

If Seattle remained a friend to the Americans, he had no intention of embracing their stupidity, and in subsequent meetings he became increasingly blunt. At a great council east of the mountains, Indians were said to have debated resuming the war, but Simmons noted that if chiefs west of the mountains had been invited, none had gone. In April, Seattle told him eastern Indians would attack after the berries were ripe, emphasizing that this came from his sources, and that he wished Simmons to have advance warning. He had already told Paige that the Yakama had asked him to join in a renewed war against the whites if Leschi was hanged. The Americans needed to be reminded who their friends were and why they had enemies.[41]

Indeed, Leschi had become a cause célèbre among both Indians and whites, and his trial commanded attention. He had been indicted for the murder of A. Benton Moses, a soldier who was killed while delivering dispatches from Captain Maloney to Olympia. When his trial, held at Steilacoom Barracks on November 17, 1856, resulted in a hung jury, a second trial took place in Olympia on March 18, 1857. Pioneer Ezra Meeker wrote that the change of venue had allowed Stevens's supporters to pack the jury, and after Leschi was found guilty, Judge Lander sentenced him to hang. Immediately, his attorneys, William Wallace and Frank Clark, prepared an appeal to be heard by the territorial supreme court in December, and, in the interim, Leschi was returned to prison at the Steilacoom Barracks to await the court's decision.[42]

Traveling to Port Townsend in April 1857, Simmons saw a huge northern canoe carrying thirty to forty native men, but he could not get his frightened crew to approach close enough for him to demand that they leave. At Port Townsend, armed citizens ordered away other northerners, who left "most reluctantly." Then more canoes appeared, one carrying sixty men.[43]

At Whatcom, northern raiders bullied settler Louis Lascher, plundered his house, and announced they would have the heads of Agent Fitzhugh and Captain Pickett. A week later, they attacked a group from Fort Kitsap, killing one man and wounding two. When Paige visited the Fort Kitsap reservation in early May, he found it deserted.

Some of its residents had fled to Port Madison or Port Orchard, but others had moved to Elliott Bay, where Maynard promised protection. Paige accused him of tampering with his charges and complained that he had tried to get him dismissed after refusing Maynard payment for claims against the Bureau of Indian Affairs. Like many, Maynard had suffered financial loss during the war and had struggled to make ends meet, but he had become unpopular with many in town, and the man who had helped Seattle create a hybrid community made plans to follow the Duwamish to the west side of the bay.

David Maynard offered ammunition and timber for a blockhouse at Holderness Point, enhancing its status as a subreserve. In July, he exchanged 260 of his acres in town for 320 of Charles Terry's at New York Alki, and he left with Catherine for their new home. George Paige gave ammunition to his charges at Fort Kitsap and offered to build them a blockhouse, too, but by July only seventy-five had returned.

In July, Isaac Stevens was elected territorial delegate to Congress by a wide margin in what was regarded as a referendum on his handling of the war. At the same time, President James Buchanan appointed Virginia Congressman Fayette McMullen as Stevens's gubernatorial replacement, who would arrive in the territory when Stevens departed in August.

Meanwhile, a tense quiet prevailed on the Sound until the evening of August 11, when northerners landed on Whidbey Island and approached Isaac Ebey's house. At about one in the morning, his dog began to bark, and when he went out to check, the raiders shot him down and sawed his head off with a knife. Having avenged Port Gamble with the death of a white tyee, they vanished, taking the head with them. It remained for the Hudson's Bay Company to retrieve his scalp and return it to his grieving family three years later. As it had after the death of Lieutenant Slaughter, a wave of horror rippled through the white community.

Among native people crowded in the camps, influenza raged as summer gave way to fall, and children died of whooping cough. For those who had returned to their traditional villages, drought ravaged the potato crop, and repeating the previous year's lapse, salmon failed to enter rivers in large numbers. Shamans were blamed for the mortality. With murder already in the air, Simmons reported famine from Cape Flattery to the head of the Sound and noted ruefully that many of his charges sought the oblivion offered by the liquor trade, "in its usual flourishing state."

In December, Michael Simmons called the groups named in the Medicine Creek Treaty to assemble at Squaxin Island near Olympia for the first distribution of annuities. Seattle and others came to observe, and on January 8, 1858, in the presence of Simmons and McMullen, the new governor, native interpreter John Hiton called householders forward to receive a blanket and four and a half yards of cloth for each person in their house, an amount worth not quite three dollars. Hiton told McMullen that the people wanted the next payment in money but cautioned him about the influence of whiskey sellers.

Then Seattle, Duke of York, and ten other headmen approached McMullen and asked him to pardon Leschi. McMullen put them off, saying he had not decided what to do in the case, but that strict justice would be his guide.

Even though the Medicine Creek treaty had been ratified in March 1855, less than three months after it was signed, it took the government nearly three years to meet its first obligation. Although the Point Elliott Treaty was signed less than a month after Medicine Creek, it would not even be ratified until 1859. Simmons wrote to Indian affairs superintendent James Nesmith, noting in disgust that while those who had murdered and waged war had gotten their treaty ratified and received annuities, those who had risked much to remain faithful allies were put off by promises.[44]

By then, Paige had convinced nearly four hundred Indians to return to Fort Kitsap, but the Duwamish remained at Holderness Point with Maynard. Seattle resumed his old itinerary, traveling from Fort Kitsap to town to exercise his authority among the Duwamish, to restore his leadership among his disaffected people and maintain contacts with Indian agents, farmers, and merchants.

In December, the territorial supreme court denied Leschi's appeal, but when it came time to hang him, sympathetic settlers and army officers had the Pierce County sheriff and hangman arrested for selling liquor to the Indians, holding them until the time of execution had passed. The trick gave Leschi a few more weeks but infuriated those who wanted the sentence carried out.

In the meantime, Colonel Silas Casey, commander of Fort Steilacoom, condemned the planned execution as "murder at best" and refused to allow it at the fort, forcing territorial officials to erect a gallows in a nearby gully. In jail, Leschi took religious instruction from Father Louis Rossi, an Italian missionary priest, and was baptized a Catholic.

On the morning of February 19, 1858, Leschi of the Nisquallies, who twelve years earlier had offered incoming Americans the hand of friendship, climbed the gallows. He went calmly and without assistance before a silent crowd of whites and Indians, according to his jailer, Charles Granger. Arms tied, he bowed his head in prayer for ten minutes and then addressed the crowd. He said he had made his peace with God and forgave all except the man whose perjury resulted in his guilty verdict. On him, he called down the judgment of heaven. The rope was adjusted around his neck, a cap drawn over his eyes, and at 11:35 a.m., the trapdoor was sprung.

---

Winter's doldrums gripped the territory until word of new gold strikes blew in from the Fraser River in what would soon become the British Crown Colony of British Columbia. In early March, local papers announced that permits to enter the mining district could be obtained in

Victoria. Bellingham Bay coal miners were among the first to join the stampede; soldiers abandoned their posts, and by April, lumber mills along the Sound had shut down for want of workers. In only six weeks, Victoria had turned into a latter-day San Francisco as thousands poured in, the overflow sloshing back to Whatcom, which mushroomed into a tent city of ten thousand.

Word of attacks on travelers to the goldfields fueled concern about undefeated native forces east of the mountains. Anxiety spiked in early May, when Major Edward Steptoe and 164 soldiers were defeated at the Battle of Pine Creek by Spokane and Coeur d'Alene warriors. But dispatches from the war ground were swamped by news from the new El Dorado, and the region seemed poised to boom. The Fraser River Stampede, as this gold rush would come to be known, was an extravaganza that diverted attention from painful realities and allowed settlers to ignore problems that wouldn't go away.

Seattle did not escape criticism, as bitter voices complained that once his Americans got hold of the land, they conveniently forgot their promises. In May, Michael Simmons visited native groups on the Sound to laud their patience and hear their grievances. At Fort Kitsap, Seattle confronted him. He had no one to speak for him now. Despite the filter of the Jargon, his fury and despair are palpable.[45]

> I want you to understand what I say. I do not drink rum; neither does New-e-ches, and we constantly advise our people not to do so. I am not a bad man. I am and always have been a friend of the whites. I listen to what Mr. Paige says to me and I do not steal—nor do I or any of my people kill the whites. Oh! Mr. Simmons! why don't our papers come back to us? You always say you hear they will come back, but they do not. I fear we are forgotton or are to be cheated out of our lands. I have been very poor and hungry all winter and am very sick now. In a little while I will die. I would like to be paid for my land before I die. Many of my people died during the cold, scarce winter, without getting their pay. When I die my people will be very poor—they will have no property, no chief, and no one to talk for them. You must not forget them, Mr. Simmons, when I am gone. We are

ashamed when we think that the Puyallups have their papers. They fought against the whites, whilst we, who have never been angry with them, get nothing. When we get our pay we want it in money. The Indians are not bad. It is the mean white men who are bad to us. If any person writes that we do not want our papers returned: they lie. Oh! Mr. Simmons! you see I am very sick. I want you to write quickly to your great Chief what I say I have done.

# CHAPTER EIGHT

___

*"Shake hands with me before I am laid in the ground."*

On February 27, 1860, Abraham Lincoln delivered a speech in the Great Hall of Cooper Union in New York City. It was meticulously researched, logical as a legal brief, and arguably one of his greatest speeches. In a city not easily impressed, the words of a frontier politician revealed a figure of national consequence. Read nationally, it assured Lincoln's candidacy for US president. The Civil War caused the deaths of nearly a million. It destroyed a region larger than Western Europe, and its wounds have lasted to the present. But if a line connecting events is drawn, neither the speech nor perhaps even the man can be judged causal. Causation derived from ancient hopes facing brutal contradictions that drove antagonists beyond reason to kill or be killed. Yet Lincoln's words defined a moment in that fatal era. Who now can recall a single line from that mighty speech? Yet the spoken word written down gains peculiar power. Lincoln's speech at Cooper Union bequeathed immortality to his later words and to the man himself. Like the stars at night whose patterns recall ancient heroes, written words last and crown those who weave them into meaning.

In the summer of 1858, Colonel George Wright defeated the Spokane, Coeur d'Alene, and Palouse Indians at Spokane Plains and Four Lakes, slaughtered their horses, destroyed their winter stores, and hanged their chiefs. Unarmed, the Upper Yakama leader Owhi was killed during a desperate escape, and his brother, the Yakama leader Kamiakin, wounded, fled across the border. The war was over, and the Americans had won. West of the mountains, Kitsap's own Green River people murdered him, and in late November, Patkanim, that most controversial and agile practitioner of frontier realpolitik, was murdered in Seattle. His people maintain he was assassinated because of his failure to gain them a reservation, but he had sired many enemies during his turbulent life. The *Pioneer and Democrat* sneered at his death. "It is well enough

188

perhaps," the paper said, "that 'Pat Kanim' is out of the way. We never had a particle of confidence in his professions of friendship." But Henry Yesler, who knew better, paid the funeral costs and buried him in Seattle, the town he helped defend.[1]

After prospectors winnowed the easy pickings from the Fraser River, the gold fever faded quickly. As the approach of civil war gripped Americans' minds, Oregon faded from the national gaze, and distant Washington Territory licked its wounds in a regional depression. Frustrated when the Indians at Muckleshoot were added to his already onerous responsibilities, George Paige left Fort Kitsap, and Michael Simmons hired David Maynard to replace him as subagent at sixty dollars a month. Assured of a sinecure, however slim, Maynard focused on his Alki farm, relying on Seattle and his subchiefs to keep their scattered people in line. In a November letter to his son, he described the old chief in his house "continually putling in his clack of jargon. I have the agency over them & therefore must treat him well."[2]

Of the head chiefs signing the Treaty of Point Elliott, only Seattle and Chowitsuit remained, and Chowitsuit had not long to live. Consumed by impending crisis, Congress did not ratify the treaty until March 8, 1859, and it took nearly two years before functioning reservations could be organized. During that time, Fort Kitsap became the Port Madison Reservation, and temporary subagencies, such as that at Holderness Point, were subsumed into the designated reservations, leaving Duwamish hopes hanging for one along their river.[3]

Ratification abolished slavery among signatory groups. By the time the Denny-Low party landed in 1851, Seattle was said to have had eight slaves, but many chose to remain with him in the years following. Ratification also started the clock ticking for the planned removal of thousands of natives to reservations. As the Medicine Creek ratification drew traders eager to profit from removals on the upper Sound, the Point Elliott Treaty reservations promised attractive markets. Maine logger Charles Matthews settled near Agate Point at the northern tip of Bainbridge Island near George Meigs's mill in 1857. The following year, he was joined by his brother to fish and open a trading post to supply native needs.[4]

The Oblates also made plans. Father Eugene Casimir Chirouse built a cabin near the mouth of the Snohomish in September 1857. Father

Pierre-Paul Durieu and Brother Celestin Verney joined him on the reservation, but a year later they all moved west to a point inevitably named Priest Point. There they cleared land, dedicated a chapel to Saint Francis Savier [Xavier] des Snohomis, established a cemetery, built a school, and planted a garden. As anxious natives arrived to find good house sites, Chirouse celebrated Easter Sunday 1859 with a High Mass, where he baptized four hundred. In a scene reminiscent of Blanchet's and Demers's earlier triumphs, he inspired more than five hundred to publicly renounce gambling, conjuring, fighting, and murder, and to heap their gambling pieces, weapons, and shamanic paraphernalia at his feet. One of these was Wahelchu, related to the Suquamish head chief Kitsap, baptized Jacob. Asking Chirouse to visit, the priest celebrated Mass in Jacob's home, near Old Man House. Chirouse and d'Herbomez had done the same with Seattle in 1856, and encouraged by native sincerity, Chirouse began visits to Port Madison.[5]

In these religious developments, no mention is made of Seattle, despite his recent baptism. It is risky to impute motive based on lack of information, as if to say, "We do not know what Seattle was doing, therefore, he must have been doing thus and so," but it is warranted here. Seattle had authority over native Christians and non-Christians. Despite his very public baptism, he encouraged Jacob Wahelchu to assume religious leadership, because, as head chief, Seattle needed to be open to all those for whom he was responsible, for much the same reason he had remained silent during the lead-up to the Yakima War.

As the Fraser River Stampede subsided, the reflux of Americans to the San Juan Islands where the HBC farmed gained international notice in the late spring of 1859, when a recent arrival, Lyman Cutler, shot an English pig rooting in his garden. Fatally wounded, the pig let out a squeal heard round the world. An ill-defined international border, conflicting claims, and the prickly truculence of the governor of Vancouver Island, James Douglas—still resentful of American acquisition of HBC holdings south of the border—became tinder to the idiotic jingoism of Brigadier General William Harney, US military commander of the Pacific Northwest.

To tin-pot generals and nervous diplomats, this rustic potshot threatened war, and hundreds of troops and several warships rushed to the islands to defend the honor of their respective flags, diverting settlers on both sides, eager for excitement. The comedy, dubbed the Pig War, ended well enough, but like the stampede, it deflected attention from the region's unresolved disputes. Thus began a pattern of immigrations that served to erase unpleasant memories, leading to bouts of historical amnesia.[6]

Threats to this most distant corner of the country prompted Congress to fund a military road from Fort Steilacoom to Fort Bellingham, and several Steilacoom settlers, eager to profit from expected traffic, founded a settlement where they assumed the road would cross the Snohomish River. A path had been blazed to the farther Stillaguamish River when the Pig War petered out and Congress canceled funding, but the little place called Cadyville—then, hopefully, Snohomish City—eventually settled down to just Snohomish. Shortly thereafter, entrepreneurs Morris Frost and Jacob Fowler built a cabin, store, and saloon down at Point Elliott, rendering its native name as Mukilteo.

On June 1, 1859, the Presbyterian minister Edward Geary replaced James Nesmith as territorial superintendent of Indian affairs and moved Michael Simmons from Olympia to the reservation across from Mukilteo, intended as the central reservation on the Sound, to better carry out treaty provisions. Simmons chose a sheltered cove called Txwli'lap, anglicized into Tulalip, meaning "Sand Flat," where an old sawmill still stood from the time of the Point Elliott Treaty, and got it back in operation, cutting lumber for his house and other buildings. In his report to Geary, he applied the name to the timbered reserve he described as "a perfect jungle" and began opening roads to various points, including the Saint Francis Xavier Mission.[7]

On New Year's Day 1861, Chirouse was officially appointed by the government as a teacher at Tulalip, and that spring he requested permission to erect a school at the new location. By July, a handful of native scholars—twenty boys and five girls—assembled for lessons and to cultivate a vegetable garden for help feeding boarders. Initially, classes were held in the priests' cabin or in one of the longhouses erected nearby, but Chirouse thought the longhouse inadequate, since it left "teacher and scholars entirely unprotected from wind and rain." Observing how closely Indians imitated whites, he believed it was essential to keep them away from "the evil disposed and immoral" and put in the charge of government employees who would be "men of good character and, as far as possible, <u>married men</u>" [his underlining].[8]

The spartan vision of uniformed children toiling in the fields at a centralized boarding school required the separation of families. "By this means they will not be obliged to go with their parents to fish, etc. and can devote all their time to the school," Chirouse wrote. He also wanted to increase the number of girls at school, to combat what he believed were the mercenary intentions of their parents. "The chief reason is that the parents of these unfortunate creatures devote them at an early age to the prostitution of the depraved among the Whites for gain." Simmons came to the same conclusion after observing groups from the central Sound selling game and fish to prospectors at Bellingham Bay "and another article that all their women have for sale."[9]

The native people's need to purchase food had become critical when salmon runs failed in the fall of '57 and '58, and the situation worsened as the influx of prospectors drove prices through the roof. Chirouse saw the breakup of native families as a rescue mission, and Gosnell was even more explicit in a report to William Miller, Geary's replacement as territorial superintendent of Indian affairs, appointed in February 1861, stating that the only way to assimilate Indian children was to separate them completely from their parents "and not allow the influences of their savage home to counteract those of the schoolroom." Already, on reservations, native children were being purged of their language and culture, a devastating process happening not just on Puget Sound, but nationally. These were the progeny that Seattle had said would become like the Changers, and this was the school that had been promised, but is this what he had envisioned?[10]

During the war, Indians had accused whites of turning native women into prostitutes. Although Chirouse and Simmons assumed that prostitution was a way native people got money to buy liquor, the charge that they prostituted their young women to do so was overblown. In native society, intermarriage allowed differing groups to lessen potential hostility and develop connections that allowed them to share in each other's resource base. As whites arrived, native people sought to intermarry with them. Now that Americans had the land and were arriving in ever greater numbers, the need to develop connections with them was even more pressing.

Most Americans were young single males, a rambunctious group that the emerging elites looked upon with a jaundiced eye. Eligible white females were few and sedulously guarded. If intermarriage was going to happen, it would be between young white men and native women, which shocked the racial sensibilities of educated middle-class whites like the Blaines. It was easy to interpret a white man paying a bride price in cash as prostitution. In 1855, in an effort to stem miscegenation, the legislature had amended the 1854 Act to Regulate Marriage, banning interracial marriages by levying a fine of as much as $500 on such unions, a law that remained in effect until 1868. But it did little to halt their inception.[11]

The protean researcher and historian Eldridge Morse, a Connecticut native who settled in Washington Territory, published Snohomish County's first newspaper, the *Northern Star*, and practiced law, estimated that between 1855 and 1870, fully 75 percent of the white men in the Puget Sound region outside of major towns were living with native women. We can surmise that at the saloons and bordellos of embryo towns and at outlying sawmills, many native girls were directed by their families to seek white partners. As settlers claimed the best and most productive lands, such liaisons allowed native kin, especially those on isolated reservations, to regain access to resources and connect with white trading networks. In addition, while native men could not vote, the male issue of interracial unions, legitimate or not, could—an important political consequence. Such arrangements were a steep price to pay for membership in the emerging American community, but many native families were willing to pay it, as were Seattle and Curley.[12]

Seattle's plea to Leschi not to kill those whites who had Indian wives underscores the value he placed on such unions. As he aged, he actively encouraged marriages and enjoyed attending wedding ceremonies. His own words and actions suggest that it was through marriage that he thought future generations of his people would become like the Changers. It was, in fact, what he was seeing happen.

The Oblates had developed the school at the Saint Joseph of Newmarket Mission and were building another at Tulalip. Seattle had brought his family to Saint Joseph's to prepare them for baptism, and he accompanied other native children at his Confirmation at Saint Francis Xavier, but these were for brief periods and did not require the rupture of family bonds as Chirouse and Geary envisioned. Since he was a family man himself, his own participation in anything that did would have been at variance with the social engineering planned by Chirouse and Geary.

---

Native people still outnumbered American settlers, and on Elliott Bay, Seattle's hybrid community remained a vital, exotic place through the 1860s. Despite the order to remove themselves to reservations, many native people remained, providing labor and trade to whites happy for their business. Residents recalled native shelters dotting the shore from the Nose north to Madison Street. On the bluffs near Spring Street, a native burial ground still in use was marked by strips of red flannel fluttering from poles above baskets and pails left as grave goods. In the fall of 1859, when twenty-one-year-old Dillis Ward arrived in Seattle, he estimated that about one hundred whites lived in town with an equal number of natives, but he said that the latter number swelled when outlying groups arrived for social and ceremonial events. Another newcomer, David Kellogg, remembered it as "a very small village, really more Indian than white."[13]

An engraving depicting Chief Seattle, center, acting as judge, which appeared in the *Seattle Telegraph* newspaper.

If new white residents found the native presence unsettling, others valued it. Store owner Henry Yesler and his wife, Sarah, appreciated that their Indian customers paid in cash. How well the natives adapted to a cash economy may in part be measured by the success of an Indian counterfeiter who copied the brass tokens Yesler issued his workers in lieu of scarce coin.[14]

The written history of these "dull and quiet times," as historian Frederick Grant labeled them, focused on what would have later meaning: a road over the mountains, the birth of a university, and the effort by Ohio immigrant Asa Mercer, the university's first president, to import marriageable young white women into the territory. But after the chaos of war and gold fever, a hiatus marked by the slower and more predictable familial rhythm of birth, marriage, and death brought peace if not prosperity, and Chief Seattle labored to see that it benefited both native and white.

Working at Yesler's mill, Dillis Ward witnessed Seattle in action amid a native crowd gathered on the waterfront, calling him "a square shouldered, deep chested, stockily built Indian, with a voice like a trumpet." He remembered him wearing trousers, a shirt, and a heavy blanket thrown over his left shoulder, leaving his right arm free to emphasize his words.

In the summer of 1862, Samuel Coombs recalled "an unusually large number of Indians in town; over 100," on the beach, gathered around a circle of seated elders, where Seattle acted as judge, an event sketched from Coombs's recollection by his son Raphael. "I was greatly impressed with the calm and dignified manner in which the old judge disposed of the matter in dispute," Coombs wrote, "and the great attention and respect shown him while speaking." Clarence Bagley, later one of the city's first historians, watched Indians turn their heads to listen to Seattle speak "although he was nearly half a mile away, such was the resonance and carrying power of his voice." Such, too, was the pervading quiet on those soft summer evenings.[15]

In the instance recounted by Bagley, Seattle was engaging in an open-air adult version of what Twana ethnographer William Elmendorf described as "evening lecturing," when children were brought into the longhouse to hear formal instruction in matters of deportment and ethics.[16]

Of these sessions, Samuel Coombs wrote that Seattle "reprimanded them often for drunkenness, fighting, and loose sexual relations with the whites," adding that he militated against blood feud and sought to promote Christian principles among his people. Yet, another of Coombs's descriptions reveals a frankness regarding the body: "During the summer months and when I first saw him he wore but a single garment. That was a Hudson's Bay Company blanket, the folds of which he held together with one hand, and from their midst appeared the broad chest and strong arm of bronze which grasped his staff." Replicated in bronze, with an upraised arm in lieu of a staff, this image of Seattle would be celebrated in the town's first example of public art.

While Seattle could act authoritatively, he was no dictator. A story about him during this time reveals how open his people were with him. While he was on the way to Tulalip to discuss a land issue with the agent, a bowman in one of his canoes was drunk and boastful, and could not steer properly. Because it was winter and travel was dangerous, Seattle bellowed at him to knock it off and behave himself. Unrepentant, the man asked if Seattle would like to see a demonstration of his power. A clap of the drunk man's hands produced a crash of thunder, a bolt of lightning struck the water between the canoes, and a wind brought so much hail, rain, and sleet that the entourage was forced to land and take shelter beneath their canoes. As they huddled and shivered, his people upbraided Seattle, asking, "Why did you not leave him alone? Look what misery your reprimanding him has brought on us!"[17]

We have observed Seattle as a survivor of cataclysm, as an unsettling presence at Fort Nisqually, as a ruthless war leader, as a single-minded impresario, as an influential head chief, and as a Christian convert who successfully navigated the transformation of his world. As more people left written records toward the end of his life, recollections of him became more frequent and personal. Often tinged with rosy sentiment, they describe an old man in the different roles he assumed as arbiter, teacher, judge, and patriarch. Like Muskrat of old, one of the mythic creators of the world, he brought up enough earth from the chaotic sea to make a place for his people to live.

In the process, he endured many humiliations. Around 1860, when Clarence Bagley's future wife, Alice, was about ten years old, she left

Dexter Horton's general store at what is now the intersection of South Washington Street and First Avenue South to go back to her home a block away. The store stood on pilings above mudflats and piles of sawdust from the mill. Two long planks provided a ramp to the street, and as little Alice Mercer raced down the ramp, she saw Seattle coming up, dressed in trousers, a shirt, vest, and coat—in Clarence Bagley's recollection, "each of a different color and texture, and considerably worse for wear," and a high silk "stovepipe" hat. But when Seattle ignored her request to stand aside, she knocked him off into the sawdust. "His top hat flew one way, his staff another." Laughing, his companions helped him up, picked up his hat and staff, and brushed the sawdust off while Alice raced home. Her wretched act, I surmise, acted out the antipathy many adult whites felt toward Indians.[18]

When not in town or at Herring House, Seattle presided at Port Madison, where he worked with agents in charge, but agents came and went, and their authority waxed or waned depending on bureaucratic policy. Beginning with Isaac Stevens, eleven superintendents administered Indian affairs in Washington Territory over the course of twenty-two years, a turnover reflecting local difficulties and changes of administration in Washington, DC.[19]

Management was further complicated by the hodgepodge of districts administered by agents, each with its own unique history. During Michael Simmons's long tenure as agent in charge of the Puget Sound district, as many as eight subagencies, like the one at Holderness Point, were administered by special or local agents.

After ratification, when native people began moving to the reservations, the number of special or local agents was reduced in the interests of economy. During and after the Civil War, Congress was loath to spend money on its native wards, and poverty exacerbated poor conditions on the isolated reserves. In 1861, Benjamin Shaw, agent in charge at Tulalip, dismissed David Maynard from his job as subagent at Fort Kitsap, claiming he had not spent more than two months on the reservation and done little more than "draw his salary." Superintendent Samuel Howe replaced Shaw a year later and appointed E. S. Dyer as assistant farmer at Port Madison, but Dyer never showed up, and Howe asked Hillory Butler, a local settler and King County sheriff, to do what he could.

Confronting this disarray, Seattle sought out private individuals for more dependable support. Since the Yakima War, when George Meigs had watched over his charges, Seattle had become good friends with this considerate man, who ran his straitlaced, teetotaling sawmill settlement at Port Madison in a paternal manner, much like the Hudson's Bay Company. Seattle and Meigs visited frequently, enjoying long and pleasant conversations. Because Meigs treated him with kindness and respect, Seattle directed his people to work at the mill and nearby logging camps. Native houses stood on the west shore, and young native women serving in pioneer homes ended up marrying young white men and raising pioneer families.

Another figure who would prove useful was William DeShaw, a Texan born in 1834 and recently arrived from California. A family inheritance had allowed him to outfit a packtrain and trade through Mexico and Central America, and during the California gold rush he exported goat hides from Baja California to Alta California. He eventually found his way to Puget Sound, where he clerked in a Port Townsend store. In the winter of 1860–61, he purchased the Matthews brothers' fishing gear and trading post and settled at Agate Point. His colorful, edgy character reveals itself in the luggage he unloaded on the beach, which included "a sword, pistols, a bunch of Comanche scalps, a Mexican officer's uniform with shining epaulets and a large cotton flag which had waved above William Walker, a filibusterer lately defeated in Mexico." DeShaw reopened the trading post as the Bonanza Store and ardently engaged his native clientele.[20]

He married Seattle's surviving granddaughter, Mary Talesa. We may see in this union a repeat of Seattle's and Curley's practice of offering female members of their families to white men in order to establish kin links with influential newcomers. The couple had a daughter, Enna, in 1863. After Mary's death in 1869, DeShaw married successively two other native women and received the honorary name Qui-Alk—possibly taken from the phrase "How much do you have?" or from "Come on in!," a typical welcome voiced from the counter—which Enna took as her native name. In the local papers, he advertised dried cod and oil, produced by his native neighbors, rendered from dogfish livers, used to grease logging skids.

By nurturing these friendships and working with agents, Seattle aided his people. Contracted out to mills and local farms and trading with those he could trust, they participated in the cash economy well enough to survive the troubles they faced. A payoff of sorts came when agents finally announced the first distribution of annuities mandated by the Treaty of Point Elliott.

In September 1861, more than 3,700 people assembled at Tulalip to receive a boatload of dry goods and hardware. With Seattle and other headmen, reservation agent Benjamin Shaw identified heads of families in a census and hosted them with rations as recipients came forward to receive goods in a distribution that resembled a traditional *sgwi'gwi*. But rather than gifts to demonstrate a host's generosity, these goods were payment for lands that had been ceded more than five years before. In 1858, an angry Seattle had told Simmons that his people wanted their pay in cash, but the government distributed agricultural tools, stock, and seed to promote self-sufficiency. Shaw observed that scythes and sickles were of little use to people who did not farm. And some of the goods sent by clerks ignorant of Coast Salish culture had recipients shaking their heads, such as black-and-white wampum, an eastern shell currency unknown to the West Coast, and hair pipes—decorative tubular beads used in the Midwest.

The aggregate value fell far short of the $15,000 stipulated for the first installment, and agents were humiliated to distribute cheap blankets that compared poorly to the finer product traded by the Hudson's Bay Company. Nevertheless, Shaw noted, "many of the Indians [who] came to Payment believing that they would receive nothing more than a small piece of cloth were agreeably surprised to find themselves in possession of so much."[21]

The infusion of goods fueled a resurgence of traditional native activity that officials found unsettling. Among Medicine Creek Treaty groups, an agent observed that over half the annuities distributed were immediately wagered in rousing gambling matches. In Seattle, the revival saw the construction of a longhouse at the Nose that could shelter large groups.

Native people had resolutely maintained their presence along the shore. Samuel Coombs noted that during the solar eclipse of July 18,

1860, a time when most were at seasonal camps, "the howling and pounding of drums . . . where the Indians were assembled, could be heard all over town." That year, another observer, David Kellogg, described the secret-society initiation of a native man, Bunty Charley, in a house at the Nose in the presence of Seattle. A year later, another newcomer, Joseph Crow, recalled a structure sixty feet long and more than thirty wide standing near what is now First Avenue South and South King Street, the same location as the house described by Benjamin Shaw in 1850 and the location of Tecumseh's camp in 1856. Joseph Crow described the wide earthen floor as "a regular circus track," allowing those seated against the walls to observe dances and rites. The "small interior room" he observed was probably the same "special room" in a large building used for secret-society initiations later described by Suquamish informant Wilson George.[22]

The longhouse was built with Seattle's and Curley's knowledge, and it may be the house on the waterfront that settlers recalled was owned by Seattle. In the early '60s, it was the scene of many traditional rites for which, despite his Catholicism, Seattle made himself present to mediate between traditionalists and Christians among his people.

The traditionalist revival received a setback in the spring of 1862, when smallpox reappeared. Brought from San Francisco to Victoria by the steamship *Brother Jonathan*, it ravaged native groups there before spreading throughout the Sound. Vaccinations saved most whites and many Indians, but the removal of Indians to isolated reservations away from white communities possessing the vaccine exacerbated the disease's effects. Father Chirouse managed to inoculate most people at Tulalip, but in Seattle, Joseph Crow remembered that the longhouse he called the "Tamanus House," his version of the Jargon word "Ta-ma-no-us," having to do with curing rites, was being used as an "Indian hospital." Patients who had sweated in small lodges and chilled in Puget Sound were then laid on the ground in the house while a shaman repeatedly bled them and assistants kept up a loud chant, accompanied by rhythmic pounding on planks. The patients' prognosis was not good, and Crow recalled that because a shaman was killed if three of his patients died, after the epidemic he saw no more shamans.

Government parsimony led agents to economize. In 1862, Alfred R. Elder, appointed agent for the Medicine Creek and Point Elliott Treaty groups, put forward his eleven-year-old adopted son, Wells Drury, for the position of interpreter. Others who wanted the job, which paid $500 a year, complained that Drury was too young, so Elder wrote to longtime friend Abraham Lincoln for advice, and President Lincoln suggested that the matter be resolved through a competitive examination. Seattle and two other Indians, along with territorial superintendent of Indian affairs Calvin Hale and an ex–HBC employee made up the jury. A series of questions asked rapidly in the Jargon severely tested the candidates, but the judges voted four to three in Drury's favor. Only Seattle objected, saying that he "was entirely too young." But Seattle was not one to belabor an issue once settled, and Drury received the appointment.[23]

Among his own people, Seattle could still act with frightening energy. During an October *sgwi'gwi* at Port Madison in 1862, a group of young Indian men who had purchased a barrel of whiskey from a floating peddler joined in a drunken brawl that led to injury. According to Keokuck, a native resident on the reservation, despite his seventy-odd years, Seattle broke up the fight, smashed the barrel, threw a large white man into Agate Passage, and chased the young Indian men back to their village. In his report, Howe added that Indians seized the whiskey boat and set it on fire, calling it "the best act I have known them to do for some time."[24]

Seattle's temper also rages in an incident from that period recalled by DeShaw. At a native funeral, several mourners plotted to murder a slave named Huston, along with his wife, on the grave of his noble master, Ska-ga-ti-quis. Alerted, De Shaw hid the couple in his store, but a mob of armed native men soon stormed inside and demanded Huston. DeShaw began to parlay and got them to lay their guns on the counter. Just then, Seattle burst in, bellowing, "Whoo, Whoo, do I hear; what do I hear." The men backed away, mute. At that point, DeShaw's little daughter, Seattle's granddaughter, said, "Grandpa, they are going to kill the Hustons over Ska-ga-ti-quis' grave."[25]

In a fury, Seattle grabbed one of the muskets, shouting, "Whoo, Whoo," as the mob bolted out the door. Outside, he threw the musket down and grabbed a large fence rail, swinging it at the men as he chased them to the beach. Jumping in a canoe, they paddled furiously across Agate Passage, but Seattle commanded others to take him over to the village, where he called the entire population out to hear his thunderous disapproval. He could be heard clearly from the other side, expounding on the evil of slave murder. "Mr. Deshaw, the big white medicine, did not want it done, Governor Stevens did not want it, Colonel Simmons did not want it, and the great chief at Washington City did not want it, and it must stop!" DeShaw was a noted storyteller, and Stevens had been gone for years, but the description of the old man's wrath has the ring of truth. The Hustons stayed in hiding for a week, but no one dared to defy Seattle.

On Christmas Eve, 1862, forty-five-year-old Henry Van Asselt, the Dutch pioneer, married Catherine Elizabeth Jane Maple, the daughter of neighbor John Maple. A highlight of the wedding, recalled locally as one of the most widely attended social events of the decade, was a grand visit by Seattle. The account of the event is woven from many recollections. Invitations were sent out in October by post, by personal delivery, and by native messengers in canoes. Local Indians had a special regard for Van Asselt, who, with a bullet in him from a hunting accident in California, was said to be invulnerable to gunshot. Whether native people believed it or not, it was a good story, and Van Asselt's warm relations with his native neighbors elicited Seattle's friendship.[26]

His arrival at Van Asselt's home, at the head of his people, was sensational. His crew brought him to the riverbank in his great canoe and sang a song of greeting similar to the one that had greeted Vancouver years before, keeping time by striking the gunwales with their paddles. Stepping ashore, Seattle formally wished the couple happiness and joy as his retinue displayed his gifts, including "the skins of cougar and mink, some moccasins . . . fish and salmon eggs." Coming down to shake hands with the chief, Van Asselt invited Seattle's people in to meet his bride, and seven hundred "passed in gaudy costumes through the house and looked with awe at the great white "squaw," or "klootchman," who had become the wife of their friend Henry Van Asselt."

This may have been a stop on the way to a *sgwi'gwi* that Seattle hosted on the Duwamish River that winter, which lasted a week. According to Eva Greenslit Anderson, who authored a children's biography of Seattle, "he gave away everything he owned: old clothes, a horseshoe, a mule shoe, fish hooks, gunny sacks, tin cans, boxes, food morsels, and many other hoarded knickknacks." Robert Maple Norman, John Maple's great-grandson, later wrote that the people at the *sgwi'gwi* performed "weird aborigine dances while the tribe sorcerer stood over pots stirring strange stews in the caldrons to the rhythm of ghoulish sounds." However bowdlerized, this sounds much like what happened at curing ceremonies held in the longhouse at the Nose when it was believed that the evil spirits driven by a shaman from a patient's body fled into a conveniently placed container of cold water, into which the shaman dropped hot rocks, making it boil and driving them away.

Gambling matches also took place, on the sandspit dividing the lagoon at Dzidzəla'ləch from the mudflats. A player from one team sat facing another and shuffled decorated chips from hand to hand out of sight. Bringing his closed hands forward, he asked his opponent which hand held them. Throughout, team members chanting loud songs that called on their gambling powers were joined by energized supporters. If these were held during Seattle's *sgwi'gwi*, we can imagine that many of the annuity goods that had been distributed at Tulalip were wagered.

Anderson wrote that Seattle hosted his *sgwi'gwi* "as a sort of crowning highlight of his sunset years," but Norman wrote that "the Chief reported afterward that he authorized more weddings during that celebration than any other in his memory." Marriages were often announced during a *sgwi'gwi*, and evidence to support Norman's claim is the large number of marriages recorded during the following spring and summer of 1863 in the Oblate's sacramental register.

On March 10, Chirouse married two Suquamish men to Twana and Suquamish brides. On August 15, Father Louis Jayol married five couples, all from the "Seattle" tribe, and the following day, in the little wooden chapel built at Port Madison, Chirouse married a Duwamish man to a Suquamish woman, with Seattle serving as a witness. Rather than just highlighting his sunset years, the *sgwi'gwi* he hosted and the marriages he announced appear to be part of his effort to reestablish his authority among the disaffected Duwamish.[27]

Despite the order to move to reservations, census counts showed many native people living at old village sites along the river well into the 1880s. Agents agreed that reservations provided neither the room nor resources for all the people, and did not discourage farmers needing labor from encouraging many to remain nearby.

The original Port Madison Reservation enclosed two sections of land (two square miles), and Seattle argued that these were not enough. Unable to farm the forested land, the Indians grew fruit trees and hoped to raise stock, but the acreage included no pasture. He also complained that settlers had claimed land in the reserved area and that agents had sold some to Meigs. On June 27, 1863, Indian agent Samuel Howe sent Seattle with assistant farmer Butler and others to visit territorial superintendent Calvin Hale in Olympia, where they made their case well enough that the reservation was enlarged the next year, and again in 1873, to encompass eleven square miles of land with seven miles of shoreline.[28]

In the meantime, the Duwamish continued to press for a reservation. In 1857, Congress approved the Muckleshoot Reservation for their upriver kin living along the Green, upper White, and Stuck Rivers—groups that had fought the Americans. When William Waterman became territorial superintendent of Indian affairs in 1864, he was receptive to the idea of a Duwamish reservation along their river and lobbied his superiors in Washington, DC. But when word of this got back to the territory, virtually the entire voting population of Seattle and King County—156 white males, including David Maynard, Henry Yesler, David Denny, and Henry Smith—petitioned newly elected territorial delegate to Congress Arthur Denny to "prevent this . . . unjust and unnecessary action," arguing that a reservation would only benefit sixteen families, "whose interests and wants have always been justly and kindly presented by the settlers of the Black River country." Fear that future investments would be threatened by a federal withdrawal of land quashed the effort once again. The words "justly and kindly" would come back to haunt the petitioners' descendants.[29]

Seattle found silent ways to express his disapproval of white obstruction. Clarence Bagley mentioned that the chief's clothing was made up of pieces, "each of a different color and texture, and considerably worse for wear," and a sensitive local observer, pioneer Caroline Leighton, described him looking old and dignified but poor. Compared with Patkanim's finery, his humble dress appears as a visual protest of the continuing injustice that rendered his people paupers, who were once lords of the land.

That he did not scold Alice Mercer or upbraid her parents when she knocked him to the ground bespoke his sense of dignity, as his refusal to hold grudges in old age bespoke a clear-minded humility. Young interpreter Wells Drury wrote that he won Seattle's regard by learning to speak to him in his own language. He also pleased him by reading aloud in the Jargon from Theodore Winthrop's recently published book, *The Canoe and the Saddle*, that writer's account of his 1853 northwestern odyssey. We can only imagine the memories kindled as Seattle heard Winthrop's descriptions of Chetzamoka, Owhi, and Kamiakin, leaders he knew in their youth, when they all enjoyed the freedom of the land, and who had also struggled to lead their people. And he would have relished Winthrop's descriptions of the great land itself: the silvery *whulj*; the gloomy forests, broad rivers, and tremendous, supernal Təko'bad, Mount Rainier; a country whose grand dimensions shaped the ancient memories of his people. In the evening of Seattle's life, Winthrop's panorama would have recalled in him still earlier scenes of an even grander world unknown to Drury, which had passed away but was stirring to remember. We are left to wonder if Drury ever asked Seattle about himself and his own memories, a lot to ask of a boy. Catherine Maynard asked, and Samuel Coombs. What is so sad is that no one else did.

Goliah and Patkanim were gone. Chowitsuit was gone; even Seattle's nemesis, Isaac Stevens, was gone, shot while leading a charge on the battlefield of Chantilly in 1862. Longevity, vision, and vitality enabled Seattle to accomplish a great deal, what no other headman did. By acts of will and force of personality, he nurtured a hybrid experiment that took his name and helped to create a community destined for greatness. Defying convention and distrust, he gained the renown which he had sought from his earliest days and cultivated until his death, of a man who parlayed a checkered inheritance into a property whose soaring value would remain forever attached to his person.

In town, Seattle stayed at his waterfront dwelling, attended by his wife and retinue. They slept on a plank bench built along the wall. Mats woven from thick cattail stalks made a springy mattress beneath blankets like those he wore. As with most saltwater folk, their day began after a morning purge and a bracing bath in the Sound. In most households, the oldest man went about smacking the walls with a switch to signal that it was time to get up. Given Seattle's temperament, we can imagine he enjoyed this. Breakfast was hot coffee and leftovers from the day before. One full meal a day was prepared in the afternoon, in several courses served separately. If it was a kettle of stew, he would dip his broad horn spoon into it and sup from its tip. For the remainder of the day, he ate when he was hungry from what was available. At the end of a meal, he rinsed his mouth out with water and spat onto the earthen floor.

Well along in years, he no longer hunted. An existing decorated Yakama flat bag, woven from plant fiber, said to have been his hunting bag, was probably used by those gathering for him. He spent his days visiting friends and acquaintances, adjudicating disputes, and doing business with merchants, farmers, and government officials in and out of town. He became a familiar sight, and as the population grew, the editor of the *Seattle Weekly Gazette*, the town's first newspaper, taught newcomers how to properly pronounce his name: "Se-at-tle is a word of three syllables accented strongly on the second or middle syllable." Questions were being asked about the "Indian chief who daily patrols our streets, with many of his tribe, in the most dignified manner, and primitive costume." This costume included many hats: a billed military hat, a stovepipe hat, and a low waterproof traditional cone of tightly woven cedar bark.[30]

He was wearing the cedar-bark cone when photographer E. M. Sammis saw him walking down Front Street, today's First Avenue, one August day. Young Clarence Bagley, who assisted Sammis, remembered him exclaiming "There's Seattle!" and rushing down from his studio to greet him in the Jargon and invite him to his parlor.[31]

The town had grown some by then. More wooden buildings fronted rutted streets, and although the forest had been pushed back, ragged growth still cloaked the crowding hills. Seating him in an armchair next to an incongruous urn, Sammis prepared the photographic plate, asking Seattle to sit quietly until Bagley said he had snapped the bulb. Flashbulbs were not yet in use, and Sammis likely produced the flash by running a battery's current through a trough of lycopodium powder.

At that moment, Seattle had folded his arms, clasped his powerful hands, and lowered his eyelids. A blanket covered his trousers and feet, and his conical hat rested on one knee, atop his walking stick. His hickory shirt collar was open at the throat and partly covered by his long, wavy hair. His face still showed the fine features that had so impressed William Fraser Tolmie. Bagley noted that Seattle left as quietly as he had entered and never asked to see the result. Sammis sent one hundred copies to a New York dealer, who painted his eyes open and added designs to the shirt and hat.

Most days in town, Seattle heard people's problems and advised them, motioning his lieutenants to move them along. This continued until late afternoon, when a particular issue might cause him to call his people together and hear him out. His authority was limited, but his opinions were grounded in a long life and sharp wisdom, and his powerful voice still commanded attention. At night, coffee with sugar elicited conversations by the house fire. In the wavering ember light arose the judgments of the day, memorable incidents, concerns, and the constant effort to answer the question, "What do we do now?" At last, he disrobed, lay on the cattail mats, and pulled blankets over himself, as coals glowed and snores mingled with the susurrous waves.

In June 1864, Seattle publicly celebrated his Catholic faith by receiving the sacrament of Confirmation at Tulalip, administered by Bishop Augustin Blanchet, Francis Norbert Blanchet's brother and head of the diocese of Nisqually, which replaced the diocese of Walla Walla abandoned after the Cayuse War. Confirmation was given to strengthen the faith of those likely to suffer persecution and temptations against their faith, or who were in danger of death. Generally administered by a bishop to children at the age of reason, thought to begin after age seven, and to the old and ill, the sacrament was believed to secure seven spiritual gifts from the Holy Spirit: wisdom, understanding, counsel, fortitude, knowledge, piety, and fear of the Lord.[32]

A desire to be right with God would not have been unusual in an old man after a long and turbulent life. One of his sons had died violently at the fortified Chemakum village of Tsit'tsibus, and Seattle had recently watched another son, George, who he had hoped would succeed him, waste away with consumption until he died and was buried in the town's first cemetery, located at what is now Second Avenue and Stewart Street. The old war leader had also observed that a *sia'b* who embraced the newcomers' religion was more likely to gain the support of trust-worthy white men, like George Meigs and Father Chirouse. So as his end approached, and determined to provide a model for guidance after his death, he asked to be confirmed.[33]

If he embraced his faith more fully, Seattle did not entirely abandon the old ways. The guardian power Thunder had been steadfast through-out his life, and Seattle continued to honor it. Since the time during his youth when he had fasted by a lake deep in the forest and dove to meet it, Thunder had taught him its song, and during the winter dances he had risen before the people, shaking the duck-shaped rattles as he sang the song in his booming voice. Seattle had paid homage to Thunder with feats of intelligence, bravery, and terror, becoming respected and feared by native groups and Company men alike. He had made his people's cause his own, seeking connection with Americans and representing the native people's interests to the new tyees. Thunder had made Seattle's voice one that peo-ple listened to, and even now, having put his rattles away, he did not forget the song that promised danger and power. He taught it to relatives so that after he was dead it could still be sung, and its hearers would know the power that had come to Seattle and made him the man he was.[34]

Seattle set an extraordinary example of humility by being confirmed with the young. On Monday, June 20, Bishop Augustin Blanchet arrived to greet over one hundred confirmands. About thirty were students at the Tulalip school; the rest came from among the Snohomish, Lummi, and Suquamish, the latter identified in the sacramental register as Etakmur, recalling the old name, meaning "Mixed People." Blanchet spent the day reviewing the lessons given by priests and catechists and exhorting his listeners to model Christian lives. The presence of Chief Seattle in the front pew focused attention on the bishop's words.

The next morning, as the boys' brass band—which Chirouse had organized and taken on successful fund-raising tours—played hymns, confirmands and their families filled the newly dedicated Saint Anne's Church. Dressed in episcopal vestments and attended by Fathers Chirouse and Durieu, Bishop Blanchet intoned prayers at the foot of the altar. After a sermon repeating the sacrament's spiritual gifts, Blanchet called the confirmands forward and addressed each one in Latin, with Chirouse and Durieu prompting their responses. The bishop called upon the Holy Spirit to provide each with a new birth, forgiveness of sins, and the seven spiritual gifts. Then he motioned for Seattle to stand before him and asked him his baptismal name.[35]

"Noah," Seattle said.

Holding his crosier with his left hand, the bishop dipped his right thumb in chrism, placed his hand on Seattle's head, and marked the sign of the cross on his forehead with his thumb.

"I sign you with the sign of the cross and I confirm you with the Chrism of Salvation," the bishop said. "In the name of the Father, and of the Son and of the Holy Spirit."

"Amen."

As the rite prescribed, Blanchet then struck Seattle's left cheek with his right hand to remind him of the blows that Christ had suffered and that, as a believer, he should expect to receive. This may shock readers unfamiliar with the rite, and even those who have experienced it as a soft pat rather than a thoughtful slap, but I believe Seattle received it quite aware of its meaning.

Blanchet concluded the rite with the hopeful valediction "Peace be with you." After the confirmands returned to the pews, Blanchet consecrated the bread and wine and distributed Holy Communion as they knelt at the altar rail.

There was a feast afterward, and then Seattle and his retinue returned in his great canoe to Port Madison. There he joined others in the chapel for morning and evening prayers. When priests came, he attended Mass and witnessed baptisms, marriages, and funerals.

In his late seventies now, Seattle continued to visit the Duwamish on the eastern shore. The 1860 census had counted 302 people in the town of Seattle, but by the middle of the decade, whites began to outnumber native residents even during native celebrations. Once they did, the vision of a white town led to discussions about what it should look like, and white residents pushed for the physical reordering of native activities.

In January 1865, the territorial legislature granted the town a municipal charter, authorizing the creation of a board of elected trustees who would appoint the town's clerk, marshal, and magistrate, with the power to tax and legislate. When the trustees met later that month and elected Charles Terry as president of the board, they began issuing ordinances to regulate town life. Ordinance Number 5 forbade Indians from building houses on streets and open areas in town and required residents using Indian labor to provide them with housing. Other towns issued similar calls for eviction. If the longhouse at the Nose survived the smallpox outbreak, lack of any later description suggests its being razed around this time. Along with Joseph Crow's mention that he saw no more shamans, its disappearance marks the passage of an ancient world.[36]

Once again, Seattle was exiled from his town, but like his people, he remained close. Although they were no longer permitted to live as groups within the town limits, they set up camps at its boundaries, at Herring House, at Baba′kwəb and southern Lake Union, and at West Point, called Pka′dzultshu, "Thrust Far Out," at today's Discovery Park. At the turn of the century, a native fishing camp called the "light house colony" existed here, a place where, when the wind blew from the north, people took their canoes to the south of the point, and when it blew from the south, they took them to the north side. The Nose itself disappeared as ships shoveled out their bilges at the point's south end, extending the shoreline. But since this contiguous addition extended beyond the town's limits generally south of King Street, native people camped on the rough spoil—named after its originating material, Ballast Island. But wherever they camped, the old man remained their chief.[37]

As we approach Seattle's final year, a Sacramental Register provides continuing evidence of his surprising ability to adapt traditional customs to Western practice. On March 10, 1863, Father Chirouse visited Port Madison and baptized three Duwamish people in the chapel: Marie, forty years old; her father, Meratlash; and his wife, Kerparebilesh. The next day, Chirouse married Marie to Noah Seattle—Chief Seattle—in the presence of two witnesses, Jacob Wahelchu and Andrie. Seattle's third wife had died, and her Duwamish family had provided him with another, following the form of a traditional sba′lusəd marriage, to take care of him in his final days. Weaving the warp of tradition on the weft of Christian monogamy, Seattle created new fabric to clothe himself and his people in a changing world.[38]

Late in 1865, the writer Caroline Leighton and her husband, Rufus, a customs collector, caught a last glimpse of Seattle on the street. She described him as "a very dignified Indian, old and poor, but with something about him that led us to suspect that he was a chief." She said he was accompanied by his grandson, "a little brown sprite, that seemed an embodiment of the wind—such a swift, elastic little creature—with no clothes about him, though it was a cold November day."[39]

At last, Seattle's people brought him back to Port Madison in his storied canoe, where we have a glimpse of him in his frame house near that of his granddaughter Mary DeShaw. As a child at Port Madison in the 1860s, Sam Snider, also known as Sublaht, was given the chore of bringing water to his family from a small stream just north of Old Man House. Near the stream, a small house built from sawn lumber stood on a low bank. When it was warm, Sam used to see an old man sitting quietly in a wooden Western-style chair looking out over Puget Sound. One day as he collected water, the old man beckoned to him and called out, "Come here, boy." While Sam was climbing the bluff to the house, the old man asked him who his father and mother were. Sam told him. He nodded and asked nothing more, but Sam sensed something unusually kind and impressive about him. Back home, when he described him to his mother, she stopped what she was doing and said with pride in her voice, "Sublaht, that man who wanted to know about us is Chief Seattle."[40]

In the spring of 1866, Seattle grew weaker. Wilson George, born in 1872, said that his mother took care of Seattle. "She was related to him but not closely," he said. "She called him Sapa [Grandfather]. She used to cook his food and take it over to him. [She used] to say, Chief Seʔał has got lots of relations, but here I am taking care of him until he dies." We know that Sam Snider continued to bring him water in his final days. There is no further mention of Marie. If she was still in the picture, being Seattle's wife may have inclined her to leave the fetching and carrying to others. Near the end, Jacob Wahelchu and other local headmen gathered beside his bed. He was dying; they asked what he wanted done. Seattle spoke his last recorded words:[41]

It is well. My heart is good. I have only one thing to ask: and that is, for my good friend—always my friend—to come to my funeral, and shake hands with me before I am laid in the ground.

It had been a blustery spring, and in early June low clouds swept north, hiding the Olympics and the Cascades from view. It rained and rained. Seattle had spent his eighty years within the confines of this lustrous world—from the mudflats at the head of the Sound to the oak-studded Nisqually Prairie, where the old fort decayed beneath eternal Ta-qo-bəd, to the lovely islands hemmed by clay cliffs. Crowned with forests, they divided the Sound as it opened onto the wider strait, where mountains rested their knees in the ocean, island after island, all the way to the blue, threatening north. A few massive timbers of Old Man House still reminded observers of earlier days—those turbulent, tremendous days when a man who called down the thunder led his people into a new age. Now his world had become the smoky interior of a small room and the arc of anxious faces hovering over him. On Sunday, Jacob led family prayers beside the dying man. On Thursday, June 7, the wind blew and rain pelted the roof. Gulls called from over the water. He died that afternoon.

Silence pervaded the village. An observer noted that "every member of his tribe seemed to be deeply afflicted." William DeShaw purchased new black pants, a shirt, a vest, and a coat for Seattle. The family dressed the body and pulled new calf shoes onto his calloused feet. A hat on his head, and a handkerchief, possibly his baptismal cloth, tucked stylishly in his coat pocket, completed the tableau. He departed the world as he had hoped to be seen in it: as a respected member of a prosperous hybrid community—a hope deferred, but still green. They laid him on a pair of blankets padding a coffin fashioned by carpenter Charles Morris from broad, varnished cedar boards fitted with handles. It all came to ninety-six dollars and thirty-eight cents, about three months' wages for a worker.[42]

A messenger carried Seattle's last request to Port Madison, and the next day George Meigs shut down his mill and brought everyone over on the steam tug *Resolute*. Four hundred people, native and white, assembled at the chapel in the morning rain, and many knelt as Jacob led prayers. The rain ceased. Sun broke through the clouds. Birdsong and the hum of insects filled the air. Then Jacob rose and broke the ancient taboo forbidding use of the deceased's name. The old man had wanted his people to live in the new way. Even in death, he was managing events.

Seattle! Seattle! The spirit of our great Chief has gone—
gone to the good land a great way off. His heart was always
good—'twas like the sun; not like the moon for that is changing.
Seattle was a great Chief. He knew better what was good for us
than we knew ourselves. But why do I speak?—for his son is
here—he knows best about our good chief—he is his own flesh
and blood—let him talk.

Then Seattle's son Jim, who would follow in his father's footsteps
as chief, delivered his eulogy.[43]

My father's remains lie before us: they are going to yonder
hill, to be buried deep in the earth. Ages ago this mode of
burial would have appalled us, for the dead bodies of our
ancestors were elevated on trees, or were laid in canoes above
the ground; but the priest came among us, and taught us the
prayer. We are Christians now. Before he came, the Seattles
were the first in the chase, and the first to draw the bow and
knife in time of war: but the godly man learned us how to
build good houses; how to cultivate the soil, and how to get
money, like the White Men. He has told us, too, that when the
Son of God was buried in the earth, a great stone was rolled
over his grave; but when God called him to heaven, the stone
rolled back, and His Son came forth. We know that my father
was the last great Chief of the Seattles. They were all his
friends—so were many Indians of other tribes—so were many
White Men his friends—because he was just to all. In the last
strife with the Whites, my father was threatened because he
would not fight; but he feared no one but God. Some of the
White Men made threats: the Chief of the Seattles told them
all, that when there was cause for shedding blood, they would
find him, night and day, on the war-path. We are all glad that
those troublesome times have passed. We are glad that the
great Chief's hands were never stained with a White Man's
blood. He is dead now, but his name will live in the memory
of all good Indians, as a wise, brave and Christian Chief.

He reached inside his coat and drew out a copy of the Sammis photograph. The man born at the capsizing of the world had gained photographic celebrity.

> The White Men will not forget him, for here is his picture, made by the light of the heavens. The older it grows, the more it will be prized. When the Seattles are no more, their chief will be remembered and revered by the generations to come.

When Jim had finished, Meigs stood up, walked to the coffin, and gravely shook Seattle's cold, stiff hand. Pallbearers lowered the lid, lifted the coffin, and carried it at the head of a long procession to the cemetery, where it was lowered four and a half feet into the ground. Earth was shoveled on top, and a simple wooden cross pushed into the mound. The great and terrifying old man was gone, but in his town, the town named after him, and in every other town the Americans were building on Puget Sound, not a single newspaper mentioned his passing.

# CHAPTER NINE

TO 1887

*"Dead, did I say?"*

By June 1866, the Civil War had been over for a year. The South lay prostrate, but the North boomed. Despite the slaughter, its population soared; immigrants poured into its flourishing cities as industries and wealth proliferated. In the decade ending in 1870, the North's per capita income doubled and the wealth of New York State alone grew to more than twice that of all the states of the old Confederacy. But wealth threatened to divide American society as deeply as had slavery. The monstrous progeny of the war—corporations and financial institutions—wielded a lash as violent as any slave master. "Who shall hold in behemoth?" asked poet Walt Whitman, "who bridle leviathan?" Leviathan would arise, as US Supreme Court justice John Harlan warned, "from the aggregations of capital in the hands of the few." Out west, these few were the captains of industry and finance who built the transcontinental railroads. On Puget Sound, no question weighed more heavily on the public mind than where the northern route would reach tidewater. In every ragged settlement hacked out of forests facing the

Dr. Henry Allen Smith sitting in his garden in the early twentieth century. His version of Chief Seattle's 1854 speech gained worldwide fame.

tide, residents dreamed of the wealth that would come when the western terminus would make them *the* city. There was no dream if it did not.[1]

In Washington Territory, a city was said to be a place with a store, a blacksmith, two or three saloons, and a weekly newspaper. In 1866, Seattle had two papers—the *Puget Sound Weekly* and the *Puget Sound Daily,* titles more hopeful than real—both of which appeared intermittently from April to August. Neither mentioned Chief Seattle's death, but if his passing was not thought printworthy, it had not gone unnoticed. In August, Catherine Leighton and her husband returned to town after a three-month absence and heard that he had died. The memory, she wrote, hung on the macabre detail of mill owner George Meigs honoring the old chief's request to "take him by the hand and bid him farewell."[2]

After Seattle's death, the Suquamish deposed his son Jim as head chief, because, it was said, he "talked rough to the people" and was "quick tempered and easily offended." In his place, they selected Jacob Wahelchu. Like Seattle, he was a Catholic, but he was less tolerant of traditional practices. Suquamish informant Wilson George recalled never seeing an initiation, "because in his day the Catholics were very strong and they forbid these ceremonies." In the town named after Seattle, few cared.[3]

News considered worth printing focused on future hopes. On the day Seattle died, the *Daily* printed a letter from Harriet S. Stevens, one of a small number of young eastern women pioneers Asa Mercer was importing into Washington Territory. Her literate account of their voyage from New York via Panama was one of the few stories originating locally that made national news, an endeavor Mercer hoped would reflect well on his distant community, where marriageable women were supposedly few. Native women were available, but educated Americans like Mercer regarded racial mixing as "detrimental to the moral tone of the community."

The papers also reported Dr. Henry Allen Smith's election to the territorial assembly as a representative from Snohomish County. He was one of only a few early Seattle pioneers to gain renown during his lifetime as a writer, due particularly to the famous speech he attributed to Seattle. Because of the speech and the controversy surrounding it, we need now to focus on Smith and his writing and why he chose to present the speech when and how he did. More than any other writer, Smith lifted Seattle the man out of history and transformed him into Seattle the myth, the icon, whose renown has grown as his city flourished.

Smith was descended from the Von Schmidts of Rhineland-Palatinate, who had arrived with other Germans in Philadelphia in the mid-1700s and migrated westward to Ohio. By then, the name had softened to Smith, and on April 11, 1830, Henry was born to the Reverend Coppelton Smith and his wife, Abigail, the tenth of eleven children, in Wooster Township. His prosperous family lived in a three-story stone house, and at the age of fifteen, Smith entered Allegheny College in Meadville, Pennsylvania, to prepare for the ministry. But when his father died a year later and left him an inheritance, Henry traveled to Cincinnati to study medicine at Dr. Charles Roode's Physio-Medical Institute.[4]

There he developed a case of gold rush fever as news from California swept the nation. For $200 and an agreement to serve as assistant physician, Smith bought a place on a wagon train in 1852.

"People die on those trips," said his fretting mother.

"That's just why I'm going," he reassured her. "To keep people from dying."

Inspired by his optimism, she had him purchase passage for her and his sister, Ellender, just finishing primary school.

A desire to get to the diggings coupled with a hard midwestern winter drove fifty-two thousand emigrants over the Oregon Trail that year, nearly double the previous year's count. A diarist, Smith preserved in writing the memories of his epic journey and the drama of pioneering that shaped his life. Decades later, he would describe prairie fires this way: "when the long, waving lines of flame flared and flashed their red light against the low, fleecy clouds till they blossomed into roseate beauty, looking like vast spectral flower gardens." A description of a lightning storm near the Platte River fairly collapses under the weight of images: "when all the windows of the sky and a good many doors opened at once and the cloud-masked batteries of the invisible hosts of the air volleyed and thundered till the earth fairly reeled beneath the terrific cannonade that tore its quivering bosom with red-hot bombs until awe-stricken humanity shriveled into utter nothingness in the presence of the mad fury of the mightiest forces of nature." It is typical Smith—his descriptive sentences overlong and overwhelming.[5]

He arrived in Portland on October 26. By then, the easy gold had been winnowed from California's streams, and Portland businessmen, anxious to keep local customers, rhapsodized about lands north of the Columbia. Smith decided to have a look. Leaving mother and sister comfortably placed in Portland, he shouldered his blanket roll, and started out on a bright morning, but the rains came and poured all day as he stumbled through the endless forest. Eventually, with the help of acquaintances he made on the way, he reached Olympia, the largest American settlement on the Sound, whose residents assured him the railroad terminus would come to them.[6]

As Smith later wrote, he and several fellow travelers met Luther Collins, who worked a homestead on the Duwamish. In one account, Smith presents Collins, whom we know as a proponent of vigilante justice and murderer of Indians, as a jovial booster. "What the hell are you doing here?" Collins bellowed. "This is no place for young men to settle in; pack up your duds and come down to my scow, the finest craft on Puget Sound, by God! and in three days time I will land you in the Garden of Eden or give you my head for a football." The name of his boat, *About Half Way Up*, advertised to the credulous as a "clipper-scow," identified his homestead's location on the Sound. Persuaded and with little to lose but time, Smith and friends clambered aboard.

On Elliott Bay, Collins introduced them to David Maynard and Arthur Denny. "Dr. Maynard," Collins joshed, according to Smith, "look out for your laurels; here are a couple of youngsters hunting the 'terminus'; you had better keep an eye on them."

Smith spent that first night in Arthur Denny's cabin with Arthur's wife, Mary Ann, and their three children. The next morning, Denny showed him around the rough settlement, extolling its virtues, especially the horse trail that led east over the mountains and whose route the railroad would surely follow. The town was half the size of Olympia, but its deep, great bay, the friendliness of the native people, and the energy of their chief inspired optimism.

Smith staked a claim on a narrow isthmus dividing a bay cove from a narrow inlet, Salmon Bay, and brought his mother, Abigail, and his sister, Ellender, from Portland to lodge in town until he could raise a "shake-built shanty" on his land.

He was among those greeting Isaac Stevens in January 1854 as the governor's entourage came down the Duwamish in a flotilla of canoes after visiting the newly discovered coal mine. Smith remembered how Stevens electrified the crowd that night, telling them that the sound of rivers rushing down the western slopes of the Cascades would soon echo the sound of a locomotive's whistle as it approached the terminus in their town. And Smith was on the beach the next morning, under the dangerous moon, penciling into his diary translations of what Chief Seattle said.

Given the date's proximity to the winter solstice, when the native people believed the road to the land of the dead lay open, ghosts figured prominently in Seattle's speech, but they were on Americans' minds as well. Far from their eastern kin, the settlers felt the pang of separation. Less than a year after Smith arrived, the *Pioneer and Democrat* printed a short, sentimental piece called "The Immortal Dead." "How unchanging is their love for us," wrote the anonymous author. "How tenderly they look down upon us, and how closely they surround us."[7]

Smith bought chickens, cleared land, planted vegetables, and built a two-story house with some of the first lumber cut at Yesler's mill. When news of the White River killings arrived, he rowed his mother and sister to town with muffled oars. He served as surgeon in Company A of the Washington Territorial Volunteers from January until July 1856, when he won election as a Democratic representative from King County to the territorial assembly in Olympia and was reelected the following year. As debate over slavery and the union grew rancorous, he became a Republican.

Hungry for real estate, he purchased a lot in town and built another house. At the cove, he raised sheep, dairy cattle, and horses, and planted the county's first orchard of grafted apple trees. Rents, wool, milk, apples, and doctoring provided income, and with his father's inheritance, he bought land from settlers who left after the Yakima War, amassing more than one thousand acres, the cove becoming Smith Cove. Everyone expected land values to increase once the railroad came, but as the wait grew and hope dimmed, Smith settled in.

In 1862, he married Mary Ann Phelan, a beautiful Irish Catholic brunette from Steilacoom, whose prosperous family had sent her to the

Saint Ann's convent in Victoria for her education. He was thirty-two; she was seventeen. And two years after Smith brought his new bride to the cove, their first child, Lula, was born.

Civil War politics directed the first transcontinental railroad to California to keep the Golden State in the Union camp, but even before the great project was completed, plans were afoot to send other railroads west. To improve his chance of profiting wherever the northern line reached tidewater, Smith explored the Snohomish River valley north of Seattle. In 1861, Snohomish County had been carved out of Island County, with tiny Mukilteo as its county seat. Surveyors mapped the valley, and steamboats made their way from tidewater all the way up to Snohomish City. Relatively untouched by the war, the county offered new chances for gentlemen farmers, and Smith described its advantages in the *Washington Gazette* after a tour in December 1863.

In the piece, after leaving Seattle, he arrived at Mukilteo, where merchants Morris Frost and Jacob Fowler were packing twenty tons of salmon for the San Francisco market. Across the river at Tulalip, Smith noted that Indian agent Samuel Howe and Father Chirouse had made the reservation "look more like a civilized village than a rendezvous for savages." At the river mouth, Smith described "thousands of acres of fresh-water tide lands with a luxuriant growth of indigenous clover, red top and pea-vine" that settlers billed hopefully as "New Holland." From there, he traveled up to the falls he described in his hallmark style as the "younger brother of Niagara . . . truly a sublime spectacle . . . eternal rainbows circle round in gorgeous beauty, losing themselves ever and anon in snowy columns of spray that continually rise and ascend far over the gigantic pines above." He assured readers that the bottomlands were as rich as those in King County, "than which there is none more productive in the world."[8]

He purchased six hundred acres on a delta island, later named Smith Island, and built another comfortable home for his family, thinking that if a railroad should arrive at Elliott Bay or Port Gardner Bay, he would greet it at either location. To advertise the Snohomish estuary, he wrote articles in the *Seattle Gazette* about farming tidal lands. He had three acres diked by the late spring of 1864, too late to plant a crop, but fall tides washed it out "as freely as if it had been constructed of loose bricks."

The next spring, he had workers widen the dike and pack the earth on top. It held. In the spring of 1866, he planted an acre in vegetables and heeled in apple, plum, cherry, and pear trees. The potatoes did poorly, the cabbage better, the turnips very well, the peas amazingly, and neighbors marveled at his ripening tomatoes and his mangel-wurzels, a field beet used to feed livestock, grown a foot wide and three feet long. He grazed livestock and sowed timothy and redtop grass, yielding two tons of hay per acre. Barley, spring wheat, and oats also flourished. Elated by his success, he hired Indians to dike seventy-five more acres and expanded his orchard. Few settlers were as avid as Smith in promoting improvements.

He frequently traveled between Smith Island and Smith Cove to develop his properties until May of 1866, when, while clearing a lot purchased at Second Avenue and James Street, near his town house in Seattle, he drove an ax into his foot. It was a serious wound, but he still managed to hobble around effectively enough to win election as Snohomish County's legislative representative in June and to the Board of County Commissioners for Snohomish, Whatcom, and Island Counties in July.[9]

Like Maynard and DeShaw, he located near native communities to benefit from trade and encouraged native farm workers to camp on his island. Across the channel at Tulalip, Chirouse opened a girls' school in 1868, staffed by the Sisters of Providence, where the Smiths eventually enrolled their daughter Lula and her younger sister Luma in the primary grades. On April 1, 1871, Henry Smith was hired as resident physician at Tulalip to treat Indians with tuberculosis, measles, diphtheria, and typhus, and he moved his family into a large government-built house there.

Tulalip had grown into a village of neat clapboard homes built of sawn lumber, with frame and sash windows and hinged doors. Surrounded by fields, stock pens, and orchards, it modeled an American farming community, in keeping with government efforts to hasten assimilation. However picturesque, the Tulalip winter villages—sheltering extended families and crammed with nets, fishing gear, drying sheds, and canoes drawn up on the waterside—recalled a seminomadic life settlers remembered only from Bible stories and folklore.

By their definition, civilized people lived in cities, and because the Indians on Puget Sound did not build cities, they were considered uncivilized and possessing none of civilization's gifts. Americans, the builders of many cities, believed themselves to possess these gifts in abundance and felt duty-bound to propagate them. Blessed with liberty, law, and wealth, they saw themselves as the children of God, the sons of light and bearers of the future. Savagery was what their northern European ancestors had emerged from a thousand years before, and they supported the notion that delivering Indians from barbarism was part of the national project. That native people differed from Americans materially and culturally was obvious. That the stage that had been reached by settlers was intrinsically better and, in the nature of things, inevitable, even necessary, was a judgment few Americans questioned—and certainly not Henry Smith.

An enthusiastic agrarian who was anxious to prosper, Smith continued writing, describing further efforts to farm tidal prairies in the *Washington Standard*, claiming "that the tide lands on the Sound are the best lands in the Territory when reclaimed." In 1869, when it was obvious that few cared, he alerted readers to a minor gold rush on the Sultan River, a tributary of the Skykomish, forty miles above Snohomish City, hoping that it would hasten "the glorious sunburst of a brighter day." It didn't.[10]

The stories Smith wrote—his orotund descriptions of traveling west, settling the land, fighting Indians, building community, and developing farms in what he and his fellow pioneers regarded as a wilderness—celebrate individual courage and the rugged challenges of frontier life. Today we regard pioneers like Smith more ambiguously, as actors in a national epic bearing as much guilt as glory, but to them their actions were proof of human progress in a physical and moral drama played on a national stage.

Ironically, the connection they so eagerly sought with the industrial East brought their pioneering epic to a close. Replacing its comprehensible challenges were the less familiar legal and managerial efforts required to deal with huge distant corporations and massive financial institutions. Pioneers rarely possessed such abilities, and they looked to incoming attorneys, accountants, and entrepreneurs to take advantage of opportunities, less dependent now on free land than in professional success in an emerging urban setting. The image of a frontiersman—handy with an ax, a plow, and a gun—building a home and raising a family in the wilderness no longer sufficed. Economic challenges required the skills of lawyers, bankers, and managers, and the more imaginative arts of marketing. Boosters lauded Seattle's central location and the energy of its citizens, but one asset that the little town on Elliott Bay was slow to utilize was its name.

It speaks to how blinkered by determination residents were that outsiders were the first to take an interest in the town's namesake. The first article to mention Chief Seattle after his death appeared in Olympia's *Washington Standard* in April 1868, describing his early activity at Chinook Street. The first biographical sketch of him, "Old Seattle, and His Tribe," written by whaler, naturalist, and author Charles Melville Scammon, appeared in April 1870 in Bret Harte's literary journal, the *Overland Monthly*. Scammon's scientific curiosity led him to research and write *The Marine Mammals of the North-western Coast of North America*, considered a classic even today. Another career as an officer in the United States Revenue Cutter Service—today's US Coast Guard—made Scammon familiar with Puget Sound and its native peoples.

Visiting the Port Madison Reservation a few months after Seattle's funeral in 1866, Scammon went with his Suquamish hosts, Jacob Wahelchu and Seattle's son Jim, to the chapel and the cemetery, "inclosed by heavy palings," that held the chief's grave. Scammon described it as "a bare clay-mound with a plain wooden cross, without a letter or other mark." Despite the ruined state of Old Man House, its remaining uprights and rafters impressed him, as did the reservation's native residents, which he identified as the "Seattles." He mentioned that little agriculture was done there, but he described the Seattles as "practical lumbermen" who "proved themselves to be shrewd hands at driving a bargain." After interviewing locals like George Meigs and noting how quickly native people had adopted Western customs, Scammon described them as the most advanced such group on the Sound, and their late chief as their most noble representative. Seeing Jim's photograph, Scammon described how Seattle's "countenance beamed with an expression of pleasant dignity, rarely met with among the race."

He was the first to outline Seattle's life and describe his final days. But echoing the social Darwinism of his time, Scammon ended the article with a valedictory, that "ere long, the Seattles will all have passed away, giving place to a superior class, who will occupy and improve their lands."[11]

The *Overland Monthly*, printed in San Francisco, enjoyed a national audience, but the town of Seattle would have no suitable public library for decades, and local subscribers were few. Closer to home, Portland's version of the *Monthly*, the *West Shore* magazine, sometimes referenced Chief Seattle and his people, but to town residents what happened on the reservation might as well happen on the moon.[12]

Still, the distant moon stirred deep tides. The new subagent appointed to Port Madison, William DeShaw, had what remained of Old Man House burned to the ground as his first order of business. The United States' Indian policy sought to end communal living and put people into separate family houses, à la Tulalip. Yet even after the building was gone, the native community kept the name Old Man House for years, and DeShaw's journal entries identifying Indians he characterized as "bad" revealed the stubborn persistence of local traditional celebrations such as secret-society initiations and journeys to the land of the dead.

At Tulalip, traditional celebrations continued, too. Indians rescheduled winter dances to July, telling the agent they were simply honoring American independence, but Father Chirouse knew that traditional rites took place in secret and warned off his students, condemning them as "the Devil's work." At Port Madison, as long as the rites took place off the reservation, DeShaw ignored them.[13]

At a well-attended Spirit Canoe ceremony in the winter of 1871, a ceremonialist found a captured soul, and his crew staged a combat with the ghosts to possess it. Afterward, he displayed a red jellylike mass on one of the spears, claiming it was the blood of a ghost. Drawing it off, he placed it into the cupped hands of Jim Seattle's wife. Nine months later, she bore a son, baptized Moses Seattle, who had a condition that stunted his growth so that he was later known as the "dwarf from the land of the dead." Through this grandson, memory of Chief Seattle gained a spectral dimension.[14]

On his island at the Snohomish River delta, Henry Smith employed all his skills to attract settlers to Snohomish County. In a florid three-part travelogue in Seattle's *Weekly Intelligencer*, he celebrated features such as Blackmans Lake near Snohomish City, which he said was "framed in immortal green, ablaze with trout and musical with the bass of the goose, the alto of the mallard and the soprano of ten thousand teal and canvass backs." He envisioned the wealthy purchasing lands even on sandy soil, "for retired villas, ornate with orchards and flower gardens." But despite his efforts, no one was biting. In July 1871, the *Weekly Intelligencer* noted that "Dr. H. A. Smith . . . paid us a visit last week. He informed us that nothing of interest was transpiring in that locality."[15]

While he had once described Tulalip as looking like "a civilized village," Smith came to regard the reservation at the mouth of the river as an impediment to settlement, "an eyesore to claim seekers and loggers who can only view its enchantment from afar . . . and whose . . . suspension and withdrawal from our country is a source of regret to all our citizens." Seeking anything of interest to promote the county, he focused on its native people in an 1873 article, "Our Aborigines."[16]

In the piece, a grab bag of tidbits about native religions, customs, and folklore, Smith made creative stabs at terms such as "Zuj-wa," his version of the Xwəljutsid *dzə'gwə*, which he described as the chief of a race of supernatural imps; *ner-hood-ams*, their priests (from "xu'da'b," the category of shamanic powers); and *tam-amins*, his early version of *tamanowis*, a Jargon word for "supernatural power." He prophesied that the people "now so rapidly passing away . . . whose deepening twilight will soon merge into a night so dark that the historian's pen alone will be able to cast a single ray upon the voiceless gloom." Noting that over a twelve-year period more than half of the Indians administered by reservation officials had died, he predicted that "at this death-rate, in the year 1885 not a solitary siwash will be left to chant a dirge over the 'loved and gone.'" We will see Smith use much the same phrasing and imagery in his later Seattle speech.

To augment his farm and reservation doctor's income, Smith took in the county poor, but the county commissioners were slow to pay. He had grown tired of watching patients die and of scraping by on a government salary, and at the end of his article, he called down a final, Darwinian judgment upon the native race, complaining that "with such opportunities, if the rising generation of 'redskins' is not able to hold its own against white aggression, it . . . ought to take the warpath in search of its sires." If the presence of Indians was discouraging whites from settling in the county, in his writing he could make the natives go away.

Hopes that the Northern Pacific Railway might locate its terminus at Mukilteo or Seattle died in July 1873, when the corporation announced that it would locate the terminus on Commencement Bay, beside a swatch of rough cabins called Tacoma, farther up the Sound. Adding humiliation, Seattle's *Weekly Intelligencer* announced that Smith was a tax delinquent, owing twenty-three dollars and eight cents on three lots. Unable to support his family on a government salary of $1,200 per annum, he resigned as resident physician at Tulalip on April 22, 1873.[17]

In his last report to Indian agent and priest Eugene Chirouse, Henry Smith argued that inadequate pay prevented physicians from ensuring the health of Indians, saying that "so rapidly are they passing away that the question as to their ultimate extinction often forces itself upon my mind. Is the Indian race on this continent really in its dotage, and if so, why? Do races of men like individuals attain a meridian vigor and then necessarily pass into senility and decay, and are the Indians as a race now in their wane, soon to pass entirely from the face of the earth to remain here only with the things that have been?" By answering his first question with another for the man of God, Smith showed that he was wrestling with deeper issues. If the Indian race was dying away, what about the other races? Would Smith's own race suffer the same fate? And if disease destroyed the Indians, what would bring about the demise of the white race? An ominous repetition of events would present Smith with a plausible answer.[18]

While growth had stalled on the Snohomish, it puttered along in Seattle, whose timber and coal made it a destination for boatmen and traders. In 1869, the legislature had granted Seattle a city charter, granting it the power to tax. Local investors had financed a rickety narrow-gauge rail and barge connection from mines near Lake Washington to Lake Union and the Seattle waterfront, and despite the decision of the Northern Pacific to locate its terminus at Tacoma, Seattle residents vowed to build a transcontinental railroad of their own.

During a May Day picnic in 1873, most of the town's able-bodied men brushed out part of the right of way. At first, the narrow-gauge Seattle & Walla Walla Railroad (S&WWR) advanced only twelve miles, to the Renton mines, but that modest stretch made Seattle a prime coaling port in the eastern Pacific. Residents coined the term "Seattle spirit" to celebrate their refusal to die at the command of a powerful corporation, but its admiration society was decidedly local.

One year later, travel writer Charles Nordhoff wrote a nationally popular account of the West Coast, featuring California, Hawaii, and Oregon. The single page devoted to Washington Territory began "When . . . you enter Washington Territory, your ears begin to be assaulted by the most barbarous names imaginable." Of the last towns on his list of towns with native names, he writes, "Seattle is sufficiently barbarous; Steilacoom is no better; and I suspect that the Northern Pacific Railroad terminus has been fixed at Tacoma—if it has been fixed—because that is one of the few places on Puget Sound whose name does not inspire horror and disgust."[19]

Many hired to build the S&WWR were Chinese, and here we come to a time when themes from Seattle's beginning were reshuffled and dealt into an arrangement presenting a cruelly familiar pattern. Present since the maritime fur trade, many Chinese arrived in California during the gold rush and traveled in search of other El Dorados or paying jobs throughout the West.

Leaving Guangdong Province during the Taiping Rebellion, Chin Chun Hock had traveled to America in 1861 and worked at Yesler's mill, where he met Curley and his daughter Mary Curley. As was often the case for native people of her generation, Westerners made her father's name her last name. In 1868, Chin opened the Wa Chong Company, selling imported cigars, rice, tea, sugar, opium, and fireworks. On April 16, 1869, he married sixteen-year-old Mary. In the weird alchemy of Xwəljutsid, English, and Cantonese, Mary Curley became Mary Kelly or Kerry, while her Cantonese name was Mei Lee.[20]

Developing close ties with the Suquamish, Chin purchased land at Port Orchard, renting part to logger George Harmon, who married one of Mary's sisters, Jeannie. At Port Orchard, Mary bore Chin three sons and a daughter. Accompanying Chin on a trip to China months after the birth of her third son, Mary developed a lung infection in the hot, humid south of the country and died on July 13, 1885. She was buried next to Chin's first wife in Guangzhou, the provincial capital, taking the story of her extraordinary odyssey with her.

Many Chinese became unemployed when the Northern Pacific, which had hired them, went bankrupt in 1873, beginning what became known nationally as the Long Depression. As unemployment spread throughout the West, white workers came to fear the Chinese as economic rivals.

In 1870, there were eleven hundred residents in Seattle; by 1880, a few more than three thousand—still small potatoes but a sign of steady growth. The collapse of the Northern Pacific delayed completion of its transcontinental line, but because small vessels carried most local commerce and it was cheaper to make short trips to and from Seattle than from outlying towns, Seattle became commercially dominant. Its deep harbor and "mosquito fleet" attracted shipyards, foundries, and banks, and even though larger mills cut and exported more lumber, Seattle's considerable production was consumed largely by its own growth.[21]

Meanwhile, on his island, Smith had to deal with a dike that had broken and flooded his farm. In 1878, he gathered up his papers and diary and brought his family back to Seattle to send his children to school and participate in the town's rebirth.

By then, civic leadership came increasingly from a new class emigrating from the urban East and Midwest. Better educated and more cosmopolitan, their ascendancy reflected a change in the definition of "wealth" from land ownership to investment capital. Seattle's middle class divided into "Old Seattle," the landowning pioneer elite, and a "New Seattle" made up of professionals and businesspeople. With different backgrounds and outlooks, their interests inevitably clashed. Pioneer historian Eldridge Morse accused Arthur Denny's family and his colleagues of a narrowness of thinking that negatively impacted the town. Denny responded by branding come-lately critics as "degenerate scrubs, too cowardly to face the same dangers that our pioneer men and women did, and too lazy to perform an honest day's work if it would procure them a homestead in paradise."[22]

In his town house on the corner of Second and James, Smith opened a medical office, but he still spent summers at the cove, tending his farm. Two years later, he erected the London House hotel—just up from Smith's Wharf, a waterfront property, which he purchased and extended from the foot of Pike Street, near today's Pike Place Market. In the spring of 1879, the Smiths' last child, Lillian, was born at the cove as prosperity seemed imminent.

But hope was again delayed. On the eve of the '80s, the Long Depression was still felt nationwide, and on Puget Sound, mills and mines suffered frequent closures. In the summer of 1880, efforts by the S&WWR's directors to obtain financial help from Wall Street resulted in the railroad being purchased by German immigrant, journalist, and entrepreneur Henry Villard, who—with financial genius and a famous "blind pool" of investors—also gained control of Seattle's nemesis, the Northern Pacific. Like a rube at a rigged poker game, residents feared their ace in the hole had become a losing hand. The town was maturing but dividing, and it appeared that outsiders were now calling the shots.

---

Curley died in 1879. On February 16, 1881, Chief Seattle's last son, Jim, died at the Port Madison Reservation. As at his father's death, no local paper noted his passing, except a small short-lived sheet, the *Tri-Weekly Seattle Fin-Back*, which made random, colorful mention of local Indians.

Two weeks later, the *Fin-Back* printed a tale set "long, long years ago, when the mighty trees of the forest, protected the soil which we now occupy, from the ardent gaze of the sun" and introduced its characters, "a primitive child of the forest, an old Indian . . . beloved by his tribe for his quiet and peaceable ways," and his daughter. Approaching death, the old Indian reveals a final vision to her: "I see men with pale faces hurrying here and there through the woods, and as they go, the trees fall before them . . . in their places are built great wigwams . . . the water is covered with great canoes with sails; and I see coming in the speed of the wind great wagons drawn by horses of iron, and it brings many people." In time, the story concluded, the old Indian's people pass away, and "the last of our once great tribe—the father of his people—is taken away, and the pale faced men carry him to his place of rest saying, 'Great was this man of the forest, and great was his people, but they are gone, and with this man dies the last of his name and his tribe—Seattle.'"[23]

It is a strange little tale told at a remarkable time. It calls up a familiar name, but this Seattle has the prophetic ability to see the future. His people pass away, and the pale faces arrive to bury the man who saw images of the world to come. The piece sounds like Smith but lacks the tidal surge of his prose. It marries the railroad's promise with

Indian removal—vivid hope eclipsing a guilty conscience. The pale faces bury the chief but keep his talismanic name. An anonymous tale printed in an ephemeral publication captures a pivotal moment in the evolution of a myth.

Cities anxious, even desperate, to succeed use whatever resources are at hand, and someone took this man's potent name to craft a compelling image. Seattle, dead these many years, grandfather of Moses, the dwarf from the land of the dead, had returned as a prophet. He would be recalled in settings marked by troublingly familiar events: a lynching, a farcical trial, and the tragic expulsion of a reviled people. And to an angry community raging against itself, he would deliver a haunting speech.

That August, Mary Ann Smith died. In town with the children while her husband helped farmhands bring in the harvest at the cove, she felt feverish and, fearing contagion, left the older children in charge and walked up First Hill to check into Grace Hospital. Henry Smith learned this at midnight but, not overly concerned, waited until morning to visit. When he arrived, she was dead. She had been given chloroform to help her sleep, and a heedless spill on her pillow had suffocated her.

Smith worked out his stunned grief at the cove, adding a wing to the dormitory, where he moved his family to protect them from the town's charlatans. The next year, he gave land at the cove for a schoolhouse used for church services and Sunday school, hired a cook, and employed a young woman to homeschool his children.

By this time, the town had spread east to the crest dividing Elliott Bay from Lake Washington. A period diorama shows long piers servicing steam and sailing vessels, backed by hulking brick and frame buildings atop rubble that had buried the little crossing place. Upslope, houses of vaguely Italianate style merged with farmsteads and forlorn trees, but the artist left out the stumps, garbage, and smoke, whose stench gave the city away long before one actually saw it.

Growth attracted transient newcomers, mostly young men, who made up the bulk of the working population. And by the mid-1880s, the Chinese population had grown to 13 percent of Seattle's adult male workforce. They ran small groceries, restaurants, and drugstores, manufactured cigars, slippers, and coffins, and collected scrap. In the working-class district taking shape south of Yesler's mill, "Chinatown" occupied the blocks from Mill Street (now Yesler Way) to Main and from Commercial Street (now First Avenue) to Fourth Avenue—where the Duwamish once lived.

An adjacent patch, called "the Lava Beds," became a vice district, infamous for saloons, dance halls, brothels, and crime. Orange Jacobs, a University of Michigan graduate who headed west with a law degree in 1852 and ended up in Seattle, where he served a year as mayor in 1880, recalled that after nightfall, holdups were so common that a knock on the door was typically met by homeowners brandishing pistols.[24]

In October 1881, George Payne, a denizen of the Lava Beds, shot down police officer David Sires, who became Seattle's first police fatality. Payne was jailed pending trial in January of 1882, when popular businessman George Reynolds was shot and killed by two thugs downtown. The fire bell rang, and a crowd dubbing itself a "Committee of Safety" found them hiding in a hayrick. The King County sheriff, Louis Wyckoff, and Seattle's chief of police, John McGraw, marched them before Justice Samuel Coombs, elected justice of the peace in 1881, who remanded them for trial in the morning, but officers had to threaten the crowd with drawn weapons to get them safely back to jail.

The next morning, the crowd stormed the court, dragged out the pair, and hanged them from scantlings lodged in the branches of some maple trees fronting Henry Yesler's house. Then they dragged Payne out of jail and hanged him, too, cheered on by most of the town's male population. Territorial supreme court chief justice Roger Greene, a resident of Seattle, waded into the crowd to cut the nooses with his knife, but he was roughly turned away. In shock, Wyckoff died of a heart attack the next day, and the scantlings remained aloft as a warning.

Yesler joked that his maples had never yielded better fruit, and Mayor Jacobs defended the action as necessary in the raw frontier, but Greene called the public lynching "an explosion of savagery," and the event troubled those who did not want their town with its odd name depicted as some blighted outpost.[25]

The affair opened a new and worrisome division between middle-class property owners, old and new, and a large, turbulent workforce. Alarmed civic leaders organized the Law and Order League, heavy with names of Old Seattle, which called for an end to municipal corruption and elimination of the vice district. This echoed national calls for reform, but in advance of the national effort, locals also sought political power by convincing territorial legislators to give women the right to vote and serve on juries, which they did in the fall of 1883.

A grand jury called that year to hear evidence of lax liquor law enforcement returned indictments that led to convictions, but the liquor trade continued. When the grand jury was recalled to issue more indictments that led to more convictions but with the same null effect, many citizens concluded that officials were in cahoots with saloon owners. The serpents from the Lava Beds had slithered into city hall.

By December 1883, Seattle's population was approaching eight thousand. On New Year's Day 1884, the *Weekly Intelligencer*, soon to be the *Seattle Post-Intelligencer* (nicknamed the *P-I*), reprinted Scammon's description of Seattle's funeral eighteen years before. Compared to the *Fin-Back*'s elegy for Seattle the prophet, the *Weekly Intelligencer*'s decision to provide a more factual account of his funeral reminded residents how far they had come—from a time when such an important role was played by a native chief, the city's namesake, who had fathered and nurtured their vulnerable settlement at the time of a dangerous moon.

In June, the Law and Order League called on supporters to assemble in Arthur Denny's apple orchard at Fourth Avenue and Marion Street to support a slate of candidates favoring "the enforcement of existing laws and ordinances." Four hundred stalwarts assembled, most of them Old Seattle—branded as naive "Apple Orchardists" by their opponents, represented by members of the Business Men's Club, the Young Men's Independent Club, and the Protective Association, who self-identified as New Seattle. In the spirited elections of '84, supported by women voters, law and order won.

But that summer, the failure of several New York banks incited panic on Wall Street, and nervous investors held on to their cash. As investment dried up, industries across the country fired workers, and mills shut down. Like the native people who did not imagine the trouble trade with Westerners would bring, few old settlers could fathom the instability and turmoil that would come with industrialization or the powerlessness they would feel when decisions made by faceless operatives thousands of miles away killed their dreams and blighted their lives.

Henry Villard had promised Seattle rail connection to the east, and that summer standard-gauge tracks from town reached the main line, but he had overspent and was removed as head of the Northern Pacific. After that, corporate officers offered minimal rail service from Tacoma to Seattle: one trip a day at inconvenient times. When townspeople complained, service was canceled.

Adding to unemployment, the shutdown of the vice district worsened Seattle's economic woes as the still-employed went elsewhere to buy a drink and a good time. New Seattle turned the sharp slump into a campaign issue, and their slate of candidates drove most of the Apple Orchardists from office in 1885. The saloons were back in business, but a darker threat loomed.

As mills and mines closed, wages fell to half of what they were at the decade's start. The railroad had employed thousands of Chinese men, willing to work for less than whites, and when they showed up unemployed in Seattle and elsewhere, tensions grew. Unable to vote, the Chinese became more convenient targets than distant corporations armed with lawyers, private armies like the Pinkertons, and well-tended politicians.

In the summer of 1885, anger and racism exploded against them in Wyoming and spread rapidly. West of the Cascades, miners drove Chinese workers from the Newcastle and Renton mines in September, and white and Indian laborers together drove them from Andy Wold's hops farm in the settlement of Issaquah, east of Seattle, killing three. More Chinese fled to the towns, but in Tacoma a group called the Anti-Chinese League met to drive them out. Led by Mayor Jacob Weisbach, and supported by the Knights of Labor, the league, under a banner demanding "The Chinese Must Go," called for a regional Anti-Chinese Congress to meet in centrally located Seattle on September 28. Their intention echoed pastor David Blaine's dark wish regarding the Indians back in 1854: "It is supposed they will be removed from our midst. What a blessing it will be both to them and the whites, if this can be effected."

A brass band greeted the anti-Chinese delegates, who were led by torchlight to Seattle's new brick Occidental Hotel. They set November 1 as the date at which Chinese residents must leave. Towns organized committees to expel them, and on October 3 a group called the

Committee of Fifteen met at Seattle's Yesler Hall to plan action. But as they met, others fearing the movement's revolutionary rhetoric met at Frye's Opera House to deputize an armed militia, the Home Guard, to protect property.

The city began to divide along economic and class lines: New Seattle from Old Seattle, and both from an angry working class. All had grievances, but many feared that as passions rose, violence would be inevitable, fears eerily similar to those in 1855 when residents had argued over whether to keep or expel the Duwamish in town. Support for the Chinese rarely went beyond business owners' defense of private property, but some sought to distinguish between the residents who were here legally, thought to deserve protection, and those brought in illegally. Some Chinese left; most who owned businesses remained. Chin Chun Hock moved to Port Orchard to wait out the trouble.

In late October at the Seattle District Court, whites, Indians, and Chinese were brought in to testify at the trial of Perry Bayne, a logger and one of three indicted for the murders of the Chinese workers in Issaquah. The first few days of the trial came and went without incident as Chinese from several towns left for Victoria. Then on November 2, after six days of prosecutorial incompetence and evident bribery, the jury at the Bayne murder trial issued the same verdict as had jurors at the 1854 Messachie Jim murder trial: acquittal. The next day, as mill whistles blew, Tacoma's committeemen entered its Chinatown, smashed down doors, pulled men and families out into a driving rain, and herded them under armed guard to the railroad tracks. Before the eyes of silent authority, hundreds of Chinese residents, clutching what little they could carry, climbed into freight cars destined for Portland.[26]

Observing their fate, many Chinese in Seattle agreed to leave, and Henry Yesler, serving a second one-year term as mayor, called a meeting at Frye's Opera House on November 6 to announce the Chinese's plans. Prominent lawyer Thomas Burke blamed the Tacoma trouble on its German-born mayor and made himself a target of working-class ire by castigating the anti-Chinese as anti-American, but businessman John Leary announced that the Chinese had agreed to leave, and the crowd left generally satisfied that the issue had been resolved.

But as 1886 began, some 350 Chinese remained, and Chin Chun Hock's Wa Chong Company still advertised in the *P-I*. On February 7, in collusion with the Seattle police, vigilantes entered Chinatown and ordered residents to pack, and teamsters hauled them to the steamer *Queen of the Pacific*, bound for San Francisco. As a crowd grew and word reached city and territorial officials, Governor Watson Squire wired a request for federal troops and imposed martial law, calling on citizens to stay home. The Home Guard, the Seattle Rifles, and Company D of the territorial militia were mobilized, and Chief Justice Greene issued a writ of habeas corpus, ordering the captain of the *Queen* and the Chinese on board to show up at his court the next day.

At seven in the morning, the anti-Chinese leaders were arrested. Chief Justice Greene told the Chinese assembled in his courtroom that if they chose to stay, they would be protected. Hearing a mob shouting outside, most decided to leave if they could get passage, and after $1,400 was collected, 200 boarded the *Queen* while another 150 remained at the dock awaiting later passage. When it was decided that these could return home, John McGraw, elected sheriff after the death of Wyckoff, began leading them back, followed by the Home Guard. But the crowd, thinking it had been double-crossed, blocked the way. Shouts grew to a roar, shots were fired, and five in the blocking crowd fell wounded, one fatally. For forty-five terrible minutes, screaming men faced the rifles of a panicky Home Guard, which was forming a square around terrified Chinese. Then the militia arrived on the run, leveled loaded rifles at the mob, and, after officials shouted out what had been agreed to, the angry crowd drifted away.

Massacre had been averted, but passions boiled. At the cove, Henry Smith spent those terrible days after the incident following accounts in local papers. He read accusations hurled later during bitter municipal and county elections, when the community seemed intent on devouring itself.

In July, members of the Anti-Chinese Congress formed the People's Party and ran a slate of candidates against their opposition, called the Loyal League. Visceral arguments over the rights of property versus the rights of labor pitted class against class, race against race, and men against women all through that lacerating period.

Smith and other old settlers, grown wealthy from sales of their land, endured a stream of abuse, branded as "old mud sills" and "dog salmon aristocrats" by critics scornful of their rustic, old-fashioned ways. "They have got to be brushed out of the way," Arthur Denny wrote bitterly, summing up the critics' sentiment, "before the country or the place can ever amount to anything. They have had their day and a few first class funerals will cause us to prosper."[27]

In the November elections, supported by angry women voters, the People's Party won by a landslide. Those opposing female suffrage, knowing they would not find support in the legislature, sought to have it revoked in the courts, where they eventually prevailed with the argument that, like earlier slaves and present-day Indians, women were not citizens and, therefore, could not vote. In February 1887, the territorial supreme court, all male, agreed and took away the women's vote.

This was the early pioneers' last effort to direct Seattle's affairs, and with it the town's pioneering period ends. Once again, through acts of violence and injustice, whites had driven out a vulnerable people they had come to despise. But the anger and hatred that engulfed the city was not unique to the Pacific Northwest or even the wider West. Chicago's bloody 1886 Haymarket Riot highlighted a growing fear of immigrants that excited the nation's first "Red Scare" and threatened economic rebellion, the so-called "Great Uprising of Labor," more violent even than the Civil War.

---

Out at the cove, Henry Smith penned a series of essays for the *Seattle Sunday Star*, a weekly catering to families. The first, "Coming North in 1852," appearing in the summer of 1887, began with an evocation of a lost world and departing pioneers, "from whose slowly dimming memories may be rescued much that might be of interest to future generations."[28]

Nine essays followed, describing wilderness glories, the coming of Governor Stevens, the Yakima War, and other topics incident to the region's development. In the tenth and final essay, "Scraps from a Diary," Smith called on Chief Seattle to deliver a warning. The doctor had watched a race once dominant decline from disease to the point of disappearance. Among his own people, he had observed a different malady growing in virulence. Thirty-three years after hearing Seattle's speech in translation, Dr. Smith worked his penciled notes into a dire prognosis as one race passed the baton of history to another. It appeared in the *Star* on October 29, 1887, as a supplement to Sabbath reading.[29]

### EARLY REMINISCENCES
#### Number Ten
### SCRAPS FROM A DIARY

Chief Seattle—A Gentleman by Instinct—His Native Eloquence, Etc., Etc.

Old Chief Seattle was the largest Indian I ever saw, and by far the noblest looking. He stood six feet full in his moccasins, was broad shouldered, deep chested, and finely proportioned. His eyes were large, intelligent, expressive, and friendly when in repose, and faithfully mirrored the varying moods of the great soul that looked through them. He was usually solemn, silent and dignified, but on great occasions moved among assembled multitudes like a Titian [sic] among, Lilliputians, and his lightest word was law.

When rising to speak in council or to tender advice, all eyes were turned upon him, and deep-toned, sonorous and eloquent sentences rolled from his lips like the ceaseless thunders of cataracts flowing from exhaustless fountains, and

HIS MAGNIFICENT BEARING

was as noble as that of the most cultivated military chieftain in command of forces of a continent. Neither his eloquence, his dignity or his grace, were acquired. They were as native to his manhood as leaves and blossoms are to a flowering almond.

His influence was marvelous. He might have been an emperor but all his instincts were democratic, and he ruled his loyal subjects with kindness and paternal benignity.

He was always flattered by marked attention from white men, and never so much as when seated at their tables, and on such occasions he manifested more than anywhere else the genuine instincts of a gentleman.

When Governor Stevens first arrived in Seattle and told the natives he had been appointed commissioner of Indian affairs for

Washington Territory, they gave him a demonstrative reception in front of Dr. Maynard's office, near the water front on Main street. The Bay swarmed with canoes and the shore was lined with a living mass of swaying, writhing, dusky humanity until

OLD CHIEF SEATTLE'S

trumpet-toned voice rolled over the immense multitude, like a startling reveille of a bass drum, when silence became as instantaneous and perfect as that which follows a clap of thunder from a clear sky.

The governor was then introduced to the native multitude by Dr. Maynard, and at once commenced, in a conversational, plain and straightforward style, an explanation of his mission among them, which is too well understood to require recapitulation.

When he sat down, Chief Seattle arose with all the dignity of a senator, who carries the responsibilities of a great nation on his shoulders. Placing one hand on the governor's head and slowly pointing heavenward with the index finger of the other, he commenced his memorable address in solemn and impressive tones.

Yonder sky that has wept tears of compassion on our fathers for centuries untold, and which, to us, looks eternal, may change. Today it is fair, tomorrow it may be overcast with clouds. My words are like the stars that never set. What Seattle says, the great chief, Washington, ([Smith's insert] The Indians in early times thought that Washington was still alive. They knew the name to be that of a president, and when they heard of the president at Washington they mistook the name of the city for the name of the reigning chief. They thought, also, that King George was still England's monarch, because the Hudson bay traders called themselves "King George men." This innocent deception the company was shrewd enough not to explain away for the Indians had more respect for them than they would have had, had they known England was ruled by a woman. Some of us have learned better.) can rely upon, with as much certainty as our pale-face brothers can rely upon the return of the seasons.

The son of the white chief says his father sends us greetings of friendship and good will. This is kind, for we know he has little need of our friendship in return, because his people are many. They are like the grass that covers the vast prairies, while my people are few, and resemble the scattering trees of a storm-swept plain.

The great, and I presume also good, white chief sends us word that he wants to buy our lands but is willing to allow us to reserve enough to live on comfortably. This indeed appears generous, for the red man no longer has rights that he need respect, and the offer may be wise, also, for we are no longer in need of a great country.

THERE WAS A TIME

when our people covered the whole land, as the waves of a wind-ruffled sea cover its shell-paved floor. But that time has long since passed away with the greatness of tribes now almost forgotten. I will not mourn over our untimely decay, nor reproach my pale-face brothers for hastening it, for we, too, may have been somewhat to blame.

When our young men grow angry at some real or imaginary wrong, and disfigure their faces with black paint, their hearts, also, are disfigured and turn black, and then their cruelty is relentless and knows no bounds, and our old men are not able to restrain them.

But let us hope that hostilities between the red-man and his pale-face brothers may never return. We would have everything to lose and nothing to gain.

True it is, that revenge, and with our young braves, is considered gain, even at the cost of their own lives, but old men who stay at home in times of war, and old women, who have sons to lose, know better.

Our great father Washington, for I presume he is now our father as well as yours, since George has moved his boundaries to the north; our great and good father, I say, sends us word by his son, who, no doubt, is a great chief among his people, that if we do as he desires, he will protect us. His brave armies will be to us as a bristling wall of strength, and his great ships of war will fill our harbors so that our ancient enemies far to the northward, the Simsians and Hydas, will no longer frighten our women and old men. Then he will be our father and we will be his children.

BUT CAN THIS EVER BE?

Your God loves your people and hates mine; he folds his strong arms lovingly around the white man and leads him as a father leads his infant son, but he has forsaken his red children; he makes your people wax strong every day, and soon they will fill the land; while my people are ebbing away like a fast-receding tide, that will never flow again. The white man's God cannot love his red children or he would protect them. They seem to be orphans and can look nowhere for help. How then can we become brothers? How can your father become our father and bring us prosperity and awaken in us dreams of returning greatness?

Your God seems to us to be partial. He came to the white man. We never saw Him; never even heard His voice: He gave the white man laws but He had no word for His red children whose teeming millions filled this vast continent as the stars fill the firmament. No, we are two distinct races and must ever remain so. There is little in common between us. The ashes of our ancestors are sacred and their final resting place is hallowed ground, while you wander away from the tombs of your fathers seemingly without regret.

Your religion was written on tables of stone by the iron finger of an angry God, lest you might forget it. The red-man could never remember nor comprehend it.

Our religion is the traditions of our ancestors, the dreams of our old men, given them by the great Spirit, and the visions of our sachems, and is written in the hearts of our people.

Your dead cease to love you and the homes of their nativity as soon as they pass the portals of the tomb. They wander far off beyond the stars, are soon forgotten, and never return. Our dead never forget the beautiful world that gave them being. They still love its winding rivers, its great mountains and its sequestered vales, and they ever yearn in tenderest affection over the lonely hearted living and return often to visit and comfort them.

Day and night cannot dwell together. The red man has ever fled the approach of the white man, as the changing mists on the mountain side flee before the blazing morning sun.

However, your proposition seems a just one, and I think my folks will accept it and will retire to the reservation you offer them, and we will dwell apart and in peace, for the words of the great white chief seem to be the voice of nature speaking to my people out of the thick darkness that is fast gathering around them like a dense fog floating inward from a midnight sea.

It matters but little where we pass the remainder of our days.

THEY ARE NOT MANY.

The Indian's night promises to be dark. No bright star hovers about the horizon. Sad-voiced winds moan in the distance. Some grim Nemesis of our race is on the red-man's trail, and wherever he goes he will still hear the sure approaching footsteps of the fell destroyer and prepare to meet his doom, as does the wounded doe that hears the approaching footsteps of the hunter. A few more moons, a few more winters and not one of all the mighty hosts that once filled this broad land or that now roam in fragmentary bands through these vast solitudes will remain to weep over the tombs of a people once as powerful and hopeful as your own.

But why should we repine? Why should I murmur at the fate of my people? Tribes are made up of individuals and are no better than they. Men come and go like the waves of the sea. A tear, a tamanawus, a dirge, and they are gone from our longing eyes forever. Even the white man, whose God walked and talked with him, as friend to friend, is not exempt from the common destiny. We may be brothers after all. We shall see.

We will ponder your proposition, and when we have decided we will tell you. But should we accept it, I here and now make this the first condition: That we will not be denied the privilege, without molestation, of visiting at will the graves of our ancestors and friends. Every part of this country is sacred to my people. Every hill-side, every valley, every plain and grove has been hallowed by some fond memory or some sad experience of my tribe.

EVEN THE ROCKS

That seem to lie dumb as they swelter in the sun along the silent seashore in solemn grandeur thrill with memories of past events connected with the fate of my people, and the very dust under your feet responds more lovingly to our footsteps than to yours, because it is the ashes of our ancestors, and our bare feet are conscious of the sympathetic touch, for the soil is rich with the life of our kindred.

The sable braves, and fond mothers, and glad-hearted maidens, and the little children who lived and rejoiced here, and whose very names are now forgotten, still love these solitudes, and their deep fastnesses at eventide grow shadowy with the presence of dusky spirits. And when the last red man shall have perished from the earth and his memory among white men shall have become a myth, these shores shall swarm with the invisible dead of my tribe, and when your children's children shall think themselves alone in the field, the store, the shop, upon the highway or in the silence of the woods they will not be alone. In all the earth there is no place dedicated to solitude. At night, when the streets of your cities and villages shall be silent, and you think them deserted, they will throng with the returning hosts that once filled and still love this beautiful land. The white man will never be alone. Let him be just and deal kindly with my people, for the dead are not altogether powerless.

Other speakers followed, but I took no notes. Governor Stevens' reply was brief. He merely promised to meet them in general council on some future occasion to discuss the proposed treaty. Chief Seattle's promise to adhere to the treaty, should one be ratified, was observed to the letter, for he was ever the unswerving and faithful friend of the white man. The above is but a fragment of his speech, and lacks all the charm lent by the grace and earnestness of the sable old orator, and the occasion.

*H. A. Smith*

# CHAPTER TEN

*"The dead are not altogether powerless."*

Seattle's evocation of the Indian dead wandering the land can lift the hairs up on the back of your neck. But are the words Chief Seattle's or Henry Smith's? In the 1990s, teacher and writer Eli Gifford analyzed the 1887 speech. He interviewed Marilyn Jones, curator of the Suquamish Museum, at Port Madison, who told him that Suquamish elders believed that Smith began work on the speech eight months after he heard it and during the following five years worked with Seattle to "get it as accurate as possible." If Smith worked from notes, Seattle relied on memory, and Smith stated in the *Star* that what he wrote was only a fragment of Seattle's speech.[1]

Smith's earlier writings often feature idiosyncratic word forms—for example, he uses *tam-amins*, "supernatural rites," for the more generally used Jargon word *tamanowus*, the slight variant of which is found in the published speech. In the speech, he also uses the names "Simsians" and "Hydas," not commonly used in the 1850s, to identify northern raiders. It is also not likely that, in snowy January, Seattle would have described beach boulders as "the rocks that . . . swelter in the sun along the silent seashore." All of this suggests at least a later editing. But the speech's unique rhetorical structure appears in none of Smith's other writings, and the fact that it is the best thing he ever wrote points to a powerful original.

To claim his hearers' attention, Smith has Seattle begin by announcing that he speaks reliable truth. He brushes aside Governor Isaac Stevens's claim that the president sent him out of a desire for friendship, pointing out that a president of a great and numerous people had no need for friendship from a group so small. Seattle praises the offer to buy his people's lands while leaving them enough to live comfortably on as generous and wise.

Seattle asserts that his people were once far more numerous and allows that their wars contributed to their decline but, shockingly, rejects the notion that the Great White Father would protect them as he would his own children. He lists the differences between them, particularly in their relationship to God, who demonstrably cares more for his white children. Americans, he continues, wander far from their ancestors' graves without regret (Benjamin Shaw had him say much the same thing). And just as Americans leave their dead behind, their dead themselves wander off, to a distant heaven beyond the stars, unconcerned for their living kin. In contrast, the native dead, Seattle tells Stevens, love their land and return to visit and comfort their living kin. As a precondition for acceptance of the treaty, Seattle demands that his people be guaranteed unhindered access to the graves of their ancestors and friends. No, his people and the Americans are as different as night from day, he says, so how can the president be the father of both; how can they become as brothers? It is a rhetorical question.

Although his living people are few and the Americans many, he reminds them that both groups are made up of individuals who "come and go like the waves of the sea," and that Americans who would die and be buried here will be surrounded by the Indian dead. The long native presence in this land, he says, ensures that their dead are many, but unlike the Americans' ancestral dead, the native dead remain in the homeland they love. Marshaling a spectral vision of this potent host in its paradoxical vitality, Seattle insists that American authority must "be just and deal kindly with my people, for the dead are not altogether powerless." In Seattle's vivid and compelling image, the native living and the dead are one. Americans might think they could buy and sell the land, he argues, but it could only be shared, not possessed; at death, the land would possess them as it has untold generations of native people.

Smith knew of other famous native orators such as Logan, the late-eighteenth-century Cayuga war leader whom he mentioned in a poem printed a week later in the *Star*. Lines in the speech also echo those made in 1805 by Red Jacket, a famous Seneca chief in upstate New York:

There was a time when our forefathers owned this great island.
Their seats extended from the rising to the setting sun. . . .
Brother, our seats were once large, and yours were small. You

have now become a great people and we have scarcely a place left to spread our blankets. . . . Brother, the Great Spirit made us all; but he has made a great difference between his white and red children.[2]

These sentiments are common in the native oratory written down by conquering whites, and Smith may have colored what he had heard Seattle say in the shades of these earlier forms. But Red Jacket's words also voiced the genuine grief and alarm native groups felt as they dealt with the calamity of white invasion, feelings that became familiar to Seattle and his people, the leitmotifs of the dispossessed.

But after saying that "tribes are made up of individuals" who "come and go like the waves of the sea," the crucial following line, "Even the white man . . . is not exempt from the common destiny," voices the idea Henry Smith proposed to Father Eugene Chirouse: that entire races, not just individuals, grow old, weaken, and die. Smith parallels the sense of crisis attending Seattle's speech in January 1854, when Governor Stevens announced upcoming treaty councils, with the bloody communal violence that preceded his publication of the speech on October 29, 1887. It is likely, too, that Smith sought to balance the season in which Seattle spoke—near the solstice, when the road to the land of the dead lay open—by publishing his version near All Hallows' Eve on October 31, knowing, likely via his Irish-American wife, that ghosts were also said to prowl the land during the Celtic feast of Samhain, prior to the remembrances of the dead on the Christian feasts of All Saints' Day and All Souls' Day on November 1 and 2.

Seattle sought to impress upon Stevens that his people, while few in number, could rely on the hosts of their dead, who were not powerless, Smith also has Seattle suggest that the demise of his race prefigures the decline of the Americans. Seattle's rhetorical question "How then can we become brothers?"—which bespeaks kinship's requirement of justice and kindness—translates in Smith's writing to a warning of fraternal doom: "We may be brothers after all."

But Seattle was too invested in his hybrid community to portray his people as anything other than the vigorous partners they were. Speaking to his people as much as to Stevens, he sought to hearten them, not bewail their demise. By his constant efforts to involve them in an emerging economy, we understand that he did not see them disappearing anytime soon. In Amelia Snaetlum's recollection, his call to his people to "observe the changers" closely was not meant to be a pathetic diversion but a spur to learn. He accepted American authority despite its failings and was openly baptized and confirmed in a Western faith, but his efforts to promote native success on and off the reservation did not presume that his people would disappear, as Smith and his colleagues assumed they would.

Other speeches given by Seattle and contemporary headmen—however traduced by the Jargon—evidence a vivid, pithy discourse, direct and engaged, even defiant. Smith's orotund, recessional tone, weighted by doom, overlays a spare and robust original.

A single tattered copy of "Scraps from a Diary" from the *Seattle Sunday Star* survives. In a note at the top, someone has written, "One of the greatest speeches in history." Most of Smith's nine preceding essays are lost or survive only in rarely recalled fragments, yet the speech has never lost its acclaim as being one of the greatest delivered by a Native American.

I have described the elections of 1886 as the end of Seattle's pioneering period, although the great fire of June 6, 1889, is more often made the marker. The ashen vistas left after the fire prompted British writer Rudyard Kipling, on tour, to write that he knew then what being "rubbed out" meant. But citizens made the disaster a part of the city's plucky image of itself and enjoyed telling how, with smoke still rising, a call to redirect money collected for the victims of Pennsylvania's recent Johnstown Flood toward its own needs was shouted down.

Washington became a state on November 11, rounding out the year as a curtain between acts. And after decades of slow growth, Seattle's population took off as railroads transformed the raw outpost into a flourishing city.[3]

The publication of Seattle's speech inspired surviving pioneers to mark the chief's unadorned grave. With the Suquamish and Duwamish, they erected a marble cross engraved with the Latin acronym *IHS* (*In Hoc Spiritus*), "In His Spirit," on his grave mound. At its public dedication on June 28, 1890, tribal members danced a slow *samanowash* around it to honor their patriarch. On its base was inscribed:

SEATTLE
Chief of the
Suquampsh, and
Allied tribes.
DIED JUNE 7, 1866.
The firm friend of
the whites, and for him the
CITY of SEATTLE
was named by its
FOUNDERS.

Baptismal name
NOAH SEALTH,
AGE PROBABLY
80 YEARS.

---

The inscription answered the basic questions about who Seattle was and why the city was named after him. In the meantime, the city and Henry Smith prospered. In March of '89, the Seattle, Lake Shore and Eastern Railway, another local enterprise, purchased 611 acres of Smith's cove property for $75,000, making him a wealthy man.[4]

Seattle's population surpassed Walla Walla's in the '80s and bypassed rival Tacoma in 1890, to become the largest city in the state. A year later, local businessman Frederick Grant, a New Seattle booster, produced the city's first comprehensive history, which emphasized that "we who reside in Seattle today do not regard ourselves in any way as pioneers." An account of the town's first forty years and sketches of leading figures filled his book's more than five hundred pages. In "Settlement and Pioneer Times," his second chapter, Grant turns the native world into a stage for the American drama, writing, "some brief description of the tribes about Elliott Bay with their noted men will make a more definite background for the historical scene." He describes Seattle as "short and heavy, as much as 180 pounds, and round shouldered. His face was refined and benevolent but not particularly strong." Grant belittles Seattle's friendship with the whites, noting that during the Yakima War, "he did not manifest the concern of Pat Kanim for their safety."[5]

Grant's portrayal is not as negative as Hubert Howe Bancroft's in the latter's *History of Washington, Idaho and Montana*, which had been published the previous year, in which he describes Seattle as "a naked savage who conversed only in signs and grunts." Bancroft also derides Seattle's recollection of Captain George Vancouver, which Grant gives credit to, as a "stretch of the imagination." Grant copied the Seattle speech from the *Star* with minor changes, but he included it in his brief biographical sketch of Smith. By doing so, he associated it with Smith rather than Seattle.[6]

As the modern city became more reflective, articles about its namesake finally and more frequently appeared in its press. At the dedication of Seattle's grave marker, the *Post-Intelligencer*, by now the city's paper of record, quoted Arthur Denny, about the chief: "His disposition was not of the turbulent and aggressive kind, but was of the mildest and most generous type with all the firmness and courage necessary to defend and maintain the rights of his people against unfriendly tribes." Denny was not the scholar Samuel Coombs was, however, and in "Good Chief Seattle," printed by the *P-I* in 1893, Coombs described Seattle's ambush of the White River raiders, which his son Raphael—Ray—sketched along with a portrait of Seattle in council.[7]

In her 1884 memoir, *Life at Puget Sound*, writer Caroline Leighton described one of Seattle's great-grandchildren as "a swift, elastic little creature . . . with no clothes about him, though it was a cold November day." This was likely Angeline's daughter Mary Telasa's boy. The progeny of Mary and William DeShaw—two girls and several boys—married into several pioneer families, several of whom were mentioned by Grant.[8]

Angeline reminded the city of its earliest past. After her daughter Betsy hanged herself in 1854, her child by Joe Foster, Joe Jr., stayed with his father until the older Joe made plans to leave the area. He wanted his son to come with him, but Joe Jr. refused unless his father gave Angeline $1,000. When he couldn't or wouldn't, Angeline became Joe's guardian.

During the Yakima War, she and Joe followed her father and step-mother to Port Madison, where she made ends meet selling pitch wood and clams on trips to Seattle and did laundry for resident families. In the early 1870s, after native dwellings were forbidden on vacant lands, she moved to a small plank house north of town. Pioneer historian Clarence Bagley wrote that she served as many families as there were days of the week, his included, which allowed him to observe her closely. Just as in San Francisco humorous deference was shown the eccentric Joshua Abraham Norton, the self-declared "Emperor of the United States and Protector of Mexico," Angeline became something of a town mascot, garnering the nickname "Princess Angeline."[9]

Suffering neither fools nor critics gladly, she was known to dump laundry on the floor if the woman of the house complained. Pioneers recalled her volatile temper, a family trait, and Bagley wrote that, despite her name, "her disposition was anything but angelic, even in her younger days." Once, he wrote, carrying a basket of clams to the Wyckoff home, she passed under a ladder, holding a neighbor boy who spattered her with paint. Dropping her basket, she began pelting him with clams, bruising him and shattering windowpanes amid a shower of invective. She would not abide teasing, especially of her grandson, Joe, and she was proud. When a pioneer woman whose house she visited made the mistake of asking, "What do you want?" she indignantly spat out, "Watcher want? Watcher want?" and left.

A source of solace in her troubled life was Angeline's strong religious beliefs. She attended Mass said by visiting priests or by Canadian missionary Father Francis X. Prefontaine in his private chapel, and later at Our Lady of Good Help, at Third Avenue South and South Washington Street, Seattle's first Catholic church. Around 1880, she moved with Joe and many small dogs to a single-room beach house on Western Avenue between Pike and Pine Streets. She was often seen striding the downtown sidewalks or resting on a curb, saying her Rosary. Once, when Angeline was working in a home, a young girl asked her mother if Angeline knew God. Overhearing the question, Seattle's daughter responded strongly in the Jargon, "You tell that girl that I know that God sees me all the time; I might lie or steal and you would never find it out, but God would see me do it."

In 1891, President Benjamin Harrison visited Seattle, and organizers made sure Angeline sat near the triumphal arch at Pioneer Place in a brilliant-blue gingham dress, a white checkered shawl, and a flaming-red bandanna. Subsequent accounts depicted her as barefoot, grasping the president's hand, and offering a hearty *"Klahowya!"* ("Welcome!"), but the *P-I* noted that "the Siwash Queen . . . shriveled and almost bent double with age, . . . [a] piece of withered royalty gazed from the other side with a wondering air at the chief magistrate, while he . . . returned the gaze with every appearance of being interested."[10]

Angeline's is the most reproduced face from Seattle's past, showing up on postcards, ads, and crockery. But when city officials thought to make her a roving ambassador by sending her around the world with eccentric entrepreneur and world traveler George Francis Train, she refused, saying that her father's spirit would be angry. "You tell the newspapers that Angeline does not want any truck with George Francis Train or any other fool."[11]

She relied on the generosity of her friends but never asked for more than she needed and tried to take care of herself. What she saved from her small wages went to pay fines or bail for Joe's misadventures. Asked in 1891 how many years she had lived in her house, she held up ten fingers, inadvertently revealing a broken wrist caused by a fall. The injury ended her ability to take in laundry, and she became a county ward, receiving food and clothing from designated stores. Her monthly bill never exceeded three dollars. Henry Yesler always helped her when she asked, and after his death in 1892, merchants continued to be generous. The owners of the Fulton Market, at Second Avenue and Cherry Street, told young clerk Billy Myers to give her whatever she wanted without charge, even when she noted her displeasure at the cut of meat that had been offered by pounding her cane on the floor.[12]

In 1894, the chamber of commerce commissioned Ray Coombs, a *Seattle Press-Times* engraver, to paint a portrait of Seattle. Guided by the Sammis photo,

A photograph of Chief Seattle's daughter Angeline taken toward the end of her life. She died in 1896.

he depicted him life-size, standing on a beach wearing a blue-bordered Hudson's Bay Company blanket, hand raised in greeting. In August, Ray's father, Samuel Coombs, asked Angeline to accompany him to the Second Avenue storefront displaying Ray's work. Recognizing her father, she burst into tears, gasping between sobs, *"Utch-i-dah! Utch-i-dah! Nika papa hias closhe."* ("Wonderful, wonderful, my father, very good.") Inside, she leaned against the counter and cried, and she returned many times to gaze and weep at his image.[13]

Stories suggest that Angeline harbored deep ambivalence toward the pioneers. Sophie Frye Bass, Emily Inez Denny's cousin, recalled a meeting between David Denny and Angeline when she rushed up, grabbed his arms, and blurted out, "God damn you Dave Denny! Oh, God damn you!" Bass thought Angeline was comically confused and meant to say "God bless you, Dave Denny." But a recollection from Episcopal priest Robert William Summers implies otherwise. Summers recalled how Angeline, addressing a room of seated churchwomen before a map of King County, protested injustice. "With eyes aflame and violent stamping, [she] pours out such a voluble denunciation of things in general and the present occasion in particular [that] her father had hiu illihie (much country) . . . he had much mountain land and many valleys and lakes; all these, here and here and here . . . pointing to them all on the map as she went along."[14]

Many whites routinely disdained native people. At Port Madison, a *Seattle Telegraph* reporter interviewing agent William DeShaw wrote, "He has without doubt during the last twenty-five years talked twice as much Chinook and pure Siwash as English, yet he uses the strongest expletives of the English tongue in speaking of his present Indian neighbors."[15]

"They never would work and never will," DeShaw told the reporter. "Kindness is wasted on them; every kind act done them is returned with an injury."

The reporter added, "He thinks it a great pity that 14,800 acres of land should be kept exclusively for a few shiftless and unworthy Indians to live on to the exclusion of white men."

They were "cultus [worthless] people. . . . run out of and off other reservations . . . veritable Indian tramps." And this was the man who had been appointed by the government to represent native people.

His views were not unique. Frederick Grant ends his Indian chapter by writing, "It would be unfair and untrue to regard these tribes of natives as altogether an evil and a hindrance to settlement . . . nevertheless, they were not pleasant neighbors."

Yet native people and their cultures continued to provoke widespread interest. George Gibbs's 1854 report was printed as the territory's first general ethnography in 1874, and a collection of myths followed. Catholic missionaries published dictionaries, ethnographies, and folklore in English and French, to aid in conversion, and Protestant missionaries published similar work, notably the Reverend Myron Eells, pastor and agent at the Skokomish Reservation, on Hood Canal. He collected much ethnographic information on the Twana, S'Klallam, and Chemakum, but excepting news stories, these appeared in academic journals read by few, and the peoples they described lived in some of the most isolated and least developed parts of the state.

In contrast, *The Siwash: Their Life, Legends and Tales* by *P-I* reporter Joseph Costello, published in 1895, combined accounts of exploration and settlement with legends, origin stories, and short chapters on the Shilshole Tribe, Sealth and the Allied Tribes, and the Old Man House Tribe. He identified Seattle's father as Sealth the First and Seattle as Sealth the Second, misnomers that persisted for decades and a miswriting of his name that vexes us still. Despite its limitations, however, Costello's book was readable and filled a gap.[16]

------

Angeline's final days captured public attention. When neighbors found her lying in the street, they took her to a hospital, where she became hysterical and refused to stay at the Skookum House ("House of Ghosts"). In 1895, the *P-I* campaigned to build her a finer house. The old house and its contents were carted off, and a new one the same size was built in its place, changes whose shock probably hastened her death.[17]

Angeline's son-in-law Joe Foster brought word of her decline to the *P-I* office late in May 1896. Staff sent Dr. G. B. McCulloch, who diagnosed her as in the final stages of consumption, complicated by heart trouble. Intent on dying at home, she refused medications but had Joe bring her traditional palliatives. On May 30, her condition worsened. The next evening, a grieving Joe returned to say she had passed away at five o'clock.

Following her request, Arthur Denny, Hillory Butler, and others had made arrangements with the Bonney & Stewart mortuary, but her body was carted off by Butterfield & Sons, which claimed others had asked them to bury her. Whether an honest mistake or a battle over advertising, Bonney & Stewart eventually regained the corpse.

Newspapers printed extensive eulogies. The *P-I* printed the beginning and ending of Smith's Chief Seattle speech and an earlier plea from local writer Hezekiah Butterworth that the city honor her father with a monument, "that he may see that he is kindly remembered when he comes back to visit the associations of his name and life, or better for his shade, the city should kindly care for his daughter, poor old Angeline Seattle, who . . . is a beggar in the streets of uplifting commercial palaces and lovely homes." The *Seattle Times* echoed the critique, saying, "her life was a protest and not always a silent one against the new order of things."[18]

Mortician James Green shaped Angeline's coffin as a canoe, and on June 5, the curious viewed her at Bonney & Stewart's chapel. The *P-I* couldn't resist noting that "Angeline looks better dead than alive." At ten o'clock that morning, black horses arrived, pulling an elegant black hearse, into which six nonnative pallbearers loaded the coffin. Two carriages—one carrying mortuary staff and city officials and the other with just Joe Foster—clip-clopped to Our Lady of Good Help church where Father Prefontaine pulled out all the stops. Recently enlarged to hold seven hundred, it was packed. Flickering candles, stained glass, thick incense, and liturgical music sung by a full choir enriched the High Requiem Mass celebrated by Prefontaine and two other priests. Afterward, at Lake View Cemetery, graveside services were held next to the tomb of her friend Henry Yesler, dead three years.[19]

Lack of a native presence save Joe at her funeral is troubling. Because she chose to live with her white *tilikums* and be buried with them, her people appear to have let her go. The city's appropriation of her as a bathetic icon, a princess clothed in rags who lived from hand to mouth, is hard to bear. The money that merchants made using her image stayed in their pockets, and her grandiose send-off stood in stark contrast to the town's indifference to her father's death.

Angeline's long life reached from a world of natural grandeur to grubby modernity, smoky by day and electrically lit at night. Seattle's grandson Moses lived in the latter time, and his short lifespan mirrored his people's struggle. The "dwarf from the land of the dead" was believed born with no bones, but while his lower body never fully developed, his upper body grew normally. He could float easily, and upper-body strength enabled him, lying flat, to spring upright, enhancing a penchant for comedic showmanship. He played baseball on children's teams even as an adult,

A newspaper engraving depicting Seattle's grandson Moses Seattle (left) and Suquamish Chief Chico.

and when they teased him he would fly into a feigned rage and chase them at a rapid, ungainly gait that invariably provoked laughter.[20]

Baptized a Catholic, Moses lived near Old Man House, attended schools near the community of Chico, named after Suquamish headman Chico on Dyes Inlet at Tulalip, and boarded at the Chemawa Indian School in Salem, Oregon. When a skiff in which he ferried a girl and her brother to school capsized, the boy drowned, but Moses saved the girl and became a hero. When a canoe in which he ferried a man through Port Washington Narrows capsized, the man drowned, but Moses floated like a cork until rescued. A skilled accordionist, he played square dances, waltzes, and polkas at lumber camps. Plied with liquor, he punctuated his music with manic shouts, which increased the more he drank.

Years later, in the winter of 1905, during a drunken party near Bremerton, Moses Seattle was shoved into a beach fire. He leaped out quickly in his unique way, but partygoers threw him back repeatedly. As historian Ernest Bertelson described it, "a crazy drunken game had become a ghastly dance of death, enlivened by burning clothing, shouts of laughter, agonized screaming." Eventually, others intervened to take him to the Puget Sound Naval Hospital, where he died on February 25. It made the news in Bremerton but not in Seattle. In Seattle, drunken Indians made serious news only if they reflected poorly on the city.[21]

On January 9, 1899, Arthur Denny, the tyee of Seattle's original white settlers, died. Less than three months later, his family asked the *P-I* to critique a recent work of fiction, *Rex's Adventures among the Olympics: A Thrilling Treasure Hunt*, written by local author H. A. Stanley, detailing the adventures of Rex Wayland, a young Swedish immigrant. The tale involved a diary kept by Andres Tonorio, a fictitious sailor on the 1794 expedition of Spanish explorer Juan Pérez, captured and enslaved by the Duwamish led by a young Chief Seattle. In the diary, Tonorio describes a buried treasure in the Olympics. Rex and his sidekick, Uncle Festus, retrieve the diary and follow its clues into the mountains.[22]

In the course of the tale, Stanley has Uncle Festus tell how Seattle's famous picture was taken. According to Festus, Seattle was "fraid we'd steal his spirit outen his body," so Arthur Denny and other settlers got him drunk. "The ole feller liked it—we could see that—and as he never drunk much, it was quick about affectin' him. Wall, we purtended to be jealous, an' we all got him to pledge us—there was seven of us, I think—an' we got seven drinks inter his ole hide." In the end, Rex and Uncle Festus find the gold, and Rex uses his share to pay his tuition at the University of Washington.[23]

We recall Seattle angrily protesting to Michael Simmons in 1858 at being called a drunk. Here was the slur again, repeated in a potboiler presenting Denny as a willing participant. The *P-I* labeled the story "vicious" and noted occasions when Denny had opposed the use and sale of liquor. The next day, it posted Stanley's reply. He argued that he had "done Seattle a greater service by [his] authorship of this book than thousands of dollars of paid advertising could have done," pointing out that he had only repeated what Joseph Costello had written in his book.[24]

To counter such historical indifference in a city anxious to be taken seriously, Edmond Meany, a professor of botany and history at the University of Washington, encouraged graduate student Frank Carlson to research Seattle's life. Much of Carlson's information came from written sources, but he also interviewed pioneers who knew Seattle and, more importantly, native informants at Port Madison, who correctly identified

Seattle's parents as Shxwiye'hub and Shxila'tsa. Quoting extensively from Samuel Coombs's account of the battle on White River, Carlson also acknowledged that Seattle's leadership derived from later efforts to protect his people from other raids, and "by his wisdom and prudence in council and by his ability to appreciate and value the new ideas that were constantly being brought in by civilized people." He quoted Seattle's words at the Point Elliott Council in 1855 to Michael Simmons in 1858, but ignored Henry Smith's speech. Carlson wrote a detailed description of the Old Man House, for which he calculated at a length of nine hundred feet. He also described Seattle's physical appearance and debunked Costello's and Stanley's accusations of drunkenness.[25]

But Carlson's corrective, printed in *University of Washington Publications in Anthropology* in 1903, drew little interest from a distracted public. Travelers making journeys via the Inside Passage during the Yukon and Alaskan gold rushes made known the monumental art produced by native peoples farther north up the coast. Reports and pictures of great mortuary poles erected at native villages inspired plundering raids by American collectors, most notably the Harriman Alaska Expedition, which left Seattle in May 1899, and motivated the city's chamber of commerce to collect a pole of its own that same year, chopped down and carted off from the southeastern Alaska village of Tongass. Erected in Pioneer Place, it and other examples of Northwest Coast native art served as spectacular trophies to mark Seattle's advent as a world metropolis.

In its bid for international attention, the city sponsored its first world's fair, the Alaska-Yukon-Pacific Exposition (AYP) in 1909, where forests of garish totem poles, locally carved and some lit electrically, guarded the gates. That same year, Emily Inez Denny, daughter of David and Louisa Denny, published her compendium of pioneer lore, *Blazing the Way: True Stories, Songs and Sketches of Puget Sound and Other Pioneers*. In it, she printed parts of Smith's Chief Seattle speech with Grant's changes, but made no mention of Carlson's work.

The city's uncritical mixing of its authentic native past with Northwest Coastal art forms continued during the Golden Potlatch, a summer extravaganza begun in 1911, when images of Seattle and Angeline stared from romantic evocations of British Columbian and Alaskan native art.

During the AYP, a bronze bust of a grimacing Seattle with a flattened head, jutting cheekbones, and a massive jaw, cast by local sculptor James Wehn, was installed above a water fountain in Pioneer Place. The fountain was a gift from the Woman's Christian Temperance Union, which made Chief Seattle its spokesman. Edward Clayson, publisher of the short-lived local newspaper the *Patriarch*, collector of Indian legends, promoter of the Jargon, and defender of Seattle, proposed that since "Chief Seattle was never known to touch whiskey . . . I would suggest a Chinook inscription . . . which should make the old Indian Chief shout out at the crowd to come and drink."

> *Nah! Klosh mika charco spose mika tickie muck-a-muck delate klosh chuck; spose mika muck-a-muck hiyu pe ococe mika halo iskum pottle. Cumtux?*
>
> (Say! Good you come if you want drink truly good water; if you drink much of this, you will not want to get drunk. Understand?)

The city demurred.[26]

Wehn also cast a bronze statue of Seattle, the city's first public art, in November 1912. The business community wanted one of Hermes, god of merchants and thieves, but more thoughtful citizens chose Seattle. The *P-I*'s publisher, Thomas Prosch, ensured that the life-size bronze statue, modeled after Coombs's painting, identified Seattle as chief of the Suquamish rather than the suggested Nisquallies. The Duwamish were ignored.[27]

Even at this late date, available sources and surviving contemporaries would have made an in-depth biography of Seattle possible. We would know far more about him if someone had done the work, but as the premier city of the Pacific Northwest advertised itself to the world as a modern, civilized metropolis, no one did.

These years took their toll on Henry Smith. He lost most of his fortune and property in the panic of 1903. His son Ralph, determined to participate in Alaska's gold rush, disappeared in a ship off the Aleutians, and Smith's daughter Maude died in surgery. Stoically, he built another home and office on property he still owned on Queen

Anne Hill. Two years later, he moved to his last house, at 1300 Roy Street, where he tended a lush orchard and cleared some lots to sell. A photograph shows the beautiful old man, resting in his sunny garden beneath a wide straw hat.

In the winter of 1914–15, he caught a flu he could not shake. The following summer, soaked by a rain while transplanting tomatoes, he developed pneumonia. His surviving daughters cared for him, and old friends visited. Neighbor Vivian Carkeek, a local attorney and president of the Seattle Historical Society, brought a copy of Smith's Seattle speech and asked him about its origin. Smith told him "that he had made extensive notes of the address at the time it was given and from those notes he reconstructed the entire address."[28]

On August 16, 1915, the old pioneer died at home. His cremated remains were placed in the columbarium at Saint Mark's Episcopal Cathedral, and local papers printed long eulogies beside his photo.

None mentioned the speech; indeed, it appears to have been largely forgotten. When Clarence Bagley published his multivolume history of Seattle a year later, he made no mention of it. His account of local native groups followed Frederick Grant's format, even to the disparaging ending: "White man's habits never took kindly to the Indian and it was far better for the latter that he should be removed as much as possible from the demoralization attendant upon intercourse between the two races."[29]

By 1920, Seattle had surpassed Portland, Oregon, in population, and by midcentury it was the largest city west of Chicago and north of San Francisco. That year's federal census counted only 9,061 native people in Washington, less than 1 percent of its total population.

Bagley finally printed Smith's Seattle speech in 1929 in his multivolume *History of King County, Washington*, and again two years later in a short biography of Seattle and Angeline. After ignoring it in his city history, what explains the its reappearance? The year 1929 marked the seventy-fifth anniversary of the speech's delivery, but Eli Gifford argues that there was more to its appearance than timing. Bagley had moved west as a child in 1852, with his pioneer parents by wagon train. A politically progressive businessman and prolific historian, he was proud of his city and eager to extol its progress. His county history included much native material from his city volumes, with additions from Costello and

Clayson. Throughout, he allowed sources to voice disdainful views of native people, and Gifford argues that he might not have included the speech at all except that a Seattle dentist, John Rich, brought it to his attention. During an excursion on the Sound at the time of Angeline's funeral, Rich had read the parts of the speech that were printed in the *P-I*. In his words, "The ecstasy held him speechless and still!"[30]

He obtained a complete copy and researched sources. Over the years, he edited a version of his own, and on August 10, 1928, he had a copy of it placed in the Northern Life Insurance Building cornerstone and spoke at its laying. Three of Rich's undated letters rest in the Bagley Papers at the University of Washington. In the first, Rich writes that when he brought the speech to him, Bagley said he was unaware of it. Rich planned to print his version, but when he learned that Bagley was going to include a version in his county history, he requested that Bagley delay publication until his version was published, or at least credit him with its rediscovery. Bagley did neither.[31]

In 1931, Arthur Denny's granddaughter Roberta Frye Watt printed Bagley's version with few changes in *4 Wagons West: The Story of Seattle*, her affectionate history of the town's founding from the Denny-Boren party's departure from Illinois, in 1851, to the May Day picnic in 1874. Compared to Grant's and Bagley's thick tomes, her popular and less expensive book made the speech widely available. Where Bagley included the speech as one more specimen in his cabinet of Native American curiosities, Watt presented it as "the swan song of a vanishing race."[32]

When Rich had his booklet, *Chief Seattle's Unanswered Challenge*, printed in 1932, he described Seattle's speech similarly, as "the Funeral Oration of the dying Indian Race." Outdoing Smith in purple prose, he suggests Seattle as the voice of destiny: "Who art thou, O man, that can answer his accusings of Fate, or reveal the purpose of the Cosmic Plan?" But following Smith's and the *Fin-Back*'s lead, Rich characterizes him as a mournful prophet.[33]

Rich's and Bagley's versions of Smith's speech differ. Gifford notes that while Rich changed about half of Smith's sentences, Bagley changed most of them—determined, it would seem, to give it his mark. Henry Smith wrote:

But why should we repine? Why should I murmur at the fate of my people? Tribes are made up of individuals and are no better than they. Men come and go like the waves of the sea. A tear, a tamanawus, a dirge, and they are gone from our longing eyes forever. Even the white man, whose God walked and talked with him, as friend to friend, is not exempt from the common destiny. We may be brothers after all. We shall see.

Bagley wrote:

But why should I mourn at the untimely fate of my people? Tribe follows tribe, and nation follows nation, like the waves of the sea. It is the order of nature, and regret is useless. Your time of decay may be distant—but it will surely come, for even the White Man whose God walked and talked with him as friend with friend, can not be exempt from the common destiny. We may be brothers after all. We shall see.

And John Rich wrote:

But why should I repine? Why should I murmur at the fate of my people? Tribes are made up of individuals and are no better than they. Men come and go like the waves of the sea. A tear, a tama-namus a dirge, and they are gone from our longing eyes forever. It is the order of Nature. Even the white man, whose God walked and talked with him as friend to friend, is not exempt from the common destiny. We may be brothers, after all. We shall see.

Bagley and Rich also added an ending not in Smith's original. Bagley writes, "Dead—I say? There is no death. Only a Change of Worlds"; Rich writes, "Dead—did I say? There is no death. Only a change of worlds!" The words appear to come from the late Roman writer Decimus Magnus Ausonius: "Sprinkle wine and perfumed oil on my ashes / oh guest and add balsam to the red roses. / My unmourned urn enjoys perpetual spring. / I am not dead; I have only changed worlds." Either Rich or Bagley had not forgotten their Latin lessons.[34]

Rich's book was published near the depth of the Great Depression, and few cities were so distressed as Seattle. By 1935, more than 25 percent of its workforce was unemployed, and among ages twenty to twenty-nine, it was 42.5 percent. Growth ceased, homelessness soared, and construction did not alter the skyline until the 1960s. Seattle's putative words "We may be brothers after all"—now printed in several publications—resounded with harsh irony.[35]

Those who later wrote about Seattle—man or city—felt obliged to cite the speech. Educators included it in their curricula, and translators reprinted it into languages as diverse as Serbian and Norwegian. In his 1941 book, *Northwest Gateway: The Story of the Port of Seattle*, regional author Archie Binns, quoting extensively from Bagley's version, repeated Smith's portrayal of Seattle as a prophet of doom, his speech "grim with meanings that outlasted his race and may outlast all the generations of men."[36]

A few years later, Edna Ferber, one of America's most celebrated writers, credited Binns as a source in the foreword to her novel *Great Son*, depicting the Melendy family, a pioneering brood grown rich and discontented in Seattle on the eve of Pearl Harbor. Near the end, a young Mike Melendy describes Chief Seattle to Regina Dresden, a young Jewish refugee from Nazi Germany. He tells her that Seattle was "over six feet . . . Gray hair down to his shoulders, loose like the prophets in the Bible, not braided, and looked like a philosopher." He reads her part of the speech, adding, "We learned it in school. Every kid in Seattle learns it in school. It didn't mean much to me then. But in the last year or two I kind of remembered it and I began to think, gosh! Wow! Gives you the chills." Ferber's Seattle warned Americans that they were to be severely tested, a warning made just before the bombs began to fall.[37]

During World War II, Eva Greenslit Anderson, a Nebraskan who moved west and became Washington State supervisor for adult education, wrote her biography of Seattle for a young audience, depicting him accurately as a warrior turned peacemaker. She drew on historical and biographical sources but, more importantly, from work carried out on the Northwest Coast by anthropologist Franz Boas in the 1880s and his students after him—in particular Hermann Haeberlin's work on the Tulalip Reservation in 1916–17. Salted with ethnographic material, her narrative sounds contrived at times, and native conversations are marred by her use of a truncated diction made simple like the Jargon. For example, following the hanging of Messachie Jim, she has Seattle say, "White men poke nose in wrong place! Why don't white men mind own business? Like storm on sea, great trouble will come." But Anderson was the first to present Seattle in a reasonable historical and ethnographic context, and more than any other writer, she introduced Seattle to a broad audience. Despite its shortcomings, her is a complete life.[38]

After a war whose violence and horror surpassed description, postwar writers and historians, abjuring the pioneering ethos, shied away from Seattle and the speech. In the city's best-known history, the 1951 classic *Skid Road*, Northwest writer Murray Morgan mentions only that Seattle spoke "well and with dignity . . . [and] that the Indians had no choice but to accept" Stevens's offer of money, schools, and workshops for their lands.[39]

In a more recent interpretive retelling, *Seattle: Past to Present*, published in 1976, Seattle historian Roger Sale quotes Binns in *Northwest Gateway*, who said, "As the amiable follies of the white race become less amiable, the iron rumble of old Seattle's speech sounds louder and more ominous." Dealing with the native people, Sale echoes Smith's mournful tone, describing Seattle's story as "inexpressibly sad," and Seattle's words as a "magnificent farewell speech."[40]

If Chief Seattle's prophetic role in the national drama no longer invited much interest, others found him intriguing as a cultural figure. In 1964, a Belgian missionary priest on temporary assignment to the Roman Catholic Archdiocese of Seattle, Father Felix Verwilghen, had James Vernon Metcalfe, a law professor at Seattle University, read a paper to the Seattle Pioneer Society in which Verwilghen argued that Chiefs Seattle and Challacum were the same person. This was during the Second Vatican Council in Rome, an historic assembly covered by the international press. It had been called by Pope John XXIII, the popular successor of Pius XII, to revitalize relations between the Roman Catholic Church and the modern world and to reassess the role of the laity. In the spirit of the Council and to make the church more relevant, Verwilghen presented Seattle as a pivotal lay leader.

He based his research largely on the letters of Bishops Francis Blanchet and Modeste Demers, but missed references in the *Journal of Occurrences at Nisqually House*, where Seattle and Challacum are clearly identified separately. Professor Metcalfe nevertheless adopted Verwilghen's thesis in a biographical sketch of Seattle later published in the *Catholic Northwest Progress*, which he said was aimed at "giving the story of his life the true Catholic emphasis . . . which . . . has been forgotten at times." It affirmed the church's importance in a region where it had long been suspect, but needlessly muddled popular understanding of the man. Local historian and journalist Lucile McDonald caught the error, but lack of local reader interest evidenced a shrugging acceptance that little could be done to present a more accurate account.[41]

Others outside the region continued to find Seattle's words compelling, accurate or not. In the late 1960s, while working at the Battelle Memorial Institute in Seattle, William Arrowsmith, a professor of classics at the University of Texas at Austin, read parts of the speech in a collection of essays and said it reminded him of Pindar, a lyric poet from ancient Greece. After finding a complete copy and consulting native traditionalists, Arrowsmith pruned the speech of what he judged to be its "dense patina of nineteenth-century literary diction and syntax." For example, Smith wrote:

> Your God loves your people and hates mine; he folds his strong arms lovingly around the white man and leads him as a father leads his infant son, but he has forsaken his red children; he makes your people wax strong every day, and soon they will fill the land; while my people are ebbing away like a fast-receding tide, that will never flow again.

But Arrowsmith wrote:

> Your God loves your people and hates mine. He puts his strong arm around the white man and leads him by the hand, as a father would his little boy. He has abandoned his red children. He makes your people stronger every day. Soon they will flood all the land. But my people are an ebb tide, we will never return.

Arrowsmith breaks Smith's long line "The ashes of our ancestors are sacred and their final resting place is hallowed ground, while you wander away from the tombs of your fathers seemingly without regret" into lyric stanzas: "To us the ashes of our fathers are sacred. Their graves are holy ground. But you are wanderers, you leave your fathers' graves behind you, and you do not care."

On April 22, 1970, the first Earth Day, Arrowsmith read his version of Chief Seattle's speech at a rally on the University of Texas's Main Mall, beneath the UT Tower, the scene of a mass shooting four years earlier. Hearing its majestic cadences in a place haunted by evil made a great impact on a young colleague, Ted Perry.[42]

Perry taught theater arts at the university, and under contract with the Southern Baptist Radio and Television Commission in Fort Worth, he was working on *Home*, a film about pollution. He got Arrowsmith's permission to use his version of the speech as the basis for his script, with the idea that Seattle's voice would inspire viewers' sense of ecological responsibility. If Arrowsmith pruned Smith's hybrid ornamental, Perry clipped it into an exotic topiary. Seattle's demand for his people's access to burial grounds became "The white man must treat the beasts of this land as his brothers." He salted the script with catchy ecological slogans: "All things are connected. The earth does not belong to man; man belongs to the earth. Whatever befalls the earth befalls the sons of the earth. Man did not weave the web of life; he is merely a strand in it. Whatever he does to the web, he does to himself." Seattle's original plea for just and compassionate treatment of his people became a plug for environmental sensitivity.

---

The 1960s and '70s marked a sea change in relations between Native Americans and the white power structure throughout the Pacific Northwest. To the surprise of many except themselves, the native people had survived, and by joining together, as Kitsap had instructed more than a century earlier, they forced a legal showdown with the state of Washington and the federal government over treaty rights. This took place during the "Fish Wars," when Indians, defending their right to fish, hunt, and gather in the "usual and accustomed" places reserved for them in treaties, fought the state, which argued that the treaties were, in essence, real estate agreements that conferred no rights beyond those enjoyed by other citizens. When tribal members persisted, state and local officials confiscated the Indians' gear and threatened violence, which became real when police beat and gassed protesters.

Eventually, the tribes' protest was heard in the US District Court for the Western District of Washington, where, in 1974, federal judge George Boldt ruled, in the case of *United States v. Washington*, that the treaty clause "The right of taking fish, at all usual and accustomed grounds and stations, is further secured to said Indians in common with all citizens in the Territory" meant that Indians had the right to half the catch each year. The Ninth Circuit Court of Appeals upheld Boldt's decision in 1975, and the US Supreme Court reaffirmed it in 1979. For the Native Americans, this was justice begun.[43]

The Fish Wars coincided with the growth of widespread public concern about human threats to the natural environment, spurred by the 1962 publication of Dr. Rachel Carson's *Silent Spring*, which alerted readers to the danger of pesticides. A catastrophic oil spill in California's Santa Barbara channel in 1965 and another caused by the breakup of the oil tanker *Torrey Canyon* in the English Channel in 1969 raised alarms. The sense of national crisis accompanying shocking political assassinations, the disastrous war in Vietnam, and the Watergate scandal and the resignation of President Richard Nixon coincided with a local economic crash when the Boeing Company, the largest employer in the Puget Sound region, laid off more than eighty thousand workers after the failure of its supersonic transport program. The so-called "Boeing Bust" crippled Seattle's economy and resulted in its population shrinking by one hundred thousand. As long-cherished positive assumptions about the American way of life were called into question, words attributed to Seattle once again called Americans to account.

In the November 1972 issue of the journal *Environmental Action*, Chief Seattle is quoted:

How can you buy or sell the sky—the warmth of the land? The idea is strange to us. How can you buy them from us? We will decide in our time. Every part of the earth is sacred to my people. Every shining pine needle, every sandy shore, every mist in the dark woods, every clearing, and humming insect is holy in the memory and experience of my people. We know that the white man does not understand our ways. Our portion of the land is the same to him as the next, for he is a stranger who comes in the night and takes from the land whatever he needs. The earth is not his brother but his enemy, and when he has conquered it, he moves on. He leaves his fathers' graves, and his children's birthright is forgotten. The sight of your city pains the eyes of the redman. But perhaps it is because the red man is savage and does not understand.[44]

What were we to make of this? Some said Seattle's words came from a letter written to President Franklin Pierce, and some of us spent a great deal of time fruitlessly searching the papers of President Pierce, looking for this extraordinary letter. Similar words appeared at the 1974 Spokane World's Fair and in Northwest Orient Airlines' in-flight reading in an essay titled, with unintended irony, "The Decidedly Unforked Message of Chief Seattle." His fame was spreading worldwide.

European Catholic groups aware of Father Verwilghen's and Professor Metcalfe's work celebrated these new writings, and enthusiasts likened them to a fifth Gospel. On the 1988 PBS series *Joseph Campbell and the Power of Myth*, author Joseph Campbell described them to host Bill Moyers as "the last echo of the Paleolithic mind." Inventor and visionary Buckminster Fuller quoted them, as did Vice President Al Gore in the 2006 documentary film *An Inconvenient Truth*.

It remained for a careful German historian, Rudolph Kaiser, to track the writings back to Ted Perry's script and later adapters. But like Frank Carlson's 1903 thesis, accuracy took a back seat to the popular demand for uplifting messages. In Susan Jeffers's best-selling 1991 children's book *Brother Eagle, Sister Sky: A Message from Chief Seattle*, Perry's words were altered even further, nested in images having little to do with Seattle or his people. In justification, Jeffers wrote, "What matters is that Chief Seattle's words inspired—and continue to inspire—a most compelling truth: In our zeal to build and possess, we may lose all that we have." Predictably, many pastors employ Seattle's apocryphal messages in their sermons, and educators have used Perry's and Jeffers's words in environmental lesson plans.[45]

That today's modern Native American groups, and not just those along Puget Sound, find it useful to quote from Smith's Seattle speech and its subsequent permutations speaks to the hold the chief's words have on the public mind. The boundary between accurate history and compelling myth is elastic, but to say Henry Smith's Seattle speech is not historically accurate and therefore false is as extreme as saying that as long as they are meant well, it does not matter what words are put into Seattle's mouth.

History is not myth, but neither are these terms antithetical or mutually exclusive, any more than prose is from poetry. The tensions between them plumb deeper sensibilities and needs. Our sense of past, present, and future, of the real and the unreal, derives from an understanding of our place in the world. Perhaps it is in keeping with Seattle's plea for justice that the authors of his apocryphal messages should make him a spokesman for the endangered earth.

In his 1997 book, *Answering Chief Seattle*, historian Albert Furtwangler examines the cultural trajectory of Seattle's speech and the central issue its theme addresses: the relationship of people to where they live. Furtwangler finds resonance between the speech and the writings of Seattle's contemporaries—Thomas Jefferson, Nathaniel Hawthorne, Walt Whitman, and Isaac Stevens himself—whose writings "shaped the kind of listening" Seattle's audiences exercised then and now. He presents these Americans' views as answers to Chief Seattle's ideas about the role of the land. Furtwangler ends, as all discussions on the speech must, with more questions: "How does anyone, in our time, grow into a homeland? And when a homeland can be lightly swept away, what will endure?"[46]

We ask similar questions about the role of justice and compassion in our vision of community. As historical experience deepens, and races that once fought and killed each other learn to work together for a common good, we lay claim to wisdom and kindness. In 1987, Lutheran, Episcopal, Roman Catholic, and Baptist bishops, as well as ministers from many other denominations throughout the region, publicly apologized to Indians and Eskimos in the Pacific Northwest and

Alaska for their churches' participation "in the destruction of Native American traditional ways and practices." This was unprecedented and well-received in native communities. In March 2004, Washington State's legislature passed resolutions exonerating Leschi of the charges that led to his hanging: justice delayed but justice still. Today the Evangelical Lutheran Church in America dedicates June 7 to Chief Seattle in its liturgical calendar.[47]

In my research I have come to regard Seattle the man as greater and more significant than his alleged words. I have written this biography to demonstrate this. If Smith's Seattle speech, with its permutations and controversies, has obscured him, it has not erased evidence of his genuine contributions, even at this late date.

A formidable war leader, the vital impresario who courted and brought Americans to his homeland, the indispensable man who anchored the first Western commercial endeavor on Elliott Bay—he was all of these. During the Yakima War, he stood by the Americans at no little risk to himself and kept contact with both sides in an effort to mediate the conflict. He cultivated relationships with whites he could trust, to gain his people a stake in an industrial economy and a measure of autonomy in a hostile white world. Since then, the ongoing efforts undertaken by native people have made it possible for recognized tribes like the Suquamish to govern themselves and enjoy a greater measure of prosperity. I believe this was Seattle's goal for all his people.

Today the city of Seattle, the hybrid community he helped birth, enjoys wealth and international acclaim as its population approaches seven hundred thousand. When the president of China meets with Seattle citizens before visiting Washington, DC, as happened in 2015, the pioneer dream of a world-class city would appear to have been realized. But because by name this is Chief Seattle's city, we have a responsibility to search out and deal with the past's unfinished business.

Foremost is the continuing struggle of the Duwamish, Seattle's mother's people, to achieve federal recognition. Despite being ordered to move to several reservations, most Duwamish chose instead to remain near the river that had given them life and identity for thousands of years. But those Indians who did not live on reservations were categorized by the federal government as "landless," and as part of his 1974 fishing-rights decision,

Judge Boldt denied the Duwamish, along with other landless groups like them, federal recognition as tribes having the rights and protections promised in the Treaty of Point Elliott.

It was not the Duwamish peoples' choice that made them landless in their traditional homeland, but a historically consistent effort by city residents and leaders to keep them so. Their actions mock the settlers' claim made in the 1864 petition protesting a Duwamish reservation, of having treated the Duwamish "Justly and kindly," words and actions that themselves mock Seattle's plea. For the last forty years, the Duwamish and their tribal chairwoman, Cecile Hansen, have patiently submitted documents demanded by the federal government for recognition. For a fleeting moment in 2000, in the waning hours of President Bill Clinton's administration, the Department of the Interior finally approved their petition. But the official responsible did so three days after leaving office, and incoming George W. Bush officials tabled the petition and overturned it. Shortly after this profound disappointment, Hansen said, "It is painful for me, for any Native American to have to prove who they are."[48]

The Duwamish have no plans to disappear. In her four decades as chairwoman, Hansen has sought to meet with every mayor of Seattle to ask their support for the tribe's petition. In all that time, as of press time, not a single mayor has agreed to meet with her. In 2009, however, helped by pioneer descendants, the Duwamish purchased land on West Marginal Way in West Seattle and opened a handsome tribal and cultural center across from the ancient Duwamish village site of Ha'apus, also known as the archaeological site 45K123, inhabited since the seventh century. Yet neither the city nor the Port of Seattle, which owns the river frontage there, has gone out of its way to help them.[49]

Port officials had allowed the Duwamish to display artifacts excavated from the village site at the cultural center, so when the officials decided to loan those artifacts to recognized tribes instead, the Duwamish protested. The tribe even offered to purchase them, but the artifacts—including jasper and jade tools that I helped excavate—were snatched from display cases and hustled out the door. For a city now easy with its name, that advertises itself as world-class, this was shameful.

Having grown rich on Duwamish land, the city has consistently made sure that not one square inch of it would be reserved for the people who nurtured and protected settlers in their hours of greatest need. That is the city's original sin. Seattle's request that his people be treated with justice and kindness falls on deaf ears. The hand of friendship offered by the Duwamish is met with blank stares and double-talk. Seattle is indeed a worthy eponym for the city, but is the city worthy of its eponym? Chief Seattle's trust in Americans' sense of justice was willed, and his claim upon our better nature has yet to be vindicated.

Some may question what the city could do that the federal government has not. With abundant wealth and resources, a city that claims to have its own foreign policy could develop economic ties with the Duwamish as a tribe and actively support their continuing quest for recognition. If the city insists on wearing the chief's name, it must answer his request for justice and kindness in meaningful ways. That is the path to repentance and reconciliation, the city's unfinished business. That would be just and kind. That would be world-class.

The demography of Seattle, the state, and the country is changing. By 2060, minorities in nearly half the states, including Washington, will become the majority. We are a continental civilization in the process of becoming a great universal nation, a mix of individuals from every race, ethnicity, nationality, culture, and religion, bearing painful memories of the past while seeking liberty and prosperity together. It is instructive to learn that from the town's beginning, Chief Seattle's hybrid experiment on Elliott Bay was conceived of with that in mind. For him, it was common sense drawn from ancient and pragmatic native traditions, and it continues to be his greatest contribution to our well-being.

The life of Seattle, the living man, means more than the words of his ghost. Only now have we begun to appreciate his vision and understand that our city draws its greatest strength from the character, energy, and dreams of all its residents—living, loving, and working together in the house of his name. He lived with that hope and died still believing it. If we believe that life and hope are greater than death, honoring his deeds, answering his request, and attending to his vision will be the proof.

# ACKNOWLEDGMENTS

Of all the people who helped in the research and writing of this book, Mary Anne Callaghan served as sounding board, adviser, critic, researcher, and translator. Without her help and support, this book would never have been written. The fact that I am lucky enough to be married to her in no way detracts from her contribution. Next is Dr. Nile Thompson, the finest linguist and ethnographer working in the Pacific Northwest today, who helped me decipher the social and cultural complexities of native groups and their languages. Best of all were our long conversations on rarefied aspects of local history and language. As he often said, "Are there any other people in the world talking about these things?" Special thanks, too, for the support and professional advice of Dr. Carolyn Marr, who also happens to be Nile's wife.

I am forever indebted to Cecile Hansen, chairwoman of the Duwamish Tribe, whose constant support, encouragement, and friendship gave me the confidence to carry on and finish this work. Among many tribal members also to be honored is the late Lottie Fenton, the first Duwamish to whom I was introduced. Happily, alive are her fellow tribal members Cindy Williams, Kathie Zuckerburg, James Rassmussen, Jeri Marie Bennett, Edie Loyer Nelson, and Kenneth Workman. More recently, I have benefited from the advice and guidance provided by the Suquamish Tribe.

During the decades of my research, I have been the beneficiary of the wonderful librarians and staff at Suzzallo-Allen Library. Among them, Susan Cunningham, Carla Rickerson, Sandy Kroupa, Richard Engeman, Glenda Pearson, and Cassandra Hartnet were never too busy to help me ferret out the most arcane information. At the various places to which Special Collections has migrated to over the years, the constant interest and encouragement of the staff made wherever it was the most pleasant of destinations.

David Brewster has overseen my evolution as a writer since I first saw him, necktie flying in the wind, as I peered up from an archaeological pit where I was a student at the Archaeological Field School held in the summer of 1980 at the Duwamish No. 1 Site, 45K123, on West

Marginal Way. He asked if I'd be interested in writing for the *Seattle Weekly*, and his generosity, professional advice, and faith in this book has meant the world to me. His editorial mantra—"Take more out; put more in"—has been my constant guide.

I must also thank Ranjit Arab, whose judgment after reading the initial manuscript of approximately seven hundred pages—"Cut it in half and we'll get back to you"—turned a sprawling epic into a workable biography. Sasquatch Books publisher Gary Luke deserves many thanks for taking on the project, and for his patience and his expert eye that saw the path to its conclusion, aided by his excellent book editor Em Gale and the astonishingly capable copyeditor Elizabeth Johnson.

To those who helped me along my way—Ralph Wigington, Giovanni Costigan, Sisters Barbara Mattson and Francine Barber, OP, Peter Henning Jr., Ed Peterson, and others too many to name—I thank you all.

# A NOTE ON THE SPELLING OF NATIVE WORDS

There are several systems that have been used to spell native names and words in historic times. This is complicated by the fact that as native languages changed, the systems have changed with them. This can lead to confusion among readers who, like myself, are not linguists. I confess I have moved blithely between these systems, choosing spellings that are easier for the reader to approximate the spoken names and words. In this effort, I wish to express my gratitude to Dr. Nile Thompson, who has patiently pointed out to me some of my more egregious errors.

The vowel sounds are as follows: **a** as in "hot," **ä** as in "hat," **e** as in "hate," **i** as in "heat," **o** as in "hole," **u** as in "hoot," the schwa, **ǝ**, as in "hug," and **ai**, as in "height."

Consonants that are glottalized, that is, sound more emphatic than they are in English, are followed by an exclamation point, **!**, as are the glottalized paired consonants **ts**, **ch**, and **sh**, and the rounded consonants **gw**, **kw**, **tw**, and **xw**. The barred *l*, **ł**, is the *l* sound made by blowing air around the place in the mouth touched by the tip of the tongue. The barred lambda, **ƛ**, is a combined *tl* sound. A glottalized barred lambda, **ƛ!**, is an emphatic *tl* sound. **X** sounds rather like the *ch* in the north German *ach*. **Txw** at the beginning and end of names are whispered.

Finally, there is the glottal stop, not a sound at all but a silence "heard," for example, between the two syllables of the English exclamation, "uh-oh." I use the glottal stop, **ʔ**, specifically regarding Seattle's name. Linguistically, his name is written as "Siʔaʔł," with the gap heard between the *Si* and the *a'*.

# APPENDIX OF NATIVE NAMES AND WORDS

Agate Passage, **Txwchə′kup**

Alki Point, **Sbə′kwabəks**

Angeline, Seattle's daughter, **Sabolits!a**

Angeline's first husband, **Daxwsəb**

Changer, **Du′kwibał**

Cousin of opposite sex, **alsh**

Duwamish chief, **Kwia′xtəd**

Duwamish head, **Skwədks**

Duwamish lower river village, **Txwkwi′ltəd**

Duwamish lower river village people, **K!elka′kubiu**

Duwamish main village, **Txwxudaw**

Duwamish River (Duwamish, Black, and Cedar), **Txwda′w**

Duwamish River people, **Duwa′bsh**

Duwamish village where Black River meets
    White River, **Skoa′lko**

End of the myth time, **gwal**

Equestrian interior traders, **Tu′bshədəd**

Flea's House village, **Ch!ut!əp!altxw**

Freight canoe, **sti′wəł**

Grandfather, **Tsa′pa**

Guardian spirit, **skala′lətut**

Herring House village, **T!ula′ltu**

Herring House headman, "Old Dick," **Tsutsa′lptəd**

Indian pink, **Ch!ti′lkw**

It is I, Seattle!, **ətsa′ Si?a′l!**

Keokuck, Duwamish judge, **Xasi′dut**

Kitsap, **K!tsä′p**

Kitsap's brother, **Təli′but**

Kitsap's supernatural power, **Tubcha′dad**

Kitsap's younger brother, **Lə′k!lax**

Lake Burien, **Xwi′yəkw**

Lake Washington village, **Sa′tsakał**

Leschi, **Lə′shai**

Levirate marriage, **sba′lusəd**

Little Crossing Place village, **Dzidzəla′ləch**

Logjam village, **Stək!**

Logjam village people, **Stək!a′bsh**

Meadow, **ba′qwəb**

Meadow village, **Baba′kwəb**

Medicine Creek, **Sxuda′dap**

Merman, **Skaita′w**

Merman's people, **Skaitil′babsh**

Mixed people (Suquamish), **Ita′kəbixw**

Mount Rainier, **Təko′bad**

Mukilteo, **Bəka′ltiu**

Nelson, **Pialchəd**

Noble, **sia′b**

Old house, **Lu′luλ! Al′al**

Olympia native group, **St!əch!a′sabsh**

Olympia native village, **St!əch!a′s**

Potlatch, Whuljutsid word, **sgwi′gwi**

Pritchard Island, **λ!i′łchus**

Salmon Bay, **Shə′lshol**

Salmon Bay people, **Shəlshola′bsh**

Salt water, **Xwa′lch**

Salt water language, **Xwəlju′tsid**

Sammamish people, **Sts'apa′bsh**

Sammamish River people, **Sts!apa′bsh**

Seattle, **Siʔa′ł**

Seattle's brother, or half brother, Curley, **Ts!agwəł**

Seattle's brother, baptized David, **Xtsha′tshidax**

Seattle's father, **Shxwiye′həb**

Seattle's half brother, **K!ubaii**

Seattle's half brother, **Xoxwa′tkəb**

Seattle's mother, **Sxila′ts!a**

Seattle's trusted warrior, **Wyab**

Seattle's warrior son, **Sa′kw!al**

Secret society, **sxədxədəb**

Shaman power, **xuda′b**

S'Klallam headman, **Skəbiaks**

S'Klallam village, **Yə′nus**

Snoqualmie chief, Patkanim, **Patkinəm**

Snoqualmie chief, **Xotik!edəb**

South Whidbey village, **Degwadzk**

Steilacoom, **Ch!ti′lkwəb**

Steilacoom people, **Ch!tilkwəbsh**

Stuck River, **Stə′x**

Sooke people, **S!o′ksun**

Supernatural being, **dzə′gwə**

Suquamish people, **Dxwsə′q!wəb**

Suquamish subchief, **Walak**

Tabu, **xa′xa**

Tecumseh, Duwamish headman, **Kwilsk!edub**

Thunder power, **Xwi′kwadi**

Tulalip, **Txwli′lap**

Upriver portion, **Tskwa′litsh**

Vashon Island people, **Sxomamish**

West Point, **Pka′dzultshu**

Whidbey Island people, **Skä′häkachet**

White River village, **Yəla′lkwo**

William, **Stoda′**

Winter dance, **spegpugud**

Wonderful, **əchidaa**

# ENDNOTES

## INTRODUCTION

1.　William Fraser Tolmie, *The Journals of William Fraser Tolmie Physician and Fur Trader*, Ed. Janet R. Mitchell (Vancouver, Canada: Mitchell Press, Limited, 1963), entry for Sunday, August 4, 223–224. Edmund A. Starling to Isaac Stevens, December 4, 1853. *The Records Of The Washington Superintendency Of Indian Affairs, 1853–1874*. Roll 1, (b), Copies and Drafts of Letters Sent, March 1853–March 31, 1856.

## CHAPTER ONE

1.　Arthur Ballard, "Mythology of Southern Puget Sound," *University of Washington Publications in Anthropology*, vol. 3, no. 2 (Seattle: 1929), 31–150, p. 41.

2.　Thomas Talbot Waterman, notes in *The Papers of John Peabody Harrington In the Smithsonian Institution 1907–1957*, vol. 1, reel 30, Alaska Northwest Coast, frame 184 (Millwood, New York: Kraus International Publications, a Division of Kraus-Thompson Organization Limited, 1981), frames 250–1. Dr. Thompson believes "Place of Clear Saltwater" is more a folk etymology told to Waterman rather than a linguistic analysis of the place name. Dr. Thompson, personal communications in author's possession, 1/28/2013 and 10/10/2016. Twana oral history tells how the canoe bearing the Suquamish ancestors drifted eastward to their present-day homeland. According to Henry Allen, William Elmendorf's Twana informant, the name for the Suquamish came from the Twana word *wuq'wa't b*, "drifted away." Allen claimed the Suquamish were not aware that their name was meaningful in the Twana language, which differs from Whuljootseed. Elmendorf, "The Structure of Twana Culture," Ibid, p. 292.

3.　Marian Wesley Smith, *The Puyallup-Nisqually* (New York: Columbia University Press, 1940), 4, 15–17. Herbert Haeberlin and Erna Gunther, *The Indians of Puget Sound* (Seattle and London: University of Washington Press, 1973), 10–15. Until recently, no ethnographies have been written about the Duwamish and Suquamish. Smith and Haeberlin provide a general understanding of these two groups, and other reports and monographs dealing with various aspects of the central Puget Sound peoples appear below.

4.　Marian Wesley Smith, *The Puyallup-Nisqually* (New York: Columbia University Press, 1940), p. 175–6.

5.　Arthur Ballard, "Calendric Terms of the Southern Puget Sound Salish," *Southwestern Journal of Anthropology*, 6 (1) 1950. Unless otherwise noted, calendric terms come from Ballard. Caroline C. Leighton, *West Coast Journeys 1865–1879* (Seattle: Sasquatch Books, 1995), p. 27. Ballard, "Mythology," Op. Cit., 123–125. Arthur Ballard, "Mythology," Op. Cit., 123–125.

6.　Waterman, "Notes on the Ethnology of the Indians of Puget Sound," *Museum of the American Indian Heye Foundation Indian Notes and Monographs Miscellaneous Series 59* (New York: 1920), p. 52.

7.　Frank Carlson, "Chief Sealth," *The Bulleting Of The University of Washington*, series III, no. 2, 1903, History Series, p. 14.

8.　Harriet Turner, *Ethnozoology of the Snoqualmie*, second ed., revised, Ms, ts, Seattle, 1976, p. 17.

9.　Smith, Op. Cit., p. 196.

10.　Ballard, "Mythology," Op. Cit., 69–80.

11.　Smith, Op. Cit., 4–5.

12.　Deposition of George Alexander, *Duwamish, Lummi, Whidbey Island, Skagit, Upper Skagit, Swinomish, et. al. versus USA Court of Claims of the United States*, LXXIX, 530 (Wash. DC, Govt. Printing Office 1935). Printed in two volumes (Seattle, Washington: Argus Press) p. 315.

13.    *Indian Journal of Rev. R. W. Summers*, trans. Fr. Martinus Cawley, OCSO, Book One, Seattle and Puget Sound, January 2, 1871 to Fall of 1873 (Lafayette, Oregon: Browsers' Edition, Guadelupe Translations, 1994), p. 4. Arthur Ballard, "The Salmon Weir on Green River in Western Washington," *Davidson Journal of Anthropology* 3:37–53 (Seattle: 1957).

14.    T. T. Waterman, "Notes on the Ethnology of the Indians of Puget Sound," Op. Cit., 62–63. Lu'q'lax was Kitsap's younger brother. Waterman, *Puget Sound Marriages and Genealogies*, Bancroft Library, University of California at Berkeley, p. 18.

15.    Harrington, 1907–1957, Op. Cit., frame 183. Warren Snyder, "Southern Puget Sound Salish Texts, Place Names and Dictionary," *Sacramento Anthropological Society Papers*, 9 (Sacramento: 1968), p. 167.

16.    Thomas Talbot (T. T.) Waterman in *The Papers of John Peabody Harrington In the Smithsonian Institution 1907–1957*, vol. 1, reel 30, Alaska Northwest Coast (Millwood, New York: Kraus International Publications A Division of Kraus-Thompson Organization Limited, 1981), frame 184.

17.    The 1870 Seattle census gives Curly's age as 60. His grandmother was enslaved sometime around the mid- to late 1700s. For the names of Seattle's near kin see T. T. Waterman, "Puget Sound Marriages and Genealogies," c. 1920, p. 24, microfilm, Bancroft Library, University of California at Berkeley. Also, Waterman's notes in *The Papers of John Peabody Harrington*, Ibid. fr. 232. Snyder, *NARN*, Ibid, p. 130. For Curly's native name see Waterman, "Duwamish Villages," *Puget Sound Geography*, 1920, manuscript no. 1864 in the National Anthropological Archives, Smithsonian Institution, Washington, DC, reel 30, frame 242.

18.    I use the southern Puget Salish name for *potlatch* from Smith, Op. Cit. p, 107.

19.    Elmendorf, "The Structure of Twana Culture," Ibid, 337–343. Hermann Haeberlin and Erna Gunther, "The Indians of Puget Sound," *University of Washington Publications in Anthropology*, vol. IV, no. 1, (Seattle: 1930), 59–61. Smith, Ibid, 107–112. Waterman, "Notes," Op. Cit., 75–82.

20.    Smith, Op Cit., 92–94. Snyder, Op. Cit.,

151–154. Waterman, *Puget Sound Geography*, Op. Cit., "Names of Places on the West Side of the Sound," frame 328, #82a.

21.    Haeberlin and Gunther, Ibid, 67–75.

22.    Ibid, p. 61.

23.    George Dorsey, "The Duwamish Indian Spirit Boat And Its Use," *Bulletin of the Free Museum of Science and Art at the University of Pennsylvania* 3(4): 227–238, 1902. Hermann Haeberlin, "SbEtEtda'q, a Shamanic Performance of the Coast Salish," *American Anthropologist* 20(3), 1918: 249–257. T. T. Waterman, "The Paraphernalia of the Duwamish 'Spirit Canoe' Ceremony," *Indian Notes* 7(2) 129-312, (4): 535–561 (Museum of the American Indian, Heye Foundation, New York, 1930), p. 144.

24.    Ballard, Mythology, Op. Cit., p. 51, 55–69. Ella Clark, *Indian Legends Of The Pacific Northwest* (Berkeley, Los Angeles, London: University of California Press, 1973), 39–42.

25.    Clark, Ibid, 44–45. Elmendorf, "Skokomish and Other Coast Salish Tales," Washington State University. Research Studies, XXIX: March, 1, 1961 (Pullman, Washington), 21, 24. In S'klallam folklore, the ancestral Duwamish drifted to their homeland during the great flood after the rope tying their canoe to a mountain parted. Ella E.Clark, *Indian Legends of the Pacific Northwest* (Berkeley: University of California Press, 1953), 44–45. I have come across no Duwamish legend about this, but many Duwamish myths have been lost.

26.    Warren Snyder, "Autobiography of Amelia Snaetlum," "Southern Puget Sound Salish: Texts, Place Names and Dictionary," *Sacramento Anthropological Society Papers* 9 (Sacramento, CA: 1968), p. 134. Smith, Op. Cit., p. 19. Elmendorf, Ibid, p. 57.

27.    Ballard "Mythology of Central Puget Sound," Op. Cit., 87–89.

28.    Robert Boyd, *The Coming of the Spirit of Pestilence* (Vancouver and Toronto: UBC Press; Seattle and London: University of Washington Press, 1999). Elizabeth Fenn, *Pox Americana The Great Smallpox Epidemic of 1775–82* (Phoenix Mill-Thrupp-Stroud-Gloucestershire-GL52BU: Sutton Publishing Limited, 2004).

29.    Martin Sampson, *Indians of Skagit County* (Skagit County Historical Series, no. 2, Mount

Vernon: Skagit County Historical Society, 1972), p. 28.

**30.** Waterman, "Names of Places on the White River," #213, 214. *Puget Sound Geography*, Op. Cit. Harrington translates *tsqwa'litch* as the "up-river portion;" Harrington, Ibid, frame 365. Arthur A. Ballard, *Listen My Nephew*, ts., nd., np. When I read it in the 1980s, only two hand- and type-written copies of this Ballard manuscript existed, each possessed by two stubborn descendants, one in a closet in the town of Orting and the other in a Los Angeles warehouse. Neither would donate them to a proper institution nor have them published for fear of the other. The account of the log jam, narrated by Stuck Jack, a native of the village of Stuq, born about 1845 (see Ballard, "Puget Sound Mythology," Op. Cit., p. 39), to Ballard early in this century are in the section, pp. 47–51. My paraphrase and a direct quote from the account follows: The logjam was one mile long and covered with sand, bushes, and trees. The people caught salmon there for their winter use. They spent the winter in the valley and the summer at Three Tree Point, where they dug clams. Sometimes they went across to Colby. "A long time before I was born, many of the people of Stuck died of smallpox." Another native informant, Alex Kittle, told Ballard about the move from Black River to Stuck. My paraphrase of his remarks follows: Five upper-class families from Black River removed themselves up the White River to the site of the logjam, Stuck. Those who remained behind on Black River called this group the Stuckabish or "logjam people." The Stuckabish considered the *chutapal'tuahbsh* low class.

**31.** Ballard, "Mythology," Op. Cit., p. 89.

**32.** John Peabody Harrington, *John Peabody Harrington Papers, Alaska/Northwest Coast*, in National Anthropological Archives, Smithsonian Institution (Washington, D.C.), Reel 15, frame 493.

**33.** Of the residents of Flea's House, Ballard writes, "A certain group having a tradition of endogamy was regarded as low class by its neighbors." Arthur C. Ballard, "Southern Puget Sound Salish Kinship Terms," American Anthropologist. 37(1): 111–116, 1935, p. 111. This information about Flea's House was provided by Alex Kittle, one of Arthur Ballard's Duwamish informants. Ballard, *Listen My Nephew*, Op. Cit., p. 47. One of Harrington's informants elaborated, "White River bad place, poor people, no account. Stakabic Indians were all chiefs. Stakabic Indians would say to White River Indians who visited them—wash my feet *cudca'dabic* Footprints as White River Indians who had been visiting was about to return the stakabic would say wash your footprints away from the beach + they would comply." Harrington, *John Peabody Harrington Papers, Alaska/Northwest Coast*, reel 15, Op. Cit., frame 328.

**34.** Harrington, reel 30, Ibid, frames 232–233, 510. Waterman, microfilm 109 (Berkeley, CA: Bancroft Library). Snyder, Op. Cit, p. 109, 113. Julia Anne Allain, *Duwamish History in Duwamish Voices: Weaving Our Family Stories Since Colonization* (University of Victoria, PhD Thesis, 2024), p. 66.

**35.** T. T. Waterman, *Puget Sound Marriages and Genealogies*, Op. Cit., p. 24. Cornelius Holgate Hanford, *Seattle and Environs 1852–1924* (Chicago & Seattle: Pioneer Historical Publishing Co., 1924), p. 148. Thomas W. Prosch, David S. Maynard, and Catherine T. Maynard (Seattle: Lowman & Hanford Stationer & Printing Co., 1906), p. 74. *History of Seattle, Washington*, ed. Frederick James Grant (New York: American Publishing and Engraving Co., 1891), p. 61. Roberta Frye Watt, *4 Wagons West* (Portland, Binfords & Mort, Publishers, 1931), p. 237. Clarence B. Bagley, *History Of Seattle From The Earliest Times To The Present* (Chicago: The S. J. Clarke Publishing Company, 1916), p. 72.

**36.** Harrington, reel 15, Op. Cit., frame 489.

**37.** Ernest Bertelson, "The Story of the Blackfish," Ibid. Frank Carlson, Op. Cit., p. 14. Snyder, *NARN*, Op. Cit., p. 108. Eva [Greenslit] Anderson, *George Adams, Indian Legislator* (Published by Earl Coe, secretary of state, 1951 [?]), p. 30.

**38.** June McCormick Collins, *Valley of the Spirits* (Seattle: University of Washington Press, 1974), p. 31.

**39.** Harrington, reel 15, Op. Cit., frame 502. The recollection of Kitsap's prophecy comes from informant James George. The memory of the peoples' fear that Hat/Gedney Island had come adrift comes from Suquamish elder Sam Wilson. Evelyn T. Bowen, *Kitsap County History: A Story of Kitsap County and Its Pioneers* (Kitsap County Historical Society Book Committee, 1977. Book II), p. 150.

**40.** George Vancouver, *A Voyage of Discovery to the North Pacific Ocean and Round the World 1791–1795*, ed. W. Kaye Lamb, vol. 2 (London: The Haklyut Society, 1984), p. 545.

**41.** Clarence Bagley, *Indian Myths of the Northwest* (Seattle: Lowman and Hanford Company, 1930), 102–3.

**42.** Oliver Dunn and James E. Kelly Jr., *The Diario of Christopher Columbus's First Voyage To America 1492–1493* (Norman And London: University of Oklahoma Press, 1989), p. 75.

**43.** Archibald Menzies, *Journal of Vancouver's Voyage*, ed. C. F. Newcombe, MD (Victoria, BC: William H. Cullen, 1923), p. 42.

**44.** Vancouver, Ibid, p. 546.

**45.** "A New Vancouver Journal," n.a., ed. Edmund S. Meany, *Washington Historical Quarterly*, vol. VI, June 1914, p. 215. Many articles the British received in trade at Restoration Point are in the George Goodman Hewitt collection in the British Museum and detailed in *Erna Gunther, Indian Life On The Northwest Coast Of North America: As seen by the Early Explorers and Fur Traders during the Last Decades of the Eighteenth Century*, (Chicago and London: The University of Chicago Press, 1972), Appendix 1, 204–248.

## CHAPTER TWO

**1.** Manuel Quimper, "Journal," in Henry A. Wagner, *Spanish Explorations In the Strait of Juan De Fuca* (Santa Anna, CA: Fine Arts Press, 1933), 110, 190. Juan Pantoja, "Extracto," Wagner, Ibid, p. 188, 181, fn. 76.

**2.** Joseph Baker, *A log of His Majesty's ship Discovery from 22d December 1790 to July 1st, 1795*, Public Record Office, London and Vancouver, Op. Cit., p. 163.

**3.** Bernhard J. Stern, "How The Lummi Came To Their Present Abode," *The Lummi Indians Of Northwest Washington* (New York: Columbia University Press, 1934), pp. 115–120. Brian Ferguson, "Tribal Warfare," *Scientific American*, January, 1992, pp. 108–113.

**4.** Chief Martin Sampson, *Indians of Skagit County* (Mount Vernon: Skagit County Historical Series no. 2, 1972), p. 25. June McCormick Collins, "Distribution Of The Chemakum Language," in "Indians of the Urban Northwest," ed. Marion W. Smith, *Columbia University Contributions to Anthropology*, 36 (New York). Reprinted AMS Press, New York, 1969, 147–160.

**5.** Sampson, Ibid, pp. 56–58. Hermann Haeberlin, "The Mythology Of Puget Sound," *Journal of American Folk-Lore* 37 (145–146): 371–438, p. 378.

**6.** Frank Carlson, "Chief Sealth," *The Bulletin of the University of Washington*, series III, no. 2 (Seattle: December, 1903), p. 14.

**7.** Clarence Bagley, "Chief Seattle And Angeline," *Washington Historical Quarterly*, vol. 22, 1931, p. 265. Carlson, Ibid, p. 26. Emily Inez Denny, *Blazing The Way: True Stories, Songs And Sketches Of Puget Sound And Other Pioneers* (Seattle: Rainier Publishing Company, Inc., 1909), reprinted by the King County Museum of History and Industry, Dec. 1984, p. 359. Ernest B. Bertelson, "The Story of the Blackfish," Accession #946, box 1, folder; Speeches and Writings—Manuscripts, p. 26. Ernest B. Bertelson Collection, Special Collections, University of Washington Libraries. George Gibbs, MD, "Tribes Of Western Washington And Northwestern Oregon," *Contributions to the North American Ethnologist*, vol. 1, 1877 (US Govt. Printing Office), 184–185. Harrington, Op. Cit., frame 186. Sub-Qualth, one of Seattle's cousins, recalled that Seattle's aged father occupied the third ranking position in Old Man House after Seattle and Kitsap, suggesting, perhaps that Schweabe sired Seattle when he was fairly old. J. A. Costello, *The Siwash: Their Life, Legends and Tales: Puget Sound and Pacific Northwest* (Seattle: n.p., 1895). Facsimile Reproduction 1967 (The Shorey Book Store, 815 Third Avenue, 1967), p. 19.

**8.** "With Solemn Rites," the *Seattle Times*, Friday, June 5, 1896, p. 5, c. 3. Abbey Denny-Lindsley, "When Seattle Was An Indian Camp

Forty-Five Years Ago," the *Seattle Post-Intelligencer*, magazine section, Sunday, April 16, 1906, p. 6, c. 2. Thomas Talbot Waterman, "The Geographical Names Used By The Indians Of The Pacific Coast," *The Geographical Review*, vol. 12, pt. 2 (1922), p. 187, #4.

**9.** Warren A. Snyder, "Southern Puget Sound Salish: Texts, Place Names and Dictionary," *Sacramento Anthropological Society Papers*, 9 (Sacramento: California, 1968), p. 119. Marian Wesely Smith, *The Puyallup-Nisqually* (New York: Columbia University Press, 1940), p. 70. Warren Snyder, Suquamish field notes, "Suquamish Traditions," *Northwest Anthropological Research Notes*, Spring, 1999, vol. 33, no. 1, ed. Jay Miller (University of Idaho), p. 156, hearafter cited as *NARN*.

**10.** Thomas Talbott Waterman, "Indian Names for places about Seattle, Map A," *Puget Sound Geography* (Manuscript no. 1864, National Anthropological Archives, Smithsonian Institution, Washington, DC, 1920), p. 150, #43. David Buerge, "Isle Of Myth: How the exotic beasts of Native American legend shaped the geography around Sea-Tac," the *Seattle Weekly*, January 4, 1989, pp. 24–31. Snyder, "Southern Puget Sound Salish," Ibid, p. 119.

**11.** The translation "Honorable One" comes from Puyallup informants via Roxanne Thayer, personal communication, 1998. Linguist Nile Thomson suggests a variation: "Good Blood Child," from the Puget Salish morphemes, `I `a'b, meaning wealth, and the suffix, "-al," indicating class membership. Dawn Bates, Thom Hess, and Vi Hilbert, *Lushootseed Dictionary* (Seattle and London: University of Washington Press, 1994), pp. 15, 29.

**12.** Conversation with Harriet Turner, c. January 1989.

**13.** Samuel F. Coombs, "Good Chief Seattle How a Young Warrior Became Ruler of Many Tribes," the *Seattle Post-Intelligencer*, Sunday, March 26, 1893, p. 9, c 1–4, p. 10, c. 2–3.

**14.** Divers found these while looking for antique bottles in what is now the Green River, and in the absence of any other aboriginal artifacts, but these suggests a battle site rather than debris from a midden. Personal communication with William Ribovik in David M. Buerge, "Giant Fish and Supernatural

Dwarfs," *EastsideWeek*, February 17, 1993, 12–19. Snyder, Ibid, p. 166.

**15.** Frank Carlson, Op. Cit., p. 16. Warren Snyder, *NARN*, Op. Cit., 108–9. Roberta Frye Watt, *4 Wagons West The Story of Seattle* (Portland: Binfords & Mort, Publishers, 1931) 50–51.

**16.** Haeberlin And Gunther, Ibid, p. 48, 51. George Gibbs, MD. *Niskwalli—English English—Niskwalli Dictionary*, Washington, DC, *Contributions to North American Ethnology* I. 1876, p. 312. Smith, Op. Cit., p. 173.

**17.** In her biography of Seattle, Eva Greenslit Anderson took La Daila, "Girlie," for the name of Seattle's first wife, from a list of names in Hermann Haeberlin and Erna Gunther's "The Indians of Puget Sound," *University of Washington Publications in Anthropology*, vol. IV, no. 1, 1930, reprinted by University of Washington Press (Seattle and London, 1973), 47–48. Eva Greenslit Anderson, *Chief Seattle* (Caldwell, Idaho: The Caxton Printers, Ltd., 1943), p. 78, footnote #3, p. 349. A native name for Angeline, Sabolits!a, comes from Mrs. James Garrison, one of Waterman's Suquamish informants. Waterman, *Puget Sound Marriages and Genealogies*, Bancroft Library, University of California at Berkeley, CA, p. 8. The names Wee-wy-eke and Kick-is-om-lo come from Clarence Bagley, "Chief Seattle And Angeline," *Washington Historical Quarterly*, vol. 22, 1931, p. 269. Kickesimla is from Carlson, Op Cit., p. 16. Ka-ki-is-il-ma comes from Emily Inez Denny, daughter of David Denny and Louisa Boren, Emily Inez Denny, *Blazing The Way or True Stories, Songs and Sketches Of Puget Sound And Other Pioneers* (Seattle: Rainier Printing Company, Inc., 1909), reprinted by Historical Society of King County, 1984, p. 378. Costello writes that Kakii-Silma was how she named herself. Costello, Op. Cit., p. 108. The suffixial ending "omlo," "ilma," was the Anglicization of "ublu," a common ending of many women's names that Dr. Thompson believes has to do with cedar. Thompson, personal communication, 5/14/13.

**18.** Waterman, "Names of Places along Lake Washington," *Puget Sound Geography*, Op. Cit., #123 (94). John Peabody Harrington, *The Papers of John Peabody Harrington In the Smithsonian Institution, 1907–1957* (Millwood, New Jersey:

Kraus International Publications, a Division of Kraus-Thompson Organization, Limited, 1981), reel 15. Duwamish Field Notes-Lecture Notes, frames 374, 417, 421, 424. Don Sherwood, "Atlantic City Park," *Interpretive Essays Of The Histories of Seattle's Parks & Playgrounds*, vol. 1, A-C. Tłił-cus, "small island," in Waterman, "The Geographical Names Used By The Indians Of The Pacific Coast," *The Geographical Review*, vol. 12, pt. 2 (1922), p. 191, #99, is probably the village of Kla-Hu-Chus identified in Claimants Exhibit W-2 in *Duwamish, Lummi, Whidbey Island, Skagit, Upper Skagit, Swinomish et. al. versus USA Court of Claims of the United States*. LXXIX, 530. Wash., DC: Govt. Printing Office, 1935. Reprinted in two volumes by Argus Press, Seattle. Harrington, Ibid., frames 374, 417, 421, 424.

**19.** For information about Seattle's second wife and their sons and daughters see Emily Inez Denny, Ibid, p. 367; the Sackman Family Tree on file in the Duwamish Tribal Office (xerox copy in author's possession), Tom Speer, "Chief Seattle's Wives and children," information researched and compiled for the Duwamish Tribal Services Board of Directors, July 14, 2004 (copy in author's possession), and Julia Anne Allain, *Duwamish History in Duwamish Voices Weaving Our Family Stories Since Colonization* (Victoria, British Columbia: University of Victoria, PhD Thesis, 2014), p. 201. Seattle's son, Sa'kw!al, was killed during the raid on the Chemakum fort at *tse'tsibus*. William W. Elmendorf, *Twana Narratives: Native Historical Accounts of a Coast Salish Culture* (Seattle and London: University of Washington Press, 1993), p. 144. George Seattle's native name, See-an-ump-kun, comes from Emily Inez Denny, *Blazing The Way* (Seattle: Rainier Printing Company, 1909), p. 367. Sloo-noksh-tan, the native name for James, better known as Jim, is found on the Treaty of Point Elliott document, where, in the list of signatories, he is one of five, excluding Seattle, that signed for the Suquamish. The baptismal name Ann is recorded in Jay Miller, Ibid, p. 9. The name for the Sammamish comes from Waterman, "Names on the Sammamish River and Lake Sammamish," *Puget Sound Geography*, Op. Cit., #91A. We do not know the names of Seattle's concubines, but Mary Sam Seattle, well known to the pioneers, may have been the daughter of one. Mary seems her baptismal name; Sam her husband's name, but her last name suggests she was the daughter of a concubine who took Seattle's name as her own. The same may be true of John Seattle, cited as Seattle's nephew. "Nephew" was commonly used to cite distant kin connections, and John's assumption of the name during a *sgwe'gwe* he hosted in 1908 suggests it came from his mother, another concubine who took it as her own. "Mary Seattle Is Badly Hurt," the *Seattle Times*, April 15, 1906, p. 5, c. 3; "Chief Seattle's Nephew Leaves $50,000 Estate," *Auburn Globe Republican*, January 25, 1924, p. 1, c. 2–3, p. 8, c. 5.

**20.** *Duwamish et. al. versus USA*, Ibid, p. 281, 299. The dimensions of the West Seattle house come from the village list submitted in *The Duwamish, et. al*, Claimants Exhibit W-2, ibid., in the author's possession.

**21.** George C. Shaw, *The Chinook Jargon And How To Use It* (Seattle: Rainier Printing Company Inc., 1909), p. 19. Harrington, Op. Cit., *Alaska Northwest Coast*, reel 30, frame 339, 433. E. E. Riddell, *History of Suquamish: Excerpts From a Manuscript Compiled by E. E. Riddell for the North End Improvement Council of Kitsap County*. n.d. in *The Suquamish Tribe: A History From Manuscripts and Memory* (A Project of the Suquamish and Klallam Tribes Title IV Committee and the North Kitsap School District, 1975), p. 57. James Vernon Metcalf, *Chief Seattle*, Supplement to the Catholic Northwest Progress, c1970, p. 4.

**22.** Joseph Perry Sanford, "Journal of Passed Midshipman Joseph Perry Sanford aboard the Vincennes and the Porpoise, August 19, 1838– July 22, 1841." *Records of the United States Exploring Expedition Under The Command Of Lieutenant Charles Wilkes, 1838–42*, reel 19. Charles Wilkes, *Narrative of the United States Exploring Expedition during the Years 1838, 1839, 1840, 1841, 1842*, vol. IV, p. 480. Goldsborough's measurement of the Oleman is in George Gibbs, Op. Cit., p. 215. George Gibbs, "Report To Captain Mc'Clellan, on the Indian Tribes of the Territory of Washington," 402–434, in "Report of the Explorations for a Route . . . from St. Paul to Puget Sound by I. I. Stevens," vol. 1. *Reports of Explorations and Surveys . . .*

from the Mississippi River to the Pacific Ocean ... 1853–54 [etc.]. 33rd Congress, 2nd Sess. Senate Executive Document No. 78 (Serial no. 758), Washington: Beverly Tucker, Printer. Reprinted as *Indians Tribes of Washington Territory* (Ye Galleon Press, Fairfield, WA, 1972), p. 215.

**23.**     Ernest B. Bertelson. "Piece Of Cedar Recalls Chief's Dream," the *Seattle Times*. *Pacific Parade Magazine*, Sunday, December 19, 1948, p. 3. Ernest Bertelson, "The Suquamish," 5–7. File: Notes—Indians. Ernest Bertelson Collection, Accession # 946, Box 1. University of Washington Libraries Special Collections.

**24.**     Carlson, Ibid, 22–25. Bertelson Collection, Ibid, p. 2. Costello, Op. Cit., 19–20. Elmendorf, *Twana Narratives*, Op. Cit., p. 152. Warren Jefferson, *The World Of Chief Seattle How Can One Sell the Air* (Summertown, Tennessee: Native Voices Book Publishing Co., 2001), 69–70. R. S. Ludwin, C. P. Thrush, K. James, D. Buerge, C. Jonientz-Trisler, J. Rasmussen, K. Troost, and A. de los Angeles, "Serpent Spirit-power Stories along the Seattle Fault," *Seismological Research Letters*, vol. 76, no. 4 (Albany, California: Seismological Research Society, July/August, 2005), 426–431.

**25.**     Smith, Ibid, p. 18. Itakbʷ, Harrington, reel 30, Ibid, frame 251. Etakmurh in Sacramental Register, Tulalip and Puget Sound, October 15, 1857 to April 1868, vol. II, p. 205. Dennis E. Lewarch to Gary Luke, February 23, 2017, p. 4.

**26.**     Harrington, Ibid, frame 338. Haeberlin and Gunther, Op. Cit., pp. 17–18. Carlson, Op. Cit., p. 24. Herbert Hunt, *Tacoma: Its History and its Builders* (Chicago: S. J. Clarke Publishing Company, 1919), vol. 1, p. 21. Beth and Ray Hill, *Indian Petroglyphs of the Pacific Northwest* (Seattle: University of Washington Press, 1974), p. 21, 45–46.

**27.**     T. T. Waterman, "Names of places on the southern shore of the sound from Johnson point to the vicinity of Tacoma," *Puget Sound Geography*, Op. Cit., 33–35, p. 35, #175.

**28.**     Murray Morgan, *Puget's Sound: A Narrative of Early Tacoma and the Southern Sound* (Seattle and London: University of Washington Press, 1980), 11–12. Francis Annance, "Journey thro. The Land," 1 28 Y. 1824, in "Opening The Pacific Slope," ed. Nile

Thompson, *Cowlitz Historical Quarterly*, 1991, vol. XXXIII, no. 1, 17–19. John Work, "Journal of John Work, November And December, 1824," ed. T. C. Elliott, *Washington Historical Quarterly*, vol. 3, 1912, 198–228, 214.

**29.**     Bruce Alistair McKelvie, *Fort Langley Birthplace of British Columbia* (Victoria, BC: Porcépic Books Limited, 1991), 9–16.

**30.**     Bertelson, "The Story of the Blackfish," Ibid, p. 26.

**31.**     Edward S. Curtis, *The North American Indian: Being a Series of Volumes Picturing and Describing the Indians of the United States, the Dominion of Canada and Alaska*, ed. Frederick W. Hodge (Norwood, Mass: Plimpton Press, 1970), vol. IX, pp. 13–16. Snyder, Op. Cit., 170–172. Theodore O. Williams, "Documents: The Indian Chief Kitsap," *Washington Historical Quarterly*, 25, no. 4. October 1934, p. 298. Elmendorf, Op. Cit., p. 148, 152. Smith, Op. Cit., p. 158.

**32.**     William Elmendorf, *Twana Narratives Native Historical Accounts Of A Coast Salish Culture* (Seattle and London: University of Washington Press, 1993), 148–9, 152.

**33.**     William Fraser Tolmie, *The Journals of William Fraser Tolmie Physician and Fur Trader*, ed. Janet R. Mitchell (Vancouver, Canada: Mitchell Press, Limited, 1963), entry for Sunday, August 4, 1833, p. 223. Sarah Robinson, whose native name was Neesemu, was the sister of Seattle's first wife, born in 1825, who married Thomas Robinson, a.k.a. "Lopson" or "Stotmish," a native of Chemainus, a Cowichan village in British Columbia. Descendants of Sarah Robinson t.s. n.d., in author's possession. Seattle's annual trips to the Fraser River, remembered by White River settler John Thomas, were recalled by Mrs. Elizabeth Lossee, his granddaughter. Conversation with Mrs. Elizabeth Lossee, March 9, 1986; notes in author's possession.

**34.**     George Barneston, no. 76, *Fort Langley Journal, 1827–28. Journal of the voyage of the Party to form an establishment at the entrance of Fraser River, and of the proceedings and other occurrences[sic] at Fort Langley, the whole commencing with the 27th of June 1827 and carried up to this 16th February, 1828*. B, 113/a/1, reel no. 1M70 (Hudson's Bay Company Archives).

**35.** Curtis, Ibid, 24–25. Mary Anne Lambert, "Mystery Solved," *Shadows of Our Ancestors: Readings in the History of Klallam-White Relations*, ed. Jerry Gorsline (Port Townsend: Empty Bowl, 1992), 23–29. George Simpson to Andrew Colville, August 9, 1824 in *Fur Trade and Empire*, ed. Frederick Merck (Cambridge: MA, 1931), p. 23. McLoughlin To the Governor, Deputy Governor and Committee, July 10, 1828 in *The Letters of John McLoughllin From Fort Vancouver To the Governor, Deputy Governor and Committee. First Series, 1825–38*, ed. E. E. Rich, MA (Toronto: The Chaplain Society, 1941), p. 57.

**36.** Francis Ermatinger, "Earliest Expedition Against Puget Sound Indians," ed. Eva Emory Dye, *The Washington Historical Quarterly*, vol. 1, no. 2 (Jan. 1907), 16–29.

**37.** Snyder, "Suquamish Traditions," *NARN*, Op. Cit., p. 130.

**38.** McLoughlin to the Governor, Deputy Governor and Committee, *Letters*, Op. Cit., p. 88. Tolmie, Ibid, p. 288. Sampson, Op. Cit., p. 25. Robert T. Boyd, *The Coming of the Spirit of Pestilence* (Vancouver and Toronto: UBC Press, Seattle and London: University of Washington Press, 1999), 110–113. Chief Martin J. Sampson, *Indians Of Skagit County*, Skagit County Historical Series no. 2 (Mount Vernon, WA: Skagit County Historical Society, 1972), p. 25. Washington Irving, *Astoria, Or Anecdotes Of An Enterprise Beyond The Rocky Mountains*, ed. Richard Dilworth Rust (Lincoln and London: University of Nebraska Press, 1976), 80–81. Tolmie, Op. Cit., entry for Sunday, June 9, p. 201.Entry for Wednesday, July 3, p. 214, Hunt, Op. Cit., 37–41. Tolmie, Ibid, p. 242.

**39.** Tolmie, Op. Cit., entry for Wednesday, June 5, 1833, 198–199. Cecilia Svinth Carpenter, *Fort Nisqually A Documented History of Indian and British Interaction* (Tacoma, Washington: Tahoma Research Service, 1986), p. 36.

**40.** Tolmie, Op. Cit., entry for Sunday, June 9, p. 201. Entry for Wednesday, July 3, p. 214,

**41.** Herbert Hunt, *Tacoma: Its History and its Builders* (Chicago: S. J. Clarke Publishing Company, 1919), vol. 1, 37–41. Tolmie, Ibid, p. 242. Smith, Op. Cit., p. 12. Conversations with Dr. Nile Thompson. Hermann Haeberlin and Erna Gunther, *The Indians Of Puget Sound* (Seattle and London: University of Washington Press, 1973), p. 47.

**42.** Riddell, Op. Cit., p. 60. William Kitsap in "Indians Feared Chief Kitsap More Than Whites, *The Bainbridge Review*, Thursday, July 2, 1953.

**43.** Waterman, "The Geographic Names Used By Indians Of The Pacific Coast," *The Geographical Review*, vol. 12, pt. 2 (1922), p. 188, #25. Tolmie, Op. Cit., entry for July 9, 1833, p. 216.

**44.** Tolmie, Ibid, p. 214.

**45.** Ibid, p. 214.

## CHAPTER THREE

**1.** Gray Whaley, *Oregon and the Collapse of Illahee* (Chapel Hill: University of North Carolina Press, 2010), p. 13.

**2.** William Welcome Elmendorf, "The Structure of Twana Culture," *Washington State University, Research Studies* 28(3), *Monograph Supplement* 2, Pullman. Reprinted in: *A Garland Series: American Indian Ethnohistory: Indians of the Northwest/Coast Salish and Western Washington Indians, IV* (New York & London: Garland Publishing, Inc., 1974), 313–314.

**3.** *The Journal of Occurrences At Fort Nisqually* (hereafter cited as *JOFN*), vol. 1, sec. 1, May 30, 1833 to April 25, 1835, trans. and ed. George Dickey, 1989 (Published by the Fort Nisqually Association). Entry for May 13, p. 3; August 29, p. 9; August 30, 9–10.

**4.** Tolmie, Ibid, entry for Thursday, September 11, 235–236.

**5.** Ibid, entries for September 29 to Friday, October 18, 238–242.

**6.** Emily Inez Denny, *Blazing The Way True Stories, Songs And Sketches Of Puget Sound And Other Pioneers* (Seattle: Rainier Printing Company, 1909), p. 358–359.

**7.** Samuel Coombs, "Good Chief Seattle," the *Seattle Post-Intelligencer*, March 26, 1893, p. 9, c. 2.

**8.** Zephyrin Englehardt, OFM, *The Missions and Missionaries Of California* (San Francisco: The James H. Barrie Company, 1908), vol. 1, p. 99; vol. p. 2, 242–256.

9. Wilfred P. Schoenberg, SJ, *A History Of The Catholic Church In The Pacific Northwest: 1743–1983* (Washington, DC: The Pastoral Press, 1987), p. 13, 20.

10. Schoenberg, Ibid, p. 13, 20.

11. *JOFN*, Ibid, entries for January 21, 1835, p. 50; February 10, p. 52; February 19, 22, p. 53; March 21, p. 56.

12. *JOFN*, Ibid, Section 2, April 25, 1835 to August 14, 1836. Entry for October 18, 1835, p 15–16.

13. *JOFN*, Ibid, entry for October 18, 1835, p 18. Bagley, "Chief Seattle and Angeline," Op. Cit., p. 269. Snyder, Op. Cit., p. 140, 156. I am convinced the description mentioned in Snyder, p. 156, describes Seattle's action. Julia Anne Allain, *Duwamish History in Duwamish Voices Weaving Our Family Stories Since Colonization* (Victoria, BC: University of Victoria, PhD Thesis, 2014), p. 205.

14. Robert F. Boyd, "Demographic History, 1774–1874," *Handbook of North American Indians*, vol. 7, *Northwest Coast*, ed. Wayne Suttles (Washington: Smithsonian Institution, 1990), 135–148, p. 141. *JOFN*, Ibid, entry for March 1–6, 9, 15, 1836, 32–33.

15. Elmendorf, *Twana Narratives: Native Historical Accounts of a Coast Salish Culture* (Seattle and London: University of Washington Press, 1993), 128–129. Colin E. Tweddel, "A Historical and Ethnographic Study of the Snohomish Indian People: A Report Specifically Their Aboriginal and Traditional Existence and Their Effective Occupation of a Definable Territory," *A Garland Series: American Indian Ethnohistory: Indians of the Northwest/Coast Salish and Western Washington Indians* II, comp. and ed. by David Agee Horr, Brandeis University (New York & London: Garland Publishing, Inc., 1974), 544–547.

16. Edward Curtis, *The North American Indian: being a series of volumes picturing and describing the Indians of the United States and Alaska.* University Press (Cambridge, MA), printer: Plimpton Press, printer, 1907–1930 Seattle, vol. 9, p. 14. *JOFN*, Op. Cit., Section 3, September 1, 1836 to October 31, 1857. Entries for February 11 to 19, 16–17.

17. Snyder, Op. Cit., p. 168.

18. *JOFN*, Op. Cit., Section 4, November 1,

1837 to May 31, 1839. Entries for December 6, 1837, p. 4; January 9, 1838, p. 7; April 9, 10, p. 13

19. June McCormick Collins, "The Influence Of White Contact On Class Distinctions And Political Authority Among The Indians Of Puget Sound," *A Garland Series: American Indian Ethnohistory: Indians of the Northwest/Coast Salish and Western Washington Indians* II, comp. and ed. by David Agee Horr, Brandeis University (New York & London: Garland Publishing, Inc., 1974), 89–204, 132–133.

20. "Diary of Wilkes In The Northwest," ed. Edmund Meany, *Washington Historical Quarterly*, vol. XVI, January, 1925, 290–301, p. 297.

21. Schoenberg, *A Chronicle Of the Catholic History Of the Pacific Northwest, 1743–1960* (Portland, OR: Catholic Sentinel Printery, 1962), 48, p. 8.

22. Rev. Francis Norbert Blanchet, *Historical Sketches of the Catholic Church in Oregon During The Past Forty Years (1838–1878)*, sketch XII, np. 1910, p. 31. Alice Esther Oksness, *Reverend Modeste Demers, Missionary in the Northwest* (Seattle: University of Washington MA Thesis, 1934), p. 14.

23. Blanchet, Ibid, sketch XVII, p. 40.

24. Collins, "John Fornsby: The Personal Document of a Coast Salish Indian," in "Indians of the Urban Northwest," ed. Marian W. Smith, 285–341, *Columbia University Contributions to Anthropology*, 36 (1949), p. 311.

25. *Notices & Voyages of the Famed Quebec Mission to the Pacific Northwest*, trans. Carl Lunderholm (Portland, OR: Oregon Historical Society, Champoeg press, Inc., 195), "Extract from A Letter of Mr. Demers to Monseigneur of Juliopolis, dated from Cowlitz, 10 November, 1841," 98–109.

26. "Historic Rock Destroyed," the *Seattle Post-Intelligencer*, October 31, 1900, p. 5, c. 2. A. J. Splawn, *Ka-mi-akin, Last Hero of the Yakimas* (Yakima, WA: 1980), p. 8, 12. James H. Teit, "The Middle Columbia Salish," *University of Washington Publications in Anthropology* (Seattle: University of Washington Press, 1928), 83–128, 108, 109. Fredi Perry, *Port Madison Washington Territory 1854–1889* (Bremerton, WA: Perry Publishing, 1989), 131–132. Elmendorf, *Twana Narratives*, Op. Cit., p. 8.

27. Inez Denny, Op. Cit., p. 360.

**28.** Marian Wesley Smith, *The Puyallup-Nisqually* (New York: Columbia Press, 1940), 150–161.

**29.** James Douglas To The Governor, Deputy Governor and Committee Hon. Hudson's Bay Company. Fort Vancouver, October 14, 1839. *McLaughlin's Fort Vancouver Letters, Second Series, 1839–1844*, Appendix A (London: Champlain Society, 1944) 205–382, p. 217. Alexander Anderson in Clarence B. Bagley, *In The Beginning: Early Days on Puget Sound* (1905). Reprinted (Historical Society of Seattle and King County, 1980), 15–16. Sir George Simpson to the Earl of Aberdeen, November 25, 1841, in Joseph Schafer, "Letters of Sir George Simpson, 1841–1843," *The American Historical Review*, XIV (1909), 78–79.

**30.** Curtis, Op. Cit., p. 105. Bruce Alistair McKelvie, *Fort Langley Birthplace of British Columbia* (Victoria, BC: Porcépic Books Limited, 1991), 53–54. Stanley Walen, *Indians Of North America/The Kwaiutl*, ed. Frank W. Porter III (New York: Chelsea House Publishers, 1992), 57-59.

**31.** Collins, Fornsby, Op. Cit., 300–301, Curtis, Op. Cit, 20–21.

**32.** *JOFN*, Op. Cit., Section 3, entry for September 27, 1837.

**33.** Charles Wilkes, *Narrative of The United States Exploring Expedition During the Years 1838, 1839, 1840, 1841, 1842* (London: Whittaker And Co., Ave Maria Lane, 1845), p. 280, 302. Patrick Haskett, *The Wilkes Expedition In Puget Sound 1841* (Olympia: The Resources Development Internship Program of the Western Interstate Commission for Higher Education and the State Capitol Museum, 1974), p. 10.

**34.** "Journal of Passed Midshipman Joseph Perry Sanford aboard the Vincennes and the Porpoise, August 19, 1838–July 22, 1841." in *Records of the United States Exploring Expedition Under The Command Of Lieutenant Charles Wilkes, 1838–42*, reel 19, entry for May 27, 1841. Wilkes, 1845, Op. Cit., p. 286. "Journal kept by George T. Sinclair, Acting Master aboard the Relief, the Porpoise, and the Flying Fish, December 19, 1838–June 26, 1842." Records, Ibid, reel 21, p. 481.

**35.** Records, Ibid, p. 286.

**36.** Bertelson, "The Suquamish," Ibid, p. 2.

**37.** Ibid, p. 7, 8. Snyder, *NARN*, Op. Cit., p.

**38.** Frank Carlson, "Chief Sealth," *The Bulletin of the University of Washington*, Series III, no. 2, December, 1903, p. 24. Hermann Haeberlin and Erna Gunther, *The Indians of Puget Sound*, vol. IV, no. 1, *University of Washington Publications in Anthropology*, 1930, reprinted (Seattle and London: University of Washington Press, 1973), p. 60. Warren A. Snyder, "Archaeological Sampling At 'Old Man House' On Puget Sound," in *Research Studies, State College of Washington* (Pullman: 1956), vol. XXIV, 17–37.

**39.** Wilkes, 1845, Op. Cit., p. 288.

**40.** John P. Richmond, letter quoted in Bagley, *In The Beginning*, Op. Cit., pp. 40–42.

**41.** Jean Baptiste Zacharie Bolduc, *Mission of the Columbia*, ed. Edward J. Kowrach (Fairfield, Washington: Ye Galleon Press, 1979), p. 111.

**42.** Bolduc, Ibid, p. 119.

**43.** *Notices & Voyages*, Ibid, 100–101, 194. Bolduc, Mission, Ibid, p. 115.

**44.** Nels Bruseth, *Indian Stories and Legends Of The Stillaguamish And Allied Tribes*, n.p., (Arlington, WA: 1926), p. 8

**45.** *Fort Nisqually Trade Shop Blotter, February 1844–December 1846*, Huntington Library Archives Manuscript FN #1247 vol. 3, 4, 5. Trans. and indexed Steven A. Anderson, p. 57, 67. June, 1848, p. 255. "To: Watzheladhee, Chief of the Sanomas, et. al, from His Excellency Joseph Lane Gov. + Sup. Ind. Aff. for Oregon War Department, Office Indian Affairs, Oct. 6, 1848," in 1848 Oregon Superintendency Collection, Microfilm 71–1, University of Washington Libraries.

**46.** *JOFN*, Op. Cit., Section Five, entries for February 6, 1846, p. 2, August 13, 1846, p. 17. Peter Skene Ogden and James Douglas to Tolmie, Fort Vancouver, July 9, 1846; in Puget Sound Agricultural Company, Box 6, Douglas, *Letters*; University of Washington Libraries, Special Collections, Accession Number, 5033-1.

**47.** Curtis. Op. Cit., pp. 33–35.

**48.** Paul Kane, *Wanderings Of An Artist Among The Indians Of North America* (Toronto: The Radisson Society of Canada, Limited, 1925), p. 155, 158.

**49.** Kane, Ibid, p. 159–161.

**50.** Myron Eells, "The Twana, Chemakum & Klallam Indians of Washington Territory,"

*Smithsonian Annual Report*, 1887, p. 607.
Edward Curtis, Op. Cit., pp. 141–142.
Elmendorf, *Twana Narratives*, Op. Cit., 143–

155. Denny, Op. Cit., 359–60. Bertelson, "The
Suquamish," Ibid, p. 15.
**51.** Elmendorf, Ibid. p. 144.

## CHAPTER FOUR

**1.** Alexis de Tocqueville, *Democracy In
America* (New York: Vintage Classics Vintage
Books, a Division Of Random House, Inc.,
1990), vol. 1, 293, 295.
**2.** "Letter of Demers to M.C., Oregon City,
March 5, 1844, from Willamette, December
20, 1845." *Notices & Voyages of the Famed
Quebec Mission to the Pacific Northwest*, trans.
Carl Lunderholm (Portland: Oregon Historical
Society, Champoeg press, Inc., 1956), p. 206,
207; 235–236.
**3.** Nile Thompson, "Grey Head, Leader of
the Steilacoom Indians," in *Steilacoom A Bi-
Annual Historical Gazette* (Centennial Souvenir
Issue, Steilacoom: Steilacoom Centennial
Committee September, 1988), 12–13.
**4.** Marian Wesley Smith, *The Puyallup-
Nisqually* (New York: Columbia University
Press, 1940), p. 332. A. J. Splawn, *Ka-Mi-Akin
The Last Hero of the Yakimas (*Caldwell, Idaho:
The Caxton Printers, 1980), p. 4. Clarence
Bagley, *In The Beginning: Early Days on Puget
Sound* (Ezra Meeker, 1905, reprinted by the
Historical Society of Seattle and King County,
1980), p. 70. Mrs. Mary Jane Hartman, née
McAllister, in, *A Small World Of Our Own*, ed.
Robert A. Bennett (Walla Walla, WA: Pioneer
Press Books, 1985), 9–19. Ezra Meeker, *The
Tragedy of Leshi* (Ezra Meeker, 1905, reprinted,
Everett: Historical Society of Seattle and King
County, New Material Copyright, 1980), p. 11.
**5.** Thomas Talbot Waterman, "Names of
Places in the so-called Nisqually and Squaxin
Areas," maps no. 26, 27, 28 (Head of Sound),
*Puget Sound Geography*, Ms 1864, Smithsonian
Anthropological Archives, p. 33, #163. Mrs.
Mary Jane Hartman, née McAllister, *A Small
World Of Our Own*, Ibid, 10–11.
**6.** Waterman, Ibid, p. 24, #124. John
M. Swan, *The Colonizations around Puget
Sd.* (Handwritten ms, Olympia, W. T., 1878,
Bancroft Library, University of California),
3–5. Edward Sylvester, *Founding of Olympia*
(Handwritten ms, *Olympia, The Pioneer Town of

*Washington, Its Socialization, Origin* Olympia,
W.T., 1878). (Handwritten ms, Olympia, W. T.,
1878), 10–18. J. C. Rathbun, *History of Thurston
Co., Washington* (Olympia, Washington,
1895), 9–10. Clinton A. Snowden, *History
of Washington The Rise and Progress of an
American State* (New York: The Century History
Company, 1909) Volume 2, p. 438.
**7.** Smith, Op. Cit., p. 31. Gray H. Whaley,
*Oregon and the Collapse of Illahee* (Chapel Hill:
University of North Carolina Press, 2010), p. 175.
Paul Kane, *Wanderings Of An Artist Among The
Indians Of North America* (Toronto: The Radisson
Society of Canada, Limited, 1925), 118–119.
**8.** Paul Kane, *Wanderings Of An Artist
Among The Indians Of North America* (Toronto:
The Radisson Society of Canada, Limited,
1925), p. 158.
**9.** "Coupeville—'Thumbnail History,'"
HistoryLink.org Essay 9587, www.historylink
.org. *Early Reminiscences of a NISQUALLY
PIONEER The McAllister Family Thurston
County, TOLD BY THE PIONEERS
Reminiscences of Pioneer Life In Washington*,
vol. 1, printed under a project directed by
secretary of state E. N. Hutchinson, 1937),
p.166–184, p. 172.
**10.** Hubert Howe Bancroft, *The Works Of
Hubert Howe Bancroft, Volume XXXI, History
Of Washington, Idaho, And Montana, 1845–
1889* (San Francisco: The History Company,
Publishers, 1890), 10–11. "Miscellaneous.
Chinook Jargon," *The Columbian*, Jan. 15, 1853,
p. 1, c. 1–2, c. 2.
**11.** Thomas Talbot Waterman, *Puget
Sound Geography*, ms. 1864 in Smithsonian
Anthropological Archives, p. 170, #207b.
William Fraser Tolmie, *History of Puget Sound
and the Northwest Coast* (Victoria, ms, 1878).
In the Bancroft Library, Berkeley, Ca. P - B 25,
29–31. Arthur Ballard, "Mythology of Southern
Puget Sound," *University of Washington
Publications in Anthropology*, vol. 3, #2, pp.
31–150, p. 37.

**12.** Joseph Thomas Heath, *Memoirs of Nisqually* (Fairfield, WA: Ye Galleon Press, 1979), p. 146, 149. William Fraser Tolmie to Peter Skene Ogden, *Correspondence Outward*, 3 letters from Tolmie to Peter Skene Ogden, Archives of British Columbia, Victoria, BC, letter of July 24, 1848.

**13.** *Oregon Spectator*, January 20, 1848. Waterman, notes in John Peabody Harrington, *The Papers of John Peabody Harrington In the Smithsonian Institution 1907–1957*, vol. 1, reel 30, Alaska Northwest Coast (Millwood, New York: Kraus International Publications, a Division of Kraus-Thompson Organization Limited, 1981), frame 249–250.

**14.** Emily Inez Denny, *Blazing The Way True Stories, Songs, Sketches Of Puget Sound And Other Pioneers* (Seattle: Rainier Publishing Company, 1909), p. 371. Jerry Kanim, in Harriet Turner, *Ethnozoology Of The Snoqualmie, Second Edition, Revised.* N.p., 1976. p. 96.

**15.** Frederick James Grant, *History of Seattle* (New York: American Publishing and Engraving Co., 1891), p. 59. Thomas Talbot Waterman, "Names of places along the Snoqualmie River," *Puget Sound Geography*, MS 1864, Smithsonian Ethnographic Collection, #9.

**16.** Elwood Evans, *History of The Pacific Northwest: Oregon and Washington* (Portland, OR: North Pacific History Company), vol. 1, p. 302. *History of Seattle*, ed. Frederick James Grant (New York: American Publishing and Engraving Co., 1891), 59–60. Bancroft, Op. Cit., p. 11. Myron Eells, *The Indians of Puget Sound: The Notebooks of Myron Eells*, ed. George Castile (Seattle and London: University of Washington Press, 1985), p. 354.

**17.** Tolmie, *History*, Op. Cit., 31–33.

**18.** Cecilia Svinth Carpenter, *Fort Nisqually: A Documented History of Indian and British Interaction* (Tacoma, WA: Tahoma Research Service, 1986), p. 143. *Washington Standard*, April 5, 1862, p. 2, c. 3., April 12, p. 2, c. 3. George Albert Kellogg, *A History of Whidbey Island* (Coupeville, WA: Island County Historical Society, 1934), 15–16.

**19.** *The Journal of Occurrences At Fort Nisqually* (hereafter cited as *JOFN*), trans. and ed. by George Dickey, 1989 (Published by the Fort Nisqually Association), Section Six, entry for April 29 to May 1, 1849, 2–6.

**20.** Heath, *Memoirs*, Op. Cit., entry for January 20, 1849. *JOFN*, Ibid, entry for May 14, 1849, p. 7.

**21.** J. E. Ayer, "George Bush the Voyageur," *Washington Historical Quarterly*, vol. VII, no. 1, January, 1916, 44–55.

**22.** Joseph Lane to Tolmie, May 17, 1849. 31st Congress, 2nd Session, *House Executive Document 1*, 156–168, p. 157.

**23.** *JOFN*, Op. Cit., entry for June 8, 1849, p. 7, p. 9.

**24.** Ibid, entry for August 21, 1849, p. 15. C. H. Hanford, *Seattle and Environs* (Chicago and Seattle: Pioneer Historical Publishing Co., 1924), vol. 1, p. 150.

**25.** Lane to the Honorable Secretary of War, October 22, 1849. 31st Congress, Ibid, 156–7. *JOFN*, Op. Cit., entries for August 21, 22, p. 15. Warren A. Snyder, "Suquamish Traditions," ed. Jay Miller, *Northwest Anthropological Research Notes* (hereafter cited as *NARN*), Spring, 1999, vol. 33, no. 1 (University of Idaho), p. 126. Lane letter, 1848, Oregon Superintendency Collection, Microfilm Reel 71–1, University of Washington libraries.

**26.** George Gibbs, *Journal*. National Archives, Records Relating to the First Northwest Boundary Survey, 1853–1869. T606. I55, roll 1–4, Miscellaneous Documents, 1854–66, frame 0011.

**27.** Wm. P. Bryant to Lane, Oct. 12, 1849, in Lane, to the Honorable Secretary of War, Ibid, 166–7.

**28.** Thomas Prosch, *A Chronological History of Seattle from 1850 to 1897*, ts, p. 15.

**29.** Inez Denny, Op. Cit., p. 378.

**30.** Sylvester, Op. Cit., p. 18. Swan, Op. Cit., 4, 7. John Swan, *Olympia, The Pioneer Town of Washington, Its Socialization, Origin and Early History From a Pioneer's Perspective* (ts. Walla Walla, 18–?), p. 9. Gordon Newell and F. George Warren, *So fair a dwelling place: a history of Olympia and Thurston County, Washington* (Olympia, WA: Warren Printing & Graphic Arts Co., 1950), p. 13. Rathbun, Op. Cit., p. 17. Bancroft, Ibid, *Washington, Idaho, and Montana, Vol. XVI*, (1890), 15–16.

**31.** Edmund Sylvester, *Founding of Olympia*, ms. (Oympia, W. T., 1878), p. 9, 19, in the

Bancroft Library, Berkeley, CA.

**32.** Samuel Hancock, *The Narrative of Samuel Hancock, 1845–1860* (New York: Robert M. McBride & Company, 1927), p. 95.

**33.** *JOFN, Section Seven, August 7, 1850 to August 31, 1851.* Entry for October 13, 1850, p. 8. Prosch, Op. Cit., p. 24. "Fay, Pierce and Willis, Commission Merchants, Battery St. near Pine," advertised in the Business Directory of the *Daily Alta California* from June 7 to November 30, 1851.

**34.** Nile Thompson, "An Atlas of Indigenous Seattle," Coll Thrush and Nile Thompson, 209–255, in Coll Thrush, *Native Seattle: Histories From The Crossing Over Place* (Seattle and London: University of Washington Press, 2007), p. 240, #74. Holgate to his sister, Portland, O. T., May 12, 1851, in "Earliest Settlers On The Sound," the *Seattle Post-Intelligencer*, April 25, 1897, p. 20, c. 1–2

**35.** B. F. Shaw, "My First Reception in Seattle," transcribed from an undated newspaper article [possibly 1904], in the Clarence Bagley Papers, Box 17, folder #17–8, University of Washington Libraries, Special Collections.

**36.** *Oregon Spectator*, October 17, 1850, no. 5, vol. 5. Lake Geneva would be named Lake Washington.

**37.** Hancock, Op. Cit., 130–131.

**38.** Prosch, Op. Cit., p. 18.

**39.** "Leaves from an Old Diary," *Washington Standard*, April 25, 1868. Rathbun, J. C., *History of Thurston Co., Washington* (Olympia, WA: 1895), p. 17. Gordon Newell and F. George Warren, *A History of Olympia And Thurston County, Washington "So Fair A Dwelling Place"* (Olympia, WA: Warren's Printing & Graphic Arts Co, 1950), p. 13. John Swan, *The Colonizations around Puget Sd.* (Olympia, WA: 1878), ms., Bancroft Library, University of California), p. 6.

**40.** Prosch, Op. Cit., p. 23. Grant, Op. Cit., p. 47. Jan Van Asselt, *In Memory Of Henry Van Asselt, one of the first four Pioneers of the Duwamish Valley, Seattle-Washington. His life story as reconstructed by Jan Van Asselt* (Ontario: ts, np, 1983), p. 12. "An Old Pioneer," *Seattle Daily Intelligencer*, June 8, 1887, p. 3, c. 2. The Laboratory Writing Classes of Cleveland High School, *The Duwamish Diary 1849–1949*

(Seattle, WA: Cleveland High School, 1949), p. 10. Robert Maple Norman, "Destination: Boeing Airfield 1851. King County's first cattle being floated in by raft," painting by Beulah Maple Norman reproduced by Robert Maple Norman in one of a series of informative cards printed in 1972, in author's possession.

**41.** Inez Denny, Op. Cit., 220–1, 413.

**42.** Prosch, Ibid, p. 24. Grant, Op. Cit., p. 66. Murray Morgan, *Puget's Sound: A Narrative of Early Tacoma and the Southern Sound* (Seattle & London: University of Washington Press, 1979), p. 50.

**43.** Frank Carlson, "Chief Seattle," *The Bulletin Of The University of Washington* (Seattle, series III, no. 2, December, 1903), p. 26.

**44.** Watt, Op. Cit., 1931, 62–63.

**45.** Hanford, Op. Cit., p. 148. Emily Inez Denny, Op. Cit., p. 48.

**46.** Inez Denny, Ibid, p. 51.

**47.** Arthur Denny. *Pioneer Days on Puget Sound (*Seattle, W. T.: C.B. Bagley, Printer, 1888), 13–14.

**48.** Waterman, *Puget Sound Geography*, ms. 1864 in Smithsonian Anthropological Archives, p. 173, #222. Denny, Op. Cit., p. 15. Emily Inez Denny, Op. Cit., p 317.

**49.** Jimmy Jean Cook, "A Particular Friend, PENNS COVE" (Coupeville, WA: Island County Historical Society, 1988), p. 35. Watt, Op. Cit., 1931, 62–63.

**50.** Watt, Ibid, p. 50.

**51.** Watt, Op. Cit., p. 51. Emily Inez Denny, Op. Cit, p. 374. Edmund S. Meany, "Story of Seattle's Nearest Indian NeighborS", the *Seattle Post-Intelligencer*, October 29, 1905, p. 6, c. 5. Waterman, Ibid, p. 139, A234. Harrington, Op. Cit., reel 15, fr. 531 "The Grizzley Bear and Rattlesnake," in Rosalie M. Whitney, *The Swinomish Totem Pole* (Bellingham, WA: Union Printing Company, 1938), 30–31. Julia Anne Allain, *Duwamish History in Duwamish Voices Weaving Our Family Stories Since Colonization* (Victoria, BC: University of Victoria, PhD Thesis, 2014), p. 201.

**52.** Abbie Denny-Lindsley, "Chelana," "When Seattle Was An Indian Camp Forty-Five Years Ago," the *Seattle Post-Intelligencer*, Sunday, April 16, 1906, Magazine Section, p. 6, c. 1–6. Op. Cit., p. 374.

**53.** Watt, Op. Cit., p. 53. Edmund Meany, "Story of Seattle's Nearest Indian Neighbors…" the *Seattle Post-Intelligencer*, October 29, 1905, p. 6, c. 5. Harrington writes, apparently from information provided by William Rogers, Tecumseh's son, that the naming of Kwaschin's sons took place at Alki. This would have been during the winter of 1851–2. John Peabody Harrington, *The Papers of John Peabody Harrington In the Smithsonian Institution 1907–1957* (Millwood, NY: Kraus International Publications, a Division of Kraus-Thompson Organization Limited, 1981), vol. 1, reel 15. Duwamish Field Notes-Lecture Notes, Frame 531. Emily Inez Denny, Op. Cit., p. 374.

**54.** "Mary Seattle Is Badly Hurt," the *Seattle Daily Times*, April 15, 1906, p. 5, c. 3.

## CHAPTER FIVE

**1.** Thomas Prosch, *A Chronological History of Seattle from 1850 to 1897*, ts, 1900–1, p. 28.

**2.** "Indian Types and Characteristics," *The West Shore*, June 1886, no. 6 (Portland, Oregon: L. Samuel, Publisher), p. 94. Bagley, "Chief Seattle and Angeline" Ibid, 260. Eva Greenslit Anderson, *Chief Seattle* (Idaho: The Caxton Printers, Ltd.), fn. # 2, p. 362. Leslie Lincoln, Coast Salish Canoes (np. 1991), 8–9. Emily Inez Denny, *Blazing the Way: True Stories, Songs And Sketches Of Puget Sound And Other Pioneers* (Seattle: Rainier Printing Company, Inc., 1909), p. 360. Frederick James Grant, *History of Seattle* (New York: History Publishing Co., 1891), p. 62.

**3.** Ernest B. Bertelson, "The Suquamish," p. 2. Ernest B. Bertelson Collection. File, "Notes," Box #1, Accession Number 946. University of Washington Libraries, Special Collections. Email communication with Dr. Nile Thompson, 9/9/16, in author's possession.

**4.** David Kellogg, "The Making of a Medicine Man," letter to Vivian Carkeek, Seattle, May 20, 1912, Museum of History and Industry (MOHAI), MS collection, folder 116. Thomas Mercer recalled 300 to 600 Indians wintering at Seattle when he arrived in October, 1852. Thomas Mercer, *Washington Territory Sketches*, 1878, (Bancroft Library Manuscript Collection, Berkeley, Ca.), p. 4.

**5.** Eli B. Maple Dictation, *Account of Experiences Crossing the Plains from Iowa, 1852, and Pioneering in Washington Territory, 1876*, (Bancroft Library), p. 11. Prosch, Op. Cit., p. 28.

**6.** Clarence Bagley, *History of King County, Washington* (Chicago-Seattle: The S. J. Clarke Publishing Company, 1929), vol. 1, p. 48.

**7.** Edward Huggins, "A Trip to 'Alki' Point Near Duwamish Bay", ts. nd., p. 1. University of Washington Libraries, Special Collections. Deposition of Mrs. Nancy Sigo, for claimant, taken at Suquamish Indians Reservation, WA, on the 12th day of March, AD 1927, *Duwamish, Lummi, Whidby Island, Skagit, Upper Skagit, Swinomish, et al. Tribes of Indians versus USA Court of Claims of the United States. LXXIX, 530* (Washington, DC: Govt. Printing Office, 1935, hereafter cited as Duwamish et. al. Republished in two volumes by Argus Press, (Seattle, Washington, vol. 1), p. 412. Deposition of Sam Tecumseh, for claimant, taken at Renton, WA., on the 28th day of March, AD 1927, Ibid, p. 683.

**8.** Watt, Op. Cit., 50–51. The late Brewster Denny, David's great, great, grandchild, says the episode provided the lyrics for several songs. Conversation with Brewster Denny, May 1999.

**9.** Watt, Op. Cit., 49–50. Inez Denny, *Blazing The Way*, Op. Cit., p. 57.

**10.** Ezra Meeker, Pioneer Reminiscences of Puget Sound (Seattle: Lowman & Hanford Stationery and Printing Company, 1905), reprinted by The Historical Society of Seattle and King County, 1980, p. 47.

**11.** Father Felix Verwilghen, CISM, *Chief Sealth ca 1786–1866 In The Letters Of The First Christian Missionaries Of The Puget Sound.* Presented to the Pioneer Association of the State of Washington, May 1964.

**12.** Watt, Op. Cit., p. 77.

**13.** A. A. Denny, *Pioneer Days On Puget Sound* (Seattle: C. B. Bagley, Printer, 1888), p. 20. "Old Chief Seattle," the *Seattle Post-Intelligencer*, June 29, 1890, p. 6, c. 1

**14.** Lottie Roeder Roth, *History of Whatcom County, Washington* (New York, Chicago: Pioneer Historical Publishing Co., 1903), vol.

1, p. 38. Hubert Howe Bancroft, *The Works of Hubert Howe Bancroft, Volume XXXI, History of Washington, Idaho and Montana 1845–1889,* (San Francisco: The History Company, Publishers, 1890), p. 23. See also Grant, *History of Seattle,* Op. Cit., p. 71. Ezra Meeker, *The Busy Life of Eighty Five Years* (Seattle: 1916), p. 203. Clarence B. Bagley, 1929, Op. Cit., p. 125. Hezekiah Butterworth, *The Log School-House On The Columbia* (New York: D. Appleton And Company, 1890), p. 241.

**15.** June M. Collins, "The Influence Of White Contact On Class Distinctions And Political Authority Among The Indians Of Northern Puget Sound," p. 35, in *Coast Salish and Western Washington Indians [1949] American Indian Ethnohistory: Indians of the Northwest Coast,* vol. 2, ( New York: Garland), 89–204, esp. p. 133.

**16.** Maple Dictation, Op. Cit., p. 12.

**17.** Statement of Nah-whil-luk in treaty council minutes, Treaty of Hahd-Skus, or Point No Point, "The Indian Treaty of Point No Point," ed. Charles Gates, *Pacific Northwest Quarterly,* April 1955, vol. 46, no. 2, 52–58. Watt, 1931, Op. Cit., p. 71.

**18.** Charles Prosch, *A Chronological History,* Op. Cit., p. 24.

**19.** James G. Swan, *The Northwest Coast Or, Three Years Residence In Washington Territory* (Seattle and London: University of Washington Press, 1982), p. 396. Peter Simpson, "We Give Our Hearts To You: A View of Chet-ze-moka," in *Shadows of Our Ancestors: Readings in the History of Klallam-White Relations,* ed. Jerry Gorsline (Port Townsend, WA: Empty Bowl, 1992), 122–163, 129–130.

**20.** The work identifying Curley's daughter was carried out by Kathie Zetterberg, the great-granddaughter of Henry Yesler's and Susan's daughter, Julia Benson Intermela. Zetterberg to Buerge, August 22, 2004.

**21.** Thomas Prosch, *David Maynard and Catherine T. Maynard* (Seattle: Lowman & Hanford Stationery and Print Co., 1906), 30–34.

**22.** Kathy M. Zetterberg and David Wilma, "Henry Yesler's Native American daughter Julia is born on June 12, 1855" (HistoryLink.org *Essay 3396,* 2001).

**23.** Delphine Haley, *Dorothy Stimson Bullitt:*

*An Uncommon Life* (Seattle: Sasquatch Books, 1995), p. 29. Armand R. Colang, *A Brief Glimpse Into The Life Of Charles Carroll Terry, 1829–1867,* ts., p. 7. University of Washington Libraries, Special Collections.

**24.** Inez-Denny, *Blazing The Way,* Op. Cit., p. 114–115, 311–312.

**25.** Clinton A. Snowden, *History of Washington The Rise and Progress of an American State,* vol. 3 (New York: The Century History Company, 1909), p. 220. George Gibbs, *Indian Tribes of Washington Territory* (Fairfield, Washington: Ye Galleon Press, 1967), 40–42.

**26.** Rebecca Ebey, "Diary of Colonel and Mrs. I. N. Ebey," *Washington Historical Quarterly,* vol. 8, October 1916. Entries for Friday, December 17 and Sunday, December 19, 1852. 56–57.

**27.** James G. Swan, *The Northwest Coast Or, Three Years Residence In Washington Territory* (New York: Harper & Brothers, 1857) reprinted (Seattle and London: University of Washington Press, 1982), 55–59. Robert H. Ruby and John H. Brown, *The Chinook Indians: Traders of the Lower Columbia* (Norman and London, University of Oklahoma Press, 1976), p. 232. Hancock, Op. Cit., p. 182.

**28.** Ebey, Op. Cit., p. 139. "Indian War," *The Columbian,* April 9, 1853, p. 2, c. 1.

**29.** *The Columbian,* "Our New Territory—Past, Present and Future," May 7, 1853, p. 2, c. 1; "Washington Territory—The Future," May 14, 1853, p. 2, c. 2.

**30.** "Indian Difficulties in Jefferson County," *The Columbian, March* 25, 1854, p. 2, c. 1. Augustine Valentine Krautz, "Extracts From The Diary of General A. V. Kautz," ed. Frances Kautz, *The Washington Historian* I (1900), 115–119, 181–196, II (1900), 12–15, p. 118.

**31.** *History of the Washington Superintendency of Indian Affairs,* 1853–1865. Charles E. Garretson, Seattle, University of Washington, MA Thesis, 1962, p. 12. E. A. Starling to I. I. Stevens, Olympia, December 4, 1853, *National Archives, The Records of the Washington Superintendency of Indian Affairs* (Hereafters cited as *RWSIA*), Roll 9, Letters from Agents Assigned to the Puget Sound District as a Whole, December 4, 1853—August 16, 1862. reel 17, December 4, 1853—July 27, 1858.

**32.** Ed. E. L. Blaine, *Letters And Papers*

*Of Reverend David E. Blaine And His Wife Catharine. Seattle 1853–1856, Oregon, 1856–1862*, (Historical Society of the Pacific Northwest Conference of the Methodist Church, 1963), pp. 68, 88 & 55.

**33.** Charles Mason to J.R.Bigelow, August 7, 1854, *RWSIA*), roll 1, reel 1, Correspondence of the Washington Superintendency printed in Annual Reports of Commissioner of Indian Affairs, 1853–1874.

**34.** Kent Richards, *Isaac Stevens, Young Man In A Hurry* (Provo, UT: Brigham Young University Press, 1979), p. 153.

**35.** "Indian Hostilities!" *The Columbian* October 8, 1853, p. 2, c. 2–3. David Blaine, letter of January 24, 1855, E. L. Blaine, Op. Cit., p. 95.

**36.** Ernest Bertelson, "The Story of the Blackfish," p. 26. File, Speeches And Writings—manuscripts. "The Suquamish," File, Notes On Seattle, p. 7. Box 1, Ernest Bertelson Collection, University of Washington Libraries, Special Collections. Warren A. Snyder, "Suquamish Traditions," ed. Jay Miller, *Northwest Anthropological Research Notes*, Spring, 1999, vol. 33, no. 1, ed. Jay Miller (University of Idaho), p. 126.

**37.** *Washington Pioneer,* "Columbia Lancaster [speaking schedule]," Saturday, January 7, 1854, p. 2, c. 4. "Governor Stevens," Saturday, January 14, 1854, p. 2, c. 2. Gibbs, Ibid, p. 38.

**38.** Henry Smith, "Early Reminiscences; Number Nine; Governor Isaac Stevens," *Seattle Sunday Star*, in Bagley Scrapbook, vol. 11, p. 18.

**39.** Henry A. Smith, "Early Reminiscences Number 10 Scraps From A Diary," *Seattle Sunday Star*, October 29, 1887, p. 3 c. 5–6.

**40.** David Blaine, letter of March 7, 1854, E. L. Blaine, Op. Cit., p. 48. George Gibbs, *Journal*, p. 0010. National Archives, Records Relating to the First Northwest Boundary Survey, 1853–1869. T606. I55, roll 1–4, Miscellaneous Documents, 1854–66.

**41.** Isaac Stevens to Michael Simmons, March 22, 1854. Isaac Stevens to George Manypenny, Dec 21, 1854, 2–3, *RWSIA*, reel 1, roll 1.

**42.** David Blaine, letter of March 7, 1854,

E. L. Blaine, Op. Cit., p. 48. George Gibbs, *Journal*, p. 0010. National Archives, Records Relating to the First Northwest Boundary Survey, 1853-1869. T606. I55, roll 1–4, Miscellaneous Documents, 1854–66. Among the chiefs Seattle selected as subchiefs of the Duwamish, a man named "Wil-lak," or "Jack," may be the Walak mentioned in Snyder, Gibbs, p. 0009. Charles M. Scammon, "Old Seattle And His Tribe." *The Overland Monthly*, vol. 4 no. 4, April 1870, 297–302, p. 298.

**43.** George Gibbs, *Journal*, Op. Cit., frames 0013, 0014. Isaac Stevens to Commissioner of Indian Affairs, Geo. W. Manypenny, Olympia, WT, December 21, 1854, RWSIA, ibid. "Indian Difficulties In Jefferson County," *Pioneer and Democrat*, March 25, 1854, p. 2, c. 1.

**44.** Watt, Op. Cit., pp. 167–8. "Hanging," *Pioneer and Democrat*, April 16 [sic] 22, 1854, p. 2, c. 2. Emily Inez Denny, Op. Cit., "The Murder Of McCormick." Chapter V, 96–104. Inez Denny gets the date wrong.

**45.** "Frontier Justice: guide to the court records of Washington Territory, 1853–1889", *Washington (State) Division of Archives and Records Management: Frontier Justice Records Project, 1987*. Thurston County (Criminal Case Files) 1850–1889.

**46.** Territory of Washington versus Heebner, William, 1854. File 35, Washington State Archives, Copy of Indictment. Territory of Washington versus Maurer, David, 1854 File 37, Washington State Archives, Copy of Indictment. Catherine Blaine to her Mother and Father, October 30, 1854, E. L. Blaine. Op. Cit., pp. 82–83. William N. Bell. P-B2, *Settlement of Seattle (Seattle 1878*), 22–23. Manuscript Collection of the Bancroft Library, Berkeley, CA.

**47.** Catherine Blaine, letter of November 23, 1854, E. L. Blaine, Op. Cit., 87–92

**48.** "Indian Depredations," *Pioneer and Democrat*, December 2, 1854, p. 2, c. 2. Stevens to Manypenny, Decmber 21, 1854, *RSWIA*, Op. Cit., Hubert Howe Bancroft, Op. Cit., 93–97.

1.   "Probable Reserves," *Reports of the Proceedings of the Commission to hold Treaties with the Indian Tribes in Washington Territory and the Blackfoot Country, December 7, 1854 to March 3, 1855*, p. 4.

2.   Marian Weseley Smith, *The Puyallup Nisqually* (New York: Columbia University Press, 1940), p. 10.

3.   David Blaine to his family, December 19, 1854, *Letters And Papers Of Rev. David E. Blaine And His Wife, Catherine, Seattle, 1853–1856, Oregon, 1856–1862*, ed. E. L. Blaine (Historical Society of the Pacific Northwest Conference of the Methodist Episcopal Church, 1963), p. 93.

4.   George Gibbs, *Journal*, in Records Relating to the First Northwest Boundary Survey Commission, 1853–1869. T606, rolls 1–4, I55, frames 0009–0048, entry for January 5, 1856, 0041.Ernest B. Bertelson, File "April 15," Box 1. Ernest B. Bertelson Collection, University of Washington Libraries, Special Collections.

5.   Thomas Talbot Waterman, "Names of Places on the Mainland in the Vicinity of Everett, Washington (Snohomish Area)," # 32, *Puget Sound Geography*, Ms 1864, National Anthropological Archives, Smithsonian Institution. Hermann Haeberlin and Erna Gunther, *The Indians of Puget Sound* (Seattle and London: The University of Washington Press, 1973), p. 7. David A. Cameron, Charles P. LeWarne, M. Allen May, Jack C. O'Donnell, and Lawrence E. O'Donnell, *Snohomish County: An Illustrated History* (Index, WA: Kelcema Books LLC, 2005), p. 62.

6.   Notes describing the Point Elliott Treaty council and the records of speeches of participants are found in the Records of Boundary and Claims Commissions and Arbitration (T-106), *Records relating to the Northwest Boundary, 1853–1901*; US Congress, Senate Ex. Doc. 37, 33rd Cong., 2nd sess., [752]. Gibbs's account is in his *Journal*, Ibid. "Indian Treaties," *Pioneer and Democrat*, February 3, 1855, p. 2, c. 1–2.

7.   *The Papers of John Peabody Harrington In The Smithsonian Institution 1907–1957*. vol. 1, reel 15, Duwamish Field Notes—Lecture

Notes. (Millwood, NY: Kraus International Publications, 1981), frames 508–9. Wilson George recalled William's effort to get a separate reservation on the Duwamish, in Warren Snyder, "Suquamish Traditions," ed. Jay Miller. *Northwest Anthropological Research Notes* (hereafter cited as *NARN*), Spring 1999, vol. 33, no. 1, p. 127, 144.

8.   Snyder, *NARN*, Ibid.

9.   *Report On Source, Nature, And Extent Of The Fishing, Hunting, And Miscellaneous Related Rights Of Certain Indian Tribes in Washington And Oregon Together With Affidavits Showing Location Of A Number Of Usual And Accustomed Fishing Grounds And Stations*. United States, Department of the Interior, Office of Indian Affairs, Division of Forestry and Grazing. Los Angeles, July, 1942. "Treaty of Hahd-Skus, or Point No Point," pp. 10 (344)–15 (349). "The Indian Treaty of Point No Point," ed. Charles Gates, *Pacific Northwest Quarterly*, April 1955, vol. 46, no. 2, 52–58.

10.   James G. Swan, *The Northwest Coast, or, Three Years Residence in Washington* Territory (New York: Harper, 1857), reprinted by Seattle and London: University of Washington Press, 1969), 348–349.

11.   Deposition of Mrs. Mary Charles, March 2–3, 1927, *Duwamish, Lummi, Whidby Island, Skagit, Upper Skagit, Swinomish, et al. Tribes of Indians versus USA Court of Claims of the United States. LXXIX, 530* (Washington, DC: Govt. Printing Office, 1935). Republished in 2 volumes by Argus Press, Seattle, WA, hereafter cited as *Duwamish et al. versus USA*, vol. 1, p. 237.

12.   Louis D'Herbomez to Pascal Ricard, Camp of the Sneomish, Snokwalmish, and Skekwamish, September 9, 1856. *Les Oblats De Marie Immaculee En Oregon 1847 A 1860*, ed. Paul Drouin, O. M. I. (Ottawa, Archives Deschatelets, 1992), #276, p.624. Hereafter referred to as *Les Oblats*.

13.   Amelia Snaetlum's recollection of Seattle words is found in Warren A. Snyder, *Southern Puget Sound Salish Texts, Place Names and Dictionary*, Sacramento Anthropological Society. Thomas Burke Memorial Museum Washington State Museum Monograph 7, ed. Robin K.

Wright (Seattle and London: University of Washington Press, 1991). p. 262.

**14.** Deposition of William Shelton, March 3, 1927, *Duwamish et al. versus USA*, Ibid, *Duwamish et al. versus USA*, Op. Cit., vol. 1, 257–258.

**15.** James Longmire, "Narrative of James Longmire: A Pioneer of 1853," in *Told By The Pioneers: Reminiscences Of Pioneer Life in Washington*, ed. F. I. Trotter, F. H. Loutzenhiser, J. R. Loutzenhiser, vol. 1. (Washington State, np., 1937) 121–143, 135–136. Emily Inez Denny, *Blazing The Way: True Stories Songs And Sketches Of Puget Sound And Other Pioneers* (Seattle: Rainier Printing Company, 1909), 67–68.

**16.** Isaac Sterett to Commodore Mervine, San Francisco, August 10, 1855, Pacific Squadron Letters, September 1854 to June, 1856. *Letters Received by the Secretary of the Navy from Commanding Officers of Squadrons, RG45, M89*, reels 36–38 (National Archives and Records Administration, Washington, DC, and College Park, MD).

**17.** Louis D'herbomez, O. M. I., "Louis D'herbomez sur l'origine de la guerre indienne [Olympia]," July 23, 1855, #252, 568–569. Louis D'jerbomez to Mgr. Eugene de Mazenod, Mission de St. Joseph, Olympia, August 25, 1856, p. 571, *Les Oblats*, Ibid.

**18.** "Letter to Col. Wm. Wallace," *Puget Sound Courier*, August 24, 1855, p. 2, c. 3.

**19.** B. F. Shaw in Ezra Meeker," *The Tragedy of Leschi* (1905; reprinted by The Historical Society of Seattle and King County, 1980), p. 47. William Fraser Tolmie, Chief Factor Hudson Bay Co., Agent, Puget Sound Agricultural Co., Nisqually, W. T. To His Excellency, Fayette McMullan, Governor, Washington Territory, Olympia, W. T., January 12, 1858 in *The Truth Teller,* February 25, 1858, p. 6, c. 3.

**20.** Clinton A. Snowden, *History of Washington: The Rise and Progress of an American State* (New York: The Century History Company, 1909, V. 3), 313–314. Emily Inez Denny, Op. Cit., p. 69. A. J. Splawn, *Ka-Mi-Akin The Last Hero of the Yakimas* (Yakima, WA: 1917; reprinted by The Caxton Printers, Caldwell, Idaho, 1980), 21–27. Peter Simpson, "We Give Our Hearts To You: A View of Chets-

ze-moka," *Shadows of Our Ancestors*, ed. Jerry Gorsline (Port Townsend, WA: Dalmo'ma VIII/Empty Bowl, 1992), 122–163, 135–136. William W. Elmendorf, *Twana Narratives Native Historical Accounts of a Coast Salish Culture* (Seattle and London: University of Washington Press, 1993), p. 154. Morda Slauson, Renton: From Coal Age to Jets (Renton: Renton Historical Society, 1976), 65.

**21.** Isaac Sterett, U. S. N., to Charles Mason, November 13, 1855, *Washington Territorial Volunteer Papers, Indian War Correspondence, 1855–1857* [hereafter noted as *WTVP*]. Washington Territorial Governor Mason, C. H. (Acting) Correspondence Incoming, November 9-13, 1855, Box 1, Folder 5 (Olympia, Washington State Archives). Watt, Op. Cit., p. 203.

**22.** Paper read by William Lane, Pierce County Historical Society on April 8, 1914, in J. A. Eckrom, *Remembered Drums A History of the Puget Sound Indian War* (Walla Walla, WA: Pioneer Press Books, 1989), p. 20, note #13, p. 177. Ed. Frederick James Grant, *History of Seattle, Washington* (New York: American Publishing and Engraving Co., 1891), p. 94.

**23.** "Treaties With The Indians at Walla Walla," *Pioneer and Democrat*, June 29, 1855, p. 2, c. 2.

**24.** Arthur Denny, *Pioneer Days On Puget Sound* (Seattle: C. B. Bagley, Printer, 1888), p. 58.

**25.** "Wars and Rumors of Wars," *Puget Sound Courier*, September 28, 1855, p. 2, c. 1. "About Indians In General," *Pioneer and Democrat*, September 28, 1855, p. 2, c. 3.

**26.** Lucullus Virgil McWhorter, *Tragedy Of The Wahk-Shum: The Death Of Andrew J. Bolon, Yakima Indian Agent, As Told By Su-El-Lil, Eyewitness; Also, The Suicide Of General George A. Custer, As Told By Owl Child, Eyewitness*. Ed. Donald Hines (Issaquah: Great Eagle Publishing, 1994), 25–32.

**27.** "War—The Yakima Indians, Etc.," *Pioneer and Democrat*, October 19, 1855, p. 2, c. 4–6; November 9, 1855, p. 2, c. 4. "Governor Stevens' War," *Puget Sound Courier*, Oct. 19, 1855, p. 2, c. 1.

**28.** The timing of Slaughter's express has confused many. Both Arthur Denny and Roberta Frye Watt write that it was sent after the White River killings on October 28, Denny, Op. Cit.,

p. 65. Roberta Frye Watt, *4 Wagons West The Story of Seattle* (Portland, OR: Binfords & Mort, Publishers), p. 222. After examining information to which they were not privy, I believe it was sent shortly after Haller's retreat on October 8.

**29.** Denny, Ibid, p. 66.

**30.** J. A. Eckrom, *Remembered Drums* (Walla Walla, WA: Pioneer Press Books, 1989), 21–24. Ezra Meeker, *The Tragedy of Leschi* (Everett, WA: The Historical Society of Seattle and King County, 1980 [originally published by author, 1905]), p. 74.

**31.** Dr. John I. King in Ezra Meeker, Ibid, p. 88. Grant, Ibid, p. 62.

**32.** Watt, Op. Cit, p. 232. *Cornelius Holgate Hanford, Seattle and its Environs* (Chicago and Seattle: Pioneer Historical Publishing Co., 1924), p. 148.

**33.** Indian Subagent Edward Haley reported to Stevens that "Mowage" [Mowitch] had killed one of the white women in the White River massacre, and "that before killing her sportingly treated her in the most barbarous manner and received a share of the plunder." Haley to Stevens, May 6, 1856. *The Records of the Washington Superintendency of Indian Affairs, 1853-1874*, hereafter referred to as *RWSIA*, reel 20, Letters from Employees Assigned to Local Agencies of the Puget Sound District. Letters from Bellingham Bay and Fort Kitsap, January 1, 1856-November 29, 1858. Roll 10, Letters from Employees Assigned to the Puget Sound District as a Whole, December 4, 1853-August 16, 1862, (2) Letters from Fort Kitsap, February 3, 1856-August 8, 1858. In the 19th century, to treat a woman "sportingly" was a euphemism for having sex with her, to rape.

**34.** Decatur logbooks, January 10, 1854–June 20, 1859, vol. 14–19, Records of the Bureau of Naval Personnel, RG 24, National Archives and Records Administration, entry for October 31, 1855.

**35.** *Log of the Decatur*, July 24, 1855–October 24, 1856, frame 7. Microfilm Uncat., 58, University of Washington Libraries, Microform & Newspapers.

**36.** Meeker, Op. Cit., p. 110.

**37.** Patrick Canam to Chas. N. Mason, Acting Governor of Washington Territory, Seattle, November 4, 1855. *WTVP*, Ibid, Indian War Correspondence, 1855–57. Washington Territorial Governor, Mason, Charles H. (Acting) Correspondence Incoming November 2, 1855 to November 8, 1855, Box 1, Folder 1.

**38.** Maynard to Simmons, Seattle, September 19, 1856. *RWSIA*, Roll 10. Letters from Employees Assigned to Local Agencies of the Puget Sound District, January 1, 1856–November 29, 1858 (2) Letters from Fort Kitsap, February 3, 1856–August 8, 1856, reel 20.

**39.** The meeting probably took place in the evening on November 16-18. Minutes of the meeting were preserved in the Indian War Correspondence, 1855–57, Box #2050, Mason to Stevens, November 18, 1855, "Minutes of Meeting with Chief Seattle and Others." Prior to its conservation with the State Archives, many documents in the collection of Indian War Correspondence disappeared. Sadly, the copy of these minutes appears to be one of these.

**40.** "The Indian Agency," Seattle, November 26, 1855, in *Puget Sound Courier*, November 30, 1855, p. 2, c. 6. Henry Yesler, David Phillips, C. C. Lewis, Dr. Sam [?] Grow, Thomas Mercer to Hon. C. H. Mason, Seattle, November 24, 1855. *W.T.V.P.*, Indian War Correspondence, 1855-57. Hewitt to Mason, Seattle, November 23, 1855. Box 1, Folder 7. Mason to Yesler, Executive Office, Olympia, November 27, 1855. W.T.V.P. Indian War Correspondence, 1855-57. Washington Territorial Governor/ Correspondence Incoming, Box 1, Folder 7.

**41.** Mason to Gansevoort, Executive Office, Olympia, WA, December 28, 1855. Washington National Guard Pamphlet, Ibid, pp. 55–56. Swartout to I. I. Stevens, Seattle, April 12, 1856, *W.T.V.P.*, Indian War Correspondence, 1855-57. Washington Territorial Governor Isaac I. Stevens/Correspondence Incoming, April 11–14, 1856, Box 2, Folder 4.

**42.** Maynard to Simmons, September 19, 1856, WSIA. Ibid.

**43.** Isaac Sterett to Chas. Mason, US Sloop of War *Decatur* off Steilacoom Nov 26th 1855, in Letters from the Decatur, *WTVP*, Indian War Correspondence, 1855-57, Washington Territorial Governor Correspondence Incoming. Isaac Sterett to J. C. Dobbins, US Sloop of War *Decatur*, Port Madison, W. T., Puget Sound, December 5, 1856. (Pacific Squadron, Com. Wm. Mervine, vol. 1, September 1854 to June 1856, no. 344).

**44.** *Pioneer and Democrat,* November 16, 1855, p. 2, c. 4–5. "Henry Yesler and the Founding of Seattle," *The Pacific Northwest Quarterly,* vol. 42, October 1951, no. 4, (Seattle: University of Washington), p. 274.

**45.** Kent D. Richards. *Isaac Stevens Young Man In A Hurry* (Provo, UT: Brigham Young University Press, 1979), 247–8.

**46.** A. J. Splawn. *KA-MI-AKIN Last Hero of the Yakimas* (Caldwell, ID: The Caxton Printers, Ltd., 1980), 56–7.

**47.** Prosch, Op. Cit., p. 74. Gansevoort to James Dobbins, Secretary of the Navy, January 31, 1856, *Letter Book of Comm. Guert Gansevoort, U.S.S. Decatur, Pacific Squadron, Oct. 30, 1855, to Feb. 9, 1856.* Microcopy of original manuscript at National Archives, A 163, University of Washington Libraries, Microform & Newspapers.

**48.** *PioneerandDemocrat,*January25,1856,p.2,c. 3. Elwood Evans, *Olympia Club Conversazione.* Filmed for the University of Washington by the Bancroft Library, 13–14.

**49.** Thomas W. Prosch, *David S. Maynard and Catherine T. Maynard* (Seattle: n.p. 1906), p. 75.

**50.** Ernest Bertelson, Op. Cit., File *April 15,* p. 1. Eanest Bertelson Collection, Accession #0946-001, Box 1. University of Washington Libraries, Special Collections.

**51.** According to Prosch, three Klikitat men and one woman arrived at the reserve a few days before the attack upon Seattle to assassinate Chief Seattle and Maynard in hopes of diverting the recently repaired Decatur to the west side of the Sound. Prosch, Ibid, p. 76.

**52.** Herman Haeberlin, "Mythology Of Puget Sound," *Journal of American Folk-lore* 37 (145–146), 371–438, 413–414.

**53.** Proceedings of the Military Commission Convened in Seattle, May 10, 1856. *W.T.V.P.* Several native witnesses called before this military commission said they thought Leschi was present, but did not recognise him. Copies of several pages of testimony were generously provided me by J. Eckrom, but the originals at the Washington State Archives are missing. Prosch, Ibid. Maynard to Simmons, September 19, 1856, *WSIA.* Ibid.

**54.** The best accounts of the battle are those written shortly after by participants: Gansevoort's report to James Dobbins, Secretary

of the Navy, on January 31, and the vivid journal entry of Lieutenant Francis Gregory Dalles written immediately after. *Letter Book of Comm. Guert Gansevoort, U.S.S. Decatur, Pacific Squadron, Oct. 30, 1855, to Feb. 9, 1856.* Microcopy of original manuscript is at National Archives. A 163, University of Washington Libraries, Microform & Newspapers. *The Papers of Francis Gregory Dalles, United States Navy, Correspondence and Journals 1837–1859,* ed. Gardner W. Allen (New York: Printed for the Naval Historical Society by the De Vinne Press, MDCCCCXVII [1917]). 203–4. Although Philip C. Johnson Jr. served on the steamer *Active,* which was not present during the battle, his comments on the aftermath and the personalities of many involved are interesting. Johnson, Op. Cit. Less accurate it would seem is Thomas Stowe Phelps's account, written many years later, which includes much speculation about the role of Indians prior to the attack. Thomas Stowe Phelps, "Reminiscences of Seattle, Washington Territory, And The U.S. Sloop-Of-War 'Decatur' During The Indian War of 1855-56," *Puget Sound Historical Series No. 2,* (Seattle: The Alice Harriman Company, 304 New York Block, 1908). An expanded version of Phelps's account is found in the appendix to Dalles's book. Similar fanciful speculation appears in the account written by Abbie J. Hanford, who was a witness to the battle. Abbie J. Hanford, *Seattle and its Indian War* (Seattle: 1878), p. 11. HHB [P-B 11] The Bancroft Library.

**55.** Prosch, Ibid, p. 74. Gansevoort to James Dobbins, Secretary of the Navy, January 31, 1856, *Letter Book of Comm. Guert Gansevoort, U.S.S. Decatur , Pacific Squadron, Oct. 30, 1855, to Feb. 9, 1856.* Microcopy of original manuscript at National Archives, A 163, University of Washington Libraries, Microform & Newspapers. Ernest Bertelson, Ibid, p. 2. In her book, *Warship Under Sail,* historian Lorraine McConaghy notes that by the time of his arrival at Seattle, ". . . he had developed a lifelong pattern of heavy drinking, alternating periods of abstinence with binges." Lorraine McConaghy, *Warship Under Sail: The USS Decatur in the Pacific West* (Seattle & London: University of Washington Press, 2009), p. 128.

**56.** Prosch, Ibid. Blaine, Op. Cit., January 29, 1865, p. 119.

1.     "Battle At Seattle," *Daily Alta California*, February 6, 1856, p. 2, c. 1. "Indian War At Puget Sound—Attack Upon Seattle," *The New York Herald*, Morning Edition, February 24, 1856, p. 1, c. 3–5.

2.     Nathanial Hill to Superintendent of Indian Affairs, Op. Cit., January 27, 1856. *Records of the Washington Superintendency of Indian Affairs*, hereafter cited as *RWSIA*, roll 10 (4), Letters from Holmes Harbor, January 27, 1856–February 8, 1857, reel 21.

3.     Maynard to Stevens, February 3, 9, 1856, Letters from Fort Kitsap, February 3, 1856–August 8, 1858. *RWSIA*, roll 10 (2), reel 20.

4.     Ernest B. Bertelson, File "April 15," p. 2, Box 1. Ernest B. Bertelson Collection, Accession #0946-001, University of Washington Libraries, Special Collections.

5.     Thomas Prosch, *David S. Maynard and Catherine T. Maynard: Biographies of Two of the Oregon Pioneers of 1850* (Seattle: Lowman & Hanford Stationers, 1906), p.76. *Pioneer and Democrat,* February 15, 1856, p. 2, c. 4. Simmons to Stevens, Patkanim's Ranch, Snohomish River, February 17, 1856 & February 20, 1856, *RWSIA*, roll 10, Letters from Employees Assigned to Local Agencies of the Puget Sound District, January 1, 1856–November 29, 1858. (7), Letters from the Sahewamish Reserve, February 18–December 1, 1856, reel 22.

6.     *Puget Sound Courier*, Feb. 15, 1856. Although this issue of the Courier is not extant, the article is pereserved in Ezra Meeker, *The Tragedy of Leschi* (1905), reprinted by The Historical Society of Seattle and King County (Everett, The Printers, 1980), 131-132.

7.     Simmons left two accounts of the battle which differ in detail. The earliest, written as the entry for February 17 at Fort Ebey, appears in the daily journal he kept during the expedition. Simmons to Stevens, Pat Kanim's Ranch, Snohomish River, Ibid. Its sentences are terse and vivid. In this, he mentions the death of only one of Patkanim's company, a Skykomish man. The second, a letter he wrote Stevens from the Sahewish Indian Reserve on Squaxon Island, is more measured and includes an expanded casualty list: nine dead among Leschi's force and five among Patkanim's. Simmons to Stevens, Indian Reserve, February 20, 1856. *WSIA*, Letters from the Sawamish Reserve, February 18–December 1, 1856, reel 22.

8.     *Puget Sound Courier*, February 29, 1856, p. 2, c. 3. Eldridge Morse, "Centennial History of Snohomish County," in *History of Snohomish County, Washington*, vol. 1, ed. Wm. Whitfield (Chicago-Seattle: Pioneer Historical Publishing Company, 1926), 87–95 (88–89).

9.     Thomas Stowe Phelps, "Reminiscences of Seattle, Washington Territory, And The U.S. Sloop-Of-War 'Decatur' During The Indian War of 1855-56," *Puget Sound Historical Series. No. 2* (Seattle: The Alice Harriman Company, 304 New York Block, 1908), p. 42.

10.    Maynard to Stevens, March 3, 4 & 8, 1856, *RWSIA*, Letters from Fort Kitsap. Op. Cit.

11.    E. D. Keyes, *Fifty Years Observation Of Men And Events Civil and Military* (New York: Charles Scribner's Sons, 1889), p. 257.

12.    Keyes, Ibid. Gilmore Hayes to Isaac Stevens, Camp Puyallup, February 29, 1856, *WTVP*, Op. Cit., Box 1, Folder 15. Ibid, Camp Connell, March 10, 1856, Box 1, Folder 16. Ezra Meeker, Op. Cit., 155–157.

13.    J. A. Eckrom, *Remembered Drums* (Walla Walla, WA: Pioneer Press Books, 1989), 141-147.

14.    Maynard to Simmons, September 21, 1856, Yesler to Stevens, April 24, 1856, *RWSIA*, Letters From Fort Kitsap, Op. Cit. Henry R. Crosbie to Stevens, Seattle, March 25, 1856. *Washington Territory Volunteer Papers*, hereafter cited as *WTVP*, Washington Territorial Governor Stevens, Isaac I., Correspondence Incoming, March 20–25, 1856. Box 1, Folder 19.

15.    Maynard to Stevens, March 28, 1856; Haley to Stevens, April 15, 1856, *RWSIA*, Letters from Fort Kitsap, Op. Cit.

16.    Proceedings of the Military Commission convened in Seattle, May 10, 1856. *WTVP*. A partial copy of this document, now missing from the Washington State Archives, was generously provided to the author by J. Eckrom.

17.    H. Haley to Stevens, June 6, 8, July 18, 1856. *RWSIA*, Letters from Fort Kitsap, Op. Cit.

18.    Clarence Bagley Papers, University

of Washington Libraries, Manuscripts and Special Collections, 0036-001, Box 21, vol. 3, *Proceedings of the Fox Island Reservation Treaty*, "Indian Council," 1–10.

**19.**   George Paige to J.W. Nesmith, Superintendent of Indian Affairs, Washington Territory, August 1, 1857. United States. Office of Indians Affairs *Annual report of the commissioner of Indian affairs for the year 1857*. G. P. O. No. 136, 329–332. http://digital.library .wisc.edu/1711.dl/History.AnnRep57.

**20.**   Meeker, Op. Cit., p. 210.

**21.**   James Goudy to George Paige, Holderness Point, Nov. 21, 1856. *RWSIA*, Letters from Fort Kitsap, Op. Cit.

**22.**   James Goudy to George Paige, Holderness Point, November 21, 1856, *RWSIA*, Letters from Fort Kitsap, Op. Cit., *Pioneer and Democrat*, October 17, 1856, p. 2, c. 3, December 12, 1856, p. 2, c., 4.

**23.**   "Battle with the Northern Indians," *Pioneer and Democrat*, December 19, 1856, p. 1, c., 2–4.

**24.**   Simmons to Stevens, Olympia, December 29, 1856, *RWSIA*, Roll 9. Letters from Agents Assigned to the Puget Sound District as a Whole, December 4, 1853–August 16, 1862. Reel 17, December 4, 1853–July 27, 1858.

**25.**   Ibid.

**26.**   Alexandra Harmon, *Indians In The Making* (Berkeley, Los Angeles, and London: University of California Press, 2000), p. 4.

**27.**   David Nicandri, *Olympia's Forgotten Pioneers (*Olympia, WA: State Capital Historical Association, 1976), 6–13.

**28.**   D'herbomez to Mazenod, St. Joseph Mission, Olympia, August 25, 1855. *Les Oblats De Marie Immaculee En Oregon 1847 a 1860.* Documents d'archives editas par Paul Drouin, O. M. I. Ottawa: Archives Deschatelets, 1992, Volume II. #254, pp. 570–580. Trans. by Mary Anne Callaghan and hereafter described as *Les Oblats*.

**29.**   Ricard to Brouillet, August 27, 1856, Seattle Archdiocesan Archives.

**30.**   D'herbomez to Ricard, Reserve de Seatle, October 16, 1856. *Les Oblats*. #283, p. 646.

**31.**   Ronald Wayne Young, O.M.I., *The Mission of the Missionary Oblates of Mary Immaculate to the Oregon Territory (1847–1860)*. Rome: Pontificia Universitas Gregoriana

Facultas Missiologiae, 2000, pp. 135–136. Paige to Stevens, Fort Kitsap, October 31, 1856. *RWSIA*, Roll 10 (2), Op. Cit.

**32.**   Louis D'herbomez a Mgr. Eugene de Mazenod, Mission de St. Joseph Olympia, le 30 Mars, 1857. *Les Oblats*. Op. Cit., #294, 690–698.

**33.**   George Paige to Stevens, Fort Kitsap, October 31, 1856; *RWSIA*, roll 10, Letters from Employees Assigned to Local Agencies of the Puget Sound District, January 1, 1856– November 29, 1858. Reel 20, no. 2, Letters from Fort Kitsap, Feb. 3, 1856–August 8, 1858. Nicandri, Op. Cit., p. 27.

**34.**   E. E. Riddell, "History Of Suquamish," *Kitsap County Herald*, October 14, 1932, p. 3, c 6. C. Elliott Pickerell, *A Goose, A Gig and a Long Kelp Horn* (Bremerton, WA: Perrypublishing, 2000), p. 115.

**35.**   Louis D'Herbomez a Mgr. Eugene de Mazenod, Mission de St. Joseph Olympia, le 30 Mars, 1857. *Les Oblats*. Op. Cit., #294, p. 692.

**36.**   *Riatuale Romanum. Pauli V. Pont. Max. Jussu Editum, Et. A Benedicto XIV, Auctum Et Castigatum, Cui Amplissima Accedit Benedictionum et Instructionum*. Tornari, Typis Societatis S. Joannis Evang. Descle'e Lefebvre Et Soc. M.DCCC.LXVIII., 13–15, 24–48.

**37.**   *Registre des cecles de baptemes, marriages & sepultrues des Missiones d St. Anne ches les Snohomish, de St. Joachim ches Les Lamys, des St. Croix ches les Semiamou . . . etc. etc. etc. defices le 15 Octobre 1857 jusqu'a.* Vol. II., Early Missionary Records for Puget Sound, Volume II (Tulalip and Puget Sound), p. 121.

**38.**   Francis Norbert Blanchet, *Historical Sketches Of The Catholic Church In Oregon and The Northwest.* (Ferndale, WA: 1910), Sketch XV, p. 36.

**39.**   Samuel Coombs, "Good Chief Seattle," the *Seattle Post-Intelligencer*, March 26, 1893, p. 9. "Deposition of Wapato John, for claimant, taken at Puyallup Indian Reservation, Washington, on the 25th day of March, AD 1927, *Duwamish, Lummi, Whidbey Island, Skagit, Upper Skagit, Swinomish, et. al. Tribes of Indians versus USA* Court of Claims of the United States. LXXIX, 530 (Washington, DC: Govt. Printing Office, 1935). Republished in two volumes by Argus Press (Seattle), vol. 667. "Deposition of Peter J. James, for claimant, taken at Renton, Wash., on the 28th day of March, 1927," Ibid, p. 709. Conversations with Dr. Nile Thompson, July, 2007.

**40.** Simmons to Stevens, Olympia, May 1, 1857. *RWSIA*, roll 9, Op. Cit., reel 17.

**41.** Paige to Stevens, Fort Kitsap Reservation, W. T., April 14, 1857. *RWSIA*, roll 10, reel 20, no. 2, Op. Cit.

**42.** Meeker, Op. Cit., p. 219.

**43.** Hubert Howe Bancroft, *Bancroft's*

*Works, Volume 31. Washington, Idaho And Montana 1845–1889* (San Francisco: 1890), p. 209. Simmons to Stevens, Ibid. *Pioneer and Democrat*, May 1, 1857, p. 2, c. 4.

**44.** *Pioneer and Democrat*, January 8, 1857, p. 2, c. 4. Simmons to Nesmith, December 31, 1857. RWSIA, roll 9, reel 17, Ibid.

**45.** *Pioneer and Democrat* October 8, 1858, p. 2, c. 2.

## CHAPTER EIGHT

**1.** "Dead," Ibid, November 26, 1858 p. 2. c. 6. "Snohomish Indians Seek Memorial to Chief Patkanim's Loyalty to Seattle Pioneers [unnamed newspaper article c1920s] Suzie Patkanim, his Sister, Age 90. University of Washington Libraries Special Collections Box N 970.1. Indians of North America—Tribes—OR & WA—Muckleshoot to N 970.1, Indians of North America—Tribes—OR & WA—Yakima Nation. File, N970.1 Indians of N.A. Tribes Oregon-Washington S-Y.

**2.** Paige to Simmons, August 8, 1858, *RWSIA*, roll 10, reel 20, no. 2, Op. Cit. Simmons to Nesmith, August 14, December 31, 1858, roll 9, reel 18, Letters from Agents Assigned to the Puget Sound District as a Whole, August 2, 1858–December 14, 1860. David Maynard to Henry Maynard, Seattle, November 28, 1858, Maynard letters, copy in Author's possession.

**3.** *Records of the Washington Superintendency of Indian Affairs*, hereafter cited as *RWSIA*, roll 1 (a), General Introduction, History of the Superintendency and Its Records, xv.

**4.** Emily Inez Denny, *Blazing The Way True Stories, Songs And Sketches Of Puget Sound And Other Pioneers* (Seattle: Rainier Printing Company, Inc., 1909), p. 359. Fredi Perry, *Port Madison Washington Territory 1854–1889* (Bremerton, WA: Perry Publishing, 19890, p. 124.

**5.** Wilfred P. Schoenberg, S. J., *A Chronicle of Catholic History of the Pacific Northwest: 1743–1960* (Portland, OR: Catholic Sentinel Printery, 1962), [253], [260], pp. 40–41. Barbara Lane "The Suquamish Tribe," from *The Suquamish Tribe: A History from Manuscripts and Memories* (Suquamish and Sklallam Tribes, Title IV Committee and the North Kitsap

School District, 1975), p. 21. *Seeing A New Day A 150 Year History Of Saint Peter Catholic Mission* (Suquamish, WA, Port Madison Indian Reservation: Archdiocese of Seattle and Suquamish Tribe, 2004), p. 7.

**6.** The best account of this affray is by Keith Murray, *The Pig War* (Tacoma, WA: Washington State Historical Society, 1968).

**7.** *RWSIA*, roll 1 (a), Ibid. viii. Simmons to Geary, Tulalip Indian Reservation, January 1, 1861. *RWSIA*, roll 9, Letters from Agents Assigned to the Puget Sound District as a Whole, January 1, 1861–August 16, 1862, reel 19. Thomas Talbot Waterman "Names of Places on the Mainland in the Vicinity of Everett, Washington (Snohomish Area)," map 11, # 6a, *Puget Sound Geography*, 1920, ms. no. 1864, National Anthropological Archives, Smithsonian Institution, Washington DC.

**8.** Chirouse to Gosnell, July 1, 1861, Simmons to Nesmith, July 27, 1858, *RWSIA*, roll 9, Op. Cit., reel 17.

**9.** Simmons to Nesmith, March 31, 1859, *RWSIA*, roll 9, Op. Cit., reel 18. Gosnell to Miller, August 1, 1861, roll 9, reel 19, Op. Cit.

**10.** J. A. Eckrom. *Remembered Drums* (Walla Walla, WA: Pioneer Press Books, 1989), p. 53. Eldridge Morse, *Notes on the History and Resources of Washington Territory Furnished to H. H. Bancroft of San Francisco, California by Eldridge Morse of Snohomish City, Snohomish County, Washington Territory.* Handwritten ms, c1880, Book 1, p. 24. P-B 30–54 Manuscript Collection, Bancroft Library, Berkeley, CA.

**11.** An Act to Amend an Act, Entitled "An Act to Regulate Marriage," passed April 20th, 1854, passed January 29, 1855. In *Laws Of*

*Washington A Publication Of The Session Laws of Washington Territory, Including The General Laws And Resolutions Of The Years 1854 To 1888 Inclusive...*, Under The Direction Of Frank Pierce (Seattle: Tribune Publishing Company. 1896), vol. 1, 651–652. An Act To Regulate Marriages, Approved January 20, 1866, In Laws of Washington..., vol. 2, 354–357.

12.    Eldridge Morse, *Notes on the History and Resources of Washington Territory Furnished to H. H. Bancroft of San Francisco, California by Eldridge Morse of Snohomish City, Snohomish County, Washington Territory.* Handwritten ms, c1880. Book 1, p. 24. P-B 30-54 Manuscript Collection, Bancroft Library, Berkeley, CA.

13.    Dillis B. Ward. "From Salem, Oregon, to Seattle, Washington, in 1859," *Washington Historical Quarterly*, vol. VI, no. 2, April, 1915, pp. 100–106. Roberta Frye Watt, *4 Wagons West* (Portland, OR: Binfords & Mort, Publishers, 1931), 58–59. David Kellogg, "The Making of a Medicine Man," letter to Vivian Carkeek, May 20, 1912. Seattle and King County Museum of History and Industry (MOHAI) MS file, 116. J. Willis Sayre, *This City Of Ours* (Seattle: Board of Directors, Seattle School District No. 1, 1936), 73–74.

14.    Sarah Yesler to Charles Plummer, Seattle, March 24, 1864, George Plummer Correspondence, 1863–1865. University of Washington Libraries Special Collections, Accession #4848001, Vertical File, 282. "The Indian Counterfeiter," in Incidents in the life of Hon. H. L. Yesler. HHB [P-B 23], Bancroft Library, Berkeley, CA. J. Willis Sayre, *This City Of Ours* (Seattle: Board of Directors, Seattle School District No. 1, 1936), 73–74.

15.    Ward, Ibid. "Good Chief Seattle," the *Seattle Post-Intelligencer*, March 26, 1893, p. 9, c. 1, 3. Clarence B. Bagley, "Chief Seattle And Angeline," *The Washington Historical Quarterly*. Seattle: vol. 22 (4), October 1931, 243–275, 263–4.

16.    Elmendorff, William W., "The Structure of Twana Culture," Monographic Supplement no. 2, *Research Studies, a Quarterly Publication of Washington State University*, vol. 28, 1960. Costello, J. A. *The Siwash, Their Life, Legends and Tales* (Seattle: Calvert Company, 1895), p. 105. Coombs, Ibid.

17.    Bertelson, "The Suquamish," p. 18, File "Notes." Eanest Bertelson Collection, Accession # 0946-001, Box 1. University of Washington Libraries, Special Collections.

18.    Bagley, Ibid, pp. 259–60.

19.    The complicated history of the Washington Superintendency is documented in *RWSIA*, roll 1 (a), General Introduction, History of the Superintendency and Its Records, Roster Of Officials In Charge Of Local Units Within The Superintendency, reel 1. Shaw to Miller, Tulalip Reservation, September 20, 1861, Howe to Hale, Seattle, October 13, 1862, *RWSIA*, roll 12, Letters from Employees Assigned to the Tulalip Agency, Serving Indians Parties to the Treaty of Point Elliott, April 24, 1861–July 1, 1874 (1) Letters from Employees Assigned to Tulalip, Muckleshoot, and Port Madison Reservations, April 24, 1861–July 1, 1874, reel 25.

20.    Perry, Op. Cit., 123–127. *Seattle Weekly Intelligencer*, September 21, 1868, p. 2, c. 1. Conversation with Dr. Nile Thompson, February 11–12, 2014.

21.    Shaw to Miller, Tulalip Reservation, September 20, 1861, *RWSIA*, roll 12, reel 25, Op. Cit., Gosnell to Miller, Squaxon Reserve, August 1, 1861, *RWSIA*, roll 9, reel 19, Op. Cit. Simmons to Geary, Olympia, WA, June 22, 1860, Portland, OR, September 1, 1860, *RWSIA*, roll 9, Op. Cit., reel 18. B. F. Kendall, Superintendent of Indian Affairs, WA, to William P. Dole, Commissioner of Indian Affairs, Olympia, January 2, 1862, Henry Webster to Calvin Hale, p. 410, in *Report of the Commissioner of Indian Affairs for The Year 1862* (Washington: Government Printing Office, 1863), p. 306.

22.    Hilman F. Jones, Typescript, Box 1, Folder 28, Hilman F. Jones Papers (TS-26), Seattle, Washington State Historical Society, Research Library (Tacoma). Kellogg, Ibid.

23.    Bagley. "Chief Seattle And Angeline," Ibid, 260–262. Wells Drury, *An Editor On The Comstock Lode* (New York: Farrar & Reinhart, 1936; reprinted in Reno by University of Nevada Press, 1984), p. xiv.

24.    "Old Indian Judge Keokuck is Dead," Bagley scrapbook #6. Manuscripts and Special Collections, University of Washington Libraries. Howe to Hale, Seattle, October 13, 1862.

*RWSIA*, roll 12, reel 25, Op. Cit.

**25.** J. A. Costello, *The Siwash, Their Life, Legends and Tales* (Seattle: Calvert Company, 1895), pp. 30–31.

**26.** "Old Letter Reveals Big Doings Way Back When," the *Seattle Times*, December 21, 1940, p. 16, c. 1. Beulah Maple Norman, *Wedding, Duwamish Settlement 1862*. Greeting card by Robert Maple Norman, 1972, in author's possession. Eva Greenslit Anderson, *Chief Seattle* (Caldwell, ID: The Caxton Printers, Ltd., 1943), p. 311. "Story of Pioneer Party In King County Forty Years Ago," the *Seattle Post-Intelligencer*, January 21, 1906, p. 16, c. 1–7. *The Duwamish Diary 1849–1949* (Seattle: Cleveland High School, 1949), pp. 23–26.

**27.** *The Suquamish Tribe: A History From Manuscripts and Memory* (A Project of the Suquamish and Klallam Tribes Title IV Committee and the North Kitsap School District, 1975), p. 60. Wilfred Schoenberg, S. J., *Chronicle of Catholic History of the Pacific Northwest 1743–1960* (Gonzaga Preparatory School 1962), 47–48 [296]. *Registre des cecles de baptemes, marriages & sepultrues des Missiones d St. Anne ches les Snohomish, de St. Joachim ches Les Lamys, des St. Croix ches les Semiamou . . . etc. etc. etc. defices le 15 Octobre 1857 jusqu'a*. Vol. II., hereafter cited as Early Missionary Records of Puget Sound, Volume II (Tulalip and Puget Sound), p. 15.

**28.** S. D. Howe to C. H. Hale, Seattle, June 27, 1863. *RWSIA*, roll 12, reel 25, Op. Cit.

**29.** Petition: To The Honorable Arthur A. Denny, Delegate to Congress from Washington Territory, July 5, 1866, National Archives Roll 909, "Letters Received by the Office of Indian Affairs, 1824–1881."

**30.** The flat bag, measuring 58 centimeters high and 39 centimeters wide (approximately 23 inches long and 15 inches wide), was woven from hemp dogbane (*Apocynum cannabinum*), false embroidered with geometric patterns of died cornhusk, and was probably used to gather roots. The Burke Museum acquired it in 1909 from an A.A. Bartow, probably for display at the Alaska Yukon Exposition. Personal communication from Rebecca Andrews, Collection Manager, Ethnology, Burke Museum, October 17, 2013. It is doubtful that Seattle gathered roots, and the bag more likely belonged to one of his wives or, perhaps, a member of his retinue. *Seattle Gazette*, January 26, 1864, p. 2 c. 2.

**31.** *Seattle Gazette*, January 26, 1864, p. 2 c. 2. Clarence Bagley, *History of Seattle From The Earliest Settlement to the Present Time* (Chicago: The S. J. Clarke Publishing Company, 1916), p. 259.

**32.** Early Missionary Records of Puget Sound, Volume II (Tulalip and Puget Sound), 205–6. Seattle Archdiocese Archives.

**33.** Elsie Franklin Marriott, *Bainbridge through bifocals* (Seattle: Gateway Printing Company, 1941), p. 33. *NARN*, Ibid, p. 126. Charles M. Scammon, "Old Seattle, And His Tribe." *The Overland Monthly* . . . (San Francisco: A. Roman and Co., Publishers, vol. 4, April, 1870, no. 4), p. 299. Grant mentions the death of two of Seattle's sons from consumption before the death of their father. Frederick James Grant, *History of Seattle Washington/ With Illustrations And Biographical Sketches Of Some Of Its Prominent Men And Pioneers* (New York: American Publishing and Engraving Co. Publishers, 1891), p. 62. The death dates for both George and James can be estimated by subtracting the times, ". . . George died over twenty years ago, and James five years ago" from the publication date of "Indian Types and Characteristics," *The West Shore* (Portland, OR: 1886), vol. 12, p. 127. Their burial in Seattle's first cemetery is mentioned in the Sackman geneaology in the Duwamish tribal archives, copy in author's possession.

**34.** Jean Dorcy, O.P. *Walk On A Rainbow Trail*, ts., nd. (c. 1960s), p. 7. The story was told by Marie Snaetlum, Amelia's daughter, to Sister Jean who taught at Tulalip in the 1940s. It is preserved in the album "Indians" in the archives of the Edmonds Dominican Sisters at Rosary Heights Convent in Woodway, WA, all of which has been pirated away by the Adrian Dominicans to Adrian, MN, and since, lost.

**35.** "De Sacramento Confirmationis, Datum Romae ex Audibus dictae Sacrae Congregationis die 23. Aprilis 1774," *Riatuale Romanum. Pauli V. Pont. Max. Jussu Editum, Et. A Benedicto XIV, Auctum Et Castigatum, Cui Amplissima Accedit Benedictionum et Instructionum*. Tornari, Typis

Societatis S. Joannis Evang. Descle'e Lefebvre Et Soc. M.DCCC.LXVIII.,

**36.** "Ordinances of the Town of Seattle," *Seattle Weekly Gazette*, vol. 1, no. 43, March 4, 1865, p. 1, c. 3.

**37.** Thomas Talbot Waterman, "The Geographic Names Used By The Indians Of The Pacific Coast," *The Geographical Review*, vol. 12, part 2, (22), 175–194, p. 187, #8. Conversation with Suquamish elder Lawrence Webster at the Suquamish Tribal Centerh, March 3, 1982, notes in author's possession.

**38.** Early Missionary Records of Puget Sound, Volume II (Tulalip and Puget Sound), March 11, 1865, Noe Siatle et Marie, p. 121.

**39.** Caroline C. Leighton, *Life At Puget Sound With Sketches of Travel in Washington Territory, British Columbia, Oregon & California, 1865–1881* (Boston: Lee & Shepherd, Publishers,

1883). Reprinted as *West Coast Journeys 1865–1879*, ed. David Buerge (Seattle: Sasquatch Books, 1995), p. 25.

**40.** Ernest B. Bertelson, "Walkin'nest Old Indian," p. 2. File, "Speech and Writings—Manuscripts," Ernest B. Bertelson Collection, Op Cit.

**41.** Warren Snyder, "Suquamish Traditions," ed. Jay Miller. *Northwest Anthropological Research Notes*, Spring 1999, vol. 33, no. 1, p. 126. Charles M. Scammon, "Old Seattle And His Tribe," *Overland Monthly*, vol. 4, April, 1870, no. 4, p. 298.

**42.** William Deshaw itemized the costs of Seattle's funeral garb and his coffin on the inside cover of his ledger. Box 1 A of 4, VO258D 1/9: Financial Records—ledgers, Manuscripts Division, Suzzallo Library.

**43.** Scammon, Ibid, 298–300.

## CHAPTER NINE

**1.** Samuel Elliot Morrison, Henry Steele Commager and William E. Leuchtenberg, *The Growth of d American Republic, Volume One* (New York, Oxford: Oxford University Press, Seventh Edition, 1980), 723–6.

**2.** Clarence B. Bagley. *History of Seattle From the Earliest Settlement to the Present Time* (Chicago: The S. J. Clarke Publishing Company, 1916), vol. 1, p. 189. Caroline C. Leighton, *West Coast Journeys 1865–1879 The Travelogue Of A Remarkable Woman*, ed. David M. Buerge, (Seattle: Sasquatch Books, 1995), p. 67.

**3.** Warren Snyder, "Suquamish Traditions," ed. Jay Miller, *Northwest Anthropological Research Notes* (hereafter cited as *NARN*), spring, 1999, vol. 30, no. 1, 125–6, 153.

**4.** Harvey Kimble Hines, D. D., *An Illustrated History of the State of Washington* (Chicago: Lewis Publishing Company, 1893), 467–468. Bagley, Ibid, vol. 2, 467–468.Herbert Hunt and Floyd C. Kaylor, *Washington West of The Cascades* (Chicago: S. J. Clarke Publishing Company, 1917), 306–310. Emily Inez Denny, *Blazing the Way* (Seattle: Rainier Printing Company, Inc. 1909. Reprinted by the Historical Society of Seattle/King County, 1984), 344–357. "C. T. Conover says Dr. Henry Smith Was Unique Influence on Early Seattle," *Seattle*

*Star*, June 11, 1947, p. 5, c. 3–5. C. T. Conover, "Just Cogitating: Dr. Henry A. Smith Tells of Early Sound Life," *Seattle Times*, Magazine Section, Sunday, August 22, 1948, p. 4. Ibid., "More Details Told of Dr. Henry Smith's Life," November 18, 1856, p. 6. Lucile McDonald, "Pioneer Doctor With Advanced Ideas,"*Seattle Times*, Magazine Section, January 29, 1960, p. 3. Ione Graf, *Dr. Henry Allen Smith and Family*, ts. np. 1955 & 1959. Anita L. Miller, Assistant Director of Development Research, Allegheny College, Personal Communication, Feb. 2, 1993.

**5.** Inez Denny, Op. Cit., 348–349.

**6.** Henry Smith, "Early Reminiscences Coming North in 1852" nd. np. *Clarence Bagley Scrapbook*, vol. II, p. 10, University of Washington Libraries, Special Collections.

**7.** "The Immortal Dead," *Pioneer And Democrat*, October 12, 1853, p. 2, c. 2.

**8.** Henry Smith, "A Trip To The Snohomish," *The Seattle Gazette*, December 10, 1863, p. 2, c. 1–2.

**9.** "Another Sad Acccident," *Puget Sound Daily*; May 12, 1866, p. 3, c. 1; *Puget Sound Weekly*, April 8, 1867, p. 2, c. 1; *The Weekly Intelligencer,* November 18, 1869, p. 3, c. 3.

**10.** H. A. Smith. "The Gold Mines," *The Weekly Intelligencer*, Septermber 6, 1869, p. 2, c. 3.

11. Charles M. Scammon, "Old Seattle And His Tribe," *Overland Monthly*, vol. 4, April, 1870, no. 4, 297–302.

12. "Indian Types and Characteristics," *The West Shore*, Portland, OR, January, 1886, no. 1, p. 197.

13. Carolyn J. Marr, *Between Two Worlds: Experiences at The Tulalip Indian Boarding School, 1905–1932* (Seattle: Upstream Productions, 1993), p. 2.

14. Warren Snyder, "Suquamish Traditions," ed. Dr. Jay Miller, *Northwest Anthropological Research Notes*, spring, 1999, vol. 33, no. 1, p. 153. Ernest Bertelson. "The Dwarf From The Land Of The Dead," *Seattle Times*, March 21, 1938, Magazine Section, 1–2.

15. H. A. Smith, M. D. "Tidelands," *Washington Standard*, Olympia, March 13, 1868, vol. VIII, no. 32, p. 2, c. 2–4. "A Desirable Locality," *Seattle Weekly Intelligencer,* February 11, 1871, p. 1, c. 3; "The Snohomish Country Part II," March 27, 1871, p. 1, c. 2; "The Snohomish Country Part III, April 3, 1871, p. 1, c. 3; July 3, 1871, p. 3, c. 4.

16. H. A. Smith. "Our Aborigines Their Destiny—Reservations, Schools, Etc., Etc.," *Seattle Weekly Intelligencer*, August 30, 1873, p. 1, c. 4–6.

17. "Delinquent Tax List," *Seattle Weekly Intelligencer*, July 8, 1872, p. 1, c. 5; Lucille McDonald, "Pioneer Doctor With Advanced Ideas," the *Seattle Times*, January 24, 1960, Magizine Section, p. 3.

18. Smith to Chirouse, Tulalip Indian Agency, September 1, 1873. *Washington Superintendency of Indian Affairs*, herafter cited as *RWSIA*. Roll 12. Letters from Employees Assigned to the Tulalip Agency, Serving Indian Parties to the Treaty of Point Elliott, April 24, 1861–July 1, 1874 (1) Letters from Employees Assigned

to Tulalip, Muckleshoot, and Port Madison Reservations, April 24, 1861–July 1, 1874. Reel 26, March 26, 1867–July 1, 1874.

19. Charles Nordhoff, *Nordhoff's West Coast California, Oregon And Hawaii* (London And New York: KPI Limited, 1987), 221–222.

20. www.timetoast.com/timelines/chin-chun-hock-timeline. Tsai Lee to David M. Buerge, August 3, 2005. Chin Chun Hock's name has different spellings, even on the Chin Chun Hock Timeline, where also he appears as Chun Ching Hock. In Seattle, many descendants write the surname as Chan.

21. David M. Buerge, *Seattle in the 1880s* (The Historical Society of Seattle and King County, 1986), p. 36.

22. Elwood Evans. *Notes on the History and Resources of Washington Territory furnished to H. H. Bancroft of San Francisco, California, by Eldridge Morse of Snohomish City, Snohomish County, Washington Territory.* Handwritten ms, Book 11, p. 119. Arthur Denny. *Pioneer Days on Puget Sound* (Seattle: C. B. Bagley, Printer, 1888), p. 16.

23. *Tri Weekly Finback,* March 1, 1881, p. 3, c. 3.

24. Orange Jacobs. *Memoirs of Orange Jacobs* (Seattle: Lowman and Hanford, 1908), p. 129.

25. Paul Dorpat, *Seattle Now & Then* (Seattle: Tartu Publications, 1984), #5, p. 16.

26. Roger Sale, *Seattle Past To Present* (Seattle and London: University of Washington Press, 1976), 42–43.

27. *Arthur Armstrong Denny Dictation*, P-B4. H. H. Bancroft Collection; Bancroft Library, p. 12.

28. H. A. Smith, "Early Reminiscences Number One, Coming North in 1852," Bagley Scrapbook, Op. Cit., vol. 11, p. 10.

29. H. A. Smith, "Early Reminiscences Number Ten, Scraps from a Dairy," *Seattle Sunday Star*, October 29, 1887, p. 3, c. 5–6.

## CHAPTER TEN

1. Eli Gifford, *The Many Speeches Of Seathl: The Manipulation Of The Record On Behalf Of Religious, Political And Environmental Causes* (California: Number One/Occasional Papers of Native American Studies/Sonoma State University, 1997), p. 73, no. 239.

2. Daniel Paul, *We Were Not The Savages,*

http://www.danielpaul.com/ChiefRedJacket.html

3. Rudyard Kipling, *From Sea to Sea and Other Sketches: Letters of Travel*, vol. 2 (Garden City, NY: Doubleday, Page & Company, 1925), 93–94.

4. "Old Chief Seattle," the *Seattle Post-Intelligencer* (June 19, 1890), p. 6, c. 1.

5.   The *Seattle Daily Intelligencer*, March 20, 1887, p. 3, c. 4.

6.   Frederick James Grant, *History of Seattle, Washington* (New York: American Publishing and Engraving Co., Publishers, 1891), p. 2, 17, 56–62. Hubert Howe Bancroft, *Bancroft's Works, Volume XXXI Washington, Idaho and Montana—1845–1889* (San Francisco: History Company, 1890), p. 23, fn. 60.

7.   "Old Chief Seattle," Op. Cit. "Good Chief Seattle," the *Seattle Post-Intelligencer*, March 26, 1893, p. 9, c. 1–3, p. 10, c. 1–2, 4.

8.   Caroline C. Leighton, *West Coast journeys 1865–1879*. Introduction and Notes by David M. Buerge (Seattle: Sasquatch Books, 1995), p. 25.

9.   Clarence B. Bagley. "Chief Seattle And Angeline," *Washington Historical Quarterly* (Seattle: University of Washington, vol. 22, 1931), 243–275.

10.   "The Welcome At The Arch. Greeting From a Children's Chorus and From the Siwash Queen," the *Seattle Post-Intelligencer*, May 7, 1891, p. 2, c. 102.

11.   "Angeline Won't Go," the *Seattle Post-Intelligencer,* March 16, 1890, p. 8, c. 3. "Who Shall Bury Her?" the *Seattle Post-Intelligencer,* June 2, 1896, p. 8, c. 5–6.

12.   John Reddin, "Free Meat For Daughter Of Chief Seattle," the *Seattle Times*, March 23, 1962, p. A, c. 5.

13.   "Old Angeline Wept," the *Seattle Telegraph*, August 12, 1894, p. 8, c. 3–5.

14.   Sophie Frye Bass, *When Seattle was A Village* (Seattle: Lowman & Handford Co. 1947), 18–19. *Indian Journal of Rev. R. W. Summers*/First Episcopal Pries of Seattle (1871–73) and of McMinnville (1873–81), transcribed by Fr. Martinus Cawley, OCSO. Book One. Seattle And Puget Sound/January 2, 1871 to fall of 1873. Ms 1–54 to I–77 (Browsers' Edition, Guadalupe Translations, P.O. Box 97, Lafayette, OR 91727, 1994), 1–2.

15.   "Wedded Into Royalty," the *Seattle Telegraph*, August 19, 1893, p. 8, c. 1–5. Frederick Grant, Ibid, p. 63.

16.   James Costello, *The Siwash, Their Life and Legends* (Seattle:1896).

17.   "Poor Old Angeline," the *Seattle Post-Intelligencer*, August 2, 1891, p. 5, c. 3–4.

18.   Hezekiah Butterworth, *The Log School-House On The Columbia* (New York: D. Appleton and Company, 1908), p. 242. "Angeline," the *Seattle Times*, June 1, 1896, p. 2, c. 2.

19.   "With Solemn Rites," the *Seattle Times*, Friday, June 5, 1896, p. 5, c. 3. "Angeline's Funeral," the *Seattle Post-Intelligencer,* June 6, 1896, p. 5, c. 5.

20.   Earnest B. Bertelson. "The Dwarf From The Land Of The Dead," the *Seattle Times Sunday Magazine Section,* May 21, 1948, p. 2, c 1–4.

21.   Bertelson, Op. Cit., c. 4. *The Bremerton News*, Friday, Feb. 11, 1905, p. 1, c. 2; Feb. 18, p. 5, c. 2; Feb. 25, p. 1, c. 5.

22.   "Denny Averse To Liquor," the *Seattle Post-Intelligencer*, March 20, 1899, p. 19 c. 1–2.

23.   H. A. Stanley, *Rex Wayland's Adventures Among The Olympics: A Thrilling Treasure Hunt* (Chicago: Laird and Leck, Publishers, nd.), p. 52–4.

24.   "A Note From Mr. Stanley," the *Seattle Post-Intelligencer*, March 20, 1899, p. 5, c. 3–4. J. A. Costello, *The Siwash, Their Life, Legends and Tales* (Seattle: np. 1895), 67–8.

25.   Frank Carlson, "Chief Seattle," *The Bulletin Of The University Of Washington* (series III, no. 2, December, 1903).

26.   Edward Clayson, Meany Pioneer File. Special Collections, Suzzallo-Allen Library, University of Washington.

27.   Thomas W. Prosch, "Seattle And The Indians Of Puget Sound," *Washington Historical Quarterly*, ed. Edward Meany, vol. II, no. 1, October 1907 (Seattle: The Washington State Historical Society), 303–308.

28.   Ione H. Graff, *Dr. Henry Allen Smith and Family*, ts., 1955. *Memoires of Dr. Henry Allen Smith by his daughter Ione—Mrs. C. F. Graff*, ts., 1959. *Memoires And Genealogy Of Representative Citizens Of The City Of Seattle And The County Of King*, n.a. (New York And Chicago: The Lewis Publishing Company, 1903), 264–267. Clark R. Belknap to J. M. Rich, *Chief Seattle's Unanswered Challenge Spoken On The Wild Forest Threshold Of The City That Bears His Name* (Seattle: Pigott-Washington Printing Company, 1932. Reprinted by Ye Galleon Press of Fairfield, WA, 1991, Rich), p. 45.

29.   Clarence C. Bagley. *History of King County Washington, Volume 1* (Chicago—

Seattle: The S. J. Clarke Publishing Company, 1929), 115–6.

**30.**    John M. Rich. *Chief Seattle's Unanswered Challenge Spoken On The Wild Forest Threshold Of The City That Bears His Name* (Seattle: Pigott-Washington Printing Company, 1932). Reprinted by Ye Galleon Press of Fairfield, Washington, 1991, 13–14.

**31.**    Rich to Bagley, 307 Pantages Building, 3rd and University, Seattle (nd—"1930?" written above heading), Bagley Collection, 0036-001, box 11. Gifford, Op. Cit., p. 80. All subsequent selections from the various permutations of Seattle's putative words come from Eli Gifford's thesis.

**32.**    Roberta Frye Watt. *4 Wagons West, The Story of Seattle* (Portland, OR: Binfords & Mort, Publishers, 1931), p. 179.

**33.**    Rich, Op Cit., p. 25.

**34.**    Decimus Magnus Ausonius, *Epistulae XXXI* (Epistole, II Cardo, Venice 1995) cited in Ivana Della Portella, *Subterranean Rome* (Venice: Arsenale Editrice, 2012), p. 46.

**35.**    Richard C. Berner, *Seattle In The 20th Century, Volume 2* (Seattle, WA: Charles Press, 1992), p. 102.

**36.**    Archie Binns, *Northwest Gateway, The Story of the Port of Seattle* (Garden City, New York: Doubleday, Doran and Garde, 1941), p. 100.

**37.**    Edna Ferber, *Native Son* (Canada: Doubleday, Doran & Company, Inc., 1944, 1945), 144–145.

**38.**    Eva Greenslit Anderson. *Chief Seattle* (Caldwell, Idaho: The Caxton Printers, Ltd., 1943), 204–5.

**39.**    Murray Morgan, *Skid Road An Informal Portrait Of Seattle* (New York: The Viking Press, 1951), p. 43.

**40.**    Roger Sale, *Seattle Past To Present* (Seattle and London: University of Washington Press, 1976), p. 27.

**41.**    Father A. Felix Verwhilgen CICM. *Chief Seattle ca. 1786–1866 In The Letters Of The First Christian Missionaries of the Puget Sound Area* (ts. np. A paper written by A. Felix Verwhilgen CICM to be presented by James Vernon Metcalf for the Pioneer Association of the State of Washington WA, 1964). James Vernon Metcalf, "Chief Seattle," *The Catholic Northwest Progress*, December 18, 1964, p. 3, c. 1. Lucile McDonald, "Historian Raises Issue: Was Tslalkom Real Name Of Chief Sealth?" the *Seattle Times*, August 7, 1964, Magazine Section, p 6.

**42.**    Gifford, Op. Cit., p. 93, Appendix F–K, 142–168.

**43.**    Alex Tizon. "The Boldt Decision/25 Years—The Fish Tale That Changed History," the *Seattle Times*, February 7, 1999, p. 1 c. 1–3, p. 16, c. 1–5, p. 17, c. 1–5.

**44.**    Ann Medlock. "Chief Seattle's Screenwriter," Huffingtonpost.com, posted 12/31/69.

**45.**    Susan Jeffers, *Brother Eagle, Sister Sky: A message from Chief Seattle* (New York: Dial Books, 1991), p. 22. Rudolph Kaiser, "Seattle's Speech(es): American Origins and European Receptions," eds. Brian Swann and Arnold Krupat, *Recovering the Word* (Berkeley: University of California Press, 1987), 497–536.

**46.**    Albert Furtwangler, *Answering Chief Seattle* (Seattle and London: University of Washington Press, 1997), p. 155.

**47.**    A Public Declaration To The Tribal Councils And Traditional Spiritual Leaders Of The Indian And Eskimo Peoples Of The Pacific Northwest c/o Jewel Praying Wolf James, Lummi, Seattle, Washington November 21, 1987.

**48.**    Linda Mapes. "Duwamish get new shot at recognition," the *Seattle Times*, March 25, 2013, p. B1, c. 1–2, B8, c. 1–3.

**49.**    Conversation with the Honorable Cecile Hansen, Secretary of the Duwamish Tribe, November 30, 2016.

# BIBLIOGRAPHY

## BOOKS, JOURNALS, MAGAZINES, AND AUTHORED ARTICLES

Allain, Julia Anne. "Duwamish History in Duwamish Voices Weaving Our Family Stories Since Colonization." PhD thesis, University of Victoria, 2014.

Anderson, Eva Greenslit. *George Adams, Indian Legislator.* Olympia, Washington: Earl Coe, Secretary of State, 1951.

Ausonius, Decimus Magnus. *Epistulae XXXI (Epistole,* II Cardo, Venice 1995) cited in Ivana Della Portella, *Subterranean Rome.* Venice: Arsenale Editrice, 2012.

Ayer, J. E. "George Bush the Voyageur," *The Washington Historical Quarterly* 7, no. 1 (1916): 40–45.

Bagley, Clarence B. *History Of Seattle From The Earliest Times To The Present.* Chicago: The S. J. Clarke Publishing Company, 1916.

———. *History of King County, Washington.* Chicago-Seattle: The S. J. Clarke Publishing Company, 1929.

———. "Chief Seattle And Angeline". *The Washington Historical Quarterly* 22, no. 4 (1931): 243–275.

———. *In The Beginning: Early Days on Puget Sound.* Historical Society of Seattle and King County, 1980.

———. *Indian Myths of the Northwest.* Seattle: Lowman and Hanford Company, 1930.

———. "Proceedings of the Fox Island Reservation Treaty". Clarence Bagley Papers, University of Washington Libraries, Manuscripts and Special Collections, 0036-001, box 21, v. 3., "Indian Council."

Ballard, Arthur. "Mythology of Southern Puget Sound." *University of Washington Publications in Anthropology* 3, no. 2 (1929): 31–150.

———. "Calendric Terms of the Southern Puget Sound Salish." *Southwestern Journal of Anthropology* 6, no. 1 (1950): 79–99.

———. "The Salmon Weir on Green River in Western Washington." *Davidson Journal of Anthropology* 3, (1957): 37–53.

Bancroft, Hubert Howe. *History Of Washington, Idaho, And Montana, 1845-1889.* The Works of Hubert Howe Bancroft, vol. 32. San Francisco: The History Company, Publishers, 1890.

Barneston, George. *No. 76, Fort Langley Journal, 1827–28. Journal of the voyage of the Party to form an establishment at the entrance of Fraser River, and of the proceedings and other occurrences*[sic] *at Fort Langley, the whole commencing with the 27th of June 1827 and carried up to this 16th February, 1828.* Hudson's Bay Company Archives B, 113/a/1. Reel No. 1M70.

Bates, Dawn. *Lushootseed Dictionary.* Seattle and London: University of Washington Press, 1994.

Bell, William N. *Settlement of Seattle: Seattle, Washington: 1878.* Manuscript Collection of the Bancroft Library, University of California, Berkeley.

Bertelson, Ernest B. "The Dwarf From The Land Of The Dead." The *Seattle Times,* Magazine Section. March 21, 1938.

———. "Piece Of Cedar Recalls Chief's Dream." *Pacific Parade Magazine,* the *Seattle Times.* December 19, 1948.

Berner, Richard C. *Seattle In The 20ᵗʰ Century.* 2 vols. Seattle, Washington: Charles Press, 1992.

Binns, Archie. *Northwest gateway, the story of the Port of Seattle.* Garden City, New York: Doubleday, Doran and Garde, 1941.

Blanchet, Francis Norbert. *Historical Sketches of the Catholic Church in Oregon During The Past Forty Years, 1838–1878.* n.p. 1910.

Bolduc, Jean Baptiste Zacharie. *Mission of the Columbia.* Edited by Edward J. Kowrach. Fairfield, Washington: Ye Galleon Press, 1979.

Boyd, Robert F. "Demographic History, 1774-1874," *Handbook of North American Indians.* Northwest Coast, edited by Wayne Suttles, vol. 7. Washington: Smithsonian Institution, 1990.

———. *The Coming of the Spirit of Pestilence.* Vancouver and Toronto: UBC Press; Seattle and London: University of Washington Press, 1999.

Bruseth, Nels. *Indian Stories and Legends Of The Stillaguamish And Allied Tribes.* Arlington, Washington: 1926.

Buerge, David M. "Giant Fish and Supernatural Dwarfs." *EastsideWeek.* Feb. 17, 1993. Personal communication with William Ribovik.

———. *Seattle in the 1880s.* The Historical

Society of Seattle and King County, 1986.

Butterworth, Hezekiah. *The Log School-House On The Columbia*. New York: D. Appleton And Company, 1890.

Cameron, David A., Charles P. LeWarne, M. Allen May, Jack C. O'Donnell and Lawrence E. O'Donnell. *Snohomish County: An Illustrated History*. Index, Washington: Kelcema Books LLC, 2005.

Carlson, Frank. "Chief Sealth." *The Bulletin Of The University of Washington* 3, no. 2 (1903).

Carpenter, Cecilia Svinth. *Fort Nisqually A Documented History of Indian and British Interaction*. Tacoma, Washington: Tahoma Research Service, 1986.

Clark, Ella. *Indian Legends of the Pacific Northwest*. Berkeley, CA: University of California Press, 1953.

Clayson, Edward. Meany Pioneer File. Special Collections. Suzzallo-Allen Library, University of Washington.

Colang, Armand R. *A Brief Glimpse Into The Life Of Charles Carroll Terry, 1829-1867*, ts. Suzzallo-Allan Library, University of Washington, Special Collections.

Collins, June McCormic. *Valley Of The Spirits The Upper Skagit Indians Of Western Washington*. Seattle and London: University Of Washington Press, 1974.

————. "John Fornsby: The Personal Document of a Coast Salish Indian." In "Indians of the Urban Northwest," edited by Marian W. Smith. *Columbia University Contributions to Anthropology*, 36 (1949).

————. "Distribution Of The Chemakum Language" in "Indians of the Urban Northwest," edited by Marian W. Smith. *Columbia University Contributions to Anthropology*, 36. New York: reprinted AMS Press, 1969.

————. "The Influence Of White Contact On Class Distinctions And Political Authority Among The Indians Of Puget Sound," in *A Garland Series: American Indian Ethnohistory: Indians of the Northwest / Coast Salish and Western Washington Indians II*, compiled and edited by David Agee Horr, Brandeis University. New York & London: Garland Publishing, Inc., 1974.

Conover, C. T. "C. T. Conover says Dr. Henry Smith Was Unique Influence on Early Seattle," *Seattle Star*, June 11, 1947, p. 5, c. 3-5.

————. "Just Cogitating: Dr. Henry A. Smith Tells of Early Sound Life." The *Seattle Times*, Magazine Section. Sunday, August 22, 1948.

Coombs, Samuel F. "Good Chief Seattle How a Young Warrior Became Ruler of Many Tribes," The *Seattle Post-Intelligencer*, Sunday, March 26, 1893.

Costello, J. A. *The Siwash: Their Life, Legends and Tales: Puget Sound and Pacific Northwest*. Seattle: 1895.

Curtis, Edward S. *The North American Indian: Being a Series of Volumes Picturing and Describing the Indians of the United States, the Dominion of Canada and Alaska*, edited by Frederick W. Hodge, Vol. IX. Norwood, Mass: Plimpton Press, 1970.

Denny, Arthur Armstrong. *Pioneer Days on Puget Sound*. Seattle: C.B. Bagley, Printer, 1888.

Denny, Emily Inez. *Blazing The Way: True Stories, Songs And Sketches Of Puget Sound And Other Pioneers*. Seattle: Rainier Publishing Company, Inc., 1909.

Denny-Lindsley, Abbey. "When Seattle Was An Indian Camp Forty-Five Years Ago." The *Seattle Post-Intelligencer*, Magazine Section. Sunday, April 16, 1906.

de Tocqueville, Alexis. *Democracy In America*, vol. 1. New York: Vintage Classics Vintage Books A Division Of Random House, Inc., 1990.

Dorsey, George. "The Duwamish Indian Spirit Boat And Its Use." *Bulletin of the Free Museum of Science and Art at the University of Pennsylvania* 3, no. 40 (1902).

Dorcy, Jean O.P. *Walk On A Rainbow Trail*, ts., c. 1960s. "Indians" in the archives (presumably) of the Adrian Dominicans, Adrian, MN.

Dorpat, Paul. *Seattle Now & Then*. Seattle: Tartu Publications, 1984.

Drury, Clifford Merill. *Henry Harmon Spalding*. Caldwell, Idaho: The Caxton Printers, Ltd., 1936.

Drury, Wells. *An Editor On The Comstock Lode*. New York: Farrar & Reinhart, 1936; reprinted in Reno by University of Nevada Press, 1984.

Dunn, Oliver and James E. Kelly, Jr. *The Diario of Christopher Columbus's First Voyage To America, 1492–1493*. Norman And London: University of Oklahoma Press, 1989.

Eckrom, J. A. *Remembered Drums A History of the Puget Sound Indian War*. Walla Walla, Washington: Pioneer Press Books, 1989.

Eells, Myron. "The Twana, Chemakum & Klallam Indians of Washington Territory." *Smithsonian Annual Report*. 1887.

Elmendorf, William Welcome. "The Structure of Twana Culture." *Washington State University Research Studies* 28, no. 3, Monographic Supplement 2 (1960).

————. *Twana Narratives: Native Historical*

*Accounts of a Coast Salish Culture*. Seattle and London: University of Washington Press, 1993.

Englehardt, Zephyrin, O. F. M. *The Missions and Missionaries Of California*. San Francisco, California: The James H. Barrie Company, 1908.

Evans, Elwood. *History of The Pacific Northwest: Oregon and Washington,* v. 1. Portland, Oregon: North Pacific History Company, 1889.

———. *Olympia Club Conversazione.* Bancroft Library, Berkeley, California: University of California.

Fenn, Elizabeth. *Pox Americana The Great Smallpox Epidemic of 1775–82.* Stroud, United Kingdom: Sutton Publishing Limited, 2004.

Ferber, Edna. *Native Son.* Canada: Doubleday, Doran & Company, Inc., 1944, 1945.

Ferguson, Brian. "Tribal Warfare." *Scientific American.* January 1992.

Frost, Robert. *Collected Poems, Prose, & Plays.* New York: Literary Classics of the United States, Inc., 1995.

Furtwangler, Albert. *Answering Chief Seattle.* Seattle and London: University of Washington Press, 1997.

Garretson, Charles E. "History of the Washington Superintendency of Indian Affairs, 1853–1865." MA Thesis, University of Washington, 1962.

Gibbs, George. "Niskwalli—English English—Niskwalli Dictionary." *Contributions to North American Ethnology* I, Washington, DC (1876).

———. "Report To Captain Mc'Clellan, on the Indian Tribes of the Territory of Washington" in "Report of the Explorations for a Route . . . from St. Paul to Puget Sound by I. I. Stevens." vol. 1, *Reports of Explorations and Surveys . . . from the Mississippi River to the Pacific Ocean, 1853–54.* 33d Congress 2nd Sess. Senate Executive Document no. 78 (serial no. 758). Washington: Beverly Tucker, Printer. Reprinted as *Indians Tribes of Washington Territory.* Fairfield, Washington: Ye Galleon Press, 1972

———. *Journal.* National Archives, Records Relating to the First Northwest Boundary Survey, 1853–1869. p. 0010. T606. I55, Roll 1-4, Miscellaneous Documents, 1854–66.

———. "Tribes of Western Washington And Northwestern Oregon." *Contributions to the North American Ethnologist* 1, Washington, DC (1877).

Gifford, Eli. *The Many Speeches Of Seathl: The Manipulation Of The Record On Behalf Of Religious, Political And Environmental Causes.* California: Occasional Papers of Native American Studies, no. 1, Sonoma State University (1997).

Graf, Ione. *Dr. Henry Allen Smith and Family.* ts. n.p., 1955 & 1959

Grant, Frederick James, ed. *History of Seattle, Washington with Illustrations And Biographical Sketches Of Some Of Its Prominent Men And Pioneers.* New York: American Publishing and Engraving Co., 1891.

Gunther, Erna. *Indian Life On The Northwest Coast Of North America: As seen by the Early Explorers and Fur Traders during the Last Decades of the Eighteenth Century.* Chicago and London: The University of Chicago Press, 1972.

Haeberlin, Hermann and Erna Gunther. "The Indians of Puget Sound." *University of Washington Publications in Anthropology* IV, no. 1 (1930).

———. "SbEtEtda'q a Shamanic Performance of the Coast Salish." *American Anthropologist* 20, no. 3 (1918).

Haley, Delphine. *Dorothy Stimson Bullitt An Uncommon Life.* Seattle: Sasquatch Books, 1995.

Hanford, Cornelius Holgate. *Seattle and Environs, 1852–1924.* Chicago & Seattle: Pioneer Historical Publishing Co., 1924.

Harmon, Alexandra. *Indians In The Making.* Berkeley, Los Angeles and London: University of California Press, 2000.

Harrington, John Peabody. *John Peabody Harrington Papers, Alaska/Northwest Coast.* National Anthropological Archives, Smithsonian Institution, Washington, DC, and Millwood, New Jersey: Kraus International Publications, A Division of Kraus-Thompson Organization, Limited, 1981.

Hartman, Mrs. James, in Bennett, Robert A., ed. *A Small World Of Our Own.* Walla Walla, Washington: Pioneer Press Books, 1985.

Haskett, Patrick. *The Wilkes Expedition In Puget Sound 1841.* Olympia: The Resources Development Internship Program of the Western Interstate Commission for Higher Education and the State Capitol Museum, 1974.

Hill, Beth and Ray Hill. *Indian Petroglyphs of the Pacific Northwest.* Seattle: University of Washington Press, 1974.

Hines, Harvey Kimble D. D. *An Illustrated History of the State of Washington.* Chicago: Lewis Publishing Company, 1893.

Hunt, Herbert and Floyd C. Kaylor. *Washington West of The Cascades.* Chicago: S. J. Clarke Publishing, 1917.

Hunt, Herbert. *Tacoma: Its History and its Builders.* Chicago: S. J. Clarke Publishing Company, 1919.

Irving, Washington. *Astoria, Or Anecdotes Of An Enterprise Beyond The Rocky Mountains,* edited by Richard Dilworth Rust. Lincoln and London: University of Nebraska Press, 1976.

Jacobs, Orange. *Memoirs of Orange Jacobs.* Seattle: Lowman and Hanford, 1908.

Jeffers, Susan. *Brother Eagle, Sister Sky: A message from Chief Seattle.* New York: Dial Books, 1991.

Kaiser, Rudolph. "Seattle's Speech(es): American Origins and European Receptions." Edited by Brian Swann and Arnold Krupat. *Recovering the Word.* Berkeley: University of California Press, 1987.

Kane, Paul. *Wanderings Of An Artist Among The Indians Of North America.* Toronto: The Radisson Society of Canada, Limited, 1925.

Kautz, Augustine Valentine. "Extracts From The Diary of General A. V. Kautz." Edited by Frances Kautz. *The Washington Historian* I, II (1900).

Keyes, E. D. *Fifty Years Observation Of Men and Events Civil And Military.* New York: Charles Scribner's Sons, 1884.

Kipling, Rudyard. *From Sea to Sea and Other Sketches: Letters of Travel,* vol. 2. Garden City, NY: Doubleday, Page & Company, 1925.

Lambert, Mary Anne. "Mystery Solved." *Shadows of Our Ancestors: Readings in the History of Klallam-White Relations.* Edited by Jerry Gorsline. Port Townsend: Empty Bowl, 1992.

Lane, Barbara. "The Suquamish Tribe." In *The Suquamish Tribe: A History from Manuscripts and Memories.* Suquamish and Sklallam Tribes, Title IV Committee and the North Kitsap School District, 1975.

Lane, William. Paper read at the Pierce County Historical Society on April 8, 1914.

Leighton, Caroline C. *West Coast Journeys 1865–1879.* Edited by David M. Buerge. Seattle: Sasquatch Books, 1995.

Longmire, James. "Narrative of James Longmire: A Pioneer of 1853." In *Told By The Pioneers: Reminiscences Of Pioneer Life in Washington,* edited by F. I. Trotter, F. H. Loutzenhiser, J. R. Loutzenhiser, vol. 1. Washington State, 1937.

Marr, Carolyn J. *Between Two Worlds: Experiences at The Tulalip Indian Boarding School, 1905–1932.* Seattle: Upstream Productions, 1993.

Marriott, Elsie Franklin. *Bainbridge through bifocals.* Seattle: Gateway Printing Company, 1941.

Meany, Edmund S. "Story of Seattle's Nearest Indian Neighbors . . . ." The *Seattle Post-Intelligencer.* October 29, 1905.

McDonald, Lucile. "Pioneer Doctor With Advanced Ideas." The *Seattle Times,* Magazine Section. January 29, 1960.

———. "Historian Raises Issue: Was Tslalkom Real Name Of Chief Sealth?" The *Seattle Times,* Magazine Section. August 7, 1964.

McKelvie, Bruce Alistair. *Fort Langley Birthplace of British Columbia.* Victoria, BC: Porcépic Books Limited, 1991.

McWhorter, Lucullus Virgil. *Tragedy Of The Wahk-Shum: The Death Of Andrew J. Bolon, Yakima Indian Agent, As Told By Su-El-Lil, Eyewitness; Also, The Suicide Of General George A. Custer, As Told By Owl Child, Eyewitness.* Edited by Donald Hines. Issaquah: Great Eagle Publishing, 1994.

Medlock, Ann. "Chief Seattle's Screenwriter." Huffingtonpost.com, 12/31/69.

Meeker, Ezra. *The Busy Life of Eighty Five Years.* Seattle, Washington: 1916.

———. *The Tragedy of Leshi.* N.p. Ezra Meeker, 1905. New Materials Copyright by The Historical Society of Seattle and King County, Everett, Washington: Printed by the Offset Printers, 1980.

———. *Pioneer Reminiscences of Puget Sound.* Seattle, Washington: Lowman & Hanford Stationery and Printing Co., 1905. New materials copyright by Historical Society of Seattle and King County.

*Memoires And Genealogy Of Representative Citizens Of The City Of Seattle And The County Of King,* n.a. New York and Chicago: The Lewis Publishing Company, 1903.

Mercer, Thomas. *Washington Territory Sketches.* 1878. Manuscript Collection of the Bancroft Library, University of California, Berkeley.

Menzies, Archibald. *Journal of Vancouver's Voyage.* Edited by C. F. Newcombe, M.D. Ed. Victoria, BC: William H. Cullen, 1923.

Metcalf, James Vernon. *Chief Seattle.* Supplement to the Catholic Northwest Progress, c1970.

Morgan, Murray. *Skid Road An Informal Portrait Of Seattle.* New York: The Viking Press, 1951.

———. *Puget's Sound: A Narrative of Early Tacoma and the Southern Sound.* Seattle and London: University of Washington Press, 1980.

Morse, Eldridge. "*Notes on the History and Resources of Washington Territory Furnished to H. H. Bancroft of San Francisco, California by Eldridge Morse of Snohomish City, Snohomish County, Washington Territory,"* handwritten ms, c1880, Book 1, p. 24. P-B 30-54. Manuscript Collection of the Bancroft

Library, University of California, Berkeley.

———. "Centennial History of Snohomish County." In *History of Snohomish County, Washington*, vol. 1. Edited by Wm. Whitfield. Chicago-Seattle: Pioneer Historical Publishing Company, 1926.

Newell, Gordon and F. George Warren. *So fair a dwelling place: a history of Olympia and Thurston County, Washington*. Olympia, WA: Warren Printing & Graphic Arts Co., 1950.

Nicandri, David. *Olympia's Forgotten Pioneers*. Olympia, Washington: State Capital Historical Association, 1976.

Nordhoff, Charles. *Nordhoff's West Coast California, Oregon And Hawaii*. London And New York: KPI Limited, 1987.

Norman, Beulah Maple. *Wedding, Duwamish Settlement 1862*. Greeting card by Robert Maple Norman, 1972, in author's possession.

Norman, Robert Maple. "Destination: Boeing Airfield 1851. King County's first cattle being floated in by raft." Painting by Beulah Maple Norman reproduced by Robert Maple Norman in one of a series of informative cards printed in 1972, in author's possession.

Oksness, Alice Esther. "Reverend Modeste Demers, Missionary in the Northwest." Masters thesis, University of Washington, 1934.

Patkanim. "Snohomish Indians Seek Memorial to Chief Patkanim's Loyalty to Seattle Pioneers." Unnamed newspaper article c1920. Suzie Paanim, his Sister, Age 90. University of Washington Suzzallo Library Special Collections Box N 970.1. Indians of North America—Tribes—OR & WA—Muckleshoot to N 970.1, Indians of North America—Tribes—OR & WA—Yakima Nation. File, N970.1 Indians of N.A. Tribes Oregon-Washington S-Y.

Paul, Daniel. *We Were Not the Savages*. http://www.danielnpaul.com/ChiefRedJacket.html.

Perry, Fredi. *Port Madison Washington Territory, 1854–1889*. Bremerton, Washington: Perry Publishing, 1989.

Phelps, Thomas Stowe. "Reminiscences of Seattle, Washington Territory, And The U.S. Sloop-Of-War 'Decatur' During The Indian War of 1855–56." *Puget Sound Historical Series, no. 2*. Seattle: The Alice Harriman Company, 304 New York Block, 1908.

Pickerell, C. Elliott. *A Goose, A Gig and a Long Kelp Horn*. Bremerton, Washington: Perrypublishing, 2000.

Polk, R. L. and R. L. Polk & Co. *Seattle City Directory*. Seattle: Polk's Seattle Directory,

Co., 1891.

Prosch, Thomas W. *David S. Maynard and Catherine T. Maynard*. Seattle: Lowman & Hanford Stationer & Printing Co., 1906.

———. *A Chronological History of Seattle from 1850 to 1897*, ts. Seattle: 1900–1901.

———. "Seattle And The Indians Of Puget Sound." *The Washington Historical Quarterly*. Edited by Edward Meany. V. 2, no. 1 (1907).

Quimper, Manuel. "Journal" in Henry A. Wagner, *Spanish Explorations In the Strait of Juan De Fuca*. Santa Anna, California: Fine Arts Press, 1933.

Rathbun, J. C. *History of Thurston Co., Washington*. Olympia, Washington: 1895.

*Riatuale Romanum. Pauli V. Pont. Max. Jussu Editum, Et. A Benedicto XIV, Auctum Et Castigatum, Cui Amplissima Accedit Benedictionum et Instructionum*. Tornari, Typis Societatis S. Joannis Evang. Descle'e Lefebvre Et Soc. M.DCCC.LXVIII. Limieux Library, Seattle University, Seattle, Washington.

Richards, Kent. *Isaac Stevens, Young Man In A Hurry*. Provo, Utah: Brigham Young University Press, 1979.

Ricard, Antoine. Ricard to Brouillet, August 27, 1856. Archives of the Catholic Archdiocesan of Seattle.

Rich, John M. *Chief Seattle's Unanswered Challenge Spoken On the Wild Forest Threshold Of The City That Bears His Name*. Seattle: Piggott-Washington Printing Company, 1932, reprinted by Ye Galleon Press, Fairfield, Washington, 1991.

Riddell, E. E. "History Of Suquamish." *Kitsap County Herald*. October 14, 1932.

———. "History of Suquamish." Excerpts From a manuscript compiled by E. E. Riddell for the North End Improvement Council of Kitsap County in *The Suquamish Tribe: A History From Manuscripts and Memory*. A Project of the Suquamish and Klallam Tribes Title IV Committee and the North Kitsap School District, 1975.

Riddle, Margaret. "Coupeville—Thumbnail History." Essay 9587. Posted September 24, 2010. www.historylink.org.Roth, Lottie Roeder. *History of Whatcom County Washington*. New York, Chicago: Pioneer Historical Publishing Co., 1903.

Ruby, Robert H. and John H. Brown. *The Chinook Indians: Traders of the Lower Columbia*. Norman and London: University of Oklahoma Press, 1976.

Sale, Roger. *Seattle Past To Present*. Seattle And London: University of Washington Press, 1976.

Sampson, Martin. *Indians Of Skagit County.* Mount Vernon, Washington: Skagit Valley Historical Society No. 2, 1972.

Sayre, J. Willis. *This City Of Ours*. Seattle: Board of Directors, Seattle School District No. 1, 1936.

Scammon, Charles M. "Old Seattle, And His Tribe." *The Overland Monthly* 4. no. 4. San Francisco: A. Roman and Co., Publishers, 1870.

Schoenberg, Wilfred P., SJ. *A Chronicle Of the Catholic History Of the Pacific Northwest, 1743–1960*. Portland, Oregon: Catholic Sentinel Printery, 1962.

———. *A History Of The Catholic Church In The Pacific Northwest: 1743–1983*. Washington, DC: The Pastoral Press, 1987.

*Seeing A New Day A 150 Year History Of Saint Peter Catholic Mission*, n.a. Suquamish, Washington, Port Madison Indian Reservation: Archdiocese of Seattle and Suquamish Tribe, 2004.

Shaw, B. F. "My First Reception in Seattle." Transcribed from an undated newspaper article [1904?], Clarence Bagley Papers, University of Washington Libraries, Manuscripts and Special Collections, Box 17, folder #17-8.

Shaw, George C. *The Chinook Jargon And How To Use It*. Seattle: Rainier Printing Company Inc., 1909.

Sherwood, Don. "Atlantic City Park." *Interpretive Essays Of The Histories of Seattle's Parks & Playgrounds* 1, A-C (1980).

Simpson, Peter. "We Give Our Hearts To You: A View of Chet-ze-moka." In *Shadows of Our Ancestors: Readings in the History of Klallam-White Relations*. Edited by Jerry Gorsline. Port Townsend, WA: Empty Bowl, 1992.

Slauson, Morda. *Renton: From Coal Age to Jets*. Renton: Renton Historical Society, 1976.

Smith, Henry A. "A Trip To The Snohomish." *The Seattle Gazette*, Dec. 10, 1863.

———. "The Gold Mines. "*The Weekly Intelligencer*, Septermber 6, 1869.

———. "Tidelands." *Washington Standard*, Olympia, March 13, 1868.

———. "A Desirable Locality." *The Weekly Intelligencer,* February 11, 1871.

———. "The Snohomish Country Part II." *Seattle Weekly Intelligencer*. March 27, 1871.

———. "The Snohomish Country Part III." *Seattle Weekly Intelligencer*. April 3, 1871, p. 1, c. 3; July 3, 1871.

———. "Our Aborigines Their Destiny— Reservations, Schools, Etc., Etc." *Seattle Weekly Intelligencer*, August 30, 1873.

———. "Early Reminiscences Coming North in 1852." *Seattle Sunday Star,* n.d. Clarence Bagley Scrapbook v. II. University of Washington, Suzzallo-Allan Library, Special Collections.

———. "Early Reminiscences; Number Nine; Governor Isaac Stevens." *Seattle Sunday Star,* Oct. 1887, in Bagley Scrapbook, University of Washington, Suzzallo-Allen Library, Special Collections.

———. "Early Reminiscences Number 10 Scraps From A Diary." *Seattle Sunday Star,* October 29, 188.

Smith, Marian Weseley. *The Puyuallup-Nisqually*. New York: Columbia University Press, 1940.

Snowden, Clinton A. *History of Washington The Rise and Progress of an American State* 2. New York: The Century History Company, 1909.

Snyder, Warren. "Archaeological Sampling At "Old Man House" On Puget Sound." in *Research Studies* XXIV. State College of Washington: Pullman, 1956.

———. *Southern Puget Sound Salish Texts, Place Names and Dictionary*. Sacramento Anthropological Society 9. Sacramento, California: 1968.

———. "Suquamish Traditions." *Northwest Anthropological Research Notes* [NARN] 33, no. 1. Edited by Jay Miller. Spring, 1999.

Splawn, A. J. *Ka-mi-akin, Last Hero of the Yakimas*. Yakima, Washington: 1917; reprinted Caldwell, Idaho: The Caxton Printers, 1980.

Stanley, H. A. *Rex Wayland's Adventures Among The Olympics: A Thrilling Treasure Hunt*. Chicago: Laird and Leck, Publishers, 1899.

Stern, Bernhard J. *The Lummi Indians Of Northwest Washington*. New York: Columbia University Press, 1934.

*The Suquamish Tribe: A History From Manuscripts and Memory*. A Project of the Suquamish and Klallam Tribes Title IV Committee and the North Kitsap School District, 1975.

Swan, John M. *The Colonizations around Puget Sd.* Handwritten manuscript. Olympia, Washington, 1878. Bancroft Library, University of California.

Swan, James G. *The Northwest Coast Or, Three Years Residence In Washington Territory*. Seattle and London: University of Washington Press, 1982.

Sylvester, Edward. *Founding of Olympia*. Handwritten manuscript in *Olympia, The Pioneer Town of Washington, Its Socialization, Origin*. Olympia, W.T. 1878.

Tacitus, Gaius Cornelius. *Agricola Germania Dialogue on Orators*. Translated by Herbert W. Benario. Indianapolis and New York: The Bobbs-Merrill Company, Inc., 1967.

Teit, James H. "The Middle Columbia Salish." Edited by Franz Boas. *University of Washington Publications in Anthropology*. Seattle: 1928.

The Laboratory Writing Classes of Cleveland High School. *The Duwamish Diary 1849–1949*. Seattle, Washington: Cleveland High School, 1949.

Thompson, Nile. "Grey Head, Leader of the Steilacoom Indians." In *Steilacoom A Bi-Annual Historical Gazette*. Centennial Souvenir Issue. Steilacoom, Washington: Steilacoom Centennial Committee September, 1988.

———. "An Atlas of Indigenous Seattle." In *Native Seattle: Histories From The Crossing Over Place* by Coll Thrush. Seattle and London: University of Washington Press, 2007.

Tolmie, William Fraser. *History of Puget Sound and the Northwest Coast*. Manuscript. Victoria, 1878. Bancroft Library, Berkeley, California. P-B 25.

———. William Fraser Tolmie, Chief Factor Hudson Bay Co., Agent, Puget Sound Agricultural Co., Nisqually, W. T. To His Excellency, Fayette McMullan, Governor, Washington Territory, Olympia, W. T., Jan. 12, 1858 in *The Truth Teller*. February 25, 1858.

Turner, Harriet. *Ethnozoology of the Snoqualmie*. Ts., manuscript, Second Edition, Revised, Seattle, 1976.

Tweddel, Colin E. "A Historical and Ethnographic Study of the Snohomish Indian People: A Report Specifically Their Aboriginal and Traditional Existence and Their Effective Occupation of a Definable Territory." *A Garland Series: American Indian Ethnohistory: Indians of the Northwest / Coast Salish and Western Washington Indians* II. Compiled and edited by David Agee Horr, Brandeis University. New York & London: Garland Publishing, Inc., 1974.

Van Asselt, Jan. *In Memory Of Henry Van Asselt, one of the first four Pioneers of the Duwamish Valley, Seattle-Washington. His life story as reconstructed by Jan Van Asselt*. Ontario, Canada, ts., 1983

Vancouver, George. *A Voyage of Discovery to the North Pacific Ocean and Round the World 1791–1795*. Edited by W. Kaye Lamb, Vol. 2. London: The Hakluyt Society, 1984.

Verwilghen, Felix CISM. *Chief Sealth ca 1786–1866 In The Letters Of The First Christian Missionaries Of The Puget Sound*. Paper presented to the Pioneer Association of the State of Washington, May, 1964.

Walen, Stanley. *Indians Of North America / The Kwaiutl*. Edited by Frank W. Porter III. New York: Chelsea House Publishers, 1992.

Ward, Dillis B. "From Salem, Oregon, to Seattle, Washington, in 1859." *The Washington Historical Quarterly* VI, no. 2 (1915).

Waterman, Thomas Talbott. "Puget Sound Geneaology." N.d. microfilm 109, Bancroft Library, University of California, Berkeley.

———. "The Geographical Names Used By The Indians Of The Pacific Coast". *The Geographical Review* 12, no. 2 (1922).

———. "The Paraphernalia of the Duwamish "Spirit Canoe" Ceremony." *Indian Notes* 7(2), (4), Museum of the American Indian, Heye Foundation, New York, 1930.

———. Notes, in "The Papers of John Peabody Harrington In the Smithsonian Institution 1907–1957." Alaska Northwest Coast, reel 30.

———. "Notes on the Ethnology of the Indians of Puget Sound." *Museum of the American Indian Heye Foundation Indian Notes and Monographs Miscellaneous* Series 59, 1920.

Watt, Roberta Frye. *4 Wagons West*. Portland, OR: Binfords & Mort, Publishers, 1931.

Whaley, Gray H. *Oregon and the Collapse of Illahee*. Chapel Hill: University of North Carolina Press, 2010.

Williams, Theodore O. "Documents: The Indian Chief Kitsap." *The Washington Historical Quarterly* 25, no. 4 (1934).

Wilkes, Charles. *Narrative of The United States Exploring Expedition During the Years 1838, 1839, 1840, 1841, 1842*. London: Whittaker And Co, Ave Maria Lane, 1845.

Yesler, H. L. *Settlement of Washington Territory*, 1878. Berkeley, CA., Bancroft Library, University of California.

———. "Henry Yesler and the Founding of Seattle." *The Pacific Northwest Quarterly* 42, no. 4 (1951).

Young, Ronald Wayne O.M.I., *The Mission of the Missionary Oblates of Mary Immaculate to the Oregon Territory (1847–1860)*. Rome: Pontificia Universitas Gregoriana Facultas Missiologiae, 2000.

Zetterberg, Kathie M. and David Wilma, "Henry Yesler's Native American daughter Julia is born on June 12, 1855." HistoryLink.org *Essay 3396*, 2001. www.HistoryLink.org.

Annance, Francis. "Journey thro. The Land,
1 28 Y. 1824." Edited by Nile Thompson
in "Opening The Pacific Slope." *Cowlitz
Historical Quarterly* XXXIII, no. 1 (1991).

*Annual report of the commissioner of Indian
affairs for the year 1857.* United States. Office
of Indians Affairs. G. P. O. No. 136, 329–332.
http://digital.library.wisc.edu/1711.dl/History.
AnnRep57

Baker, Joseph. *A log of His Majesty's ship
Discovery from 22d December 1790 to July
1st, 1795.* London and Vancouver: Public
Record Office.

Belknap, Clark R. Clark R. Belknap to J. M.
Rich, D.D.S, n.d., in Rich, *Chief Seattle's
Unanswered Challenge Spoken On the Wild
Forest Threshold Of The City That Bears His
Name.* Seattle: Piggott-Washington Printing
Company, 1932, reprinted by Ye Galleon
Press, Fairfield, Washington, 1991.

Bertelson, Ernest B. Ernest Bertelson Collection.
University of Washington Libraries, Special
Collections.

Blaine, E. L. ed. *Letters And Papers Of Reverend
David E. Blaine And His Wife Catharine.
Seattle 1853–1856, Oregon, 1856–1862.*
Historical Society of the Pacific Northwest
Conference of the Methodist Church, 1963.

Demers, Modeste. "Extract from A Letter of Mr.
Demers to Monseigneur of Juliopolis, dated
from Cowlitz, 10 November, 1841; Letter
of Demers to M.C., Oregon City, March
5, 1844." *Notices & Voyages of the Famed
Quebec Mission to the Pacific Northwest.*
Translated by Carl Lunderholm. Portland,
Oregon Historical Society: Champoeg Press,
Inc., 1956.

Deshaw, William. *Financial Records, Ledger.*
Box 1 A of 4, VO258D 1/9. University
of Washington, Suzzallo-Allan Library,
Manuscripts Division.

Dickey, George, ed. and ts. *Journal of
Occurrences At Fort Nisqually.* Fort Nisqually
Association, 1989.

Ebey, Rebecca. "Diary of Colonel and Mrs. I. N.
Ebe." *The Washington Historical Quarterly* 8,
October, 1916.

Eells, Myron. *The Indians of Puget Sound: The
Notebooks of Myron Eells.* Edited by George
Castile. Seattle and London: University of
Washington Press, 1985.

Ermatinger, Francis. "Earliest Expedition Against
Puget Sound Indians." Edited by Eva Emory

Dye. *The Washington Historical Quarterly* 1,
no. 2 (Jan 1907).

Gansevoort, Guert. *Letter Book of Comm. Guert
Gansevoort, U.S.S. Decatur, Pacific Squadron,
Oct. 30, 1855, to Feb. 9, 1856.* Gansevoort to
James Dobbins, Secretary of the Navy, January
31, 1856.

Harrington, John Peabody. *The Papers of John
Peabody Harrington In the Smithsonian
Institution, 1907–1957.* Part 1, Alaska
Northwest Coast, 30 reels. Millwood, New
York: Kraus International Publications, 1981.

Heath, Joseph Thomas. *Memoirs of Nisqually.*
Fairfield, WA: Ye Galleon Press, 1979.

Holgate, John. Holgate to his sister, Portland, O.
T., May 12, 1851 in "Earliest Settlers On The
Sound." The *Seattle Post-Intelligencer.* April
25, 1897.

Huggins, Edward. "A Trip to 'Alki' Point Near
Duwamish Bay." ts. n.d. University of
Washington Libraries, Special Collections.

Jones, Hilman F. *Hilman F. Jones Papers.* (TS-
26) ts, Box 1, Folder 28. Tacoma, Washington
State Historical Society, Research Library.

Kellogg, David. "The Making of a Medicine
Man." David Kellogg to Vivian Carkeek,
Seattle, May 20, 1912. Museum of History and
Industry, manuscript collection, folder 116.

*Les Oblats De Marie Immaculee En Oregon
1847 A 1860.* 4 vols. Edited by Paul Drouin,
O. M. I. Translated by Mary Anne Callaghan.
Ottawa, Archives Deschatelets, 1992.

*Log of the Decatur.* July 24, 1855—October 24,
1856. University of Washington Libraries,
Microform & Newspapers.

Maple, Eli B. *Account of Experiences Crossing
the Plains from Iowa, 1852, and Pioneering
in Washington Territory, 1876.* Eli B. Maple
Dictation, Bancroft Library, California.

McLoughlin, John. *The Letters of John
McLoughlin From Fort Vancouver To the
Governor, Deputy Governor and Committee.*
First Series, 1825–38. Edited by E. E. Rich,
M.A. Toronto: The Chaplain Society, 1941.

———. *McLaughlin's Fort Vancouver Letters,
Second Series, 1839–1844.* London:
Champlain Society, 1944.

Miller, Anita L. Anita L. Miller, Assistant Director
of Development Research, Allegheny College,
to David M. Buerge. Feb. 2, 1993, in author's
possession.

Ogden, Peter Skene and James Douglas to
Tolmie, Fort Vancouver, July 9, 1846; in Puget

Sound Agricultural Company, Box 6, Douglas, *Letters*; University of Washington Libraries, Special Collections, Accession Number, 5033-1.

Pantoja y Arriaga, Juan. "Extracto de la navagacion." In Cook, Warren L. *Flood Tide Of Empire Spain and the Pacific Northwest, 1543-1819.* New Haven and London: Yale University Press, 1973.

*Registre des cecles de baptemes, marriages & sepultrues des Missiones d St. Anne ches les Snohomish, de St. Joachim ches Les Lamys, des St. Croix ches les Semiamou . . . etc. etc. etc. defices le 15 Octobre 1857 jusqu'a.* Vol. II. *Sacramental Register* in the Archives Of The Catholic Archdiocese Of Seattle.

Sanford, Joseph Perry. "Journal of Passed Midshipman Joseph Perry Sanford aboard the Vincennes and the Porpoise, August 19, 1841– July 22, 1841." *Records of the United States Exploring Expedition Under The Command Of Lieutenant Charles Wilkes, 1838-42.* Microfilm reel 19.

Simpson, George. Journal in *Fur Trade and Empire, George Simpson's Journal: remark connected with the fur trade in the course of a voyage from York Factory and back to York Factory 1824–25, together with accompanying documents.* Edited by Frederick Merck. Cambridge, Mass: Harvard University Press; London: H. Milford, Oxford University Press, 1931.

———. Sir George Simpson to the Earl of Aberdeen, Nov. 25, 1841, in Joseph Schafer, "Letters of Sir George Simpson, 1841–1843." *The American Historical Review,* XIV (1909).

Sinclair, George T. "Journal kept by George T. Sinclair, Acting Master aboard the *Relief,* the *Porpoise,* and the *Flying Fish,* December 19, 1838–June 26, 1842." *Records of the United States Exploring Expedition Under The Command Of Lieutenant Charles Wilkes, 1838–42.* Microfilm reel 21.

Summers, Rev. R. W. *Indian Journal of Rev. R. W. Summers.* Transcribed by Fr. Martinus Cawley, OCSO, Book One, Seattle and Puget Sound, January 2, 1871 to Fall of 1873. Lafayette, Oregon: Browsers' Edition, Guadelupe Translations, 1994.

Sterett, Isaac. Isaac Sterett to Commodore

Mervine, San Francisco, Aug. 10, 1855. Pacific Squadron Letters, Sept. 1854 to June, 1856. *Letters Received by the Secretary of the Navy from Commanding Officers of Squadrons, RG45, M89.* Reels 36-38. National Archives and Records Administration, Washington DC, and College Park, MD.

Rich, John M. Rich to Bagley, 307 Pantages Building, 3rd and University, Seattle, Wash., n.d.—'1930?' written above heading. University of Washington, Suzzallo-Allan Library, Bagley Collection, 0036-001, box 11.

*The Records Of The Washington Superintendency Of Indian Affairs, 1853–1874.* [RWSIA] 63 reels. University of Washington Suzzallo-Allan Library.

*The Washington Territorial Volunteer Papers, 1855–1858.* [WTVP] Washington State Archives, micropublication 3.

Tolmie, William Fraser. William Fraser Tolmie to Peter Skene Ogden, July 24, 1848. *Correspondence Outward,* three letters from Tolmie to Peter Skene Ogden. Victoria, Archives of British Columbia.

———. *The Journals of William Fraser Tolmie Physician and Fur Trader.* Edited by Janet R. Mitchell. Vancouver, Canada: Mitchell Press, Limited, 1963.

Lee, Tsai. Tsai Lee to David M. Buerge, August 3, 2005, in author's possession.

Webster, Henry. Henry Webster to Calvin Hale, p. 410, in *Report of the Commissioner of Indian Affairs for The Year 1862.* Washington: Government Printing Office, 1863.

Webster, Lawrence. Notes of conversation with Suquamish elder Lawrence Webster at the Suquamish Tribal Center, March 3, 1982, in author's possession.

Wilkes, Charles. *Narrative of the United States Exploring Expedition during the Years 1838, 1839, 1840, 1841, 1842.* London: Whitaker, 1845.

———. "Diary of Wilkes In The Northwest." Edited by Edmund Meany. *The Washington Historical Quarterly* XVI, January, 1925.

Work, John. "Journal of John Work, November And December, 1824." Edited by T. C. Elliott, *The Washington Historical Quarterly* 3, 1912.

## DOCUMENTS AND COURT CASES

Chin, Chun Hock, www.timetoast.com/timelines/chin-chun-hock-timeline.

*Duwamish, Lummi, Whidby Island, Skagit, Upper*

*Skagit, Swinomish, et al. Tribes of Indians v. U.S.A. Court of Claims of the United States.* LXXIX, 530 Washington, DC: Govt. Printing

Office, *1935.* Republished in 2 vols by Argus Press, Seattle, Washington.

*The Duwamish et. al. Tribes of Indians Claimants, vs. The United States Of America Defendant,* "Number of Duwamish Villages on White River Valley." Claimants' Exhibit W-2, Oct. 3, 1927.

*The Duwamish et. al. Tribes of Indians Claimants, vs. The United States Of America Defendant,* "Villages of the Duwamish and Lak [sic] Washington." Claimants' Exhibit Y-2, Oct. 3, 1927.

"Frontier Justice: Guide To The District Court Records Of Washington Territory." http://www.sos.wa.gov/archives/ FrontierJusticeGuidestotheDistrictCourt. aspx Thurston County (Criminal Case Files) 1850–1889.

Miller, Jay. *Duwamish Tribal Recognition,* c. 1980. Duwamish Tribal Office records, copy in author's possession.

Lane, Joseph. *"*To the Honorable Secretary of War, or the Commissioner of Indian Affairs," to Tolmie, May 17, 1849, William P. Bryant to Territorial Governor Joseph Lane. Oregon City, October 10, 1849. 31st Congress, 2nd Session, *House Executive Document 1,* 156–168

Petition: To The Honorable Arthur A. Denny, Delegate to Congress from Washington Territory, July 5, 1866, National Archives Roll 909, "Letters Received by the Office of Indian Affairs, 1824–1881."

*Reports of the Proceedings of the Commission to hold Treaties with the Indian Tribes in Washington Territory and the Blackfoot Country, December 7, 1854 to March 3, 185,* "Probable Reserves."

*A Public Declaration To The Tribal Councils And Traditional Spiritual Leaders Of The Indian And Eskimo Peoples Of The Pacific Northwest,* c/o Jewel Praying Wolf James, Lummi. Seattle, Washington November 21, 1987.

*Records relating to the Northwest Boundary, 1853–1901.* US Congress, Senate Ex. Doc. 37, 33rd Cong., 2d sess., [752], "Records of Boundary and Claims Commissions and Arbitration (T-106)."

*Report On Source, Nature, And Extent Of The Fishing, Hunting, And Miscellaneous Related Rights Of Certain Indian Tribes in Washington And Oregon Together With Affidavits Showing Location Of A Number Of Usual And Accustomed Fishing Grounds And Stations.* United States, Department Of The Interior, Office Of Indian Affairs, Division Of Forestry And Grazing. Los Angeles, California, July, 1942.

Robinson, Sarah. Descendants of Sarah Robinson ts, n.d., in author's possession.

Sackman Family Tree on file in the Duwamish Tribal Office, copy in author's possession.

Speer, Tom. "Chief Seattle's Wives and children," information researched and compiled for the Duwamish Tribal Services board of Directors, on July 14, 2004, copy in author's possession.

Treaty of Hahd-Skus, or Point No Point, "The Indian Treaty of Point No Point." Edited by Charles Gates.*Pacific Northwest Quarterly* 46, no. 2 (April 1955).

Territory of Washington vs. Heebner, William, 1854. File 35, Washington State Archives, Copy of Indictment. Territory of Washington vs. Maurer, David, 1854 File 37, Washington State Archives, Copy of Indictment.

## NEWSPAPERS AND JOURNALS

The *Columbian*
*Daily Alta California*
The *New York Herald*
*Oregon Spectator*
*Pioneer and Democrat*
*Puget Sound Courier*
*Seattle Daily Intelligencer*
The *Seattle Daily Time*

The *Seattle Gazette*
The *Seattle Post-Intelligencer*
The *Seattle Telegraph*
The *Seattle Times*
The *Seattle Tri-Weekly Finback*
*Washington Standard*
The *West Shore*

# IMAGE CREDITS

**Page ii:** Photo of Chief Seattle by E. M. Sammis, c. 1864, courtesy of the Museum of History & Industry, shs67.

**Page xviii:** Chief Seattle grave site, photo by Damon Tighe.

**Page 11:** John Y. Taylor sketchbook, Beineke Library, Yale University, restored by author.

**Page 19:** Photo by author.

**Page 33:** Engraving by Raphael Coombs, the *Seattle Post-Intelligencer*, March 26, 1893, restored by author.

**Page 63:** Ink on paper, Huntingdon Library, San Marino, California.

**Page 86:** Photo of Patkanim, Snoqualmie Chief, courtesy of the Museum of History & Industry, shs1679.

**Page 95:** Island County Historical Society.

**Pages 104–105:** Clifton A. Faron, *Western Enterprise*, June, 1907, restored by author.

**Page 106:** Drawing by Steve Patricia, courtesy of Alliance for Pioneer Square.

**Page 194:** Engraving by Raphael Coombs, the *Seattle Post-Intelligencer*, March 26, 1893, restored by author.

**Page 215:** Dr. Smith of Smith's Cove, photo by Asahel Curtis, c. 1904, University of Washington Libraries, Special Collections, A. Curtis 05895, Order # CUR402.

**Page 251:** Portrait of Princess Angeline with hair uncovered, c. 1895, Seattle Public Library Portrait Collection, UW38003, #PH Coll. 844.8.

**Page 255:** The *Seattle Telegraph*, August 12, 1894, restored by author.

# INDEX

Note: Photographs and illustrations are indicated by *italics*.

# ABOUT THE AUTHOR

David M. Buerge was born on December 8, a Holy Day of Obligation, in 1945 in Oakland, California. In 1949, his family left nearby Pleasanton and moved to rural south Snohomish County, Washington. He and his older sister received a fine education from excellent and demanding teachers in the Edmonds School District. In 1964, he entered the University of Washington and graduated with a major in history, a minor in far Eastern studies, and subsequent classes in geology. In 1968, he joined the Peace Corps and spent two years in Nepal.

Returning, he developed an interest in archaeology and northwestern native mythology, in particular documenting the location of mythical sites. He began his teaching career in 1972. Three years later he married Mary Anne Callaghan and moved to Seattle, where they raised their two children. While teaching, he began researching and writing about northwestern prehistory, and during an archaeological field school on the Duwamish estuary, made the acquaintance of David Brewster, publisher of the *Seattle Weekly*, who asked if he would write for the news magazine. Thus began a second writing career produtive of hundreds of articles in local, regional, and national publications and nearly a score of books. He also became acquainted with the Duwamish tribe and became a student of their history.

Having quit teaching in 2014, he continues to write and explore other avenues of expression: poetry, watercolor painting, and carving in stone intaglio writings in Tibetan and other Central Asian scripts.